A CLAIM ON THE COUNTRYSIDE

A Claim on the Countryside

Countryside

A History of the
British Outdoor Movement

KEELEUNIVERSITY**PRESS**

First published in 1997 by
Keele University Press
22 George Square, Edinburgh

Typeset by Carnegie Publishing Ltd
18 Maynard St, Preston, England
Printed and bound in Great Britain

ISBN 1 85331 166 9

For John Taylor:
cyclist, walker and naturalist

Acknowledgements

I would like to thank the staff of the Ramblers' Association; the Cyclists' Touring Club; the Youth Hostels Association; the British Library (Bloomsbury and Colindale); County Durham Record Office; Lancashire Record Office, Preston; Public Record Office, Kew; Manchester Archive Department; Tyne and Wear Archive Department; the National Museum of Labour History, Manchester; Edinburgh Public Library; the Mitchell Library, Glasgow; the libraries of the Universities of Lancaster, Newcastle and Northumbria; and the local studies libraries of Blackburn, Bolton, Bradford, Burnley, Colne, Gateshead, Huddersfield, Leeds, Nelson, Newcastle and Sheffield.

I am also grateful to Dr Clyde Binfield of the University of Sheffield, Dr Neville Kirk of Manchester Metropolitan University, Dr Michael Winstanley of the University of Lancaster, and Mr Ken Spencer of Burnley.

Special thanks must go to Dr John K. Walton and Rita Cooper for their invaluable advice and guidance.

Contents

Contents

Abbreviations

BFC	Burnley Footpath Committee
BHA	British Holidays Association
BL	British Library
BTC	Bicyclists' Touring Club
BWSF	British Workers' Sports Federation
CCC	Clarion Cycling Club
CFC	Clarion Field Club
CHA	Co-operative Holidays Association
COS	Commons and Open Spaces Society
COSFPS	Commons Open Spaces and Footpaths Preservation Society
CPRE	Council for the Protection of Rural England
CPRW	Council for the Protection of Rural Wales
CTC	Cyclists' Touring Club
DORA	Defence of the Realm Act
EPL	Edinburgh Public Libraries
FNS	Field Naturalists' Society
FPS	Footpath Protection/Preservation Society
HF	Holiday Fellowship
ILP	Independent Labour Party
LCRO	Lancashire County Record Office
MAD	Manchester Archive Department
MFPS	Manchester Footpath Preservation Society
NCCC	National Clarion Cycling Club
NCU	National Cyclists' Union
NFPS	National Footpath Preservation Society
NHRU	National Home Reading Union
NHS	Natural History Society
NMLH	National Museum of Labour History
NRA	National Register of Archives
PD	Parliamentary Debates
PP	Parliamentary Papers
PRO	Public Record Office
RA	Ramblers' Association
SDF	Social Democratic Federation

SMC	Scottish Mountaineering Club
SYHA	Scottish Youth Hostels Association
TWAD	Tyne and Wear Archive Department
WTA	Workers' Travel Association
YRC	Yorkshire Ramblers' Club
YHA	Youth Hostels Association
YMCA	Young Men's Christian Association

Introduction

The British outdoor movement has been identified generally with the popular expansion of healthy open-air pursuits that was a feature of the interwar years. The origins of this recreational phenomenon have been located in formative influences generated within the intellectual milieu, and in the practical expression of predominantly upper-middle-class anti-industrial responses and athletic impulses during the last quarter of the nineteenth century. Existing exposition, in the form of largely unsubstantiated impressions and superficial studies, has obscured the true character of a movement which evolved to assert a widespread influence in the sphere of open-air recreation and countryside planning in the twentieth century. Helen Walker has produced the most comprehensive study of the development of an outdoor movement in Britain, but only occasionally investigates fully the themes set out in her own agenda.[1] She fails to challenge prevailing impressionistic assumptions, which have identified the origins of the substantive movement of the interwar era in the formation of upper-middle-class walking and mountaineering groups, drawn predominantly from a metropolitan professional and intellectual élite towards the end of the nineteenth century, and in contemporaneous references to an Arcadian anti-commercial rural idyll.[2] A fundamental objective of this book is to investigate the validity of some of the hitherto dominant assumptions, examining the ways in which the social and political capacity of this alliance of open-air interests was shaped through the common concerns of outdoor-orientated individuals and the associations that emerged through expansive formative stages which roughly paralleled the process of industrialization and urbanization.

In redefining the British outdoor movement in practical campaigning and politically significant terms, I do not deny the influence of wider contemporary concerns with the potential of leisure as a civilizing influence or as a counter to the consequences of large-scale urbanization. The consolidation of a capitalist system in the nineteenth century both stimulated and restricted open-air recreation. Urban industrialism created the demand for healthy and active uses of leisure time, which in turn was frustrated increasingly by the policy of exclusion that was a consequence of the growing capitalization of the agrarian sector, including the commercial exploitation of 'wilderness' areas for shooting. The trend towards rural exclusion provoked the emergence of an important campaigning dimension, which has served as a unifying focus. The active participants in this movement have been the ramblers, mountaineers and touring cyclists, who have combined to create a loosely constructed but discernible entity bonded by areas of common interest, stimulating the associational collaboration that engendered a nascent movement towards the end of the nineteenth century.

The underlying unifying ideology which evolved as a focus for a substantive twentieth-century outdoor movement was situated within a wider context of notions of 'rational' leisure as a self-improving and character-building alternative to traditional popular recreation. Rationalization of leisure is normally associated with the growth and consolidation of the serious-minded, work-orientated ethos which came to the fore as an aspect of the nineteenth-century upper-middle-class pursuit of cultural hegemony. The origins of the various contributory strands certainly fit comfortably within the compass of that emerging value system. It is also evident that working people were actively encouraged to conform to an ethos that was increasingly equated with social progress. Such notions were disseminated widely through an institutionalized 'improving' cultural structure, which, with regard to the generation of an outdoor movement, was represented initially by natural history societies and field study groups, before expanding into rambling and cycling clubs and holiday associations. This inculcation often took the form of direct patronage. The creed of hard-working respectability shaped and legitimized the challenge to mainstays of a conservative *status quo*, sustaining the radical basis of the movement as it developed. Beyond the more obvious concern with the healthy open-air use of leisure, many individuals and associations involved in the development of the outdoor movement can be seen to have adopted much of the broadly rational culture which was confronted with new challenges around the turn of the century.

The character of the British open-air recreational movement has been shaped by manifold forces: eighteenth-century Romantics; early nineteenth-century, utilitarian, urban, middle-class, liberal radical footpath campaigners; proponents of anti-capitalist organic and regenerative alternatives, such as John Ruskin and William Morris; and Christian nonconformist church- and chapel-based improving culture – all have asserted their influence, while Utopian socialists constructed their own eclectic open-air solutions, based on interpretations of pertinent ideas for popular consumption by members of groups affiliated to the Clarion movement. However, a hitherto understated popular input has also performed a crucial role in the origins and development of a movement whose character cannot be discerned accurately without a full investigation of that contribution. The fundamental ethos of the socially diverse foundations of the nascent movement was in many instances independently adopted, and adapted to suit the requirements of those elements of the urban working class whose earliest identity is defined generally as artisanal, but which came to be associated more and more with lower-middle- and upper-working-class social strata, generally incorporating clerks, small shopkeepers, and 'labour aristo-crats'. Their dominant values and institutions evolved in a community culture which formulated autonomous and distinctive versions of what is too readily assumed to be middle-class liberal culture. Moreover, the genesis of the outdoor movement depended to a significant degree on the persistence of older cultural influences, such as a recreational use of, and attachment to old routes and customs, the connection with autodidactic and self-help traditions, and the related cultural continuity of the study of natural history. Evaluation of the activities of early rambling natural historians and the concept of the 'scientific ramble', as a strand in improving culture,[3] demonstrates that the beginnings of the movement were both on a much larger scale than has been recog-nized previously and of a wider social composition, which was manifest, for example, in the 'large admixture' that participated in country walks and natural history excursions.[4] The nature and scale of the movement certainly changed as it consolidated and expanded by way of a recog-nizable core of ideas and organizations into a loose amalgamation of collaborative national bodies in the twentieth century, but the essential influences had been assimilated from substantial areas of continuity.

Notwithstanding retrospective references in its intellectual and ideo-logical growth, the tangible movement of the twentieth century was constructed from a practical and increasingly concerted pursuit of funda-mentally progressive, reforming and social democratic objectives. Persistent anti-modernist interpretations do, nevertheless, continue to distort the true picture. A recent article by Frank Trentmann, for ex-ample, perpetuates the prevalent line of analysis that has consigned this important aspect of leisure development to the quirkish neo-romantic fringes of retrogressive rural-based nostalgic nationalism. Trentmann raises some important questions regarding the motives of working-class ramblers and hikers during the interwar outdoor boom, recognizing the essential differences from the mentality of earlier open-air recreationists. However, the emergence of popular, independent, rational forms of recreation is equated erroneously with esoteric, neo-romantic concepts in an engagement with the 'debate about the ambivalence of modernity'. References such as the 'spirit of chastened humility' or the shift 'from individualist to communitarian exercises of romanticism' effectively dis-guise the simpler *raison d'être* of the ramblers and cyclists, their associations, and their increasingly unified practical campaigning lobby.

Trentmann's statement that 'English neo-romanticism refused to push anti-modernism to totalitarian extremes' is an inadequate qualification of such recurrent references as *Wandervogel* in reaction against the rationality of the prevalent *Gesellschaft*, or *Zivilisationkritik* and *Leitdisziplin* based on neo-romantic *Ideengebilde*.[5] Such inference helps to sustain a persistently misleading connection to the contemporary ultra-nationalistic movement in Germany, whereas the peculiarly British outdoor movement was rooted in the language of open-air fellowship and the rights of the free-born Englishman, or the Scottish stravaiging tradition of roaming at will, rather than atavistic romanticism.

The rejection of commercial values that characterized an important part of the development of the movement should not be equated with anti-modernism *per se*. Apparently nostalgic ruralism, most articulately presented in Morris's comprehensive criticism of capitalism, was only one element in a philosophy of social progress that was far more complex than anything conforming to theories proposing a 'decline of the industrial spirit'.[6] The popularization of pertinent aspects of Morrisian philosophy, employing a religious idiom for largely secular purposes, was instrumental in formulating fundamentally progressive ideals and strategies and transforming romantic and old Tory revulsion against utilitarianism into a social-revolutionary egalitarian creed.[7] As a Utopian doctrine, it was most widely disseminated in the Clarion movement's secular regenerative cultural fellowship, but it was also more widely adopted. For example, it was readily absorbed into the Christianity of the cooperative holiday movement. The Christian non-conformism which was so crucial to the formulation of the core philosophy of such associations was a product of the chapel-based culture that flourished towards the end of the nineteenth century in the industrial towns of the Pennine valleys. This localized influence was also converted into the religion of socialism in the secularized version of a nonconformist ethical influence which manifested itself through the Labour Church connection with Clarion-affiliated leisure groups. Many of the working people who participated in the rural camps organized by the Clarion cycling clubs (CCC) would have absorbed much of their political philosophy and their value system in the chapel. Thus the gospel that emanated from their open-air or marquee services, or from a gathering of cooperative holiday-makers on a Lake District fellside, was suited ideally to the class of people attracted to the activities offered by these institutions. However, within the philosophy of Clarion fellowship the nonconformist root was mediated by a strong anti-puritan aspect, given substance by versions of the culture of Merrie England, although the Clarion movement also built on existing reformist values.

The political and campaigning significance of a peculiarly British movement has depended upon an interaction between these diverse original influences. From as early as the 1820s radical defenders of local rights of way effectively set the agenda for an underlying conflict of fundamental political ideological principles. The lobby in support of enhanced rural recreational opportunities for an increasingly urban population was one aspect of the generation and consolidation of a broader rationalizing ideology. During those early tentative origins the right of the public to walk on long-established footpaths was adopted as an urban radical cause in a growing conflict with the representatives of the landed *status quo* and their *nouveaux riches* allies. Local challenges to the landowners' reassertion of the exclusiveness of their domains were strongly influenced by the practical utilitarian motive of improving the physical health and morals of factory workers and their families. Provision of healthy open-air exercise for the urban operative was also the primary concern of the 1833 Select Committee on Public Walks.

Those urban liberal radical origins do need to be kept in perspective. Regular recourse to the rights of the people, employed by nineteenth-century footpath defenders, was often a rhetorical device aimed at triggering sympathetic responses, although the assumption of ulterior motives should not be overplayed. In its earlier and more stridently utilitarian manifestations, the public walks issue can be seen to be coldly calculating, but the motivation became increasingly complex. Within the fundamentally progressive politics of municipalism there developed some measure of genuine and conscientious, if sometimes arrogant and condescending, belief in the overall social benefits that could accrue from broadly defined rational forms of recreation. It can be discerned, for example, in Burnley from the 1850s, where an archetypal liberal radical commercial class implemented zealously all the essential ingredients of a doctrine of municipalism and social improvement, which incorporated concern for the needs of the citizen to take exercise in the rural surroundings of the burgeoning urban district.[8] The philosophy of improvement reinforced localized municipal concern with rights of way for the public in the second half of the nineteenth century. Such socially progressive, philanthropic motives found adherents across the social spectrum, and were even adopted by members of the landed class, such as the Ashton family at Darwen in the 1890s, or, most notably, by Sir Charles Trevelyan in Northumberland during the first half of the twentieth century. The overriding ideological challenge remained, nevertheless, a conflict between urban radical-inspired community improvement and socially conservative forces defending landed property in its fullest definition.

The broader nineteenth-century socio-political confrontation had its origins in the need of a protean landowning class – reinvigorated by aristocratic and plutocratic rural alliance – to commercialize the economy of the land under the impulsion of recurrent agricultural crisis. The interests of an emerging outdoor movement came into direct conflict with a newly rationalized and market-orientated landowning demand for public exclusion, at a time when the desire for open-air recreation was taking off. This essential theme highlights the way in which the extremely politically sensitive Highland clearances became a focus for the ideological conflict over the use of Scotland's unculti-vated upland expanses. Disputes with water companies, or such specific cases as the campaign for access to Hunslet Moor to the south of Leeds (see Chapter 4), emphasize that the interests of those who sought their recreation in the open air conflicted not only with the older landed interests, but also with the more overtly commercial and increasingly regulatory concerns of modern society.

During the nineteenth century the growing urban-based outdoor lobby represented only one dimension to an urban–rural power struggle. It was a conflict which originated in the Manchester area, before escalating towards a national arena by way of other areas of Lancashire and then across into Yorkshire, although a Scottish lobby was evolving independently and roughly contemporaneously. The pursuit of rights of way, the defence of commons, and access issues, which continue to sustain the active role of the British outdoor movement, demonstrated the need for respectable organization. This was provided during an early associational formation which produced what were effectively the first countryside amenity organizations. Recourse to the law, and the financial backing necessary to fight footpath and countryside-access campaigns, was facilitated by the commitment of the urban commercial and legal classes, including members of the legal profession.

From the 1880s proponents of the multifarious benefits of open-air recreation made their own contributions to a wider critique of a per-ceived leisure problem, at a time when the question of increased leisure and its proper use came to the fore.[9] The provincial liberal radical press regularly uttered homilies on the subject, while from the 1890s *Clarion* and *Labour Prophet*, as well as local socialist publications such as *The Worker* (Huddersfield), *Workman's Times*, *Willesden Call*, and *Rochdale Labour News*, disseminated socialist views on the question of leisure. Establishment periodicals pursued their own discourse.[10] Much of the contribution to the recreation debate was declamatory, while conde-scending attitudes were adopted across the political spectrum, including some socialists, such as H. Halliday Sparling of the Socialist League, who, expounding the 'Delights of Laziness', campaigned for leisure time for the working man to be 'touched by culture [and] glorified by art'.[11] The Social Democratic Federation (SDF), founded in 1884 to campaign for democratic reforms including working-class repre-sentation in Parliament, encouraged workers to make better use of their free time: 'Educate yourself for the enjoyment of rational pleasure, agitate for opportunities of taking pleasure, and organize yourself for its final realisation.'[12] An article in *Nineteenth Century* favoured a more discriminating appraisal of specific needs; for instance, it recommended active outdoor recreations such as mountaineering for those in sedentary city occupations.[13] Although clearly different in both scale and social composition, the nascent outdoor movement was at least as relevant to the transformation of leisure which occurred around the turn of the century as was the later substantive model to post-World War One developments.

Common concerns shared by the numerous open-air associations which were formed towards the end of the nineteenth century added to the complexity of politically and ideologically significant popular cultural reformation. For example, a rejection of cruel pursuits, and dignified individual application and self-discipline, were wholly in keeping with the concept of 'muscular Christianity' and the cult of athleticism which characterized the three decades immediately prior to 1914. However, to many of the promoters of overall social improvement through recreation, athleticism itself represented both a trivial expenditure of valuable time and an unhealthy obsession with physical prowess, which echoed aspects of former 'rough' pastimes. Socialists could not deny that they shared common aims and aspirations with the more traditional philanthropic and radical liberal moralists, but this in turn made it even more difficult to reach out to the broader popular constituency to which they really needed to appeal. The Clarion clubs achieved a degree of success, but the wider field of leisure was left open for Tory populism.[14] The more popular Primrose League was less restricted by the high-minded ideals of cultural regeneration, the 'education of desire', and individual and social improvement.

A marked acceleration in the commercialization of leisure during the last two decades of the nineteenth century brought the issue of popular culture to the fore in new ways. Some degree of commercial provision of various forms of recreational activity did, of course, exist much earlier, but it really took off as a major area of enterprise as a consequence of population growth and concentration, general extension of free time and expendable income, and the consolidation of other enabling factors, such as the greater mobility afforded by improvements in transport. The proliferation of rambling and cycling clubs, and the provision of suitable holidays and rural accommodation, represented collectively an additional and less profit-orientated dimension to the changing structure of recreation. Proffered alternatives to a seemingly rapid commercialization of aspects of popular culture were ideologically sustained. To the established moralizing and rationalizing forces in society, led by the institutions of liberal middle-class philanthropy, was added the British socialists' concern with the betterment of the individual as a means to fundamental social transformation, which was redolent of one aspect of Chartist aspiration. Both of these facets were, nevertheless, basically reformist in their objectives, despite the revolutionary rhetoric employed by propounders of socialist open-air fellowship, led by Robert Blatchford and contributors to Clarion publications. From the Utopian socialist angle, the debate over the relationship between recreation, the betterment of the individual and social improvement came to prominence particularly through the development of the Clarion cycling movement, as the most popular expression of the creed of social amelioration rooted in recreational fellowship.

The radical retrospection that has tempered the progressive frame of reference found its most prominent expression in the Utopian socialist response to individual alienation. This complex interaction between traditionalism and progressivism was best encapsulated in Morris's comprehensive philosophy of social progress. The tenacious traditionalist and anti-rationalist vein sustained by the socialists can be identified in the philosophy of the historian and socialist thinker G. D. H. Cole, who was a keen walker in the southern countryside which is generally associated with the embodiment of rural England. This internationalist socialist adopted a nationalist, sentimental, and nostalgic Tory vision of England. In an account of a walk past the Highclere estate in Berkshire in the 1920s Hugh Gaitskell recalls Cole's panegyric upon the English aristocracy.[15] Cole was an admirer both of Morris and of Hilaire Belloc, a representative of the full-blown version of that Tory traditionalism which also, of course, flavoured the Clarion movement's popular contribution to the strengthening of this Tory-socialist emotional axis. This complex, often romantic socialist input contributed to a broader ideology, whose central core was dependent on a mutated liberal radical strand. It is, therefore, misleading to overemphasize the influence of a desire to return to the form of social relations ascribed to a mythical 'golden age' of organic society, notwithstanding the attractions of idealized interdependence. A maximization of opportunities for progress towards independence and self-reliance was particularly important to many of the people involved in the growth of the outdoor movement. To the escapee from urban conditions and restraint, dependence and consequent deference were the lot of the gamekeepers and hired hands employed by landowners to prevent access. Escape to, and enjoyment of, the countryside has rarely been motivated by nostalgic ruralism, and the majority have no real desire to live in the country, but merely to have easy and regular access for physical recreation and mental refreshment. Pursuit of healthy open-air recreation, and campaigns to improve access to open spaces have progressed hand in hand with the related goals of ameliorating urban conditions and removing social constraints. The social reforming character of the nonconformist ethos assumed a particularly progressive character in the form of ethical socialism, while the emphasis on the importance of leisure for the majority represents a reformist theme in itself. A further dimension to the progressive credentials of the developing movement has been an important, if sometimes overstated, contribution to the emancipation of women. During the formative period towards the end of the nineteenth century even the minority, esoteric, and often idiosyncratic aspects of the open-air idea depended on a strong progressive inclination; sexual liberation, for example, was an integral part of several schemes offering alternative lifestyles in harmony with the natural environment.

Although the underlying urge was reformist, romantic impulses cannot be discounted in the wider challenge to growing commercialization and the continuing prevalence of utilitarian values.[16] The strong conservative and nostalgic dimension also informed the emerging conservationist strand that evolved by way of such individual influences as that of Ruskin, or the novelist, environmental campaigner and 'Sunday Tramp', James Meredith, through to the vigorous interwar defence of the countryside against despoliation by developers.[17] As a popularizer of the Lakes who reacted against modern development, Ruskin in many ways assumed the mantle of Wordsworth. This obvious interest in countryside conservation connects the evolution of the outdoor movement with the early stages in the development of green politics, which has been linked by Peter Gould to the formative stages of the British political left in an ideological construct that goes beyond conservationism into a set of values underpinning a whole way of life.[18] The green connection has been relatively marginal, but does link the development of the outdoor movement to adherents of the simple life such as Edward Carpenter, cooperative agrarian socialists, and disciples of Walt Whitman and Ralph Waldo Emerson. This element of retrospective Utopianism was also nourished by the disillusioned alienation from industrial society which attracted outdoor recreationists to the Clarion movement. However, the environmentalism of the main body of the outdoor movement has been situated more generally within the sphere of conventional reformist values and concerns, which are distanced from Gould's 'catastrophist' paradigm which belongs on the green political fringes. The environmental concern within the established outdoor movement conforms with only the first element of Ralf Dahrendorf's 1981 critical definition of green politics: 'The Greens are essentially about values, an imprecise, emotional protest against the allegedly overbearing rationality of the social democratic world.'[19] The social democratic national consensus politics of planned compromise solutions to the use of the countryside have inevitably absorbed elements of a developing green agenda which has influenced that debate in the twentieth century.

In many instances it is virtually impossible to discern any real discord between liberal philanthropic and putative socialist critiques of popular cultural developments, or in the basic principles on which their alternative versions were constructed. Radical socialist mistrust of a liberal moralizing discourse, and a related fear of hegemonic motives, suggests that an ideological chasm existed between establishment middle-class liberalism and the emerging doctrine of socialism over the issue of philanthropy. In reality, substantial sections of the socialist camp recognized the value of philanthropic involvement, both in terms of essential social amelioration and as a means of gaining converts and positive publicity. Clarion club attitudes to philanthropy, for example, displayed a strong propensity to pragmatism. This area of common ground between otherwise opposed political forces is most easily discerned in the charitable involvement of the Clarion movement. The idealistic practical implementation of the notion of healthy and optimistic open-air fellowship, as a key element in the construction of an improved model of society, was indeed a major contribution made by the Clarion cycling, rambling and field naturalist clubs to a set of motivating principles which fed into a wider movement based on a diversity of individual input and associational formation.

Nonetheless, fundamental rifts in the apparently concurring liberal and socialist concerns with the revision of popular culture and the provision of broadly rational recreational pursuits do need to be exposed fully. The established body of moral reformers, who were overwhelmingly instrumental in setting the original agenda, leaned towards a primarily pessimistic Hobbesian analysis of human nature, although their response was an optimistic one, concerned with social regeneration, and founded on the belief that individual character could be reformed by way of moral instruction based partly on cultural reform. It was to that end that recreations that were perceived as character-building were promoted as one means to the improvement of the working classes, in pursuit of the larger goal of a stabilization of the social order. But, to the Utopians of socialist persuasion, the proper utilization of leisure time could be used to reinforce a challenge to the *status quo*. Education and individual improvement were mainstays of a socialist doctrine that was propagated through institutions ranging from socialist Sunday schools to Clarion clubs. The Clarion strand in the development of a larger, more eclectic movement was indeed central to an ambivalent socialist response to the problem of leisure. The pursuit of shorter working hours was an obvious plank in the campaigning platform, but the generally high-minded proselytizers of the socialist creed both abhorred mindless time-wasting and warned against the ideologically debilitating potential of commercial exploitation of available leisure. Ideologues, notably William Morris, sought a greater interpenetration of work and recreation as a reaction against the deskilling which had gone hand in hand with more and more rationalization of the processes of industrial production. The involvement of factory operatives, especially from Lancashire and Yorkshire, in the formation of open-air clubs and rational holiday associations suggests that a significant section of urban workers both reacted against deskilled work and rejected exploitative leisure, contributing independently to those associations which offered something more physically and mentally stimulating.

It can, of course, be argued that the philanthropic practice and the guiding moral tenets offered by the promoters of evolved liberal moral doctrine represented an optimistic attempt to orchestrate the construction of a common culture in the perceived long-term interests of social harmony, untainted by more profound ulterior motives of social control. However, it would be more difficult to deny ideologically stimulated motives conforming to the more flexible social theoretical construct of cultural hegemony, based on an inculcation, however benignly implemented, of a favoured set of values. The hegemony of commercialism adds to the complexity of the debate over social subordination.[20] Moreover, the notion that social stratification developed within a more flexible pattern, subject to strong cultural influences, rather than a rigid economically determined model, is supported by the evidence of collaborative common interest between members of the outdoor-orientated rational recreation associations on which the outdoor movement was founded. The relationship between recreation and class formation does, however, remain contentious. Stephen Jones, for example, stresses the importance of recreation in mediating exclusively material-based models of social delineation, whereas Gareth Stedman-Jones warns against the dangers of overemphasizing the role of leisure.[21] These cultural influences on the course of social formation were based loosely on a variable degree of identification with either the rough or the respectable elements in society. One area of mutuality influencing this form of social sub-division was a common aversion to more trivial uses of leisure. It was a dichotomy sustained by responsible walkers who distanced themselves from the urban tripper, and by touring cyclists who spurned the 'scorcher' element, although they in turn may have seen themselves as rational athletes. That agenda was consolidated in Colne by the Congregationalist minister and notably energetic open-air recreation campaigner T. A. Leonard, and found one of its more overt expressions through the anti-Blackpool motivation of the cooperative outdoor holiday associations, whose ethos was perpetuated from 1930 by the simplicity of the Youth Hostels Association (YHA).

The formative Christian connection was also instrumental in generating active involvement in such topical spiritual issues as the proper function of the Sabbath. Rambling groups associated with religious institutions arranged their open-air activities for Saturday afternoons, but more and more walkers and cyclists chose to take advantage of Sundays. Sir Leslie Stephen and his intellectual band of Sunday Tramps were partly motivated by a desire to escape the oppressive conventions imposed by social Sabbatarian moralist cant, while the cycling clubs were in the vanguard of anti-Sabbatarian action from the 1890s. The spiritual influence that was absorbed through Christian nonconformism reinforced the growing challenge to much of the negative practice of formal religion. That quietist tradition helped to sustain tenuous connections to pantheistic influences on the spiritual dimension to the appreciation of nature, discernible, for instance, in individuals as socially and politically diverse as Leslie Stephen and Ernest Evans, a self-educated Burnley weaver who rose to a position of prominence as an educationalist in the town. What is also evident is a reconciliation of the spiritual and the temporal, the romantic and the practical, antitheses that are rooted in late Victorian intellectual attempts to reconcile secular-spiritual dualism. Crucial to the underlying dilemma have been attempts to understand the character of the relationship between Man, Nature and God. The Christian contribution was certainly not confined entirely to nonconformism. It is strongly evident in a clerical propensity for energetic country walking and nature study, typified by Canon Rawnsley, whose involvement extended to defending rights of way and environmental campaigns. The fundamental conflict between scientific investigation and romantic and spiritual influences goes back to early nineteenth-century natural historians. It was articulated later in the century by intellectuals like Leslie Stephen and, influentially, Ruskin, whose updated version of an organic interdependent social model has been identified by Raymond Williams as performing a modifying role in the evolution of mainstream reformist ideology, notably through the influence of J. A. Hobson.[22] The dissemination of Ruskin's wider corpus of ideas was instrumental in embedding in the core ideology of the movement motifs that were founded on anti-utilitarian conservative notions. His country rambles were a source of the most widely circulated expression of a combination of the aesthetic and the scientific in the active appreciation of natural phenomena. Ruskin represented the quintessential Victorian attempt to mediate spiritual, aesthetic, scientific and moral responses to natural surroundings. The ethical framework that he presented manifested itself in a range of contemporary responses, which included the walk in the countryside as a spiritual renewal as well as a healthy physical escape, although the spiritual dimension should not be allowed to submerge the fundamental practical and campaigning functions of collaborative open-air interests.

The obvious pertinence of ideas and issues ramifying from a late nineteenth-century concern with urban crisis and rural decline has resulted in often vaguely defined notions of an outdoor movement, which has been equated too readily with those contemporary expressions of 'back to the land' philosophy[23] which incorporated such progressive, planned, practical concepts as public parks, garden suburbs and garden cities. This misleading connection also places too much emphasis on the sort of nostalgic pastoralism that produced sentimental ossified reproductions of landscape, represented in late Victorian artifacts for the urban kitsch market, and generating a suburban villadom attachment to an idealized representation of southern English countryside.[24] The emphasis placed on such contemporary developments depends on different interpretations of what constitutes an outdoor movement in Britain. However, it can also produce inconsistency and contradiction. While serving as important indicators of the context of ideas, practical interpretations of contemporary ruralism, such as that constructed by Ebenezer Howard,[25] were, in reality, the product of a different manifestation of an open-air philosophy. Such solutions to urban blight were based on urban and rural environmental integration rather than the leisure-based escape to the countryside, underpinned by practical campaigning aimed at facilitating recreational opportunity. Nonetheless, these differing responses to the same crisis found common ground in their contribution to the generation of growing support for the increasingly essential, mutually beneficial notion of town and country planning.

Through a concerted involvement in the construction of planned solutions to recreational amenity and land use, the emerging outdoor movement in Britain contributed to the ascendant liberal radical social democratic ideology which became the cornerstone of an all-embracing collectivist urge which was constructed by the middle decades of the twentieth century. This influence was exerted, for example, through those individuals and associations which contributed to the Addison Committee, whose official report of 1931 represented a salient element of the planners' breakthrough, and to the consequent setting-up in November 1935 of the influential Standing Committee on National Parks.[26] This planning legacy has, nonetheless, persistently been frustrated – and the role of the state limited – by ideological restraints, by the continuing influence of pressure groups such as the landed and sporting lobby, and, particularly in the early 1930s, by financial crisis and economic orthodoxy. Economic exigency was perhaps the primary factor militating against a real breakthrough being achieved before the

wider consensual situation of the war years. The mainstream social
democratic input was empowered by the inclusion of a substantial
establishment influence, asserted through the involvement in open-air
and countryside issues of a number of Labour, and some former Liberal,
politicians. Apart from the longstanding involvement of Sir Charles
Trevelyan, there was substantial parliamentary support for access bills
and the concept of national parks, as well as active participation by a
walking group of Labour MPs in the postwar development of countryside recreational amenities such as the Pennine Way.[27] The fundamental
character of the movement has conformed consistently to the compromising, but socially improving *raison d'être* of the evolving social
democratic ideological model with which it has shared common interests and basic reforming principles. Close affinity with an evolving
reformist social democracy tendency has far outweighed the more
publicized, avowedly socialist connection with rational outdoor leisure
and countryside amenity campaigning, which achieved a high profile
through episodes such as the Winter Hill or Kinder Scout mass trespasses and skirmishes. This does not deny that the influence was an
extremely important one. Indeed, in manifesting some of the key
formative elements in the intellectual and practical formation of the
movement, the Clarion strand can in many ways be seen as the embodiment of the ideal.

The socio-political environment in which areas of common interest
were generated and the main objectives formulated during the nineteenth century was one in which an ambiguous relationship developed
between cultural change, related associational formation, varying
interpretations of social progress, and the development of class consciousness. Chris Waters identifies both the emancipating and enslaving
potential of developments in the sphere of rational recreation in the
three decades up to 1914.[28] Degrees of either assimilation into the
prevailing establishment cultural and ideological milieu or independent
politicization were also often complicated by nuances of localized
subcultures and their interaction with community politics, which, in
terms of influences on the growth of the movement, found expression
in turn-of-the-century Bolton or Sheffield from the 1900s, for
example.[29] These multiple local influences counteract any facile generalization. In Lancashire in particular the development and mediation
of social and cultural relations based on liberal and socialist nonconformist respectability needs to be set against the widespread Tory
populism which ramified from paternalism in the factory and the
community.[30] Both escapist and politicized motives can be detected in
the independent autodidactic tradition, which was a particularly prominent influence on the development of popular open-air recreation
around the mill towns. Escape to the hills was a substitute for drink

long before C. E. M. Joad commented on the larger-scale phenomenon in the Manchester of the 1930s. From the 1830s and 1840s, when it was self-improvement and educational pursuits rather than Chartism which interested self-taught botanists of Lancashire, apolitical escapism, often underpinned by a love of nature, has been at least as important to the growth of a movement founded on active countryside recreation as has its ideologically-underpinned campaigning dimension.

The powerful appeal of the freedom of the open spaces cannot be separated from profound dissatisfaction with aspects of the prevailing system. That underlying desire for change can be detected both in individual responses such as that of Ernest Evans of Burnley or Allen Clarke from Bolton, and in the mass reaction of the 1920s and 1930s. To the obvious push and pull factors, such as the juxtaposition of contrasting ugly and attractive environments, have been added localized influences, shaped within parochial community culture, which have contributed significantly to the character of a national movement heavily dependent on distinct regional concentrations. This fragmented local institutional formation was gradually federated and unified in the present century. The main seedbed was in Lancashire, typified by the varied culture of Bolton, where numerous outdoor associations, as well as some of the more marginal expressions of anti-industrialism, shaped the pattern of a local collaborative movement.[31] Similar diversity was evident in the weaving towns of north-east Lancashire, where the open-air-orientated dimension to a more general self-improving popular culture stimulated contributions to the composition of the movement, which included the concept of the 'scientific ramble'. The importance of the industrial areas of Yorkshire to the scale and nature of the movement stemmed from similar local cultural diversity. G. H. B. Ward's Clarion ramblers were at the forefront of a strong local socialist input to the movement in Sheffield, where an independent, working-class, radical culture flourished,[32] although proximity to open moorland should not be underestimated as a less complicated influence on the strength of a developing movement in that area. In the more homogeneous popular cultural environment of Tyneside early professional, commercial, and spectator dimensions to recreational development went against the grain of middle-class rationalism,[33] while rational outdoor pursuits remained predominantly within the domain of the commercial and professional middle class until the advent of a popular movement in the interwar period. Activities relevant to the formation of the outdoor movement never achieved the popularity that they did in some of the other industrial areas.

A different set of legal and cultural traditions informed the development of the movement in Scotland, where a general right to roam on uncultivated land, whether for business or for pleasure, was embedded

in Highland custom until it was challenged by increased commercialization of the rural economy. The threat to customary practice became
the focus for the earliest access lobby, as well as giving substantial
momentum to the organization of the defence of public rights of way.
The customary status of the fundamental right of passage across private
land proved of little value when challenged seriously under the growing
pressure of economic exploitation and enclosure of the land by an
unconstrained landowning class.[34] The Scottish open-air culture of
'tramping' also presents the most telling challenge to the prevailing
assumption that mountain scenery was universally the subject of awe
and foreboding. Early practical and rational motives for walking
through wild landscapes, manifesting athletic, aesthetic, and scientific
motives, were particularly evident in Scotland, as part of the relatively
advanced rational culture pursued by the commercial and professional
social stratum.[35] The more general awesome reputation that was ascribed to mountain landscapes was generated by the prevalent literary
taste for a romantic idiom, which, paradoxically, was employed by men
who were themselves practical and level-headed walkers, notably Wordsworth and Keats.

In both its ideological evolution and its practical expression, the
British outdoor movement developed generically rather than specifically, and has therefore been subject to a range of definitions. However,
the character of the practical, campaigning, and large-scale popular
movement, which grew into a 'vast and rapidly increasing Brotherhood
of the open air' in the 1930s,[36] and which has continued to adapt in
response to new forces, assumed its distinctive form from contributory
strands whose origins can be traced to the early part of the nineteenth
century.

Notes

1. Walker, H., 'The Outdoor Movement in England and Wales, 1900–1939',
   unpublished Ph.D. thesis, University of Sussex, 1988.
2. Hill, H., *Freedom to Roam* (Ashbourne, 1980); Stephenson, T., *Forbidden
   Land. The Struggle for Access to Mountain and Moorland* (Manchester, 1989);
   Walker, 'The Outdoor Movement', ch. 4.
3. Buxton, R., *A Botanical Guide to the Flowering Plants, Ferns, Mosses, and
   Algae, found indigenous within sixteen miles of Manchester* (London and
   Manchester, 1859), intro.; *Burnley Express*, 13 September 1884, p. 6; Burnley Literary and Scientific Club, *Transactions*, 1874–87.
4. Manchester Field Naturalists' Society, Report, 1860, p. 4.
5. Trentmann, F., 'Civilisation and its Discontents: English Neo-Romanticism and the Transformation of Anti-Modernism in Twentieth-Century
   Western Culture', *Journal of Contemporary History* 29, 4 (October 1994),
   pp. 584, 613–14, 603, *et passim*.

6. Wiener, M. J., *English Culture and the Decline of the Industrial Spirit* (London, 1981).

7. Thompson, E. P., *William Morris: Romantic to Revolutionary* (rev. edn; London, 1977).

8. Taylor, H., 'Footpath protection societies in mid-nineteenth century textile Lancashire', *Manchester Region History Review* IX (1995), pp. 25–31.

9. Bailey, P., *Leisure and Class in Victorian England. Rational Recreation and the Contest for Control, 1830–1885* (London, 1978); Bennett, T. *et al.*, eds, *Popular Culture: Past and Present* (London, 1982); Cunningham, H., *Leisure in the Industrial Revolution, c. 1780 to c. 1880* (London, 1980); Golby, J. M. and Purdue, A. W., *The Civilisation of the Crowd. Popular Culture in England, 1750–1900* (London, 1984); Jones, S. G., *Sport, Politics and the Working Class* (Manchester, 1988); McKibbin, R., *The Ideologies of Class. Social Relations in Britain, 1880–1950* (Oxford, 1990); McKibbin, R., 'Why was there no Marxism in Great Britain?', *English Historical Review* XCIX (1984), pp. 306–10; Stedman-Jones, G., 'Class expression versus social control? A critique of recent trends in the social history of leisure', *History Workshop Journal* 4 (1977), pp. 162–70; Waters, C., *British Socialists and the Politics of Popular Culture, 1884–1914* (Manchester, 1990).

10. See *Contemporary Review* LXVIII (1895), pp. 103–13; *Westminster Review* CXXXV (1891), pp. 473–9.

11. *Commonweal*, 30 October 1886, p. 244.

12. *Justice*, 29 December 1894, p. 3.

13. *Nineteenth Century* XIV (1883), pp. 977–88.

14. Waters, *British Socialists*.

15. Gaitskell, H., 'Recollections of G. D. H. Cole', in Briggs, A. and Saville, J., eds, *Essays in Labour History* (London, 1960), pp. 12–13.

16. Shoard, M., *This Land is Our Land* (London, 1983), pp. 106ff.

17. Williams-Ellis, C., ed., *Britain and the Beast* (London, 1937); Joad, C. E. M., *The Untutored Townsman's Invasion of the Country* (London, 1946).

18. Gould, P. C., *Early Green Politics. Back to Nature, Back to the Land, and Socialism in Britain* (Brighton, 1988).

19. Quoted in Porritt, J., *Seeing Green. The Politics of Ecology Explained* (Oxford, 1984), p. 16.

20. Burns, T., 'Leisure in Industrial Society', in Smith, M. A. *et al.*, eds, *Leisure and Society in Britain* (London, 1973), p. 40; Cunningham, *Leisure in the Industrial Revolution*; McKibbin, *The Ideologies of Class*; Stedman-Jones, 'Class expression', pp. 162–70.

21. Jones, *Sport, Politics and the Working Class*.

22. Williams, R., *Culture and Society, 1780–1950* (London, 1985), ch. 7.

23. Marsh, J., *Back to the Land* (London, 1982).

24. See Colls, R. and Dodd, P., eds, *Englishness: Politics and Culture, 1880–1920* (London, 1986); Marsh, *Back to the Land*; Rich, P., 'The quest for Englishness', *History Today*, 31 June 1987, pp. 24–30.

25. Ebenezer Howard (1850–1928) was the founder of the Garden City Association and planner of England's first garden cities: Letchworth (1903) and Welwyn (1919).

26. Ministry of Town and Country Planning, Cmd. 7121, Report of the

National Parks Committee (England and Wales) (HMSO, July 1947), pp. 6–7.

27. Holt, A., ed., *Making Tracks. A Celebration of Fifty Years of the Ramblers' Association* (London, 1985).

28. Waters, *British Socialists*.

29. See Langton, J. v. Gregory, D., 'Debate. The production of regions in England's Industrial Revolution', *Journal of Historical Geography* 14 (1988), pp. 170–6.

30. Joyce, P., *Visions of the People. Industrial England and the Question of Class, 1840–1914* (Cambridge 1991); Joyce, P., *Work, Society and Politics. The Culture of the Factory in Later Victorian England* (Brighton, 1980).

31. Salveson, P., *Lancashire's Links to Walt Whitman* (Bolton, 1984); Salveson, P., *Mill Towns and Moorlands: Rural Themes in Lancashire Working Class Culture* (Salford, 1986).

32. Reid, C., 'Middle class values and working class culture in nineteenth century Sheffield. The pursuit of respectability', in Pollard, S. and Holmes, C., eds, *Essays in the Economic and Social History of South Yorkshire* (Sheffield, 1976), p. 275.

33. Taylor, 'Footpath protection societies'.

34. Shoard, *This Land is Our Land*, pp. 46–64.

35. Aitken, R., 'Stravagers and marauders', *Scottish Mountaineering Club Journal* XXX, 166 (1975), pp. 351–8; also see the small journal compiled by Adam Bald concerning Glasgow statistics, the weather, and general notes of his reading, Mitchell Library, Glasgow.

36. *The Ramblers' Handbook* (London, 1933), p. 2.

Chapter 1

The Formation of Footpath Protection Societies

Significant ideological and practical origins of the British outdoor movement, which had assumed recognizable shape by the 1930s, can be located in the defence of threatened public rights of way. This defence was orchestrated in central Scotland, Yorkshire, and, most notably, Lancashire from the 1820s. In formulating their initial campaigning agenda, the early footpath protection groups provided a unifying focus through which open-air recreational interests connect directly to the organized defence of public rights of way in the late twentieth century. Conflict over the footpaths around the burgeoning industrial towns was a product of the confrontation between the growing demand for access to open space created by urban industrialism, and of the trend towards exclusion which accompanied a process of capitalization of the agrarian sector. Neither the early emphasis on the mundane and utilitarian function of footpaths, nor the ulterior political motives of the leading rights-of-way activists, detracts from the importance of the concern of footpath preservation societies with rural amenity. In some areas local municipal involvement in the protection of rights of way was reinforced by an underlying socio-political struggle, which was informed by the philosophy of improvement.

The use of of footpaths for pleasure can be traced back to an earlier period than the formation of recreational walking groups which characterized the development of open-air leisure during the last quarter of the nineteenth century. Prevalent perceptions of the growth of recreational walking have generally connected the earliest forms of the country ramble with the coterie of literary figures who sought poetic inspiration in wild landscapes during the Romantic period.[1] Furthermore, the emergence of leisure walking as a more popular pursuit is normally associated with broader responses to specific socio-economic developments which came into full play during the last two decades of the nineteenth century. This apriorism stems partly from misconceptions regarding demographic and popular cultural aspects of the process of industrialization, exemplified by events in Lancashire. The cotton-textile districts nurtured a longer tradition of escape from urban-industrial conditions, which was situated within an independent autodidactic attitude to a diverse popular culture. The influential liberal radical Manchester newspaper proprietor Archibald Prentice pointed out the substantial numbers of factory workers who walked for pleasure during the early stages of industrial expansion in south-east Lancashire. The hyperbole of the campaigning radical journalist may be evident in Prentice's reference to the 1820s, but an important leisure phenomenon can be identified in his observation that: '… thousands and tens of thousands whose avocations render fresh air and exercise an absolute necessity of life, avail themselves of the right of footway through the meadows and cornfields and parks of the immediate neighbour-hood'.[2]

In the 1840s Dorothy Wordsworth's remark that 'a green field with buttercups would answer all the purposes of the Lancashire operatives'[3] confirmed the perceived existence of a popular dimension to country walking in the first half of the nineteenth century. It was a comment made as part of a reaction against the construction of a rail link to Windermere from the main line at Oxenholme, which afforded rela-tively easy access from the expanding Lancashire cotton towns, thereby threatening the hitherto unchallenged exclusiveness of the sublime landscape.[4] However, disputes over the 'right of footway' in 'the im-mediate neighbourhood' of Lancashire towns had led already to the establishment of footpath protection societies. Concerted campaigns to preserve the age-old rights of way were a reaction to the growing practice of excluding the public from landed estates around the urban fringes.

The first effectively organized campaign to defend a right of way as a public amenity began in the expanding commercial and industrial city of Glasgow in 1822. A trend had been established in the latter part of the eighteenth century enabling the owners of land along the banks of the Clyde to exclude the public from the popular walk which went south-eastwards up the river out of the city. Earlier challenges to this practice had foundered because of a failure to muster sufficient organized influential opposition. Nonetheless, a local radical tradition of defence of customary rights was well established, illustrated, for example, by a boycott of weaving work put out by Alexander Allen, who had closed part of the riverside footpath to the village of Carmyle. An 1829 narrative of the proceedings of an inquiry into the Clydeside rights of way indicates the recreational value of the amenity: 'These banks have afforded to the citizens at all times a delightful and quiet retreat, for health and recreation, when the labours of the day had closed; and in addition to this – for the cultivation of taste, em-bracing as they do scenes worthy of the poet and the painter.'[5] G. Adams's narrative of the local footpath defence in his *A History of*

Bridgeton and Dalmarnock confirms the recreational function of the right of way:

> It was of immense benefit to those who passed their time pent up in a crowded manufactory, to be able to enjoy fresh air by the side of the river. On the Sabbath evenings it was customary for them to take this walk with their wives and families, thus spending a portion of this day of rest in an innocent and healthful manner.[6]

In 1822 Mr Harvie, a spirit dealer, who had recently acquired the property of Westthorn, 1¼ miles above Dalmarnock Bridge, barricaded the section of the path over his land with a high stone wall, iron pikes, and *chevaux de frise*. Opposition to the closure was organized by Gabriel Neil and James Duncan, a bookseller in the city, 'gentlemen of liberal sentiments and public spirit ... They looked upon it not merely as abridging their own liberty, but as deeply affecting the rights and privileges of the whole community'.[7] Defence of the footpath was initiated and perpetuated in correspondence to the *Glasgow Chronicle* from July 1822, which called upon the public to organize measures to recover the right of way. The struggle to reinstate the Clyde walkway was marked by violent incidents, which included one person being fired on when attempting to scale the wall. Some of the crowd which set out to demolish the obstruction on 21 June 1823 carried their own firearms, prompting the intervention of a troop of Inniskillings, who seized forty-three prisoners. In the summer of 1823 a committee was set up by Duncan and on 23 July a fund was opened which eventually raised £553. 12s. 2d., including £55. 9s. 10¼d. from an exhibition of art, for the defence of the walks on the banks of the Clyde. The defence committee was highly critical of the municipal authority, which was seen as neglecting its duty as guardians of the public interest. The conviction of three weavers and a collier – sentenced to six months imprisonment, and bound over to the sum of £30 – set in motion the legal proceedings which culminated in January 1826 in a settlement in favour of the footpath campaigners, and found Harvie liable to pay expenses. A number of witnesses were called to testify to the use of the path. They included William Rankin of Camlachie, who claimed to have used the right of way for more than fifty years, and to have seen hundreds of people on the walk. In 1829 the House of Lords declared a right of access along the full length of the pathway.

The first English footpath society was set up in York in June 1824 in response to several cases of encroachment around the city. The committee of the Association for the Protection of Public Footpaths, composed of respectable members of the community, met a few weeks later at the Red Lion Inn in York, and, using their own solicitor, produced notices to be sent to offenders and 'resolved to prefer an indictment against one of them, at the ensuing Assizes'.[8] The offender pleaded guilty at the summer assizes, with the result that several ancient footpaths were immediately reopened. The series of events around York in the summer of 1824 thus prescribed the initial organized associational expression of a campaigning lobby which would adopt as one of its principal objectives the protection of the right to open-air recreation and healthy exercise.

Without discounting the original defence of footpaths around Glasgow and York, it was in the set of circumstances that pertained during the urban-industrial development of Lancashire that footpath preservation societies proliferated. Distinctive continuities in local popular culture lay behind a growing challenge to exclusion from open spaces. The received wisdom concerning Lancashire's massive industrial expansion in the first half of the nineteenth century has produced a self-perpetuating picture of large-scale immigration of Irish peasants and southern English labourers and paupers, even though such a dominant image has been regularly discredited. This view has given credence to the idea of unprecedented disruption of lifestyles and an irrevocable discontinuity from virtually every aspect of the older rural rhythms. Such oversimplification has generated the notion of the imposition of a new popular culture, divorced from its rural foundations, and devised to meet the needs of urban existence. It is assumed that there then emerged a nostalgic reversion to pre-industrial points of reference, which supposedly informed a later demand for escape to the countryside after a period of general enforced urban captivity. But insufficient attention is paid to continuities from pre-industrial recreational patterns, which were far more complex than the commonplace picture of disorderly and cruel pursuits. There was, undoubtedly, substantial rural migration to the factory towns, but Lancashire, with the highest birthrate in the country during the period in which industrial growth took off, supplied the majority of its own workforce from local, short-distance migration. John Walton's study of Lancashire has shown that during the early period of industrial growth 'the towns recruited mainly from the surrounding countryside'.[9] As a consequence of that demographic pattern, traditional culture was perpetuated rather than eradicated. New time strictures and other restrictions may have curtailed popular cultural activity, but there was also much that survived the imposition of radical change. Regular and widespread use of an intricate network of footpaths and drove-roads was part of that deeply ingrained cultural heritage, onto which were later grafted newer demands for rural recreational activities from a greatly expanded population. It is also inaccurate to assume that all migrants were immediately swallowed into giant industrial conurbations, and removed from all contact with the natural

environment, until greater access to public transport reversed the trend
at the end of the century. Before 1850 even the largest urban settlements
rarely cut off access to the countryside completely. Older traditions
survived to influence the consolidation of an autonomous popular
culture, in which walking over fields and moors was a fairly common
activity. Traditional aspects of that popular culture were transferred
into an urban environment, where they were concentrated and assumed
a larger scale. The formation of a lobby in defence of long-established
rights of way was thus stimulated by the dual motivation of protecting
age-old rights and meeting new demands for access to fresh air and
pleasant exercise in a rural environment.

Closures and diversions of traditional rights of way had become
commonplace well before any effective defence was developed, with
the scene being set for a protracted struggle as early as 1773, when
Parliament passed an act to: 'Explain, amend, and reduce into one Act
of Parliament the Statutes now in being for the Preservation of the
Public Highways in the Kingdom and for other purposes.'[10] The main
function of this act was a rationalization of existing highways and other
rights of way, in order to facilitate more efficient trade and travel as
part of a concerted modernization process. Nonetheless, a clause in
this legislation, providing for the 'stopping-up' of old rights of way and
the sale to adjacent landowners of the land and its soil, presented a
serious threat to public footpaths, putting into jeopardy their underestimated recreational role as a public amenity. The landowner was
required to provide an alternative route, but, crucially, only if two
magistrates 'find it necessary'.[11] Squirearchial dominance, ensuring collaboration between landowners and magistrates, as well as the
guaranteed cooperation of the local highways surveyor whose job it
was to apply the provisions of the act, thereby gave landowners, including the assertive parvenu element of a protean landed class, the
powers to close any right of way which interfered with their privacy
and exclusive proprietorship. The likelihood of replacement rights of
way was remote, except where passage for a neighbouring landowner
or access to the parish church were deemed essential. The regular loss
of public amenity thus dubiously obtained the sanction of the legislature
from 1773 onwards, although landowners were, in reality, transgressing
against the spirit of that law. A pattern was therefore established for a
conflict between landowning interests and the public's right to use
traditional footpaths. This cynical manipulation of legal forms was
wholly consistent with the rural hierarchy's tenacious defence of the
old order, and an abdication of duty by the governing class, particularly
in areas where urban-industrial growth accentuated the underlying
conflict of nascent class interests. The rural structure was defended just
as obstinately by a *nouveau riche* element with only superficial roots in

the land. Local ruling élites never really needed a repressive legal
structure so long as they could assert a large measure of control over
local interpretation and use of the law. Modernization was the fundamental motive of the legislators, but scope remained for conservative
retrenchment. Nonetheless, the legislation of 1773 was more of a straw
in the wind, predictive of nineteenth-century rationalization.

It was in the early part of the nineteenth century that the ruling
oligarchy embarked on a series of repressive measures which consolidated and legitimized landed interests within the structure of English
law, including the sanctioning of footpath closure. In February 1815
an act was passed which was consistent with the web of subsequent
restrictive laws which contributed to the all-embracing compass of the
post-revolutionary reaction. The Stopping-Up of Unnecessary Roads
Act complemented the Enclosure Acts in providing additional powers
to resist the pressures for rural recreation in an urbanizing society.
Application of the Stopping-Up Act became particularly widespread
around the industrial towns of Lancashire, where the practice of either
closing or diverting long-established paths was on the increase by the
1820s, as one landowner followed another in confirming the exclusiveness of their estates. The vehemence with which the old routes were
defended indicates their popular importance. Notices of footpath closures featured prominently in local newspapers; one published in the
Blackburn Mail was typical: '... the Order was signed by Charles Whi-
taker and Lawrence Halsted, Esquires, two of his Majesty's Justices of
the Peace for Stopping-Up a certain Foot-path or Foot-Way in the
township of Habergham Eaves'. This order also stated typically that
the right of way 'is become unnecessary and useless'.[12] The purpose of
these orders was reinforced by another common form of notice, which
issued warnings to trespassers: 'Notice that proceeding will be taken
against trespassers on the Manor of Colne, in the Forest of Trawden
by solicitors to the Dowager Duchess of Buccleugh and Queensberry.'[13]
The regular appearance of these notices emphasizes the Lancashire
landowners' growing obsession with keeping their domains exclusive.
In the Blackburn-Burnley area the practice of either stopping-up or
diverting traditional paths had become fashionable by 1827, some time
before the main period of urban growth of that specific area.

It seems, on the face of it, surprising that no really coordinated and
enduring response to the large-scale encroachment of rights of way
was devised until a decade after the Stopping-Up Act. What was needed
to trigger an organized campaign was the combination of certain circumstances. The essential coincidence of factors occurred first in the
mid-1820s around Manchester, where it manifested itself through the
the liberal caucus's reaction against local Tory landlords' policy of
exclusion from urban fringe landed estates;[14] footpaths became part of

the conflict between new and old ideologies. This emergence of the radicals represented a significant expression of the social consolidation of the political economy of the 'Manchester school'. The rights-of-way issue presented itself as one of the diverse rallying focuses of a broader political conflict, which was fought out almost exclusively within the expansive Manchester middle class. V. A. C. Gatrell and John Walton have both established the dearth of older landed dynasties in south-east Lancashire by the beginning of the nineteenth century, showing that commercial and industrial money was the foundation of a new Tory gentry in the Manchester area. This was the political and social milieu in which the struggle for local hegemony was fought, and which stimulated the formation and consolidation of the Manchester Society for the Preservation of Ancient Footpaths, more commonly referred to as the Manchester Footpath Preservation Society (MFPS). The creation of this first enduring public amenity lobby, at a meeting at Manchester Town Hall on 15 November 1826, was the result of a particular local dispute, but its subsequent strength and success stemmed from the solid and influential base on which it was founded.

The new plutocratic gentry of the district, whom Archibald Prentice referred to as 'tyrants of the field',[15] were typified by Ralph Wright of Flixton, which was then no more than a rural village to the south-west of Manchester. When Wright obtained the sanction of his fellow magistrates in 1824 to stop up the unnecessary footpaths which crossed his sixteen acres, he could hardly have foreseen either the protracted struggle which was to ensue or the popular movement that his actions stimulated. A minor local dispute triggered long-term and widespread reverberations. The initial reaction against the closures came from Samuel Wood, a neighbouring farmer, which suggests that the local unpopularity of a new landowner may have been as important a factor in this instance as any conflict between a landowning Tory and an urban radical. Wood enlisted the assistance of a few neighbours to break down obstructions erected on the route, and reclaimed a right of way by trampling a path through a field of oats. A succession of orders over the next two years led to legal proceedings, which proved unbearably expensive for the local footpath campaigners, with the result that an appeal for help went out to sympathetic people of influence in Manchester; this was a significant development in the construction of an organized footpath lobby: 'The case excited considerable interest outside its particular area. Some of the chief citizens of Manchester were enlisted on the side of the Flixton people.'[16] The cause had already stimulated concern in the Manchester area following its adoption by the radical press, which gave prominent and substantial coverage to the Flixton affair. The *Manchester Gazette* followed the sequence of events as they unfolded between 1824 and 1827, during which time Wright obtained a series of orders from friendly magistrates, and his opponents removed barriers, physically asserted the right of way, and fought the orders with an increasing degree of efficiency in the courts, while incurring costs reportedly amounting to £750. The ability to organize a recourse to the law of the land was a crucial milestone in those formative stages of the movement. It became a vital item on the agenda in the subsequent development of a national unified and more effective body, which would respond to greatly expanded problems at a later stage. The footpath lobbyists pursued a variety of tactics against an extremely persistent antagonist. When the third closure order was quashed in June 1826 they walked the path in procession, trampling invasive crops, cutting down obstructive fences, and levelling ditches on the line of the right of way. Nevertheless, Wright continued to be obstructive and took out a fourth order, which aroused considerable publicity and a determined campaign. The *Manchester Gazette* defended the public right and exposed the corrupt practices of the local oligarchy:

Those footways – PUBLIC footways as they are called in the notices, being in the estimation of Robert Fielden Esquire, and James Brierley Esquire, UNNECESSARY, they sign orders for stopping them up, and the inhabitants of Flixton, who think them NECESSARY, and who have already spent SEVERAL HUNDRED POUNDS to preserve them, are now again forced, in defence of their rights, to appeal against these orders; and to appeal, not to a JURY, but to Mr. Wright's brother magistrates.[17]

When the order was contested at Salford Michaelmas Quarter Sessions on 29 October 1827, dozens of witnesses were called to attest that the paths were not 'necessary'. The evidence gives some interesting insight into the wider conflict that was always just below the surface, between expanding radical forces and upholders of the local landed structure. Under cross-examination, Thomas Yates, a house carpenter, said that the roads were not necessary to him: 'I do not travel them; if I did, I must trespass and go round into the path. I live on the high road, and have no occasion to go on the foot-path. I never did break down one of the roads through Darbyshire's orchard.'[18] Joseph Howard, a weaver, had obviously at some stage associated with the footpath activists, but had been persuaded by local pressure to switch sides; he became a pawn in the underlying contest for popular support:

I have had conversation with Coupe and Bent, the appellants, on this subject. E. Coupe said he would spend a deal of money before he would give it up: and the other called me a spy ... I know there is an association at the Roebuck in Flixton, for opposing the stopping up of these roads ... [19]

When further questioned, Howard continued: 'I do not inform against carters, I have a man to inform for me, and I prove the facts. I live on Green-Lane. It is on the way to Irlam boat-house. I never was at any meeting of the society at the Roe Buck [sic].' Another witness, John Upton, denied saying to John Whitehead 'that I would swear for either side for my bellyfull [sic] of meat and drink'.[20] These and several other testimonies are indicative of the workings of contemporary society. A pattern emerged of accusation and counter-accusation, spies and informers, mistrust, and the fear which perpetuated deference. Many witnesses denied using the paths, while some attempted to deny that they had ever said that they thought that the rights of way were useful. The prevalence of bribery and coercion is apparent in the weeks leading up to the final hearing, by which the time the footpath protection lobby had attained the degree of sophistication needed to fight a successful case in courts of law, while the appellants crucially managed to retain a sufficient number of witnesses to confirm that the footpaths were both useful and popular, especially during the regular seasonal floods. The final stopping-up order was quashed.

The genesis and expansion of an effective footpath association around Manchester needs to be assessed within the context of contemporary political and ideological developments in that area. Despite Prentice's claim that the MFPS arose from a congenial alliance of Tories, Whigs and Radicals, its membership was in fact drawn overwhelmingly from those who had initiated and developed commercial and professional-based liberal radical dominance in the city. It was led by the young, successful, and largely nonconformist group, centred on Cross Street Unitarian Chapel, which fashioned the ideological and tactical emergence of the local liberal caucus. Increasingly influential local worthies, such as Richard Potter, Robert Greg, Archibald Prentice, and John Edward Taylor, were in the vanguard of this energetic and unrelenting progressive alternative to the stagnation of the old order. It is significant that several members of the MFPS committee were among the signatories of a Declaration of Protest against the violent tactics employed by the authorities during the Peterloo incident in August 1819. Some of the same men had lent support to the 'Blanketeers', and would be among the founder members of the Manchester branch of the Anti-Corn Law League in September 1838; Prentice later became the historian of the League in Manchester. This evolving emphasis on the Anti-Corn Law campaign helps to illustrate how the earliest of organized footpath activists were involved both in the formation and in the disintegration of a radical alliance in Manchester that had pragmatically transcended social stratification. From 1824 the defence of rights of way in the district had helped to forge and sustain the alliance as part of the struggle for political dominance.

The involvement of the journalists Prentice and Taylor crucially established a critical lobby in the radical Manchester press, giving a popular platform to the work of the MFPS. The ideological and political opposition, and the most persistent threat to rights of way, came in the main from the same economic stratum in Manchester society. This consisted mostly of Anglican Tories, who exerted their influence around the fringes of the city from their minor estates. Their hegemony relied on control of the magistracy and manipulation of 'Church and King' popular support, backed up by the inevitable ingredient of parochial deference. Consistent with an important ideological foundation of the contemporary radical alliance, the fundamentally reformist doctrine of the liberal radical camp was couched in the language of ancient rights and duties: 'In the year 1826, in which the deep distress of the poor and the timely benevolence of the wealthier classes were alike memorable, a society was established having for its object the preservation of a right of considerable importance to the former.'[21] In deliberately linking the importance of rights of way to a need for exercise and fresh air, Prentice was consistent with the Clydeside footpath activists' emphasis on recreational amenity. He described the unwholesomeness of Manchester as a place of residence, but counterbalanced that criticism by promoting the pleasant paths which lay within easy reach of the city, describing their environment in romantic terms. In an extensive panegyric he obviously exaggerated the facility, but certainly indicated the potential of the footpath network and the importance of its protection, at a time when the need and the demand was increasing: 'There are so many pleasant footpaths, that a pedestrian might walk completely round the town in a circle, which would seldom exceed a radius of two miles from the Exchange ... [A]ll this delightful scenery lies open to the pedestrian.'[22]

The Flixton footpaths campaign had been the opening round in the defence of these, stimulating the establishment of a solid foundation from which to fight subsequent disputes. Between 1828 and 1830 the MFPS and its solicitors were kept extremely busy, combining legal proceedings with direct action against landowners of such varied status as the Duke of Bridgewater and Messrs. Hall and Thorp (Dyers), who had erected part of their works across 'the very pleasant walk along the Irwell bank from Mr. Clowes' Bridge in Broughton Road'.[23] The *Manchester Times* confirmed both the success and the continuing importance of the local footpath lobby: 'The society has in several other instances been successful in restoring the to [sic] public, roads which had been illegally obstructed.'[24] By 1830 the MFPS had consolidated its position sufficiently to: '... strike terror in the heart of any petty tyrant who might contemplate depriving the poor man of his right to breathe the pure air in the green fields'.[25] Auxiliary branches, such as that at Marple, were formed, as the original nucleus expanded, and extensive publicity spread the fame of the MFPS further afield. As early as 1827 Mr Ellins of Bromsgrove, Worcestershire, one of the appellants against the long-standing closure of a right of way, enlisted the assistance of Richard Potter and the MFPS solicitor, Charles Wood. The closure order, which had been issued by two clerical magistrates, was quashed on a technicality in the Court of King's Bench; the advantages of an organized and publicized right-of-way lobby, particularly with a proven track record, were again evident. The success and growing reputation of the MFPS, and its capacity to organize and finance drawn-out legal proceedings, increasingly encouraged transgressors to compromise, once their encroachment on public walks was challenged seriously. During a protracted dispute at Pendleton the footpath activists were forced to apply the full range of their tactics. Mr George Jones had diverted a path to exclude the public from his newly acquired land, and to facilitate the laying of extensive lawns in front of his mansion. On receiving no satisfactory reply to 'repeated applications', the committee of the MFPS determined on direct action to reassert the right of way.[26] Jones played for time by first promising alterations and then refusing to do anything. Prentice initiated the reinstatement of the route by removing a fence and iron hurdles, and levelling an obstructive bank with the help of a hired labourer. Other workmen were brought in to complete the job:

> The workmen now having levelled down the bank, the deputation walked across the grounds directly in front of and close to Mr. Jones's newly-erected mansion, making their way through the lately laid-out shrubberies and flower parterres. Where the footway joined the carriage road at the other extremity of Mr. Jones's lawn, another bank needed to be levelled, and here again Mr. Prentice volunteered to be the first in removing the fence, repeating that no malice or unneighbourly feeling could possibly influence him ...[27]

The immediate reaction from Jones was to apply for a magistrate's order, but on reflection he gave in, and reached an agreement with the MFPS over an alternative path. The work of the MFPS, particularly the much-publicized Flixton and Pendleton cases, excited some interest across the Pennines, where the *Leeds Patriot and Yorkshire Advertiser* lent its support: '... since its formation a check has been put upon this kind of robbery (for it deserves no better name) of public property'.[28] The *Patriot* also called for a similar association to be set up in their own area, although the interest at that stage was apparently short-lived.

The 1835 General Highways Act, which replaced existing rights-of-way legislation, was a challenge to the practice of footpath encroachment. This act entered the statute books following a bill of 1833, introduced by E. B. Portman, Liberal MP for Dorset, although the direct pressure had been applied mainly by the urban radicalism of the Manchester area: 'For some time past there had been growing up in the new urban districts a volume of popular indignation against the magistrates' activity in closing public footpaths.' [29] A petition from Manchester had in fact been presented in 1831 'against the present state of the law for stopping-up Foot-Paths'.[30] Debates on both the petition and the bill emphasized strongly the restrictive costs involved in prosecuting footpath cases and the prevalence of corruption in the application of the law. Contributors to the debate pointed out that individuals were hardly likely to chance the costs of prosecution in courts which were often under the jurisdiction or influence of the same magistrates who had issued the original orders. The successful defence of footpaths had hitherto depended largely on a financial ability to advance the case to a higher court. Other speakers confirmed the fashion for footpath closures and the jobbing and patronage that were essential to the maintenance of the rural order. Mr Fyshe Palmer claimed that: '... the desire to encroach was so general, that it was a common thing to hear one magistrate saying to another "come and dine with me, and I shall expect you an hour earlier as I want to stop up a footway"'.[31] Sir Oswald Mosley, who was himself a magistrate, exposed 'the connivance between particular farmers and surveyors'.[32]

It was during the 1830s that the closure of public footpaths was given a prominent position on the agenda of a national debate on open-air amenities, which encompassed the recreational use of the threatened commons. The underlying motive was topically utilitarian, emphasized by the interest shown by Edwin Chadwick:

> In the rural districts, as well as in the vicinities of some of the towns, I have heard very strong representations of the mischiefs of the stoppage of footpaths and ancient walks, as contributing, with the extensive and indiscriminate closure of commons which were playgrounds, to drive the labouring classes to the public house.[33]

In 1833 a Select Committee on Public Walks investigated access to commons around the urban areas. Much of the evidence presented to the committee came from the Lancashire cotton towns, where the virtues of such convenient open spaces as Oldham Edge were extolled. Particular emphasis was placed on the effects of substantial population expansion. Blackburn MP William Fielden reported considerable instances of trespass, and the problems which could result from restricted access, such as: 'damage at harvest times due to residents confined to paths along turnpikes and from farm to farm and from village to village'. There were no common lands and nothing but private property around Blackburn, with its large number of factory operatives. From Bury it was reported that there was no open space, but there was 'uninclosed heath' two and a half miles away. Representatives from other towns confirmed the absence of recreational areas. A traditionalist paternalistic interest in the issue is indicated by the contribution made to the debate by Bolton's Tory authoritarian MP, William Bolling, who was responding to a question regarding open spaces to which the common people could resort: 'No, we have no part of the moor for that purpose, because all of it is inclosed, but still no person in the neighbourhood prevents them.'[34]

This concern amongst Tory factory paternalists to provide facilities for healthy recreation for their mill hands found practical expression in the Bolton district with the creation in the 1850s of a public walk in a pleasant rural environment close to Eagley Mills, where 'the art of man ... effected a promenade for the working classes'.[35] In the complex political structure of Lancashire the welfare of the workers and utilitarian concerns with early notions of rational recreation were often translated into an organic social relationship, in which the great textile magnates sustained a pre-industrial concern with the overall welfare of the community. It was a reference to past rights and duties as potent as any employed by the liberal radicals. P. A. Whittle, a local chronicler, and a supporter of Bolton's Tory MP, contrasted the town's paternalists, who had provided healthy recreational facilities for the workers, to greedy liberal capitalists: '... the capitalists and manufacturers of England have not only not fulfilled the trust committed to them in any tolerable degree, but have rather acted with a deep unconsciousness that they had any trust or duty to fulfil, beyond that of getting rich as fast as they could'.[36] Whittle described the attractive walk which had been newly created at Eagley Park:

> ... this is about fifty yards from the mills, and occupies a long slip of land, running along the valley in a southerly direction, and extending from Eagley mills nearly to Dunscar-bridge. – It is now a pleasant spot of land, made for the recreation of the people. The art of man has effected a promenade for the working classes. A notice is posted up, desiring that no one will gather the flowers, injure the shrubs, deface the seats, or injure the walks.[37]

Following the radical reconstruction of the socio-economic system, which effectively removed large numbers of people from a natural environment, representatives of the employer class, led by Lancashire factory paternalists of various ideological persuasions, set about reinstating a necessary degree of the former relationship between man and nature in order to preserve the physical and psychological well-being of the operatives in the manufacturing districts. Whittle gave full expression to that moralizing discourse in the Bolton area:

> We have always found in our rural walks great pleasure, for there it is we are taught botany, geology, dendrology; there is sublimity in every hedgerow ... the fruitful valley where the gurgling stream is running. These teachings will fill the mind with knowledge, improve the morals, render the heart more pure, make us more intelligent, and cause us to glory in the wonders of creation.[38]

The spiritual connection was pursued in a typically romantic idiom: 'We conclude the best medicine for a virtuous mind is a country walk among woodbine and sweet-blossomed hawthorns ... Hopeless indeed is the case of that man who cannot enjoy the joyous scenes of nature's God!'[39]

The repeal of the 1815 right-of-way legislation may theoretically have removed the original *raison d'être* of footpath preservation societies. However, as the use of rights of way increased, and urban expansion exerted greater pressure, many landed proprietors gradually returned to the practice of applying autocratic rule within their own domains in pursuit of continuing exclusiveness, or, in the case of commercial encroachers, merely rode roughshod over legal restraints. Abuse of traditional rights was always easier where sympathetic local government members chose to turn a blind eye. By the time that Manchester was incorporated in 1838, liberal radical hegemony in the area was so well established that the MFPS had become virtually redundant locally, but it remained essential as the model for similar groups elsewhere. Notwithstanding Tory paternalist interest in the provision of healthy leisure facilities, footpath protection had become embedded in the broadly progressive ideology that informed the evolution of municipal politics founded on civic pride. All-embracing political rivalries continued to be the fundamental driving force, but the self-styled defenders of traditional rights nevertheless left no doubt as to the importance they attached to the preservation of footpaths as a recreational amenity, which were under threat from rural retrenchment in the face of the expansion of the urban, modernizing influence.

It was during the 1850s that footpath protection entered the political agenda in Burnley, when several attempts were made either to close or divert popular rights of way. The continuing promotion of healthy pursuits for the factory operatives, and the involvement of the local liberal radicals, raised the profile of the issue in the grass-roots politics of the district. The character of the conflict around Burnley was particularly influenced by fear of a substantial rougher and unruly social stratum, which was blamed for perverting the righteous and respectable pursuit of working-class improvement, a notion which incorporated recreational activities that were perceived as rational. Rapidly expanding Burnley was notorious as a centre of general disorder, and it was the spectre of widespread rowdyism that the local landowners invoked as a welcome excuse to exclude the public from their estates.[40]

The footpath issue in the Burnley area was contested vigorously between the entrenched landed establishment and an emerging civic oligarchy. In 1856 the rector of Burnley, deciding to assert the privacy of the route to his residence at Royle Hall, had heavy doors erected under an archway on the right of way. Local radicals succeeded in mustering a large and vociferous crowd at the gates. Two local blacksmiths were hired to smash down the obstruction with their heavy hammers, and the excited crowd rushed through the gap to reassert their right to walk the route. However, the old order maintained the advantage during these early stages, and the blacksmiths were gaoled by magistrates at the Preston Quarter Sessions, who also confirmed the privatization of the route. In justifying the closure of the Royle footpath, which he and his family used on the way to church, the rector's appeal to public decency succeeded in winning some local support: '... a large sprinkling of Irish poor ... were accustomed to take athletic exercise on Sundays along this road ... [R]aces by half-naked men were an outrage to decency.'[41] 'Disgusting and revolting scenes' were reported from another threatened footpath, where 'old men in sear [sic] and yellow leaf of life ... men of depraved tastes and habits' were said to extort money from passers-by.[42] Such reasoning was, nonetheless, countered cleverly by another correspondent to the *Burnley Advertiser*, who pointed out that if the logic of those who wished to close the footpaths was adhered to, 'every time a robbery or murder is committed on the Queen's highway we ought to stop it up'.[43]

It was in response to such threats to public recreation, and to the undermining of customary rights entrenched in selected elements of an idealized pre-industrial 'moral economy', that local Burnley radicals came to form a footpath committee, similar to the MFPS. But, as in Manchester, the formation of the Burnley Footpath Committee (BFC), and its increasingly successful campaigns to preserve pleasant leisure facilities at a time of rapid urban-industrial expansion, was only one dimension to the wider political struggle evolving in the town. The organized defence of footpaths was one of the practical expressions of the intellectual ferment of Bradshaw's coffee-house, where the local group of political radicals met to discuss the questions of the day, and to formulate their challenge to the *status quo*. This intellectual circle had strong working-class connections, which sustained a Chartist link in Burnley municipalism, thereby contributing to the general liberal radical disposition towards the defence of rights of way. Its ideology was embodied in the leader of the group, Charles Owen, a disciple of John Bright and, accordingly, a pacifist critic of the Crimean War. Owen's political doctrine demonstrated that the radical alliance had in certain localized circumstances survived the Chartist period. His 'moral force' Chartism espoused the Anti-Corn Law campaign, while rejecting O'Connor's land scheme. Charles Owen, a working currier who had prospered after setting up his own business, had also rejected the communism of Robert Owen, but was a powerful advocate of an early form of municipal socialism, which developed in mid-nineteenth-century Burnley hand in hand with the simultaneous agitation for the twin goals of incorporation and separate representation in Parliament.

The optimistic objective of improvement sustained this carefully concerted preservation of pleasant public walks in tandem with the creation of the Burnley Improvement Commission, which was originally set up to establish gasworks in the town, and to improve water supply and sanitation. The persistence of the Chartist strand reinforced campaigns for universal manhood suffrage, sustaining the impetus towards the Second Reform Act. The strength of the BFC depended on its solid foundation on the principles of reform and community improvement. Its members were to assume growing influence as upholders of civic pride. For example, T. T. Wilkinson became an alderman when the town was incorporated in 1861. He was already a director of the Burnley Mechanics' Institution, and became prominent in the Literary and Philosophical Society and the Burnley Literary and Scientific Association, as well as being a member of the Burnley Reform Association, and presiding over the formation of the local branch of the Young Men's Christian Association (YMCA). The influence and respectability that this coterie of reformers represented had evolved during the political agitation of the 1850s through bodies like the BFC, which soon developed into a dedicated organization with the will and the ability both to employ direct action and to fight in a court of law. Notwithstanding an evident propensity to take the law into their own hands in removing obstacles to access, the members of the BFC were either middle-class radicals, or fitted accurately into Bright's 'Rochdale model' of the respectable working man, legitimately pursuing wider representation and participation in a progressive creed, which was characterized by a 'retrospective radicalism' rooted in the rights of the free-born Englishman.

The crucial degree of sophistication achieved by the organized defence of rights of way in Victorian Lancashire is certainly evident from the notable successes which the Burnley group achieved against firmly established landed interests. The BFC was formed in direct response to the closure of rights of way, known locally as the Rabbit Walks, which crossed the estate of major local landowner Colonel Charles Towneley. These popular footpaths were blocked towards the end of 1857 by the construction of a substantial wall and a water-filled trench. There followed a battle of attrition, which lasted for several weeks, during which the obstacles were demolished and then replaced more than once, before Towneley gave up the contest and conceded the right of way. Towneley's somewhat ambiguous position during this period of change is in some respects indicative of the adaptability of the older landed élite, whose response to ever-changing challenges was generally more flexible than that of the *nouveaux riches* who had purchased smaller estates around urban areas. The Colonel had something of a reputation as a man of relatively liberal persuasion, who was said to have fallen amongst 'evil advisers',[44] although the history of the defence of footpaths is marked by landowners' deliberate delegation of awkward areas of estate administration. Towneley, a member of the Lancashire Roman Catholic aristocracy, did, nevertheless, become prominently involved in the democracy of Burnley civic affairs.

The need for a more formal organization became more pressing when the Burnley activists set out to reinstate another footpath across the Towneley Park. The right of way from Causeway End had been truncated a few years earlier by the deliberate removal of a footbridge and the erection of a wall to block access to a tributary of the River Calder near Mere Clough. BFC member John Pennington, who had been delegated the responsibility of removing the Rabbit Walks obstructions, was called on again to remove the wall. On this occasion, however, he was arrested, convicted, and fined 4s. 6d. (22½ p), including costs. On repeating the action he was rearrested, but this time the BFC was fully prepared for a protracted legal struggle, employing the services of a Yorkshire barrister, Wasney. The BFC was fully acquainted with its legal rights, confident that solidarity and organization would produce ultimate success. During a long-running debate in the local press on the Towneley Park affair, one correspondent, the pseudonymous 'Well-Wisher to Towneley' stressed that the footpath 'cannot be stopped by any authority short of an Act of Parliament ... all their walling and barricading and bridge-cutting will not avail'. Referring to the alleged displays of indecency along the contested paths 'Well-Wisher' claimed that 'one single policeman could clear the whole park of such characters in a few minutes'.[45] Another correspondent, a Mr Robson, felt that 'Well-Wisher' would be better employed trying to raise standards of morality than writing anonymous letters. When the dispute came to court, one of the key prosecution witnesses, a local man called Redfern, claimed that no bridge had ever existed, and that he crossed the river using stones which had been washed down by a flood. However, when pushed under cross-examination as to the whereabouts of the stones, he was reported to have said, 'Well, they were just where the bridge used to be.' The prosecution against Pennington collapsed, a new footbridge was erected, and 'this picturesque walk' was saved for the public of the Burnley district.[46] A more significant longer-term consequence of the Mere Clough case was the establishment of the principle locally that rights of way could not be disturbed with impunity. Collaborative protection of public amenities was to become a feature of civic government during the second half of the nineteenth century.

Similar associations of mutual interest took up the defence of rights of way in other cotton towns. Local political nuances determined that the underlying conflict was never a straightforward clash between upholders of liberal radical civic pride and the old landed order, whether or not reinforced by a newer plutocracy of minor landowners. Lancashire Tory paternalism, which had asserted its own idiosyncratic influence on the provision of public walks for operatives, was notably evident in Blackburn, where it continued to hold sway over submissive and often inept local administration. The formation of a footpath protection association in Blackburn was the product of a conflict between defenders of local public rights and a particular form of factory paternalism. In 1864 the Dickinson brothers – cotton-spinners – had a new factory built on land which they had acquired at Bank Top, and proceeded to assert proprietorship by erecting a high wall which blocked a popular local path to Galligreaves. The route was an important link from the urban area to several beautiful walks along the banks of the River Darwen. There had been no problems over the right of way while the land that was crossed by the disputed path was owned by the Lancashire Tory paternalist, the popular and charismatic local MP, W. H. Hornby. The initial dispute over the route came to a head in a violent confrontation, which raged throughout the afternoon of Monday, 10 October 1864, when a considerable crowd fought with Dickinsons' employees, who 'flocked to the barricade'. 'Volleys of stones were thrown', and some of the operatives came over the wall on a 'sortie' during the battle which had been triggered when the Borough Surveyor had attempted to comply with his stated duty to demolish the obstructive wall.[47] Throughout a three-year dispute the local council equivocated and proved generally ineffective.

The Dickinsons were a rarity amongst Victorian factory paternalists in that they came from a genuinely working-class background, although their father had accumulated capital from his inventions with textile machinery. Their paternalist regime was, nonetheless, wholly consistent with the Blackburn area pattern, in which factory owners influenced the culture and politics of the district in which most of their operatives and their families were housed. In 1861 twenty-one of Blackburn's thirty-six town councillors were employers in cotton, iron, or engineering.[48] The successful paternalist had to be seen to protect the welfare of the community in his own particular domain, while simultaneously assuring that law and order were maintained. The day after the disorder at Bank Top, James Dickinson took out summonses against '5 or 6 persons who had been conspicuous in the work of destruction'.[49] A week later eight people were charged with riotous assembly and wilful damage, liable to sentences ranging from three years to life imprisonment. The subsequent episode indicates the pertinence of such issues as the defence of footpaths and recreational amenities to the machinations of grass-roots politics. Dickinson chose shrewdly to apply his paternalistic prerogative in a public relations exercise aimed at achieving some of the kudos enjoyed by Hornby and Fielden, the towns MPs. The summonses were withdrawn, the defendants dismissed with a warning not to offend again, and Dickinson guaranteed the costs of the case. James Dickinson later became Mayor of Blackburn, and, during the period of the right-of-way dispute, was returned unopposed as councillor for St Peter's Ward, where the 2–1 Tory majority was founded on the big Dickinson and Duckworth mills.[50] The indignation of the radicals was expressed in the *Blackburn Times*: '... great indignation has been expressed, as many burgesses in St. Peter's Ward wished for an opportunity of voting against Mr. Dickinson, owing to his having made himself very unpopular over the footpath question'.[51] Rights of way were thereby pushed into the political limelight in Blackburn. From April 1866 the Bank Top Footpath Association was established, with the intention that it would: 'by its watchfulness and continued exertions, teach the tyrannical usurpers, who have risen from the people, that the rights and privileges of the public are not to be violated and trampled upon with impunity'.[52]

As in other areas where radical groups disputed the closure or diversion of rights of way, the formation of a footpath association in Blackburn produced the organization and financial backing necessary to sustain effective campaigning. In June 1866 the Bank Top Footpath Association called on the services of the well-established MFPS in a development which contributed to the process by which a substantive and collaborative national footpath defence lobby evolved. The MFPS's solicitor, a Mr Fox, was brought in to coordinate a campaign whose impetus was maintained through letters to the Dickinsons and the local press, petitions to the council, and the collection of depositions from local people who had used the Bank Top right of way over periods of more than twenty years, including the evidence of a 93-year-old man who claimed to have used the footpath for eighty years. Fox also asserted that the removal of the obstructions would be a lawful and justifiable act, although the association's committee requested that no one should resort to violence. It took three years to regain access to the Bank Top to Galligreaves route, after which the association faded into obscurity. Before doing so, however, it successfully challenged other encroachments in the area, such as that on the footpath from Duke's Brow to Revidge, which was stopped in the summer of 1866, and the closure of a scenic walk to Moor End near Accrington.

Other footpath protection groups were established in north-central Lancashire during the 1860s. The Preston Footpath Association arose out of a response in 1866 to the closure of a right of way from Wesham to Treales to the west of the town, and it was called upon again in June of the same year, when it unsuccessfully contested the stopping-up of a route which crossed the land of Sir T. G. Hesketh MP, adjacent to Preston Cemetery. It was in a political climate more sympathetic to that which pertained in either Preston or Blackburn that the Carr Hill Road Defence Committee was formed in Nelson in February 1866. This association was 'entirely composed of working men',[53] although advice and assistance were provided by local middle-class radicals. Nelson was a smaller, more radical and homogeneous weaving town, where the successful defence of rights of way was always more likely once resistance had been properly organized. The formation of the committee was triggered by the actions of a substantial landowner, Captain Clayton. The assize courts had confirmed Clayton's authority to close a footpath which was used as a regular route to work and church, but was also particularly popular for leisure walks, allowing open access to the countryside to the north and west of Nelson: 'On Sundays and summer evenings', it was stated, 'the inhabitants of Nelson, of all ages, were to be seen enjoying the shady lane, the refreshing breeze, the beautiful landscape, and the numerous other delightful pleasures which the use of the road afforded.'[54] When the case was heard at the Manchester 1865 spring assizes, no verdict was returned, but the Lancaster assizes in July of the same year decided in favour of Clayton, and fined the seven appellants against whom the original writs were issued one shilling each. However, the newly organized lobby succeeded in reopening the case, which was prosecuted successfully by the defence in a well-publicized hearing at Lancaster in the following year, when the footpath campaigners produced witnesses to a lifelong use of the footpath, including the sworn statement of a 98-year-old man who had died the week before the hearing. Led by William Greenwood of Nelson and James Emmott of Lomeshaye, near Burnley, the Carr Hill Road Defence Committee conformed to the general pattern of such associations, adopting the tactic of establishing their campaign in the context of the wider question of public rights – 'other privileges we now enjoy'. They also acknowledged the important precedent set by the MFPS: 'Many footpaths have been closed for want of an organization formed to resist the imagined and apparent right of the owner of the property through which they led: hence the establishment of the Manchester Ancient Footpaths Association.'[55]

The main focus for footpath defence groups continued to be in areas where the process of industrialization and urbanization conflicted directly with the rural order, but rights-of-way campaigns elsewhere contributed crucially to the generation of an open-air lobby during the nineteenth century. In Scotland John Hutton Balfour, professor of botany at Edinburgh University, was one of the pioneers of a rights-of-way movement. He initiated his challenge to the *status quo* following a much-publicized incident when he and seven of his students were prevented by the Duke of Atholl and his men from traversing the old drove-road up Glen Tilt in the southern Cairngorms. The public right to use the route was established following a prolonged lawsuit, which involved the newly formed Edinburgh Association for the Protection of Rights of Roadway in Scotland, the forerunner of the Scottish Rights of Way Society. Nonetheless, the Duke continued to assert his own jurisdiction, and, in August 1850, his ghillies were involved in a minor skirmish with two Cambridge students on a botanical field trip to Glen Tilt.[56] The Scottish Rights of Way Society was subsequently involved, both through direct action and in the courts of law, in the protection of various routes in the Highlands, including the drawn-out legal action against Duncan McPherson, who, after purchasing the Glen Doll estate in the southern Cairngorms with capital accumulated in Australia, closed the well-established route over the Jock's Road to Deeside. The success of the Scottish campaigners can be attributed in some measure to the membership of the Edinburgh lawyer Thomas Gillies, who, by calling on drovers and shepherds to attest to a history of public use of a right of way, employed one of the movement's most successful tactics.[57]

Although there were a number of common strands, and a measure of associational collaboration, the moulding of a unified footpath lobby was a slow process. The response continued in predominantly piecemeal fashion, based on the spontaneous actions of dedicated individuals or élite groups, who, nevertheless, often succeeded in arousing significant levels of local interest and support. These localized campaigns only rarely managed to sustain any long-term interest, particularly in the vital underlying universal issues, once that the specific case or series of cases had been followed through, either to successful conclusion, or to a stage where constant frustration eventually induced apathy. However, concern with the issue did become more general as a response to the escalating conflict between demands for open-air recreation and the expanding 'sporting' interest. The spread of commercial and industrial encroachment, and newer demands from water companies and, in the present century, from the military, exacerbated the problem.

Greater mobility and the genesis of rambling clubs also tended to push the demands on footpaths further afield from the urban centres, thereby kindling increasing numbers of interested societies. The Derbyshire and the Hallamshire Footpath Preservation Societies (FPS) – the latter based in the rambling stronghold of Sheffield – and the Hayfield and Kinder Scout Ancient Footpaths Association, which later became the Northern Counties and Peak District FPS, fought campaigns in the Peak District which influenced considerably the crucial debate over wider open access to the countryside in the twentieth century. It was appropriate that the funds of the MFPS were transferred to the Northern Counties and Peak District FPS in 1896, as the centre of attention of an outdoor movement, with a substantial base in Manchester, switched to the Peak District.[58]

The defence of rights of way towards the end of the nineteenth century remained within the sphere of an evolving, broadly radical set of ideas and motives, frequently receiving the official sanction of local government in some areas, as part of a general promotion of public utility. The Clitheroe and District FPS, presided over by the mayor, J. H. Satterthwaite, campaigned in the 1890s to reinstate a right of way from West Bradford to Clitheroe, and also appealed specifically to local ramblers to use their footpaths on a regular basis. The Clitheroe group mooted with the council the idea of registering rights of way on maps and erecting footpath signs. Activists continued to work with sympathetic local councils against encroachers of all kinds – including commercial concerns as well as landowners. For example, amicable agreement was reached at the 1907 Manchester spring assizes, following an incident in which the local district council at Ainsworth, to the east of Bolton, had a wall breached to allow access to a path over Cockey Moor which had been blocked by Samuel Holt, manager of the co-operative stores. By the 1890s the essence of a nascent movement can be discerned in its collaborative campaigning dimension.

Although Tory paternalistic concern with the provision of healthy open-air facilities was always evident in nineteenth-century Lancashire, the body of organized and active campaigners was drawn almost exclusively from the rationalizing local liberal radicals. The re-emergence of an organized footpath defence around Blackburn in the 1890s can be attributed to the dedicated work of radically motivated prosperous tradesmen and members of the professional class. The Blackburn and District Ancient Footpaths Association was formed at the Coffee Tavern in Victoria Street in 1894, to coordinate the response to a growing threat to footpaths in the Ribble Valley. The *Northern Daily Telegraph* helped to stimulate local interest in the issue, stressing the important function of rights of way: 'The footpaths in that part of the Ribble Valley are among the most prized of the privileges the public enjoy, and it is to be hoped the effort to close them will be strenuously resisted.'[59] The footpaths referred to were threatened from a variety of sources, ranging from Mr Edgar Appleby, a corn miller and lessee of shooting rights in the vicinity of Salesbury Hall, the Queen Red Facing Brick Company of Liverpool, which was excavating at Lower Cunliffe in 1899, Mr Aspinall of Standen Hall, Clitheroe, who owned land along the Ribble near its confluence with the Hodder, and the absentee Duke of Somerset, who acquired land in the Ribble Valley in 1896. The Blackburn association also contested closures and diversions in collaboration with other outdoor organizations. In 1898 it joined with a group of ramblers from Preston and the Spring Vale Ramblers of Darwen to reopen a footpath at Osbaldeston. The *Blackburn Times* reported that a peaceful and orderly party of 230 country-lovers met no opposition, and made good their claim. Cooperation with the Preston branch of the Commons Open Spaces and Footpaths Preservation Society (COSFPS) prevented Squire Ormerod from disrupting a right of way by fencing off a portion of Nicky Nook in the Forest of Bowland in 1912.

A long-running dispute over the Hacking Boat Road, which was brought to a head in 1898, produced a joint effort with local cyclists, indicative of a growing collaboration of open-air recreational interests as a foundation of a broader integrated outdoor movement. The right of way to a ferry across the Ribble, a popular route for cyclists during the first cycling boom, had been blocked by obstacles, an action which triggered the organization of a joint demonstration in July 1898. The estimated 500 people who rendezvoused at the Tanner's Arms included about 50 cyclists. The demonstrators were of varied social standing, but generally represented a broadly based and culturally influenced social stratum, cemented together in a loose alliance of mutual interest by many of the principles which helped to underpin the construction of an outdoor movement. The *Blackburn Times* reported the presence of 'lawyers, doctors, Town Councillors, gentlemen of social position, artisans of every class and a good number of ladies'.[60] The footpath association in Blackburn had, from its inception, demonstrated an ability to raise and organize a substantial body of protesters, like the force of 1,500 people who gathered from all over the district in April 1894 to reclaim paths by direct action. No doubt this degree of support proved to be a useful bargaining agent, but a good proportion of the success of the local lobbies can be attributed to J. W. Mawdsley, a prosperous grocer, who became the leading light in the Blackburn movement, and who continued to campaign vigorously into the interwar period. Mawdsley's main tactic was to enter into civilized and often protracted correspondence with transgressors, in which he emphasized the strength of local feeling and the large numbers of ramblers who were active in the area. Successful conclusions were achieved from correspondence with the Duke of Somerset, for example, whose letters to Mawdsley and the Blackburn association illustrate urbane aristocratic skill in the art of public relations. The Duke was reluctant to upset local sensibilities when compromise could be achieved. An effective record of large-scale direct action proved to be a powerful complement to Mawdsley's eloquent appeals to the better nature of landowners.

On the other side of the Pennines, around Walshaw Dean and Castle Carr on the moorland above Hebden Bridge, Lord Savile displayed similar patrician stewardship in guarding the exclusiveness of his domains. Savile was, however, bargaining from a significantly stronger and longer-established position in the local hierarchy. Mr Lipscomb, Savile's land agent, claimed that no footpath had existed on the estate for more than fifty years, and that trespass and damage were on the increase, but made the offer, on behalf of his employer, that if the local authority in Halifax agreed not to pursue the case in a court of law, then an agreement could be reached regarding conditions under which the footpaths could be used. This stance was tantamount to an admission that long-standing routes over the moor did exist. Local government was expected to make an undertaking clearly stating that 'they now relinquished every intention of legally or otherwise contending that this was a public path'.[61] Lipscomb's exposition of the landowner's position was reported fully in the *Halifax Courier*:

> I have his Lordship's authority for saying that should such a communication be received by him, he would, in spite of the unfriendly action of these Local Authorities during the last two years, agree to a conference; and further that he would, while protecting his estate from damage endeavour as far as possible to meet the wishes of persons anxious to use this path.[62]

The dispute over Walshaw Dean and Castle Carr was brought to legal arbitration in 1898 only after the conflict had been simmering, with periodic outbursts of intensified activity, since 1869, when the original notice against trespass had been erected at Dean Head. This prolonged series of disputes exemplified most of the key common characteristics of rights-of-way conflicts, particularly those towards the end of the nineteenth century. They included:

1. A clash initiated by a landowner defending his 'sporting' interest

against a perceived threat from undisciplined urban trippers – the paths actually ran close to the grouse butts.

2. A local legal system subject to jobbery – in the Castle Carr case the magistrate and landowner were in fact one and the same person.

3. A major local landowner playing at public relations by offering a measure of compromise.

4. A dispute that dragged on until it eventually arrived at a higher court of law, with witnesses called to testify for and against regular use of the disputed routes.

5. The equivocation of local government under the influence of conflicting interests and loyalties.

6. The water supply cited as an important factor, with civic authorities torn between the defence of public rights of way and a fear of pollution of the water-gathering grounds.

7. The inclusion of the footpath question on the agenda of local grass-roots politics, with the radical element stating their position of support for open-air leisure in terms of champions of public rights. They also enlisted the help of the sympathetic section of the local press; the *Halifax Evening Courier* turned the dispute into an issue in the 1894 local election: 'In December next we elect the Parish Council, one of whose duties is to protect public foot-paths. Let us see that we send men pledged to stand up for our rights.' [63]

However, there was no footpath association to coordinate a defence of rights of way in the area, and the best outcome that could be expected was the 'amicable agreement', consistent with the development of the compromising character of the campaigning dimension to the outdoor movement, reached in May 1908, which imposed conditions relating to dogs, damage and nuisance, and the flying of red flags in season.[64]

The stance adopted by local authorities certainly became increasingly complicated by the activities and attitudes of the water boards, whose schemes were inextricably linked to the concerns of municipal government. Local government bodies in the Halifax area were influenced in their agreement with Lord Savile by the construction of corporation reservoirs at Walshaw. The question of water supply and potential pollution featured increasingly prominently in debates and local negotiations over footpaths and access to the countryside. Additional pressure in the twentieth century was exerted by military demands for the use of moorland and seashore, which was initiated in the period leading up to 1914, and subsequently escalated. The closure of more than fifty miles of paths in the Entwistle, Belmont and Rivington area of the Bolton Moors during 1915 gave rise to a sustained campaign against all categories of footpath encroachment, represented by Sir W. H. Lever of Beech House near Rivington, the Liverpool corporation water board, and the War Office's Western Division. The contended rights of way were said to present 'the finest view round Bolton', and, it was claimed, probably with a degree of licence, with 'not a factory to be seen'.[65] The dispute stimulated a public protest meeting against the Liverpool corporation, and a communication to the War Office. It was brought to a head when Alfred Gerrard, an employee of Horwich Locomotive Works, was fined five shillings (25p) after using a path that had been closed by war restrictions. The highly publicized and partially successful campaign was led and coordinated by Mr Charles Sixsmith of Adlington, an active and versatile outdoor person who was strongly involved in countryside and open-air issues and organizations right up to the time of his death in 1954. Sixsmith was a successful managing director of a Bolton cotton mill from the 1890s to 1933. However, his crucial local political influence stemmed from turn-of-the-century roots in the Utopian socialist, open-air-orientated Clarion movement, and from his broadly liberal leadership of Chorley Rural District Council. Membership of a Whitmanite group in Bolton, as well as a 'firm friendship'[66] with Edward Carpenter, the prophet of alternative lifestyles, gave Sixsmith a substantial grounding in the Lancashire mill town milieu of open-air culture. His life-long love of rural traditions led to membership of the national executive of the highly respectable Council for the Protection of Rural England (CPRE) and he was later appointed to the National Trust Executive for Rufford Old Hall. Sixsmith was typical of the influential open-air activists of the early decades of the twentieth century, whose ideology was situated within the evolution of northern English local government from its nineteenth-century liberal radical roots into a consolidated form of oligarchal municipalism. The social democratic reforming principles promoted by such local establishment reformers ensured that the defence of public rights of way and countryside recreational amenities remained prominent on local political agendas.

C. J. F. Atkinson was a contemporary of Sixsmith who enjoyed an even greater degree of the local prestige and influence that was so essential to truly successful campaigning. Atkinson was a founder member of the Leeds-based Yorkshire Ramblers' Club, an association dominated by middle-class professionals, which included in its objectives the protection of rights of way in the West Riding. The Airedale and Wharfedale area to the north-west of Leeds was the focus of much of Atkinson's attention. He painstakingly defined rights of way above the Washburn Valley, backing up his conscientious fieldwork and mapping by producing affidavits 'carefully collected from inhabitants of long residence', holding back the names of witnesses 'to protect them from annoyance',[67] and maintaining a correspondence with Wharfedale Rural District Council. As a solicitor in Leeds who was a prominent member of the area's middle-class community, Atkinson was ideally suited to the leadership of the local footpath protection lobby.

The movement took on a new dimension and gained fresh impetus towards the end of the nineteenth century. The emergence from the 1880s of uniquely British forms of socialism ensured that rights of way and a wider concern with countryside access were prominent local political issues. However, this new challenge to the landed *status quo* contributed little to the construction of a stronger united front. Any cooperation with liberals was a result of pragmatic local political manoeuvring. The socialists thrust themselves forward as the true defenders of the rights of the people, asserting their own position against predominantly Tory landownership, while simultaneously questioning the motives of liberalism as the main political expression of capitalism. This new ideological angle was beginning to assert its influence at a time when the land question generally had become a prominent national issue, and when the radical wing of liberalism was discarding many *laissez-faire* principles, which had always challenged stagnant land monopolies anyway.

There was a certain inevitability to the SDF's grass-roots involvement in Lancashire – its provincial stronghold – where it evolved into a more popular movement, adopting and promoting a range of popular campaigns as the route to local prestige, especially in enclaves where socialism achieved wider support, such as the Burnley–Nelson district, or the diverse political arena of Bolton. It was in such areas that aggressive SDF direct action formed the vanguard of a flourishing involvement from the left of the political spectrum, rooted in popular culture, and generating an open-air-orientated fraternity whose activities ramified into a variety of other contributions to the growth of an outdoor movement. Within the localized, heterogeneous, and often quirkish political milieu of Lancashire, the rhetoric of universal dogma counted far less than did an involvement in narrowly parochial issues.[68]

The best-documented instance of a socialist involvement in a right-of-way dispute arose over the closure, in 1896, of a footpath which crossed Winter Hill in the upland area to the north-west of Bolton. It was an issue which presented an ideal opportunity for the relatively well-established SDF branch in Bolton to gain significant leverage in local politics by adopting a populist and active role. Support for the footpath activists was always likely in Bolton, where a desire for open-air recreation combined with a long tradition of local footpath use and a general concern for the people's rights as part of the deeply ingrained popular local culture, described in B. Jones's history of the Holiday Fellowship (HF) in the town: 'Bolton folks have always been lovers of the open moorlands around them, and they are quick to defend any attempt to deny them access to what they considered their birthright.' [69] Spanning the turn of the century, the struggle for the Winter Hill route was to become established as a key event in the folklore of both a British outdoor movement and of the unique brand of local socialism which continues its connection with open-air recreational activities at the end of the twentieth century. The disputed right of way was closed by Colonel Ainsworth of Smithills Hall, who in many ways typified that group of south Lancashire landowner which has complicated any easy assumptions regarding the ideological and class basis of town-versus-country conflict. By the 1890s the divisions had become almost wholly obscured, undermining simplistic generalizations about a mutual dislike and perpetual rivalry between old landed interest and the pros-perous liberal industrialists, and the commercial and professional social classes based in the urban areas. As well as owning substantial estates on the Bolton Moors, Ainsworth had amassed a fortune from a bleach-ing business at Halliwell. In the view of the Conservative *Bolton Chronicle*, he was 'a good-natured, easy-going man, a kindly employer, and a good and generous citizen'.[70] Despite spending an increasing amount of time on the south coast for health reasons, or at his second estate in Northamptonshire, 'Squire' Ainsworth exerted a huge in-fluence in the Bolton area, following in the Tory paternalistic traditions of the district, despite a dubiously liberal family background, which included his uncle, Peter Ainsworth, who had been an MP for Bolton. As in Manchester during the 1820s and 1830s, the struggle underlying the footpaths conflict was for local hegemony between liberal radicals and a corrupt Tory oligarchy under the thrall of the local squirearchy. The influence of extreme parochialism and individual popularity on the composition of local government should not be underestimated.

The dynamic activism of the SDF triggered a mass trespass on the Winter Hill right of way in September 1896, followed by fur-ther demonstrations. The publicity attracted an attendance at the original demonstration which was estimated to be as high as twelve thousand. The *Bolton Chronicle*, which, as the local Tory platform, took a pro-landlord stance, was quick to question the motives of the socialists:

> Mr. Shufflebotham and his minions, trading under the name of the Social Democratic Federation, appeal to the general public for sub-scriptions to help them fight the above case ... [T]he primary motive of these discontented agitators in taking the case up is cheap adver-tisement for them and their pernicious doctrine, and, they want the public to pay for it.[71]

Indignant correspondents to the *Chronicle* sustained the attack on the

SDF, stressing the disgrace to the town, expressing horror at the desecration of the Sabbath, and lending consistent support to Ainsworth. One letter claimed that only one per cent of the local population had ever previously been on Winter Hill. *Justice*, as the national organ of the SDF, fully exploited the propaganda opportunity which the issue afforded to the socialists of Bolton, at the same time heralding the recent victory of the people of Darwen in gaining access to their moors as SDF-inspired.[72]

The socialists had certainly succeeded in promoting a substantial degree of interest in local disputes, thereby raising the profile of the footpaths issue generally. The tactic presented an obvious opportunity for Tory attacks on a revolutionary threat not only to the *status quo*, but even to social stability itself. Both of these perspectives were, in reality, grossly exaggerated, with the real agenda again sustained in the long term by progressive liberal radicals. When the establishment in Bolton gathered their forces, regained the initiative, and started to apply pressure, the SDF was easily frightened off. When it came to the crunch, it again became evident that respectable organization, and, most importantly, ample finance, were the main prerequisites for maintaining a campaign to protect rights of way. Such a vital foundation was never really achieved, as local enthusiasm waned in Bolton and campaigners' morale was dented in the period between the original excitement of September 1896 and the court hearing at Manchester on 9 March 1897. Sufficient contributions to the Defence Committee fund were not forthcoming, and, in consequence of defeat in the court of law when the appellants incurred costs of £600, the SDF withdrew from the campaign completely. The defeat had occurred in spite of massive local interest in the issue, and continuous support from the *Bolton Journal*, which vehemently challenged Ainsworth and the mendacity of landowners in general. The fact that the campaign was maintained for more than a decade can be attributed almost entirely to the efforts of one man, the local radical and journalist Solomon Partington. As part of his stubborn challenge to Ainsworth and to the widespread corruption in what he called 'Bolton's Augean Stable',[73] Partington's adoption of the footpath cause sustained his attack on what he exposed as a combination between the local council and the old ruling establishment in 'a conspiracy to defeat the ends of public justice'.[74] Winter Hill became Partington's main obsession in his 'Truth' crusade against 'our Tammany Ring' and the 'municipally corrupting caucus'[75] which he publicized through his five 'Truth' pamphlets, printed under the general heading of *Winter Hill Right of Way. Truth v. Falsehood*, and later in his election pamphlet of 1907. From 1904, Partington fought the issue as a town councillor, elected with the pragmatic support of the socialists. Prior to his election, and assisted by his lone council ally, Hutchinson, he amassed substantial new evidence to be presented to the council's General Purposes Winter Hill Sub-Committee, which decided, on 24 January 1902, that the case should not be reopened. The footpaths campaign was escalated during Partington's 1907 election campaign, to introduce an attack on both the injustice of the Horwich Moor Inclosure Act of 1815, and the loss of other local roads, including the Higher Lomax Wives Road, which rose to over a thousand feet en route to Blackburn. Persistence in the fight against encroachment by landowners did eventually appear to have some impact in the Bolton area when, in 1914, the local council reinstated footpaths over Turton Moor. By and large, however, the combination of a newly consolidated, if less aristocratic landed class, a changing emphasis in land use, and 'Duplicity in High Places' and 'the Hostility of the Oligarchs'[76] frustrated an increasing desire amongst socially diverse town-dwellers to enjoy fresh air and healthy exercise. Solomon Partington's stubborn tenacity and eloquent rhetoric in turn-of-the-century Bolton were no substitute for the crucial degree of local influence available to Prentice and Potter and colleagues around Manchester in the 1820s, while the ruling class easily discredited the eager and righteous socialist involvement as mere political chicanery which threatened the social fabric. In September 1909 a reformist social democratic interest in the Winter Hill rights of way re-emerged, albeit in reformist establishment garb, when Westhoughton's Labour MP, Tyson Wilson, raised with the board of trade the question of the public amenity which such local routes afforded.

As recreational demands expanded towards the end of the nineteenth century, socialists in the Burnley area also took up the cause of the defence of rights of way. In August 1896 the *Rossendale Free Press* reported on the serious disruption of a popular path, known locally as the 'Shady Walk', by the landowner, Colonel Starkie, who had stepping-stones over the River Calder removed, and obstacles positioned to block the path: '... a number of people connected with the local Socialist Club marched to the field with hatchets and spades, and made a gap in the hedge at the fence which had been closed with railings and barbed wire'.[77] Intervention by socialists only occurred after more traditional footpath defenders succeeded in having the stepping-stones reinstated following an agreement between Colonel Starkie and Burnley Rural District Council in May 1896. Starkie had again closed the route in August by replacing iron railings at Hargrove Farm, which had been the focus of an earlier demonstration by 'hundreds of people ... headed by Mr. Norman Bleazard (Chairman) and other members of the local Footpath Committee'.[78] The committee was also active on two occasions against Sir Ughtred Kay-Shuttleworth, who had paid lip-service to the principles of public amenity.

The episodic development of an effective footpath lobby depended heavily on the pursuit of 'respectability', which has been so essential to the evolution of a broader outdoor movement. Such concerns have influenced significantly the character and ideology of a cultural development which conforms to a social model constructed on vertical links between the different economic groups. Elements of what was perceived as an unruly social group were held responsible for subverting the respectable cause of footpath protection. That dichotomy maintained a high profile around mid-century Burnley, for example. The effectiveness of the Blackburn footpath lobby in the 1860s was patently undermined by the activities of the mob, which took the opportunity to indulge in a bit of general mayhem. The *Blackburn Standard* condemned the 'large crowd of idle and disorderly people' who deserved punishment for taking the law into their own hands.[79] General lawlessness did achieve wider publicity, but also diverted the focus of attention away from the real issues and the rational and orderly campaign to save a right of way in order to facilitate general public amenity. It became easy for James Dickinson, for example, to exploit the situation by portraying himself as the magnanimous unprejudiced upholder of social stability against the forces of chaos. It was always in the interests of rights of way campaigners, often institutionally represented by respectable footpath protection associations, to emphasize the rational and disciplined nature of their cause. Justifying the defence of the Moor End right of way near Accrington in 1866, a correspondent to the *Blackburn Times* spoke of the 'decent and respectable people ... [who] ... have realised the benefits of a pleasant walk, and the salubrious air which is to be found in this locality'.[80] The writer clearly indicated his own unflinching devotion to the pursuit of justice, and his membership of that 'respectable' stratum of society, when he signed himself 'Rhadamanthus'. The footpath campaigners in Nelson, defending the seven local men against whom writs had been served in 1865, referred to the defendants as 'respected and well-conducted young men who are teachers in our Sunday schools and much respected in the neighbourhood'.[81] The landed establishment in the Nelson area also emphasized the incidence of disorderly behaviour in their justification for footpath closure. The *Preston Guardian* countered that argument by pointing to the inevitability of an unruly element in the population of a growing industrial town, but, feeling that this did not exonerate Captain Clayton, stated the case of the respectable defenders of public rights: '... we are therefore not disposed to let the innocent suffer for the guilty'.[82]

The huge turnout for the original Winter Hill demonstration obviously owed much to general inquisitiveness for a highly publicized event, and did become the venue for mob rowdyism and a bit of excitement for the local riff-raff. The *Manchester Guardian*, reporting an 'Extraordinary Demonstration at Bolton', highlighted the important division between 'rough' and 'respectable' contributions to the episode:

> ... between eight and ten thousand people assembled to assert the public right of the user ... The main body of the vast crowd was orderly, but there were also many roughs, who, in traversing the road, knocked over Inspector Willoughby, struck Sergeant Sefton with a stone, violently kicked Mr. Jabez Walch, the landagent's son, and broke down stiles and other woodwork.[83]

The *Guardian* also adopted the establishment line that the ringleaders were from the Bolton SDF. Associating the local socialists with rabble-rousing was consistent with the ease with which the establishment was able to equate emergent socialism with the unruly and dangerous sub-stratum in contemporary society.

A vehement attack on footpath encroachers, made by Luke Garside of the Hayfield and Kinder Scout Ancient Footpaths Association in the 1880s, was careful to stress the association's intention to 'ascertain and ensure, as amicably as possible the rights of both parties'; Garside conceded that a degree of annoyance was caused by 'trespassers, often in the form of excursionists'. From this somewhat élitist perspective, which conforms with the subsequent concerns of a developing movement, it was even suggested that proprietors should furnish an 'order' to any 'well-conducted persons'.[84] The question of trippers and tourists would increasingly fuel the debate over the use of rights of way. The ambiguity of the notion of 'respectability' is also apparent in the propensity amongst nineteenth-century footpath defenders to resort to direct action. It is strongly evident, however, that the activists, whether as individuals or in association, usually paid the maximum attention to lawfulness and discipline, and to a carefully precise removal of obstacles to well-established rights. The question of what strategy should be employed by the campaigning vanguard has recurred persistently throughout each stage in the development of the outdoor movement.

The largely fragmented growth and fluctuating fortunes of an expansive movement in defence of public footpaths as a leisure amenity, in the century which culminated in the First World War, was obviously and inextricably linked to an emerging interest in open-air and country-side recreation. At the same time, tangible roots of that development can be detected in older cultural traditions which had survived the threat posed by the process of 'modernization'. The agenda was set predominantly in Lancashire, but was strongly influenced by contemporaneous developments in a different Scottish context. However, as the nineteenth century progressed, and recreational pressures expanded, other regions developed similar sets of conflictual circumstances and became subject to the pressures that generated the footpath societies, which came to represent a vital unifying strand of continuity. Rights-of-way campaigns, the defence of open spaces, and the expansion of outdoor recreational pursuits combined to elevate the issue from a series of localized squabbles to an issue of national importance. The formation in 1885 of the highly respectable National Footpath Preservation Society (NFPS) integrated a broader response by publicizing the vastly increased number of conflicts. That unifying function was consolidated through the national society's coordination of the formerly piecemeal proliferation of local associations. As rambling and general leisure walking emerged as a fashionable activity, before developing into a more popular pastime, the whole concept of footpath protection became more sophisticated. The essential institutional structure had been created, and important precedents set, nevertheless, by the earliest defenders of the traditional right to walk unhindered on public footpaths.

Notes

1. Walker, H., 'The Outdoor Movement in England and Wales, 1900–1939', unpublished Ph.D. thesis, University of Sussex, 1988.
2. Prentice, A., *Historical Sketches and Personal Recollections of Manchester* (London and Manchester, 1851), p. 289.
3. Martineau, H., *Bibliographical Sketches. 1852–1875* (new edn; London, 1885), p. 404.
4. Walton, J. K., 'The Windermere Tourist Trade in the Age of the Railway, 1847–1912' in Westall, O. M., ed., *Windermere in the Nineteenth Century* (Lancaster, 1991), pp. 19–33.
5. *Narrative of the Proceedings in the Case of Rodgers and Others versus Harvie for the Recovery of the Liberty of the Banks of the Clyde* (Glasgow, 1829), p. 1.
6. Adams, G., *A History of Bridgeton and Dalmarnock* (Glasgow, n.d.), p. 23.
7. *Ibid.*, p. 5.
8. *York Herald and General Advertiser*, 31 July 1824, p. 2.
9. Walton, J. K., *Lancashire. A Social History* (Manchester, 1987), p. 124.
10. British Sessional Papers, 1731–1800, House of Commons, Bills vol. vii, 1773, No. 229, para. 1.
11. *Ibid.*
12. *Blackburn Mail*, 21 September 1825, p. 2.
13. *Ibid.*, 3 August 1825, p. 2.
14. Prentice, *Historical Sketches*.
15. *Ibid.*, p. 290.
16. Lawson, R., *A History of Flixton, Urmston and Davyhulme* (Manchester, 1988), p. 78.
17. *Manchester Gazette*, 22 September 1827, p. 2.

18. *Ibid.*, 3 November 1827, p. 1.
19. *Ibid.*, p. 2.
20. *Ibid.*
21. Prentice, *Historical Sketches*, p. 289.
22. *Ibid.*
23. *Manchester Times*, 27 March 1830, p. 102.
24. *Ibid.*, 12 June 1830, p. 192.
25. *Ibid.*, 26 April 1830, p. 136.
26. *Ibid.*, 6 March 1830, p. 75.
27. *Ibid.*
28. *Leeds Patriot and Yorkshire Advertiser*, 6 February 1830, p. 3.
29. Webb, S. and B., *The Story of the King's Highway* (London, 1913), p. 203.
30. *PD*, 3rd Series, 5 (1831), col. 650.
31. *Ibid.*, col. 651.
32. *Ibid.*, 19 (1833), col. 1104.
33. Quoted in Cunningham, H., *Leisure in the Industrial Revolution* (London, 1980), p. 81.
34. *PP*, Report of the Select Committee on Public Walks, 1833, para. 79.
35. Whittle, P. A., *Bolton-le-Moors and the Townships in the Parish* (Bolton, 1855), p. 59.
36. *Ibid.*, pp. 373–4.
37. *Ibid.*, p. 198.
38. *Ibid.*, p. 375.
39. *Ibid.*
40. In *The History of Burnley* (Burnley, 1951) W. Bennett equates the reasoning behind local footpath closure with the unruly reputation of an element within the new urban working class: 'hooliganism was to be found everywhere, notably on the "Rabbit Walk" in Townley Holmes, at Pendle Bridge, and near Royle, so that landowners threatened to close the roads'.
41. Scrapbook of Newspaper Cuttings, 1907–1915, p. 42, Burnley Local Studies Library.
42. *Burnley Advertiser*, 1 January 1859, p. 2.
43. *Ibid.*, 8 January 1859, p. 2.
44. *Ibid.*
45. *Ibid.*
46. Scrapbook of Newspaper Cuttings, 1914–1916, p. 11, Burnley Local Studies Library.
47. *Blackburn Patriot*, 15 October 1864, p. 3.
48. Joyce, P., *Work, Society, and Politics. The Culture of the Factory in Later Victorian England* (Brighton, 1980), p. 169.
49. *Blackburn Patriot*, 15 October 1864, p. 3.
50. Joyce, *Work, Society and Politics*, p. 206.
51. *Blackburn Times*, 3 November 1866, p. 5.
52. *Ibid.*, 28 April 1866, p. 6.
53. *Preston Guardian*, 28 February 1866, p. 4.
54. *Ibid.*
55. *Ibid.*

56. Aitken, R., 'Stravagers and marauders', *Scottish Mountaineering Club Journal* XXX, 166 (1975), pp. 351–8.
57. *Ibid.*
58. Wild, H., 'The Manchester Society for the Preservation of Ancient Footpaths', *Manchester Review* 10 (Winter 1965–6), p. 242.
59. *Northern Daily Telegraph*, 24 April 1894; Records of the Work of Blackburn and District Footpath Preservation Society, 1894–1936, Blackburn Local Studies Library.
60. *Blackburn Times*, 30 July 1898, in Records of Blackburn and District Footpath Preservation Society.
61. *Halifax Courier*, 11 January 1908, p. 3.
62. *Ibid.*
63. *Halifax Evening Courier*, 4 October 1894, p. 3.
64. Turner, W., *A Springtime Saunter in Brontëland* (Halifax, 1913), p. 144.
65. *Bolton Journal*, 9 April 1915, p. 10.
66. *Chorley and Leyland Advertiser*, 26 February 1954, p. 1.
67. *Wharfedale and Airedale Observer*, 10 August 1917, p. 7.
68. See Howell, D., *British Workers and the ILP, 1885–1906* (Manchester, 1983).
69. Jones, B., *Holiday Fellowship: The First Sixty Years* (Bolton, 1983), introduction.
70. *Bolton Chronicle*, 18 September 1896, p. 3.
71. *Ibid.*
72. See Chapter 2, which distinguishes the defence of traditional rights of way from the campaign to improve open access to upland areas.
73. Partington, S., *Truth Pamphlet, No. 5* (Bolton, 1902).
74. *Idem, Truth Pamphlet, No. 1* (Bolton, 1902).
75. *Idem, My Three Years Councillorship for West Ward* (Bolton, 1907), p. 4.
76. *Ibid.*, p. 10.
77. *Rossendale Free Press*, 15 August 1896, p. 8.
78. *Nelson Chronicle*, 21 February 1896, p. 7.
79. *Blackburn Standard*, 12 October 1864, p. 3.
80. *Blackburn Times*, 30 June 1866, p. 6.
81. *Preston Guardian*, 28 February 1866, p. 4.
82. *Ibid.*
83. *Manchester Guardian*, 7 September 1896, p. 6.
84. Garside, L., *Kinder Scout with the Footpaths and Bridle Roads about Hayfield* (reprint; Oldham, 1980), pp. 9, 64.

Chapter 2

Early Walkers

Rambling as a distinct recreational activity emerged during the period of widespread anti-industrialism in the last quarter of the nineteenth century. Helen Walker comments on the specifically motivated associational formation, noting that 'the gradual emergence of clubs with rambling as their primary objective is found in the later years of the century'.[1] The emphasis on anti-commercial and anti-urban influences in the generation of open-air associations has, nonetheless, led to a tendency to depict nineteenth-century recreational walking as a relatively insignificant pursuit, confined almost exclusively to those people from the more leisured classes, who rejected many of the values on which contemporary society was constructed. This fundamental over-simplification helps to perpetuate the dominant notion that the more popular adoption of healthy open-air pursuits only emerged in the wake of radical social and cultural changes following the First World War. There was certainly a boom in outdoor leisure activities in the interwar period, but the substantial earlier involvement of individuals and groups, who are generally assumed to have had neither the means nor the inclination to participate in such forms of recreation until the 1920s, should not be neglected as a shaping influence on the character of a significant nascent movement. Howard Hill expresses the current orthodoxy when he tells us that: 'The earliest rambling clubs were not drawn from a wide stratum of British people.'[2] This prevailing overview largely ignores the evidence of extensive early popular participation in rambling, which represented one aspect of the cultural continuity that was particularly apparent in the urban and industrial south Pennine communities, where a vigorous rights-of-way movement had evolved from the 1820s. Undoubtedly the well-to-do did enjoy greater recreational opportunities, and it was from those upper strata of society that most of the literature of the open-air and the published accounts of outdoor activities emanated. It is hardly surprising that the impression has been established of an exclusive pursuit, which originated in organized form with the London-based Sunday Tramps in 1879: '... mainly from the upper echelons of Victorian society ... aesthetes, academics, and members of the legal profession'.[3] Other accounts, such as M. Marples's *Shanks's Pony*, published in 1959, have specified the

intellectual classes as the recreational walkers during the second half
of the nineteenth century.

This association of countryside leisure with urban escapees drawn
entirely from a single elevated social stratum also helps to perpetuate
unduly rigid notions of class formation. It neglects the potential for
social bonding founded on a mutual interest, which can often transcend
economic conflicts and status divisions. A significant level of social
hybridization in the sphere of leisure, engendered by a cross-fertilization
of values and interests, was a manifest influence on the formative stages
in the development of the outdoor movement. Direct links between
the walkers of the high-Victorian period and the notion of a movement
based on a common interest in recreational walking are easily discernible. However, much earlier origins can indicate some of the diverse
motivation and changing responses to differing sets of circumstances,
which contributed to the process through which the outdoor movement
evolved. The Oxford classicist A. H. Sidgwick, an exponent of both the
aesthetic and athletic attractions of countryside rambling, and a prominent member of that turn-of-the-century walking fraternity drawn from
the professional stratum of society, traced deep roots in a literature of
walking that reached right back to Graeco-Roman references.[4] Less
dubious and more tangible connections can be made with an eighteenth-
and early nineteenth-century minority of walkers who came mainly
from a literary background.

At a time when the landscapes most typically associated with open-air
recreation were recorded as the subject of awe and even dread, John
Clare gained his poetic inspiration on solitary walks in the softer pastoral
landscapes of his native English south Midlands. Clare exhibited many
of the characteristics common to later avid walkers, who ranged from
the poets of the Romantic age to the modern-day moorland rambler.
He sought both solitude and escape from the mundane. He combined
the naturalist's practicality and objectivity with romantic inclinations.
His countryside walks contained elements of the spiritual and religious
motivation suggestive of a pantheistic tendency in the spiritual dimension that was apparent in some late nineteenth-century walkers. Clare
can in some ways be seen as a herald of later country ramblers from
the lower social strata. Representative of the cultivated peasant, he
gained his fundamental education from the lanes, meadows and hedge-
rows. He walked in order to enquire, discover, and to give expression
to an advanced emotional development, which contradicted the dominant élitist perception that regarded the appreciation of beauty as the
exclusive domain of the cultivated minds of the higher social echelons.[5]

The forbidding reputation of mountain landscapes in the eighteenth
century owed much to exaggerated accounts of tours made by literary
figures, such as that of Dr Johnson in Scotland, and Daniel Defoe in

the Peak District and Westmorland – although Norman Nicholson, in *The Lakers*, questions whether the notoriously mendacious Defoe ever got as far as the Lake counties. Among the first to popularize the wilder regions was schoolteacher and cleric John Gilpin, who toured Scotland, Wales and the Lakes during the 1770s. Gilpin was the most influential promoter of a new vogue for the picturesque and the sublime; Nicholson refers to him as 'the travelling salesman of the picturesque'.[6] Others perpetuated the newly attractive images of the Lake District, but it was left to the esoteric and spiritually motivated Romantics to demonstrate that walking across the hitherto terrifying fells, and contact with wild landscape, could produce both physical and sensual rewards. From such discoveries emerged the development of a new literary genre: the Lake District guide. Many of these were produced from the later eighteenth century onwards to give impetus to the developing recreational popularity of the area. One of the best known, though by no means the first of such guides, was Wordsworth's *Guide through the District of the Lakes in the North of England*. The prodigious capacity for physical exercise for which Wordsworth was renowned was recorded by Thomas De Quincey, who estimated that the 'poet of the Lakes' had walked a total of between 175,000 and 180,000 miles. Other acquaintances of De Quincey were John Stewart, referred to as 'Walking Stewart', the vegetarian, teetotal and atheistic author of *Travels over the most interesting parts of the Globe, to discover the Source of Moral Motion*, and who, De Quincey claimed, had 'walked over the habitable globe';[7] and Allan Cunningham, a stonemason and rustic poet from Dumfriesshire, whom De Quincey likened to John Clare, and Sir Walter Scott referred to as 'Honest Allan'.[8]

Keats was another of the Romantic poets to gain inspiration from strenuous country walking. Between 25 June and 3 August 1818, at the age of twenty-two, Keats walked six hundred miles from Lancaster to Inverness. During a journey which traversed some of the wilder scenery of the British Isles, Keats, together with his companion Charles Brown, took in mountain ascents, visits to archaeological sites, and a crossing to the Isle of Mull, where he contacted a heavy cold and throat ulcers which forced him to rest in Oban for two days. Keats described this long-distance walk in some detail in his prolific correspondence.[9] In May 1798, Wordsworth was visited by the twenty-year-old William Hazlitt, another literary figure with a penchant for long walks. Like Wordsworth, Hazlitt enjoyed solitude on his rural rambles, with Nature supplying ample company, although his motivation was more to do with the freedom which that solitude represented:

I cannot see the wit of walking and talking at the same time. When I am in the country, I wish to vegetate like the country. I am not

for criticising hedge-rows and black cattle. I go out of town in order
to forget the town and all that is in it ... I like solitude when I give
myself up to it, for the sake of solitude.[10]

The picturesque harmony of the Lake District provided the main
focus for the literary coterie of walkers who drew their inspiration from
Wordsworth, although others with artistic leanings also enjoyed physical open-air pursuits in other remote areas of rugged scenery.
P. G. Hamerton, a Lancashire art critic who was later made an honorary
fellow of the Royal Society of Painter-Etchers, recorded living close
to Nature when he was in his twenties, while walking, camping and
painting at an artists' camp in the Scottish Highlands during the 1850s.
Hamerton also walked locally on the Lancashire–Yorkshire borders,
rambling and camping on the Boulsworth moors, for example, with his
uncle's servant, Jamie. Part of the inspiration for his expeditions into
wild places in all weathers came from what he called 'the Emersonian
doctrine of individualism'.[11] Emersonianism epitomized the optimistic
American version of a Romanticism which based its philosophy of
human conduct on the efficacious influences of nature on the spirit,
with an ultimate objective rooted in the idea of individual perfection.
Wordsworth's poetic evocations of romantic countryside continued to
inspire ramblers, as the pastime gained popularity, in the later nineteenth century. The Manchester writer Abraham Stansfield, who
produced literary sketches of popular culture, invoked *The White Doe
of Rylstone*, claiming that he and his walking companions had read the
poem fifty times and were 'seized with a great longing to visit the
beautiful country which it celebrates and *consecrates*'.[12] In his own poetic
idiom, Stansfield contrasted the city with Wharfedale, where he and
his party walked:

> From grimy Manchester to the green dales of Yorkshire, from a
> forest of tall chimneys to the glorious woods of Bolton, from muddy
> Medlock and inky Irwell to pellucid Aire and the clear-flowing
> Wharfe, from prosy Cottonopolis, with its noisy traffic, its striving
> and driving, its hustle and bustle, to a region of tranquil beauty,
> hallowed and glorified by the genius of the poet ...[13]

The Reverend Francis Kilvert's love of the open air, and his poetic
feeling for the picturesque, are redolent of Wordworth, and suggest a
substantial influence. Kilvert's promotion of the benefits of long upland
walks would, however, seem to apply only to men, and he was convinced
that Dorothy Wordsworth's ill health in old age was caused by too
many strenuous long walks when she was younger.[14] Kilvert was a great
walker and lover of solitude, who made extensive forays into the hills

during the 1870s from his clerical livings in the Welsh Marches. His accounts of regular and energetic rambles and mountain scrambles have the feel of the increasingly popular genre of walking guide books, which combined the utility of bald description with romantic evocation, illustrated suitably by the entry for Tuesday, 22 February 1870:

> After luncheon went for a walk with Mr. V. to the top of Drum du. When we got to the cairn Plynlimmon was quite visible, but only the ghost of Cader Idris to be seen. We went away disappointed but had not gone far before the clouds suddenly lifted and a sun burst lit up grandly the great snowslopes of round-backed Plynlimmon and the vast snowy precipices of the giant Cader Idris near 50 miles away. We hurried back to the cairn and had a glorious view to N. & W. of the Fans of Brecon and Carmarthen.[15]

Four days later Kilvert was tramping over the hills to Colva, and combining convivial sociability with escape to the open spaces:

> Very hot walking. At the Green Lane Cottage found Mrs. Jones and daughter at home sewing ... There was the brown withered heather, the elastic turf, the long green ride stretching over the hill like a green ribbon between the dark heather. There was the free, fresh, fragrant air of the hills ...[16]

Kilvert's love of the freedom of walking in the open spaces was wholly consistent with the significant numbers of nineteenth-century clergymen who enjoyed the all-round benefits of country rambles, and who displayed a common sympathy with a range of open-air concerns. This understanding was exemplified in the Reverend J. M. Mather's two volumes of *Rambles Round Rossendale*,[17] which recorded numerous rambles taken around the hills and dales of east Lancashire throughout the second half of the nineteenth century, some of them with a factory-hand walking companion. Mather criticized the narrowness of Board School education, advocating the benefits of knowledge and enjoyment of the natural environment.

Walking in the countryside was never exclusive to the poet, the artist, the aesthete, or to the spiritually inspired clergyman. Fresh air, fun and physical exercise were already well established as motives for countryside rambles during the first half of the nineteenth century, as the proliferation of footpath protection campaigns in the vicinity of the Lancashire industrial towns emphasized. An uncomplicated enjoyment of walking in the hills can be traced back into the eighteenth century. Detailed written accounts by the Glasgow dry-salter Adam Bald, of his numerous rambles taken between the 1790s and the 1830s, challenge the overweening assumption that mountains were always held in romantic awe. Trepidation for wild mountain landscapes was a predominantly southern English and metropolitan perspective, reinforced by a prevailing opinion of the Scottish Highlands which continued to be shaped by the series of events that culminated in the final quashing of the Jacobite uprising in 1745–6; the Scots' familiarity with mountain scenery, consolidated by a tradition of roaming, would most certainly have been an influence on their different attitude. What the activities of Bald and his fellow ramblers also serves to emphasize is that an outdoor movement in Scotland had earlier recognizable roots than its counterpart further south, except arguably in Lancashire. Interestingly, Bald suggested that around 1790 a change occurred in the perceived function of the healthy outdoor environment. The change was indicated in his account of a 'Ten days Ramble to the Seacoast', in July 1791: 'It was the custom for valitudinarians [sic] in the inland parts of the country to repair for the summer to the seacoast.' [18] He went on to describe how the coast of the Firth of Clyde used to be for 'convalescence and purifying their constitution', but had recently become the resort of 'the plump and jolly, sauntering the rocky shore, or climbing the heathery hill full of health and spirits, whilst the sickly race are confined to their gloomy chambers ...' [19] Bald most commonly started his frequent rambling tours by walking down the Clyde to Gourock to take the ferry to 'Rothsay' [sic] or to 'Ardontenny [sic]'. These rambling tours of up to fourteen days in duration were sometimes recorded in a range of verse forms, most commonly in rhyming couplets. Good food played an important part in the tours, on which Bald was joined by various companions – for example, John Sanderson, a 'writting master [sic]', [20] joined the five-day walk around Stirling in November 1792, and regular companions John Muire and Stephen Rowan went on the eight-day ramble to Inveraray in August 1799, when, after taking the coach to Dumbarton, they enjoyed 'adventures amongst the heath cover'd mountains of Calidonia [sic]'.[21] Bald's expeditions did have a practical scientific dimension, satisfying an obsessive interest in meteorology, which is evident from the content of his journal.

Descriptions of rambling tours in a similar vein proliferated from the middle of the nineteenth century. It was a genre which both reflected and perpetuated the popularity of the pastime, around the industrial towns of Lancashire in particular. Three volumes of W. Dobson's *Rambles by the Ribble*, the first published in 1864, or dialect poet Edwin Waugh's *Rambles in the Lake Country* (1861) were typical. Later came such accounts as P. H. Bird's *A Ramble by the Ribble and Hodder*, E. Bogg's *A Thousand Miles of Wandering along the Roman Wall, the Old Border Region, Lakeland, and Ribblesdale*, or W. H. Burnett's *Holiday Rambles by road and field-path; principally near the River Ribble*. On the other side of the Pennines, as early as 1848, G. S. Phillips's *Walks Round Huddersfield* typically contrasted the new urban ugliness with the attractions of local rural scenes: '... nature seems always to be tempting us there with her sweetest smiles, to leave the hot, dusty town, and wander with her amongst the hills, dells, and moorlands'.[22] Phillips was an Owenite radical and also a friend of Emerson, who stayed as a house guest in 1847.[23] In Scotland, Hugh MacDonald produced his *Rambles Round Glasgow*, first published in 1854 and reprinted in 1878. Mac-Donald was the eldest of eleven children whose parents had migrated early in the century from the west Highlands to the east end of Glasgow. He originally worked as a block-printer, but it was as a journalist that he produced accounts of rambles within a radius of ten miles of the city for the *Glasgow Citizen*, of which he later became subeditor. Similar descriptions, incorporating romantic rural evocation, became a common feature of the columns of local newspapers in Lancashire and Yorkshire. The *Preston Chronicle* produced such sketches as early as the 1860s. This indirect evidence of an expansion of recreational walking is complemented by accounts contained in the journals of the naturalists' associations. The painstakingly researched footpath guides produced by the pseudonymous 'Walker Miles', for instance, were invaluable aids to ramblers in such popular areas as the Surrey hills. Armed with notebook and compass, Miles pieced together the vast complex of old rights of way and wove them into continuous walks, which took into account the available facilities for rail transport and refreshment. His guides, supplemented by those produced by 'Alf Holliday' and Noah Weston, gave a new focus and added urgency to the issue of rights of way in the south-east of England.

The practical and tangible beginnings of the outdoor movement, given substance by the formation of rambling groups, were informed by a critique of those crude and often superficial values that had gained purchase in the ethos of a consolidated industrial capitalist system. Hingeing around a group of Oxbridge and professional intellectuals, the broader contemporary response ramified into peripheral expressions of an open-air ideology, which attempted to formulate alternatives to the existing system. Represented, for instance, in the ideas of Edward Carpenter, schemes were devised for a radically different *modus vivendi*.[24] Nonetheless, the social criticism was also directed from a continuing position within the mainstream of society.

Formed in 1879, the Sunday Tramps were a small, but influential association of upper-middle-class professional men, several of them academics from a range of disciplines. The Tramps were regularly entertained by the poet and novelist George Meredith at his home at Box Hill in Surrey. In a letter to Robert Louis Stevenson, Meredith described one such visit following a ramble around Tillingbourne and

Ranmore and through 'Evelyn's Wooton' [sic]: 'The Tramps visiting us were L. S. [Leslie Stephen] for leader or Pied Piper, Morison, Fredk. Pollock, Croom Robertson, Edgeworth and another.'[25] Such a group was representative of the composition of the Tramps, whose membership was drawn from the progressive vanguard of late-Victorian intelligentsia. Frederick Pollock, for example, was professor of jurisprudence, and George Croom Robertson was professor of mental philosophy and logic at University College, London. Participants in other rambles included F. W. Maitland, Downing Professor of Law at Cambridge, whose biography of Leslie Stephen was published in 1906, and James Sully, professor of philosophy at University College, whose article describing the activities of the Sunday Tramps appeared in the January 1908 edition of the *Cornhill Magazine*.[26] Meredith had himself been an avid walker, but partial paralysis curtailed his physical participation in the Tramps' activities.

The Sunday Tramps discovered their rural ideal and the means of personal renewal on these weekend walks in a natural environment, away from 'the dreary London Sabbath'.[27] The rigid conventions so essential to contemporary religious practice were rejected as unnecessarily restrictive. Their reaction to evangelical cant can be detected in Meredith's keenness that Stephen should exclude parsons and hymn-writers and other 'nonentities'[28] from the *Dictionary of National Biography*, which Stephen edited. Although not much of a physical participant in the generation of an active outdoor fellowship, Meredith's vision and influence were directly pertinent to the common concerns of a nascent movement. His widely disseminated beliefs epitomized the ideology of freedom and the open air which was the product of a profound and conscientious attempt to come to terms with personal convictions. A form of spiritualism can be identified which was steeped in the pantheon of Nature. It was akin to other direct expressions of the trenchant criticism of a disorientated society labouring under moral and spiritual torpor, such as the particularly active and radical response formulated by Edward Carpenter. These intellectual idealists were generally divorced from the reality of the majority's experience of the material world, but their perspectives offered a pertinent contribution by giving some substance to a desire for alternatives. Meredith's critique, for example, contained more than a negative reaction. There is some irony in the fact that this romantic writer presented both a more rational and a more naturalistic set of notions than did his close friend Stephen, overtly the archetypal Victorian rationalist and the athletic influence on the group, but also the suppressed sentimentalist.

From his role as convivial host and literary guru to the Tramps, Meredith articulated a version of the interdependent organic vision of

society which challenged the assumed inevitability of selfish individualism. Such ideas appear to fit comfortably into a tradition of Tory
anti-capitalist thought, but they were, by the latter part of the nineteenth century, consistent with the type of moral economy that
motivated those metropolitan professional intellectuals who made up
the membership of the Sunday Tramps. This included J. B. S. Haldane,
and later G. M. Trevelyan, underpinning the central ideological contribution to an evolving liberal radical philosophy, which added impetus
to an apparent coming together, in areas of common ground, of socially
conservative Tories, progressive, interventionist liberals, and Utopian
socialists. In reality, of course, fundamental switches were taking place
within the wider ideological *status quo*.

This was the nature of the discourse which Stephen's 'flock of cranium
tramps' [29] combined with a physical and spiritual enjoyment of the
natural environment: '... tramping with them one has the world under
review as well as pretty scenery'.[30] Their response, lucidly expressed
through Meredith, represented part of a growing reaction against *laissez-
faire* economics, adopting an environmentalist flavour which provides
a coherent link to some of the prevalent concerns of the modern-day
open-air movement in its various associational representations. A stance
was taken against the philistinism [31] that sanctioned modern development in hitherto largely unspoiled natural environments – this was a
specific focus of continuing concern to the conservationist wing amongst
countryside recreationists, which goes beyond the direct self-interest of
today's so-called 'Nimby' phenomenon. The Tramps were certainly
drawn from a social élite, and Meredith would rarely have come into
contact with factories or urban-industrial blight, but they shared with
the increasing numbers of ramblers and cyclists from the expanding
urban areas a common distaste for the product of unbridled, profit-
obsessed industrial capitalism. That environmental concern is evident
in a letter which Meredith wrote to a former Sunday Tramp, Douglas
Freshfield, in 1908. By that time much of the practical idealist dimension
to the literary contribution to an open-air response had descended into
the 'Georgian' sentimentality, which was swamped into insignificance
by a general early twentieth-century resurgence of political realism and
economic materialism: 'Those old days of the Tramps are lively in my
mind. I know you're a Keeper of Ashdown Forest. My own quarrel with
the present-day developments lies in the hectoring of lovely open
country by hideous villas.' [32] As the relatively widely disseminated voice
of an influential element from the emerging fraternity of countryside
ramblers, Meredith's environmentally concerned polemic was at times
reminiscent of Ruskin, who had objected strongly to railway development. In a letter to the *Pall Mall Gazette*, Meredith opposed the
construction of the Ambleside railway, although his position was one

that was equally scathing towards both utilitarians and sentimentalists. Meredith recognized the recreational potential of the Lake District as a national amenity, but felt that such public utilities should also remain unsullied by any form of industrial development or profit-motivated despoliation:

It cannot be thought that Englishmen will allow their one recreative holiday ground of high hill and deep dale (I would add 'consecrated by one of our noblest poets', but that I am on guard against treating the subject emotionally) to be a place of no retreat. They must have ceased to discern the quality of true utility if they permit it. The project smells of all that is vilest in English Middle-class Philistinism.[33]

This urge to preserve certainly harked back to the Wordsworthian Romantic connection with walking and countryside conservation. There is a sympathy with the common people, but also a fundamental misunderstanding of the potential value of the railways. Meredith assumed that the Ambleside project, endorsed in the House of Commons in February 1887, would favour only the moneyed classes and the shareholder: '... it does not promise to be of good use to the people'.[34] Such views, whether or not naïve or condescending, were representative of an influential continuous strand within the nascent conservationist lobby that was emerging amongst open-air ideologues, and undermined some of the overall progressive intent, although there is always some ambiguity as to what actually constitutes 'progress'. There is the continuing élitist failure to recognize the railways as an important enabling factor which would allow urban workers to escape to the countryside in growing numbers, in pursuit of fresh air and recreation; the general anti-tripper sentiments amongst all levels of the developing outdoor movement does, nevertheless, need to be remembered.

The railway network has always been important to recreational walkers from various social levels. Mancunians were encouraged to use the trains to enable them to ramble in Cheshire as early as 1862, by C. G. Smith's guide to walks in the vicinity of the Altrincham and Cheshire Midland Railways,[35] and it was certainly not just working people or general trippers who utilized them as a means of access to rural areas in the nineteenth century. Robert and Elizabeth Spence Watson were prominent members of the Tyneside upper-middle-class professional community. They obviously had no compunction about using the train to allow them to walk in the Lake District, although it is not known what their reaction was to railway construction within the boundaries of Lakeland. The Spence Watsons walked, for instance, twenty miles in the area of Eskdale on one day in April 1879, reaching the area from the station at Whitehaven. Robert Spence Watson was a Newcastle solicitor, educationalist and member of the local liberal establishment, whose Quaker principles were rooted in the lead-mining district of the Allendale area of south-west Northumberland, where the Society of Friends was firmly established by the time George Fox visited the dale in 1663. Both the Spence Watsons adopted the passion for Alpinism which seized an active element of the late-Victorian middle class (Robert was a member of the Alpine Club from 1862). Elizabeth Spence Watson was in fact complimented on her mountain proficiency by Austrian guides, and joined her husband on a mountaineering holiday to Norway in August 1880. They also took trains to such stations as Steele Road Junction and Hawick for 'hiking' tours in southern Scotland, such as that which took them to St Mary's Loch, Hermitage Castle, and Canonbie in September 1880.[36] A letter which Robert wrote to his sister in 1880 from Tibbie Shiel's bothy in the Ettrick valley commented on the growing numbers of tourists who visited the border hills. The regular recurrence of the élitist perspective within the open air fraternity is again reflected:

> I could wander about for ever and a day, always provided that I was not taken into crowds. This country is indeed tourist-ravaged from time to time. They mutilate the statues, write hideous rot in the Visitors' Books, and scrawl their vulgar names over every object of interest ...[37]

An intellectual and aesthetic response continued for some time to exert an influence on perceptions of the recreational potential of the Lake District. It led, for example, to the sort of inconsistency that is evident in Meredith's opposition to the railway and the march of progress, although he effectively qualified his position with the claim that the project only benefited capitalist enterprise. In Meredith's own words, his opposition was stated 'just a little less briefly than a vote in the urn'.[38] The outdoor and conservationist-stimulated critique of modern society that Meredith helped to articulate on behalf of the active outdoor people contained a measure of sympathy for the old Tory-led harmonious social order and a strong strain of English nationalism. It is, however, also important to stress a rejection of sentimentalism, which was defined as a disease of the human spirit, and, therefore, detrimental to human development. As J. Wilt put it: 'Meredith's view of nature, though romantic, was profoundly unsentimental.'[39] This fundamental recourse to common sense recurs regularly during the development of countryside recreation and the related enjoyment of nature. There is, nonetheless, also an element of the poseur evident in the stance adopted by Meredith. Promulgation of the simple life in harmony with nature can be contrasted with the inevitable excesses of upper-middle-class social life, of which the hospitality enjoyed by the Sunday Tramps was a part, and which some of them saw as the highlight of their excursions into the Surrey countryside. The spiritual and the material were never far apart. Chesterton called Meredith 'a sort of daintily dressed Walt Whitman';[40] according to K. Hanley, he had 'one foot in the woods and one foot in the drawing room'.[41] Gregarious conviviality has, nevertheless, had a part to play as a formative influence on that aspect of open-air recreation which has eschewed the more ascetic and puritan influences. Meredith's romantic evocations as part of his own response to natural beauty were certainly more genuine than the contrived Victorian sentimentality of the likes of Tennyson, with whom he was contrasted by Charles Sorley in 1912: 'Tennyson is most pre-eminently paltry and superficial when he sings about nature and earth. He was not long in hedging her in the shapely corsets of alliterative verbiage. Meredith was the first to break through this barrier and discover her in her truth.'[42] Notwithstanding a measure of dilettantism, at least Meredith personally experienced the genuine country-walkers' feel for their surroundings, which he reflected in his writing: 'A rapid walker practically and humourously [sic] minded gathers multitudes of images on his way. And rain, the heaviest you can meet, is a lively companion when the resolute pacer scorns discomfort and wet clothes and squealing boots.'[43] In this passage from Meredith's novel *The Egoist*, Sir Leslie Stephen is represented as Vernon Whitford, 'the long lean walker and scholar', and intellectual lover of open-air physical pursuits, who was undeterred by adverse weather conditions.[44]

The type of outdoor philosophy which was constructed from a late nineteenth-century cross-fertilization of ideas was indeed represented typically by Sir Leslie Stephen. He was the Victorian rationalist tussling with personal spiritual and moral dilemmas, and challenging *status quo* assumptions from within the ferment of ideas of the contemporary establishment. Like Carpenter, Stephen was a Cambridge intellectual, who combined the aesthetic with the athletic in an enjoyment of the outdoors that rejected ugliness and forms of restraint, although his was a different ideological contribution. Stephen's input into the development of the outdoor movement represented both a tangible contribution and a practical proposition for people of similar inclination. His formation and leadership of the Tramps was based partly on a strong propensity to purely athletic achievements for their own sake, or in order to test one's own physical limits to the full: 'Our leader, a tall man and a vigorous walker, set the pace, which, though it had an inviting look of ease, was a lofty ideal for average pedestrians.'[45] He encouraged the Sunday Tramps to cover substantial distances in all weathers; tramps of twenty miles were common. The object of most of the group, which also included philosophers, literary critics and the poet, Robert Bridges, was to combine high-minded discussion with open-air exercise on relaxed conversational rambles, although Stephen managed to retain the athletic and mildly ascetic aspects of the fellowship. The practical and rational facets of Stephen's nature came to the fore in the military precision with which the walks were conducted. He was also a keen mountaineer, whose competitive instincts were most obviously manifested in an obsession with the Alps that was initially stimulated by Ruskin's *Modern Painters*, thereby providing a reminder that his interests were also largely aesthetically inspired. However, in his rationalist mode Stephen remained sceptical of the romantic nature of Ruskin's devotions to mountain landscape.

The practical roots of such a diverse movement were generated from a complex set of motives, epitomizing the interaction between the practical, physically challenging and sentimental romantic dimensions to countryside exercise. The rural response as represented by Stephen was typically Victorian and, arguably, British in its deliberate suppression of natural emotions. Although he was sceptical about Ruskin's ornate imagery and medieval romanticism, Stephen's aesthetic and romantic impulses regularly resurfaced in, for example, passages of descriptive purple prose, in a style reminiscent of the Gothic Romantic. He also acknowledged the legacy of an open-air tradition, but denied any sentimental attachment to customary origins: 'Much as I respect Wordsworth, I don't care to see the cottage in which he lived.' [46] The nature of a Victorian intellectual dilemma which sought to reconcile spiritual and practical aspects is evident in the way in which Stephen's scientific knowledge and inquisitiveness, fed by a strong tendency towards rational analysis, placed restraints on a romantic appreciation of the natural environment.

The original Sunday Tramps attained a membership of sixty, and lasted until 1894. The group was, however, resurrected at the beginning of the twentieth century with some of the founder members, as well as new recruits including G. M. Trevelyan, who maintained the Stephen tradition of combining the aesthetic with the athletic. As an obsessive long-distance moorland walker, Trevelyan perhaps leant more towards the physical; his earliest involvement coincided with the turn-of-the-century zenith of the cult of athleticism. In an essay published in *Clio* in 1913, he promoted 'scrambling' as an integral part of the country walk. [47] The Trevelyan family was involved increasingly in the growth and consolidation of the outdoor movement throughout the first sixty years of the twentieth century.

A. H. Sidgwick was a self-proclaimed trespasser, who claimed the moral high ground in defence of ancient rights. His anthologies of essays covering various aspects of walking afford some valuable insights into the motives and philosophy underlying the popularity of the pastime amongst members of the professional and intellectual middle classes.[48] In his writing he eloquently located recreational walking in the late Victorian and Edwardian social context, and he defended the activity against establishment cant, responding to the criticism being levelled by sections of polite society that denigrated it as an unsociable and individualistic diversion from the essential duties of social intercourse. Sidgwick did in fact concede that the full appreciation and enjoyment of countryside walking was not conducive to conversation, but claimed at the same time that it laid 'the foundation of mutual respect'.[49] He questioned the notion that walking did not have as valid a social function as any of the entrenched conformities which had been created and employed as a social cement, bonding together the fundamental code with which self-styled civilized society was consolidated: 'If every one [sic] stopped obeying the law, trouble would ensue; if every one stopped going to garden parties, it is hard to see how the world would suffer permanent harm.'[50] Similar contributions to the construction of alternative interpretations of the ambiguous and dynamic notion of respectability were characteristic of the ramblers' philosophy, which can be traced to well before the high-Victorian consolidation of rigid formal social behaviour. Adam Bald, for example, stated in 1799 that he was 'convinc'd that a too rigid ceremonious behaviour does not suite [sic] those who wish to find out the disposition of mankind'.[51] Sidgwick's extremely comprehensive appraisal of recreational walking was also scathing of the contemporary athletic cult and the obsession with 'the conception of Health'.[52] He compared the lifting of dumb-bells to 'smiling on purpose in order to cultivate a habit of cheerfulness'.[53] It was a sentiment echoed by numerous lovers of healthy outdoor exercise. William Brown of the Cairngorm Club, for example, stressed that country walking 'is not a sport, because the element of competition or the incentive of a keenly pursued object is awanting'.[54] Brown was a proponent of the all-round attractions of climbing, but claimed to know 'keen climbers who would climb in a coal pit',[55] a judgement which conformed with the view of the many walkers who equated climbing with gymnastics. To Sidgwick, 'the great democracy of walkers',[56] from eighteenth-century strenuous pedestrians on the Lake District fells, such as the geologist William Budworth, to the likes of Sir Leslie Stephen and the Reverend T. A. Leonard at the end of the nineteenth century and beyond, successfully integrated a degree of athletic prowess and physical fitness with social, aesthetic, cerebral, and spiritual benefits. The idealized outcome was perceived as a generally efficacious, simple and unforced coordination of the faculties of mind and body working in harmony with the elements of Nature, as these two quotations from Sidgewick's *Walking Essays* show:

... leave the intimate character of your surroundings to penetrate slowly into your higher faculties, aided by the consciousness of physical effort, the subtle rhythm of your walk, the feel of the earth beneath your feet, and the thousand intangible influences of sense ... [57]

... if you have trained your body, and given it its due of food and drink and sun and air, then you will walk with a peculiar exaltation; you will swing your legs to the full rhythm of your physical being.[58]

The expanding vogue for walking in the countryside was equated by Sidgwick with the opportunity to liberate the physical being from the various forms of deprivation that had been imposed during the history of human development. Such a liberating motive would strike a chord with the late nineteenth- and early twentieth-century ramblers, as they began to achieve a measure of freedom from the physical and mental consequences of industrialization, and the restraints which ramifications of that structural change had imposed:

Poor, ill-used, neglected, misunderstood body! Our ancestors sodd-ened you with port: our grandfathers overlooked you while they muddled with the soul and mind which are bound up with you: ascetics starved you and hedonists cultivated you in patches: doctors analysed you until there was nothing left but a catalogue of inanimate fragments: economic forces penned you in dens and prisons: fashion clothed you in impossible garments, and kept you up at hours and in atmospheres which enraged your most sacred instincts. And now I make you sit here writing – writing! For heaven's sake, come out for a walk.[59]

Moderation is again the key, with walking the preserve of predominantly sensible people, imbued with their own vision of a better world. The walking fraternity was generally adopting a socially progressive agenda, which incorporated liberation from the less-acceptable aspects of existing convention, rejection of unsatisfying forms of leisure, and moderation of the effects of the utilitarian emphasis within still-prevalent rigid economic dogma. Sidgwick also suggested that the best way to trace the history of walking as an important social and cultural phenomenon, and its development as a pastime, was through fiction: 'Walking is one of the many things whose history is not to be found in the historians ... Literature is our only help'; and he continued: 'Walking being above all things human and intimate, is naturally neglected by the historians: it cannot be shown to have caused any political convulsions, or to have any economic effects; it is therefore ruled out.' These specific observations were also given a more universal relevance: 'History is probably the worst record of ordinary man, and memoirs are the second worst ... If we want to know our great-grandfathers we turn not to Lecky but to Miss Austen.'[60] It was Miss Austen who had reflected at the beginning of the nineteenth century on young upper-class women asserting their independence and infringing against accepted convention, by taking energetic walks.[61]

Athleticism reinforced with a measure of stoicism has certainly played some part as a motive force behind the generation of an open-air movement, but the advocates of moderation were distanced from the more excessive expressions of competitive outdoor activity. Sir Leslie Stephen was one example of the mountaineer with an urge to push himself to the limits, but who tempered his instincts in the varied and rounded motives of the rambler. The more vigorous and obsessive side of walking can be identified in its long history as a competitive activity, which developed as an early form of professional sport under the influence of the gambling instincts of the sporting 'fancy', although the competitive dimension was also manifest in the popular late nineteenth-century fashion for hillwalking. The desire to compete, if only against oneself and the natural environment, was given a focus in 1891 when Sir Hugh Munro published his 'Tables', listing 283 peaks in Scotland which exceeded 3,000 feet (the 'Munros' – which were reduced to 277 following an Ordnance Survey recalculation). An Alpine climber from the age of seventeen, Munro was a failed Conservative politician, a military man, and a founder member of the Scottish Mountaineering Club (SMC); his form of hillwalking produced a fundamental difference of opinion within the SMC, which stimulated the club president's criticism. The first successful 'Munroist' was the Reverend A. E. Robertson, who clocked up his final peak in September 1901, almost exactly ten years after the publication of the tables. Munro's tables continue to obsess a more rigorous fringe, which, in the renewed passion for physical exercise at the end of the twentieth century, has become something more than a fringe; they were reprinted with revisions in 1990.

The hard walking and the poetic appreciation of landscape which combined in the turn-of-the-century motivation towards open-air recreation can be detected in the more traditional response of Hilaire Belloc, a keen country walker who harked back to the Romantics. His interpretation of the uncomplicated joys of a simple pastime was included in *The Footpath Way* anthology in 1911: '... walking ... introduces particular sights to you in their right proportion'.[62] The strong spiritual aspect of Belloc's love of country walking led him not only to excursions in Italy and the Pyrenees, but also towards a close affinity with the Englishness of Sussex, which he identified with stability, and eulogized with Arcadian images: '... the unshaven, hard-drinking rambler through Catholic Europe was only part of the truth'.[63] Belloc was representative of the country walker whose motives were embedded in a culture of Tory Merrie England, distinctly different from the secular puritanism evident in the activities of Sir Leslie Stephen and his intellectual coterie of pedestrians.

The involvement of substantial numbers of clerics in the growth of the popularity of rambling sustained both spiritual and athletic dimensions, connecting the pastime directly to the notion of 'muscular Christianity'. The question arises of the degree to which the emerging popular movement was inculcated with that creed. Many of the Victorian and Edwardian clergy were, of course, products of the public school system, and consequently influenced by many of the principles of its underlying philosophy. But not all clerics who were keen on rambling were motivated uniformly by the same ethos, although all seemed to share some devotion to muscular exercise. For example, A. N. Cooper, who sometimes wrote pseudonymously as the 'Walking Parson', was a canon from Yorkshire with a fondness for strenuous European walking tours, which typified more obsessive and unashamedly muscular motives. In his writings Cooper combined descriptions of walking and personal philosophy, revealing ample evidence of the frustration common to many of the socially restrained clergy, who preferred a more natural existence and enjoyed the freedom which both the leisurely country ramble and the more vigorous type of walking represented:

> I do commend the freedom of the road to those who like myself, are condemned to wear black cloth, white collars and cuffs, to sit down to dinner with serviettes and finger glasses, and generally to be en grande tenue. We know it is an artificial life, and consequently it is all the more enjoyable to return to Nature and her ways.[64]

Cooper's antipathy to the artificial life of convention led him to the Spartan attractions of living on 6d. (2½p) a day while on walking tours. He recommended the benefits to health and condition, and to the eradication of sleeplessness. Cooper was an exemplar of the self-disciplined breed of 'muscular Christian'. His promulgation of the principles of strength of character, independence, rationalism, and physical and mental training incorporated the promotion of strenuous country walking: 'Nobody can appreciate the delights of walking save those who experience them. What with hours in the open-air, the body always in motion, the muscles exercise, and then the rests and the meals which you feel you have earned, all combine to make a satisfied mind.'[65]

Notwithstanding the influential doctrine of mainstream religion, the late-Victorian creed of the healthy mind and body was perhaps most clearly expressed in the nonconformist ethos, whose connection with the Christianity of the public schools was at best tenuous. It was widely disseminated as a strand in the generation of the diverse popular culture of Lancashire, whose nuances were dependent upon variations engendered by specific local traditions.

Martha Vicinus has identified the main escape from toil for the substantial numbers of intelligent Lancashire autodidacts as reading and writing, but, as with the working-class botanists, it is clear that local writers and poets appreciated the benefits to be gained from the escape that countryside walks afforded them. Open-air recreation accounted for a significant proportion of the regional writers' record of the local popular culture. Not surprisingly, self-educated writers resorted to the style of inflated romantic poeticism – the characteristic idiom of the literary products of high culture which were the main available source of reading. It was a romantic flavour that was, nevertheless, often expressed in a popular vernacular form. From the mid-nineteenth century, Lancashire writers articulated a desire to get out into the fresh air. The relief felt on escaping from Manchester was expressed in John Critchley Prince's essay entitled 'Rambles of a Rhymester', which in 1842 appeared in the short-lived *Bradshaw's Journal*, which published working people's literary offerings: 'What relief it was for me, after vegetating for twelve months amid the gloom, the filth, the squalid poverty, and the dissipation of Manchester, to find myself surrounded by green fields, luxuriant hedgerows, and trees just opening to the breath of Spring!'[66] The athletic pedestrian impulse also proved to be an influence, even at that early stage, and Prince, drawn by business to London, walked there from Manchester, motivated by the pleasure of passing through changing landscapes. Working long hours in the dying trade of reed-maker, Prince walked mainly in the country around Manchester. His predominantly spiritual and aesthetic motives were consistent with those of so many of the nineteenth-century country walkers, for whom the activity always meant much more than a physically satisfying pursuit. The Romantic poets' influence on the autodidactic Lancashire writers and versifiers stimulated the corresponding rural imagery within the overall corpus of their work, which incorporated storytelling and descriptions of local life and character. Classical Arcadian images, which evoked visions of a rural idyll, were a feature of the writing of Ben Brierley, whose work included a description of 'a day's ramble in the country ... [from] ... the teeming streets of our great commercial Babel, Manchester', during 1855, the year of the siege of Sebastopol, in the semi-fictional *A Day Out*.[67]

Although a rural influence on responses to urban-industrial expansion was far more typical of the last quarter of the nineteenth century, romantic literature in praise of the local countryside was readily available to Lancashire people several decades earlier. From the 1820s the *Blackburn Mail*, widely circulated in the cotton towns to the north of the county, contained romantic rural verse in every edition. It is impossible to quantify the effects of such journalism, but some degree of permeation of rural images into an urban readership, which was encouraged to take leisure in the fresh air in natural surroundings, was inevitable. The genre was the precursor of the prolific countryside writing which punctuated the columns of local newspapers from the 1880s. The early work of one such journalist was acknowledged in the *Burnley News* after the First World War: '"The Lone Tramp" – James Ashworth – who has so often delighted our readers with vivid descriptions of his rambles by hill and dale ...'[68]

The popular dialect writing of Edwin Waugh, the 'Lancashire laureate', covered the whole gamut of local culture, but also regularly reflected his own love of walking in his native hills around Rochdale and beyond. Waugh's countryside evocations and accounts of rambles combined dialect with a more conventional romantic idiom. The language, the imagery and the emotions were consistent with a particular genre of writing which is rooted in Wordsworth and the Romantic Movement, and has continued right up to the present day in less original and more hackneyed forms. Part of his appeal in the industrial communities of Lancashire – referred to by Waugh as 'the toilful district'[69] – was in evoking a recent rural past to a population whose cultural roots were planted in that past; the inspiration lay close at hand. Much of Waugh's record of walking in the hills harked back to the 1850s, when he worked as a printer, and when the moors and cloughs were even more accessible from the mills and smoke of Rochdale. He would spend his spare time roaming the hills, physically and emotionally distanced from the drudgery of working life and the mundane. Accounts of his rambles began to appear in Manchester newspapers. In the early days he would often walk alone, or 'with a young friend of mine in Rochdale, whose tastes were congenial to my own'.[70] As the opportunities increased for more and more people to enjoy country walks, Waugh became a well-known figure amongst Lancashire outdoor people, and he recorded meetings with groups of ramblers from other towns. In *A Rossendale Anthology*, R. Digby relates the reminiscences of an elderly friend who recalled Waugh joining a party of Haslingden ramblers: 'We had monthly rambles throughout the summer, some of which Edwin Waugh joined ...'[71] Waugh would regularly walk twenty to thirty miles, and even as far as fifty miles. These expeditions featured in his *Lancashire Sketches*, which indicated the popularity of the pursuit at a time when it is generally assumed that such outdoor recreation was restricted to an insignificant minority. In sketches such as 'Ramble from Bury to Rochdale' and 'Ramble from Rochdale to the top of Blackstone Edge', Waugh described the countryside walks of inhabitants of the mill towns. When, for example, he and a companion 'wore the afternoon far away in rambling about the high and open part of Blackstone Edge ...', he related that: 'Turvin is becoming a resort of ramblers from the border towns and villages of the two counties, on account of the picturesque wildness of the scenery.'[72] After moving to Manchester, Waugh commented on the squalid and unhealthy environment of that city – a sentiment echoed at various stages by other promoters of country exercise. He did, nevertheless, record simultaneously the ease of escape at a time before the suburbs sprouted. The description was prompted by a trip, in April 1857, from Oxford Road Station to what was then the agricultural village of Stretford:

> We left the huge manufactories, and the miserable chimney tops of 'Little Ireland' down by the dirty Medlock; we ran over a web of dingy streets; we flitted by the end of Deansgate and over the top of Knot Mill ... we left the black stagnant canal ... we left the cotton mills and dyeworks and chemical manufactories of Cornbrook.[73]

Leopold Hartley Grindon was another lover of the open air to provide a reminder of the world from which increasing numbers sought escape. Grindon's promotion of regular respite from the industrial and commercial system maintained an optimistic tone:

> Manchester itself, grim, flat, smoky Manchester, with its gigantic suburb ever on the roll further into the plain, and scouts from its great army of masons posted on every spot available for hostile purposes – Manchester itself denies to no one of its 500,000 who is blessed with health and strength, the amenities and genial influence of the country.[74]

Grindon was also keen to influence future generations, addressing himself 'especially to the young, who have ductile material in them, and are the hope of the future for us all'.[75] Primary motivation towards self-improvement and independence was thereby linked to an ideology which would generate an improved society, incorporating a wider adoption of educative, healthy and fulfilling pursuits, while rejecting environmental ugliness, and promoting the benefits of the rural sojourn. Encouragement to take a break from the town was also contained in William Dobson's stated aim, in 1864, to 'attempt to make the public better acquainted with the scenic beauties of a most picturesque district'.[76]

The time and the facilities were increasingly available to more and more town-dwellers to take their outdoor leisure further afield. A letter to the *Manchester Guardian* in 1895 encouraged people from the city to leave 'the heavy, smoky atmosphere of Manchester' by taking the train to Glossop and 'walking over the Moss to the Snake, past Kinderscout'.[77] One group from Manchester which did travel further afield was the Ancoats Brotherhood, which was formed in 1882 by Charles Rowley, founder of the Sunday Recreation Movement. The philosophy of Rowley and the Brotherhood was very much in line with the generally high-minded ideals which influenced the ethical construction of the outdoor movement. The overall aim was to raise the moral and intellectual tone of the workers of Ancoats – which the *Labour Annual* of 1897 referred to as 'the Cinder Heap of Manchester'.[78] The *Labour Annual* outlined the object of the Ancoats Brotherhood: it was 'to afford opportunity to the workers of this industrial part of Manchester to see and hear something of what is best worth seeing and hearing in the world'; there was 'No patronage and no charge.'[79] Speakers at Brotherhood meetings included William Morris, Peter Kropotkin, and Ford Madox Brown. Summer rambles and weekends in the countryside formed an important part of the improving object of the Brotherhood's itinerary. Rowley recalled 'rambling with a bevy of chums', and the 'inexpensive rambles', which included weekends in Wales or the Lake District at a cost of £1.[80] The writings which emerged from such activities were published in the local press and affordable pamphlets. They reflected all aspects of a popular local culture, helping to perpetuate deeply rooted rural traditions. As Vicinus and others have shown, representatives of local communities also mingled with the business and professional classes in societies such as the Manchester Literary Club, to produce the local cultural identity which went beyond basic class models.

Interwoven with these narratives of rural activities were the representative sentiments and hopes which were spun together to form a consistent thread in the development of the movement. A literary record of the influence of the outdoor movement on urban culture found its most characteristic expression in the work of Allen Clarke, whose success as a journalist and writer enabled him to move from the pollution of Bolton to the fresh air of Blackpool. As an energetic and eclectic contributor to the growth of the movement in Lancashire, and as a regular rambler and cyclist, Clarke produced a valuable first-hand record of an outdoor culture that flourished, particularly in the Bolton area. Much of his prolific literary output was produced in the present century, and provided a stimulus to later generations which fuelled the interwar outdoor craze, but much of his writing recorded the activities of the earlier, formative period.

Clarke, the son of millhands, himself worked in a mill at the age of thirteen and fourteen. The *Bolton Review* in 1897 praised his 'broad humanity', 'hatred of cant and hypocrisy', and 'belief in the "Brotherhood of Man"'.[81] Through articles in the *Bolton Journal*, the *Liverpool Weekly Post* and his own publications, the *Northern Weekly* and *Teddy Ashton's Journal*, he both reflected and helped to popularize diverse, but similarly motivated contributions to an emerging outdoor movement in Lancashire, which included the walking clubs of the district. Clarke commented on the 'Ramble Clubs' which existed around turn-of-the-century 'Manchester and most Lancashire towns';[82] he joined in the activities of some of them, including the Bolton Pedestrian Club, and a group connected with the Bolton Sunday Afternoon Class of the Labour Church. Reports of his rambles included a meeting with walkers from Bolton on Darwen Moors, and a gathering at Pendle Hill in the 1890s of clubs from all parts of Lancashire, including a group from Padiham, Edwin Waugh and friends, and a contingent led by Joe Bates, another of the Lancashire writers to record the popularity of open-air recreation. Bates adopted the pseudo-Romany name 'Boshemengro', reflecting the existence of a romantic response to gypsy culture amongst some of the more marginal elements within the nascent movement, although this represented only one aspect of a generally ambivalent attitude to gypsies during the latter part of the nineteenth century.[83] Clarke himself recorded having 'gypsy teas made by spirit kettle on the moors' when rambling with a Sunday Afternoon Class group, led by 'that sturdy reformer and rambler, John Kirkman, and by that clever collier-botanist John Fletcher of Westhoughton ...'[84]

Many of Clarke's articles were later included in *Moorlands and Memories*, which sold 1,300 copies in three editions. His *Out O' Doors* sketches helped to spawn a number of outdoor associations, such as the Daisy Out O' Doors Rambling and Cycling Clubs, based at Bolton, and connected to the Daisy Colony Scheme, which formed part of the popular local expression of the wider 'back to the land' movement.[85] Expanding to thirty-one branches spread throughout industrial Lancashire and north-east Cheshire, the Daisy Colony Scheme formed part of a locally influenced libertarian and Utopian socialist reaction against the unnaturalness which industrial capitalism had imposed on the lives of the majority of people. In line with early socialist solutions to prevailing urban social problems, Clarke and others projected a vision in which the countryside, healthy recreation and fellowship would play a significant role in the creation of a new social order. It was, however, a doctrine which remained out of touch with an evolving popular culture, whose character was shaped increasingly by commercial enterprise. Clarke himself remained critical of what he perceived as the millhands' misuse of leisure-time amongst Blackpool's burgeoning popular holiday amenities.[86] His enthusiastic promotion of countryside walking and cycling was part of a wider mission to awaken in the Lancashire factory worker an awareness to the realization that there was more to life than what was offered by the mill and the smoky town, relieved only by the occasional works trip. He was addressing the same people whom the founder of the Clarion movement, Robert Blatchford, represented as the fictional John Smith of Oldham, projecting the stereotypical working man of *Merrie England*.[87] Many of the Lancashire operatives had indeed taken the opportunity throughout the nineteenth century to walk in the country as a respite from the effects of the increasingly dominant economic system, but Clarke's comments in 1899 served both to keep the scale of active outdoor recreation in proportion, and as a counter to the generally optimistic tone of the leisure-based social revolution,which he and others were actively propagating; he was referring to the workers of Bolton: 'They have no true idea of life. They believe they are bound to work; they do not see that work is but a means to life ... They honestly believe that if there were no mills and workshops the poor people would all perish.'[88]

Part of the role of the outdoor groups was envisaged idealistically as contributing to the fulfilment of a democratic vision, which sought to break the stranglehold of dependence upon industrial capitalism. This visionary aspect to the formation of a movement was promoting much more than escape into the countryside for a few hours. As with the wider message being promulgated by the Utopian strand in British socialism, it was a vision that most commonly appealed to members of the expanding professional class. Bruce Glasier, for example, found inspiration in the beauties of nature, which he experienced while roaming the hills of Scotland. In Lancashire, a romantic literary form of socialist response manifested itself through the gathering together in Bolton of a group of disciples of Walt Whitman. The Whitmanite circle of friends, who referred to themselves as 'The College',[89] included Dr James Johnston, a Labour Church man and an ILP councillor in Manchester, who reported the 'Comradeship and Brotherhood' of the 'Whitman Day' celebrations in 1911 to the *Annandale Observer* in his native Dumfriesshire. The Bolton Whitmanites were predominantly middle class, but did attract some members from the upper stratum of workers, as well as others from working-class backgrounds, notably J. W. Wallace of Anderton, a socialist mystic, whose father was a mill-wright, and Allen Clarke himself. Several members were active in both the ILP and the Labour Church, while some, such as Johnston and Charles Sixsmith, the successful footpath campaigner who later became a Chorley councillor, were also members of Bolton Clarion Cycling Club. 'Whitman Day' took place on 31 May, when events were to be held in the open air. Allen Clarke recalled taking part in the 'Whitman

Day' ramble to Rivington in 1913, when a range of topics including religion and philosophy were covered. Serious discussion was an important feature of many of the socialist-led group rambles around the turn of the century, in contrast to the quiet appreciation of nature and the meditative mode preferred by many country walkers. On a Sunday Afternoon Class walk, undertaken by more than fifty men, women and children over Winter Hill on 6 August 1904, the subjects included socialism and Tolstoyanism, and the group sang Edward Carpenter's hymn of the socialist movement. The Bolton Whitmanites maintained a close relationship with Carpenter, who shared their admiration for the American prophet of the open-air philosophy. In July 1890, James Johnston visited Whitman in Pennsylvania, and later referred to the American poet's work as being 'saturated with "out-of-doors"'.[90] Other literary influences on the Whitmanites included Burns, Carlyle and Ruskin.

The involvement of Lancashire ILPers in the promotion of countryside and leisure-based solutions to social problems contradicts the widely held belief that fundamental conflicts over the proper role of leisure created an unbridgeable divide between the conviviality of the Clarion movement and the dry, serious politicking of the ILP and SDF. Clarion involvement in outdoor recreation was chiefly through their popular cycling clubs,[91] although by 1913 there were Clarion rambling clubs in Blackburn, Burnley, Bolton and Glasgow, as well as the founding Sheffield group led by G. H. B. Ward, which, with 470 members, was the largest rambling club in the north of England.[92] The ILP-backed *Blackburn Labour Journal* recognized the benefits of nature and rural leisure pursuits, a sentiment that was expressed, for instance, by a columnist, 'Amicus', in 1904:

'All work and no play makes Jack a dull boy.' After deciding in my own mind that this maxim was a good one, I betook myself into the country. And what a contrast to the humdrum, monotonous toil of everyday lives. There is no artificiality about Nature. No production of shoddy! No vitiated atmosphere; but everything to make the heart gay.[93]

F. W. Jowett recalled the early socialist fellowship in the West Riding of Yorkshire, which combined political proselytization with enjoyment of walking in the countryside: 'Sometimes in summer-time the joint forces of Leeds and Bradford Socialism tramped together to spread the gospel by printed and spoken word in neighbouring villages, and at eventide, on the way home, as we walked in country lanes or on river bank, we sang ...'[94]

Ambivalence in the SDF attitude to the function of leisure qualifies their general reputation as an organization exclusively concerned with political activism and propaganda. In 1893 *Justice* appealed for 'more joy and fun', claiming that 'High spirits breed high courage and high aims.'[95] It was a dispute that re-emerged in the socialist press in the 1930s. The objective expressed in *Justice* was to attract more young people to the overall cause. The Glasgow Socialist Rambling Club, formed in 1893, was one group which entered fully into that vigorous and optimistic spirit of comradeship. Their membership was drawn mainly from the local SDF, but also included Fabians, anarchists, and what *Justice* referred to as a 'sprinkling of Labour Party men'.[96] The Glasgow socialist ramblers did propagandize widely on their group rambles outside the city, but combined the dissemination of the message with the pursuit of good fun. They carried socialist songbooks, which included such titles as 'When leisure and pleasure shall be free'; they whistled the 'Marseillaise'; they distributed literature; they wrote slogans on walls; and they unfurled their banner bearing the inscription, 'Ye Rambling Socialistes of Auld Sanct Mungo'.[97] On a ramble to Renfrew and Paisley in July 1893 they were interrupted by drunks, Liberal and Tory hecklers, and a Tory party agent who was also an Orangeman. The occasion was attended by a *Justice* correspondent, who expressed his admiration for the ramblers: 'Rarely have I seen the pleasure of a summer Saturday's country ramble and the dull slogging work of Socialist propaganda so effectively combined.'[98] This reporter called on Lancashire and Midland branches to follow suit. The theme of walking and enjoying the benefits of a pleasant environment was also evident in the *Justice* report of a socialist 'beano' at Windsor Castle during the same month: '... the park and the river afforded our party a full measure of pure physical enjoyment. Lovely walks ...'[99] And elsewhere in the country – for example, the Bristol Socialist Rambling and Propaganda Society – countryside recreation was mixed with campaigning, good fellowship and intellectual discourse.[100]

The vigorous ILP branch in Nelson was especially keen to encourage a local interest in open-air recreation, and influenced strongly the development of the outdoor movement in the area. Formed on 21 January 1893 at the Weavers' Institute, Nelson ILP typically combined elements of socialism with nonconformist religious principles, in a local cultural formation which incorporated the fundamental tenets of improvement, self-culture, individual freedom, temperance and healthy, rewarding outdoor leisure. In 1900 the Nelson ILPers took a ten-year lease on a summer residence – Nab's House – for the use of walkers and those 'who desire to get away from the never ending vista of bricks and mortar'.[101]

Apart from the significant socialist involvement in the formation of rambling groups, the main movers were the churches and chapels, although the degree of mutual interdependence which existed between the socialist and nonconformist motivating ethos and core values should not be underestimated. Allen Clarke referred to rambling clubs 'in connection with a place of worship',[102] such as Albert Place United Methodist Ramble Club in Bolton. The Saturday half-day holiday that was firmly established in Lancashire from the 1870s enabled organized groups from many of the churches and chapels in the cotton towns to utilize the time for rambles in the surrounding countryside, as a respite from the mills and the cramped, smoky towns. In 1879 an article in the first issue of the biannual journal *Biograph* reflected on the use of the Saturday half-day by early ramblers. More recent assumptions that open-air recreation was necessarily socially exclusive before the First World War have failed to consider sufficiently the combined influence in many of the industrial towns of a free afternoon and the proximity of open countryside. Rambling groups of the late nineteenth century clearly intended to present alternatives to wasteful and trivial uses of leisure time, and helped to consolidate the various ways in which religious denominations asserted their influence on the community. The chapels were important institutional focuses for the community social life of the mill towns. These predominantly nonconformist Christian ramblers represented one of the most substantial contributions to the development of a more popular dimension to the expansion of outdoor recreation, both numerically and ethically. The rambling groups with church and chapel connections were supplemented by those from the temperance movement. They were extremely active in the strongly nonconformist weaving towns of north-east Lancashire, an area in which they were particularly prolific, often based on the Congregationalist churches which flourished in the district. Local groups included those from the Holy Trinity Congregational church in Burnley, from Nelson and Brierfield Congregational churches, and from the Colne Congregationalist and parish churches. The same period – from about 1890 to 1910 – saw the formation of the Mount Zion Baptist Band of Hope Rambling Club of Nelson, the Colne and District Temperance Cycling and Rambling Club, and outings organized by Nelson Temperance Union and by the Colne branch of the Women's Temperance Association. In the main, these groups took advantage of the stimulating local countryside, whose elevation made it easily visible from the unhealthy mill towns, but they also used trams to get as far as the Ribble Valley, or ventured further afield on such trips as the Colne Congregational church ramble to Bolton Abbey in Wharfedale in September 1892.

Underlying religious motives provided much of the impetus for the popular expansion of countryside rambling. YMCA rambling clubs were formed in Liverpool in 1874 and in Manchester in 1880, while the one in Sheffield was reported to have been 'a strong and virile club' in the 1880s and 1890s.[103] The generally 'improving' motives of many of the rambling groups ramified into spiritual and educative functions, although such idealism was very often subordinate to a popular third role as social clubs. The activities of the Huddersfield Co-operative Holidays Association (CHA) Rambling Club epitomized that tripartite role. Formed in 1907 as the Huddersfield Rambling and Reading Club, 'with Christian ideals, to provide the man in the street with leisure activities',[104] its expeditions were supplemented by educational activities which ranged from literary study to astronomy, and by socials and dances at the Temperance Hall. This rambling club, with an early membership of around fifty, had superficial links with the ILP. It was said to be 'obsessed with the concept of enlightened democracy with cultural, ethical, and spiritual promptings',[105] and pursued typically high-minded ideals. Nonetheless, a prominent social *raison d'être* is emphasized by the corruption of CHA to 'Catching Husbands Association', while HF became 'Husbands Found'.[106]

Apart from the obvious social attractions of the popular rambling clubs, the idealistic strain which informed their fundamentally improving ideology continued to absorb serious intellectual influences, such as the anti-utilitarian creed of John Ruskin. Bolton and Darwen Rambling Clubs, for example, received a lecture on Ruskin following their joint outing to Edgeworth in 1907. A Ruskin Hall Conference of West Riding Education Leagues, in June 1905, included rambles within a broadly educative syllabus, whose primary function was to encourage independence. The stated aims were to 'educate more broadly than commerce or profession', and to fit the students 'to become more capable citizens individually and less dependent upon the guiding strings of party, sect, or newspaper bias'.[107] This was the type of doctrine disseminated through the University Extension Scheme, to which Edward Carpenter contributed, and which included lectures on Ruskin. The Yorkshireman W. Turner picked up the theme in his articles on rambling and the countryside for the *Halifax Courier* in 1905, some of which were published in 1913 in *A Springtime Saunter in Brontëland*. Turner quoted Ruskin on the beauties of the natural world, and generally reflected a relatively common contemporary reaction, which suggested the influence of Ruskin's idealism: '... men are coming to know that there are greater possessions than those which can be measured by the surveyor's chain or locked in iron safes'.[108]

The thriving and deeply rooted walking culture of Scotland was also shaped continuously by diverse influences, which focused generally on 'improving' ideals. The popularity of walking as a pastime had been established some time before it developed its collaborative aspect through the formation in the Glasgow area in 1892 of the West of

Scotland Ramblers' Alliance, which initially affiliated ten clubs. The élite SMC and the Cairngorm Club were predated by more popular rambling clubs, such as the Glenfield Ramblers, formed in 1884 by employees at the Glenfield and Kennedy works in Kilmarnock, who had been inspired to walk together during free afternoons by A. R. Adamson's *Rambles round Kilmarnock*, published in 1872. The potential of the rambling club as an integral part of Christian fellowship was recognized in Scotland. One such association was prominent in the wide-ranging social and cultural activities organized by the Wesleyan Methodist Mission in Edinburgh, which aimed to guide young working men in 'Christian Fellowship'.[109] The club was formed in 1896: 'To furnish healthful exercise and recreation by means of excursions in the country (mostly on foot) on Saturday afternoons during the summer.'[110] An important function of this rambling group was to sustain through the summer months a recreation-based fellowship, whose 'improving' ideals were embedded in a range of winter season activities, such as those organized by the Mission's Literary Society. The Edinburgh Wesleyans also opened a temperance public house, which provided games, literature, music and facilities for conversation.

Organized rambling took off as a popular pastime in the sub-Pennine mill towns and in the industrial and commercial central lowlands of Scotland before the turn of the century, but was slower to catch on in other urban areas with similar economic bases. The first organized rambling group on Tyneside, for example, was the CHA Rambling Club, formed in 1902 in Newcastle. This group was mixed in its social composition. Initially, most of the officers were drawn from the middle class, but the first secretary, G. H. Stafford, a 'gentleman', was superseded by A. N. Vinycomb, a clerk. A large proportion of the club's membership was drawn from the lower-middle and upper-working classes. Respectability was ensured by the nomination of potential recruits by an existing member, and they were subsequently vetted by the committee before being elected.

The nature of open-air associations like the rambling clubs did vary from district to district, shaped by the type of influences that have been intrinsic to the more general idiosyncratic milieux of local political and social variation. This localized development of the outdoor movement limited the areas of common ground which have served as unifying focuses in the creation of a wider movement. The differing social composition, ethical emphases and ideological backgrounds of outdoor associations, influencing the type of open-air culture that they represented locally, were, in fact, often quite marked, sometimes presenting a microcosm of more general regional cultural variations. This simplified general observation does, however, need to be qualified through an appraisal of the roles played by particularly influential individuals who established the initial tone. Even so, the outdoor movement in the Glasgow area, for example, inevitably mirrored the flourishing popular socialism which contributed to the 'Red Clyde' soubriquet; while north-east Lancashire rambling clubs formed one of the associational expressions of the local version of religious nonconformity.

During the formative turn-of-the-century period, a particularly significant difference was generated between the rural ideologies that flourished in both Leeds and Sheffield. This diversity stemmed directly from the roots of the two main rambling and countryside leisure associations of these similarly sized Yorkshire industrial cities. R. J. Morris has cited the absence of a strong merchant-professional élite as the significant influence on the nature of the local culture of Sheffield, where a 'radical neighbourhood culture gained substantial authority ...' from the first half of the nineteenth century.[111] The influence of key individuals was most certainly a factor in the equation, although, of course, those main actors were reflecting general developments within the evolution of the local ideology and culture, as well as asserting their own influence. In Leeds, the Yorkshire Ramblers' Club (YRC) was guided by the upper-middle-class liberal C. F. Atkinson, while the Sheffield Clarion Rambling Club owed its origins to the efforts of the working-class socialist G. H. B. Ward. Ward was employed as an engineer at Hadfield's Hecla Works in Sheffield, and became a pioneer of the Labour Representation Committee and Secretary of the Sheffield Labour Party. It was during the period in which an independent working-class socialist political consciousness evolved through a protean generative stage, before the general interwar degeneration into the obsessive fiscal orthodoxy of establishment Labour Party politics. Ward in fact was later to serve in the capacity of adviser on behalf of labour for the Sheffield district to the Ministry of Labour. Atkinson and Ward, both influential in their own local culture and politics, did, unsurprisingly, share a good deal of common ground, most notably in their roles as energetic and successful rights-of-way campaigners. Radicals and socialists shared the same adversary – the landowning class – whose interests were in direct opposition to those of the urban-based outdoor associations. However, the areas of natural affinity between local liberalism and socialism could never be constructed into an effective alliance founded on a broadly based leisure-orientated ideology, as the events around Burnley, Darwen and Bolton during the 1890s had amply demonstrated.

The YRC was a product of the respectable middle-class culture of west Leeds, 'which promoted science, art, music, literature ... and those cultural activities directed "to the improvement of the human mind and spirit"'.[112] The club was formed on 6 October 1892 at a meeting, at the Skyrack Inn in Headingley, of 13 gentlemen 'drawn together by similar tastes'.[113] By early 1893 the membership had risen to 34. The stated objectives of the YRC were: '... to organize walking and moun-taineering excursions, and to gather and promote knowledge concerning Natural History, Archaeology, Folklore ... [A]lso to strengthen the hands and further the objects of the Commons Preservation So-ciety.'[114] Membership rose consistently through the turn of the century, to over 120 in 1907, some of whom were drawn from outside the Leeds area, predominantly from the professional and commercial sectors, and including the celebrated botanist Reginald Farrer of Ingleborough Hall. Relative exclusivity was maintained by the election of members by ballot after they had first been proposed and seconded; YRC membership in 1906–7 had an apparently more exclusive flavour than the relative social mixture of the first few years, which included a minority from such occupations as commission agent, 'fetler' [sic] and clerk, although this may have been part of a process of gravitating towards a dominant peer group rather than deliberate exclusion. Churchmen, solicitors and acad-emics featured prominently in the lists of members for the first twenty years. In keeping with its own version of respectability, the YRC established a strictly non-controversial stance, founded on a 'reluctance on the part of the members to take part in any controversies of any kind'.[115] The rigidity of that position was demonstrated by withdrawal of support, in 1895, from the COSFPS, whose activities were deemed too controversial.[116]

A middle-class interest in rambling and other countryside leisure activities was also evident in the Sheffield area, where the Derbyshire Pennine Club was formed in 1906. Its first president was J. W. Putrell, geologist, naturalist and environmentalist, who had also been one of the early members, in the 1880s, of the similarly motivated Kyndwr Club. Putrell's lectures and journalism helped to sustain into the in-terwar years the high level of interest in the outdoor movement, which has been a feature of the popular culture of that area. Local literature, such as Charles H. Chandler's *More Rambles Round Sheffield*, published in 1915, highlighted the proximity of heavy industry to the south Pennine moorlands, while also picking up the cause of conservation and encouraging Sheffield people to walk in the Peak District. Howard Hill has identified a local increase in interest in walking and the outdoors, and a consequent escalation of the issue of access, as coin-ciding with the opening of the Dore and Chinley Railway in 1895. Recreational walking was sufficiently established in the Sheffield area for the idea of a federation of rambling clubs to be mooted in 1912, although confederation was not achieved until after the First World War. The roots of a unified campaigning lobby for the district were thus established fairly early.[117]

Although local inter-class collaboration over a common interest in outdoor issues was the general tendency in the formation of outdoor associations, the movement in Sheffield was shaped by a strong independent working-class socialist involvement in rambling; many of the twenty-four rambling clubs which existed in Sheffield by 1924 were formed by Clarion members. The most prominent and actively campaigning association was the Sheffield Clarion Rambling Club, which was established on a fundamentally different set of principles from those of the YRC, of which Putrell was also a stalwart. The Clarion club was formed in 1900, with a guiding ethos based on independently determined principles of working-class mental and physical improvement, which was patently in the Utopian socialist autodidactic tradition. The independence that was achieved by the Sheffield working-class ramblers does not deny the high degree of mutual sympathy that existed across the class and ideological divide. Putrell expressed his admiration for G. H. B. Ward in an article in the *Sheffield Mail* in April 1923, and the Clarion campaigned alongside the more middle-class groups, subscribing to the Northern Counties and Peak District FPS. The burgeoning of an open-air culture in the Sheffield area was, nevertheless, located in the socially and politically significant dichotomy between 'rough' and 'respectable' elements, which gave more specific definition to the working social strata. The formation and growth of the Sheffield Clarion Rambling Club fitted into a local artisanal tradition, which developed a culture independent both of middle-class domination and of the turn-of-the-century popular cultural institutions of drink, music hall and football. As early as 1842 the People's College had reinforced the growth of intellectual independence, a recreational dimension of which can be traced through Ward's father, who led rambles of a 'Young Men's Class' [118] into the Peak District, and influenced his son into a love of the open air.

The Clarion ramblers' socialist fellowship in Sheffield stemmed directly from Ward's conflict with the Church in 1897 over the use of the Sabbath, thereby fitting neatly into the local trend towards popular recreation that was both secular and independent. Here was an artisanal tradition that operated in parallel with the independent political growth of a strong, enduring, culturally underpinned local socialism. Ward's political and recreational philosophy and active involvement epitomized the development of a working-class political milieu that acted as a counter to the rise of popular conservatism, which emerged with the expansion of the more proletarianized, and consequently less independent, heavy trades in the city. The local middle-class political response to the rise of working-class socialism was the formation of the Citizens' Association, as a coalition of Conservatives and Liberals. The two dominant, and potentially conflictual, strands in early British socialism – leisure and political activism – were combined in the

flourishing Sheffield Clarion ramblers' contribution to the city's independent working-class political evolution. Caroline Reid's examination
of the relationship between working-class culture and middle-class
values in Sheffield has determined that 'neither Ruskin nor Carpenter
made much impact upon the Sheffield artisan'.[119] However, the Clarion
ramblers, who were in many ways representative of local culture and
its ethical underpinnings, certainly gained the same stimulus from the
ideas of Morris, Ruskin and Carpenter, and from the guidelines devised
by religious nonconformity, as did the rest of the Clarion movement.

The outdoor movement gained much of its momentum and formative
aspects of its character from the love of walking in the countryside,
which was shared by people from various social backgrounds. Walking
developed as a pastime enjoyed by people of all political persuasions,
who were certainly partly motivated by such important material considerations as the juxtaposition of industrial squalor with natural beauty.
Nevertheless, crucial ideological and ethical considerations were
brought into play to underpin the growth of a fellowship of common
interests. There is a frequently recurring linkage with an individually
and socially improving ethos, which stimulated a desire to cultivate
mental and physical faculties, and which found its most common expression through various interpretations of the basic philosophy of
Christian nonconformism. However, complications to this general
model were inherent in the substantial ideological and social divisions
that characterized the associational formation of the movement. These
variations ramified into the differing tactical stances that were adopted
within the evolving movement over the issues of common concern,
such as rights of way, access to the countryside and environmental
conservation. Nonetheless, unity was the dominant theme, and the
rambling clubs before the First World War set the agenda for a banding
together across class and ideological divides. Notwithstanding the evident differences of opinion, the interests of all recreational walkers were
underpinned by the unifying institutional focus of footpath protection
societies. This crucial campaigning dimension was given extra impetus
during the period of associational expansion by the parallel promotion
of the countryside-access issue. It was in fact to be regional loyalties
which caused the only real prevarication over national federation when
the matter came up in the late 1920s. The first area federation was
created in the London region in 1905, but the most important and
active campaigning federations were those in Manchester and Sheffield,
situated on either side of the increasingly controversial open countryside
of the Peak District; it was to be the Manchester Federation that held
out longest against national federation and the consequent loss of local
autonomy.[120]

Despite its evident, but sometimes overstated, élitist aspect, recreational walking developed as a democratic pursuit. The mentality of the rambler was certainly subject to competitive and athletic influences, but, in its essential contribution to the growth of an outdoor movement, the pastime remained overwhelmingly simple and natural. W. J. C. Miller, a Yorkshire rambler and writer, contrasted British country walkers with their American counterparts, who 'only walk as trials of endurance'.[121] This was a patent oversimplification, and similar attitudes did exist amongst British walkers, but it was in Britain that walking for leisure has been most commonly associated with the term rambling, with its connotations of freedom and wandering at will as dictated by personal fancy.

Freedom from convention and utility motivated many of the walkers to escape the shackles of commercial values and socially constructed restraints. It was a reaction that combined against a range of perceived ills, from the social conventions instituted by the upper-middle-class establishment, to the commercial pastimes of drink, music hall and spectator sport, which were coming to dominate the popular culture of the industrial towns by the later nineteenth century. The growth of rambling clubs needs to be considered in the context of a dynamic relationship between dominant and subordinate social groups, and the generation of a stabilized popular culture.[122] However, the significant degree of broad common interest which contributed to the formation of the nucleus of an outdoor movement cannot be interpreted simplistically in order to corroborate key concepts of social theory. A strong and persistent strand of urban working-class autonomy in open-air leisure activities resisted challenges to self-determination, although, conversely, too much emphasis should not be placed on cultural struggle.

Notes

1. Walker, H., 'The Outdoor Movement in England and Wales, 1900–1939', unpublished Ph.D. thesis, University of Sussex, p. 113.
2. Hill, H., *Freedom to Roam* (Ashbourne, 1980), p. 28.
3. Walker, 'The Outdoor Movement', p. 114.
4. Sidgwick, A. H., *Walking Essays* (London, 1912), p. 183.
5. Barrell, J., *The Idea of Landscape and the Sense of Place, 1730–1840* (Cambridge, 1972).
6. Nicholson, N., *The Lakers* (London, 1955), p. 38.
7. Masson, D., ed., *The Collected Writings of Thomas De Quincey*, vol. III (Edinburgh, 1890), p. 103.
8. *Ibid.*, p. 147.
9. Forman, M. B., ed., *The Letters of John Keats* (4th edn; London, 1952), pp. 153–212; Walker, C. K., *Walking North With Keats* (Yale, 1992).

10. Hazlitt, W., 'On Going a Journey', in Sampson, G., ed., *Hazlitt. Selected Writings* (Cambridge, 1959), p. 141.
11. Hamerton, P. G., *A Painter's Camp in the Highlands*, vol. 1 (London, 1862), p. 26.
12. Stansfield, A., *Essays and Sketches* (Manchester, 1897), pp. 173–4.
13. *Ibid.*, p. 173.
14. See Todd, R., 'Women Walkers', *Rambling Today* (Spring 1993), pp. 38–9.
15. Plomer, W., ed., *Kilvert's Diary; Selections from the Diary of the Reverend Francis Kilvert, 1 January 1870–19 August 1871* (London, 1938), pp. 39–40.
16. *Ibid.*, p. 42.
17. Mather, Rev. J. M., *Rambles Round Rossendale* (2 vols; Rawtenstall, 1880 and 1894).
18. Adam Bald journal, Mitchell Library, Glasgow, p. 21.
19. *Ibid.*
20. *Ibid.*, p. 86.
21. *Ibid.*, p. 150.
22. Phillips, G. S., *Walks Round Huddersfield* (Huddersfield, 1848), p. 15.
23. Tholfsen, T., *Working Class Radicalism in Mid-Victorian England* (London, 1976), p. 143.
24. Tsuzuki, C., *Edward Carpenter, 1844–1929. Prophet of Human Fellowship* (Cambridge, 1980).
25. Cline, C. L., ed., *The Letters of George Meredith*, vol II (Oxford, 1970), p. 601.
26. *Cornhill Magazine*, New Series, vol. XXIV, January–June 1908 (London, 1908), pp. 76–88.
27. Cline, ed., *Letters of George Meredith*, vol. II, p. 658.
28. *Ibid.*, p. 743n.
29. *Ibid.*, p. 924.
30. *Ibid.*, p. 658.
31. For the roots of the reference to cultural philistinism, see Arnold, M., *Culture and Anarchy* (London, 1869).
32. Cline, ed., *Letters of George Meredith*, vol. III, p. 1672.
33. *Ibid.*, vol. II, p. 853.
34. *Ibid.*, p. 852.
35. Smith, C. G. (pseud. Ichabod Tristram Jones), *Rural Rambles in Cheshire; or walks, rides and drives for Manchester and other people: a guide book to the scenery, antiquities, and gentlemen's seats within walking distance of the Altrincham and Cheshire Midland Railways* (Manchester, 1862).
36. Spence Watson, R., Letter to his daughter, Mabel, September 1880, in Mabel Spence Watson family letters, Accession No. 213, Tyne and Wear Archive Dept., Newcastle.
37. Corder, P., *The Life of Robert Spence Watson* (2nd edn; London, 1914), p. 172.
38. Cline, ed., *Letters of George Meredith*, vol II, p. 852.
39. Wilt, J., *The Readable People of George Meredith* (Princeton, 1975), p. 99n.
40. Chesterton, G. K., *The Victorian Age of Literature* (London, 1913), p. 88.
41. Hanley, K., ed., *George Meredith. Selected Poems* (Manchester, 1983), p. 7.
42. Quoted in Williams, R., *The Country and the City* (London, 1985), p. 251.

43. Meredith, G., *The Egoist* (London, 1947), p. 274.
44. *Ibid.*, p. 10.
45. *Cornhill Magazine*, p. 77.
46. Stephen, Sir. L., 'In Praise of Walking', in Sidgwick and Jackson, eds, *The Footpath Way: An Anthology for Walkers* (London, 1911), p. 207.
47. Quoted in MacDonald, H., *On Foot* (London, 1942), p. 17.
48. Sidgwick, *Walking Essays*, p. 191.
49. *Ibid.*, p. 147.
50. *Ibid.*, p. 156.
51. Adam Bald journal, p. 150.
52. Sidgwick, *Walking Essays*, p. 134.
53. *Ibid.*, p. 140.
54. *Cairngorm Club Journal* 2, 7 (July 1896), p. 1.
55. *Ibid.*, p. 2.
56. Sidgwick, *Walking Essays*, p. 8.
57. *Ibid.*
58. *Ibid.*, p. 132.
59. *Ibid.*, pp. 142–3.
60. *Ibid.*, pp. 181–3.
61. See Jane Austen, e.g. *Persuasion*, Ch. 10.
62. Quoted in Sidgwick and Jackson, eds, *The Footpath Way*, p. 9.
63. Wilson, A. N., *Hilaire Belloc* (London, 1984), p. 111.
64. Cooper, A. N., *With Knapsack and Notebook* (London, 1906), p. 7.
65. *Ibid.*, pp. 6–7.
66. Prince, J. C., 'Rambles of a Rhymester', *Bradshaw's Journal* III, 2 (14 May 1842), p. 1 – reproduced in Vicinus, M., *The Industrial Muse* (London, 1974), plate 14.
67. Brierley, B., *Tales and Sketches of Lancashire Life* (Manchester, n.d.), p. 4.
68. *Burnley News*, 3 July 1920, p. 5.
69. Waugh, E., *Lancashire Sketches* (Manchester and London, 1892), p. 1.
70. *Ibid.*, p. 131.
71. Digby, R., *A Rossendale Anthology* (Rawtenstall, 1969), p. 89.
72. Waugh, *Lancashire Sketches*, pp. 194–5.
73. *Ibid.*, pp. 5–6.
74. Grindon, L. H., *Country Rambles and Manchester Walks and Wild Flowers* (Manchester, 1882), p. 2.
75. *Ibid.*, p. 1.
76. Dobson, W., *Rambles by the Ribble* (1st series; Preston, 1864), introduction.
77. *Manchester Guardian*, 11 January 1895, p. 9.
78. *Labour Annual* (Manchester, 1897), p. 234.
79. *Ibid.*, p. 98.
80. Rowley, C., *Fifty Years of Work Without Wages* (London, 1911), pp. 195, 204.
81. *Bolton Review* I (1897), p. 154.
82. Salveson, P., 'When socialism was popular', *The Chartist*, June–August 1984.
83. See Mayall, D., *Gypsy-Travellers in Nineteenth Century Society* (Cambridge, 1988).

84. Clarke, A., *Moorlands and Memories* (Blackpool, 1924) pp. 120–1.
85. *Ibid.*, pp. 323–4; see also Salveson, P., *Mill Towns and Moorlands: Rural Themes in Lancashire Working Class Culture* (Salford: 1986), pp. 20ff.
86. Walton, J. K., *Lancashire. A Social History* (Manchester, 1987), pp. 296–7.
87. Blatchford, R., *Merrie England* (London, 1893).
88. Quoted in Joyce, P., *Work, Society, and Politics* (Brighton, 1980), p. 90.
89. *Bolton Journal and Guardian*, 10 June 1904, p. 8.
90. Johnston, J., *Walt Whitman: The Poet of Nature* (London, 1910), p. 1.
91. See Chapter 5.
92. Hill, H., 'Who is Bert Ward?', *The Holberry Society for the Study of Sheffield Labour History* 3 (November 1979); Walker, 'The Outdoor Movement', ch. 4.
93. *Blackburn Labour Journal*, July 1904, p. 4.
94. Quoted in Thompson, E. P., *William Morris: Romantic to Revolutionary* (rev. edn; London, 1977), pp. 667–8.
95. *Justice*, 6 May 1893, p. 6.
96. *Ibid.*, 1 July 1893, p. 2.
97. See Yeo, S., 'A new life: the religion of socialism in Britain, 1883–1896', *History Workshop Journal* 4 (1977), pp. 5–49, for the tradition of song at socialist open-air meetings in the 1890s; *The Clarion Song Book* contains contributions from Morris, Carpenter, Robert Burns, and Robert and Montague Blatchford – National Museum of Labour History, Manchester.
98. *Justice*, 1 July 1893, p. 2.
99. *Ibid.*, 22 July 1893, p. 3.
100. Yeo, 'A new life', p. 37.
101. *Nelson Leader*, 15 March 1907, p. 8.
102. Clarke, *Moorlands and Memories*, p. 339.
103. *Sheffield Daily Telegraph*, 10 January 1925, in Putrell, J. W., Collection of Newspaper Cuttings, Sheffield Local Studies Library.
104. *Huddersfield Daily Examiner*, 2 October 1987, p. 7.
105. *Ibid.*
106. *Ibid.*
107. *Halifax Courier*, 17 June 1905, p. 3.
108. Turner, W., *A Springtime Saunter in Brontëland* (Halifax, 1913), p. 239.
109. Wesleyan Methodist Mission, *Quarterly Magazine* (January–March 1891), p. 29, Edinburgh Public Library.
110. *Ibid.*, *Report* (1896), p. 23.
111. Morris, R. J., *Class, Sect, and Party: The Making of the British Middle Class: Leeds, 1820–1850* (Manchester, 1990), p. 327.
112. Fraser, D., ed., *A History of Modern Leeds* (Manchester, 1980), p. 200.
113. Yorkshire Rambler's Club, Secretary's Report to AGM, 17 October 1893, in *YRC Annual Report and List of Members, 1892–3* (Leeds, 1893), p. 9.
114. *Ibid.*, p. 1.
115. *Ibid.*, *Journal* 1–4 (1899–1902), p. 1.
116. Morris, *Class, Sect, and Party*.
117. See Sheffield Campaign for Access to Moorland, *Freedom of the Moors* (Sheffield, 1988).
118. Hill, 'Who is Bert Ward?', p. 8.

119. Reid, C., 'Middle Class Culture and Working Class Values in Nineteenth Century Sheffield. The Pursuit of Respectability', in Pollard, S. and Holmes, C., eds, *Essays in the Economic and Social History of South Yorkshire* (Sheffield, 1976), p. 275.

120. See Chapter 7.

121. Miller, W. J. C., *Essays and Nature Studies. With Lectures* (London, 1899), p. 92.

122. See Bailey, P., *Leisure and Class in Victorian England* (London, 1978); Cunningham, H., *Leisure in the Industrial Revolution* (London, 1980); Jones, S. G., *Sport, Politics and the Working Class* (Manchester, 1988); McKibbin, R., *The Ideologies of Class* (Oxford, 1990); Waters, C., *British Socialists and the Politics of Popular Culture* (Manchester, 1990).

Chapter 3

Natural Historians

From the latter part of the eighteenth century, when the Romantics drew their inspiration from rambles in the country and botanists roamed considerable distances in search of specimens, there has always been a strong bond between the compatible activities of outdoor exercise and an interest in natural history. This connection is especially apposite when broader definitions of the naturalist are applied, such as that suggested in a paper presented to a meeting of the Yorkshire Ramblers' Club (YRC) on 3 March 1894, which defined the 'naturalist in the highest sense of the word ... a lover of nature'; the speaker referred to the 'observant man ... with an inquiring interest in the objects and phenomena around us'.[1] The long-standing connection between these two outdoor pursuits was identified by the Lancashire writer T. W. Pateman in 1948, when he claimed that 'The naturalists have always been ramblers.'[2] It could be stated with equal veracity that many ramblers, and indeed touring cyclists, have always been naturalists. Although the dominant motive for substantial numbers of lovers of the open air has certainly had more to do with a search for freedom, a desire for physical exercise and a sense of achievement, with the immediate and intimate environment being of only peripheral interest, for many outdoor recreationists aspects of natural history have presented the primary reason for getting out into the countryside.

This formative influence on the nature of the outdoor movement developed out of origins that reach back tentatively as far as the seventeenth century, thereby easily predating the more general desire for country leisure pursuits as part of a reaction against industrialization and urbanization. Keith Thomas's *Man and the Natural World* has raised the profile of the widespread appreciation of nature and the countryside, which existed across the social spectrum in pre-industrial Britain.[3] The activities of early amateur botanists, entomologists and geologists have been investigated from a variety of angles, but they have only ever been considered fleetingly as an essential element in the growth of the broadly based outdoor movement. An examination of the motives and ideals of people such as the early botanist-ramblers, and of the objectives and activities of natural history societies, which expanded as an important dimension to the nineteenth-century growth of rational institutions, show them to be important generative impulses underpinning the formation of the movement.

The interest in natural history has depended upon motives ranging from an aesthetic and romantic appreciation of the beauties of nature to a more hard-headed scientific investigation of natural phenomena, although those two aspects have rarely been mutually exclusive. Abraham Stansfield of Manchester, writing in 1897, identified the botanist-rambler's fascination with nature as both poetic and scientific.[4] An appreciation of the natural world, enhanced by its study, palpably produced a combination of romantic inclinations with practical attitudes, which was wholly consistent with the more general Victorian intellectual dilemma concerning the problem of reconciliation between the spiritual and the rational. Sheffield's 'Corn Law rhymer', Ebenezer Elliott, for example, pursued a practical study of botany in conjunction with romantic and spiritual appreciation: '... the forms of Nature impressed themselves upon his soul in these wild woodland ramblings'.[5] C. P. Hobkirk, honorary secretary of Huddersfield Literary and Scientific Society in the 1850s, conducted rambles in search of botanical specimens, and gave painstaking attention to botanical nomenclature, but he also believed in 'communion with the Spirit of Nature in her own domain'.[6] The apparent pantheistic influence on such forms of spirituality may have owed more to the inflated eloquence of the period than to genuine inclinations. Nonetheless, it is clear that a prominent underlying motive for the widespread study of natural history was founded on a desire to achieve some understanding of the 'hidden treasures of God's world'.[7] Wonder at the manifestations of creation thus gave a particular religious significance to the study of nature. A fascination with natural history was particularly common amongst practising Christians, and was a popular pursuit with members of the clergy.[8] Typical of the church group excursion was that reported in the *Nelson Chronicle* of seven young men from Cooper Street Sunday School 'botanizing' and walking in the Lake District in 1907; they had listed mosses, ferns, herbs and other local flora.[9] The Reverend W. Tuckwell promulgated the notion that the study of natural history in the field had the benefit of making people more religious. The spiritual ambiguities attached to rambling in pursuit of an understanding of nature engendered some of the more esoteric and marginal notions which have contributed to the overall philosophical and ethical construction of the outdoor movement. Nonetheless, the general inclination of seekers after all forms of scientific knowledge, however superficial, was predominantly consistent with rational and improving principles. The involvement of naturalists, especially within the various associations, reinforced the ethical development of a nascent outdoor movement with a fundamentally progressive agenda.[10]

The natural history connection grew out of a predominantly individual and self-motivated recreational phenomenon, centring on the relatively well-documented activities of early nineteenth-century autodidactic working-class botanists in Lancashire, with rapidly expanding Manchester to the fore. Even during the early stages, however, small groups of naturalists were beginning to associate together in botanical societies, which existed from the latter part of the eighteenth century, such as that formed in 1777 at Eccles, to the west of Manchester. Other south Lancashire and north Cheshire botanists formed groups at Oldham, Ashton-under-Lyne and Stalybridge, while the Tyldesley Botanical Society existed at least as early as the 1820s. The early interest in botanical rambles, representing a further assertion of Lancashire's crucial contribution to the growth of an outdoor movement, has never been explained satisfactorily. In *The Naturalist in Britain, A Social History*, D. E. Allen makes a connection with a pre-Linnaean botanical society amongst Norwich weavers, many of whom are thought to have migrated to Lancashire. Allen has also suggested that the connection may go back even further to migrant Flemish cloth-workers, who had settled in East Anglia. This apriorism is less credible than is the continuity of a local popular culture sustained by short-range migration, and the influence of a strong autodidactic propensity amongst the weavers and other groups of independent radical craftsmen.

The primary motive for collecting botanical specimens was, of course, a practical quest for useful knowledge, rooted in the enquiring energy of the Enlightenment. During the nineteenth century interest broadened into a more general obsession with both natural and scientific phenomena. Possibly the first recorded rambler-botanist served as a foot soldier under Cromwell: Thomas Willisel, 'a good botanist' and 'a lusty fellow', was employed by London botanists to collect specimens during extended walking tours of England: 'Our English itinerant presented an account of his autumnal perigrinations about England, for which we hired him.'[11] The *Dictionary of National Biography* is uncertain whether Willisel was a native of Lancashire or Northamptonshire, and leans towards the latter, but recent research has confidently located him in the Burnley area of Lancashire: 'Three Thomas Willisels were baptised locally between 1599 and 1621 and he was almost certainly one of them. The families lived at Scholebank (Padiham) and at Monk Hall and Coldweather House in Briercliffe and Marsden.'[12]

The earliest botanists could never be termed ramblers in the modern sense, but those from the Manchester area certainly walked considerable distances in search of specimens, and were direct forerunners of the later nineteenth-century natural historians, for whom walking in the countryside was an integral part of their chosen leisure pursuit. Men like James Crowther from a Manchester slum, who attended the botanical society at Eccles, and who reported several confrontations with gamekeepers during his extensive walks outside the city; or John Horsfield, a Whitefield weaver, president of Prestwich Botanical Society, who typified the Lancashire autodidactic seeker after self-culture, would serve as models for Mrs. Gaskell's

> ... class of men in Manchester ... whose existence will probably be doubted by many, who yet may claim kindred with all the noble names that science recognizes. I said in Manchester, but they are scattered all over the manufacturing districts of Lancashire ... There are botanists among them, equally familiar with either the Linnaean or the Natural system, who know the name and habitat of every plant within a day's walk from their dwellings; who steal the holiday of a day or two when any particular plant should be in flower and tying up their food in their simple pocket-handkerchiefs, set off with single purpose to fetch home the humble-looking weed.[13]

These were the intellectually inclined artisans whom the Cambridge geology professor Adam Sedgwick praised during a lecture in 1842. Significant numbers of rambling botanists and entomologists were extremely active in Lancashire during the first half of the nineteenth century, usually rambling alone, but occasionally meeting with others of the same inclination, for example at a large gathering at Newchurch-in-Pendle in July 1825. Chroniclers of local life, such as James Cash in his *Where There's a Will There's a Way!*, published in 1873, have emphasized the influence of the early naturalists on the popular cultural traditions of Lancashire. Cash identifies the recreational strand represented by the activities of Crowther and Horsfield, and of men from the Manchester area such as Edward Hobson, George Crozier, Thomas Townley, Samuel Carter, Richard Buxton, William Worsley of Middleton, Jethro Tinker of Stalybridge, John Mellor of Royton and John Martin of Tyldesley.[14] Some of these naturalists were employed as gardeners, but the majority, in keeping with the inquisitive intelligence and independence associated with their trade, were handloom weavers: '... many of the early botanists were weavers, or were engaged in some other branch of the cotton industry'.[15]

Richard Buxton, however, was a Manchester shoemaker. The autobiographical introduction to his *Botanical Guide* provides an invaluable record of some of the activities and motives of the early Manchester natural historians who roamed the local countryside. Buxton would walk twenty to thirty miles from his home in Hulme in search of botanical specimens, and in pursuit of exercise and fresh air in pleasant surroundings, away from the conditions of the industrial town. Later in life, in 1859, Buxton extolled the benefits of rambling in the countryside:

> I have now reached the age of sixty-two years; and, although by no means robust, I can yet make a ramble of thirty miles a day, and enjoy the beauties of nature with as much zest as ever I did in my life ... [I]t has preserved my health if not my life, and afforded me a fair share of happiness.[16]

Buxton was also keen to promote the importance of combining the progressive benefits of science and learning with enjoyment of the natural world. He was appealing to the factory operative, cooped up in the unhealthy manufacturing towns, to make the effort required to get into the surrounding countryside, which, by mid-century, when Buxton was putting his life's experience into writing, had become less accessible than during the heyday of his own botanical ventures:

> He sees much of what is termed the triumphs of science and art, but little of the works of nature. This renders him an intelligent, but, to a certain extent, an artificial man ... [T]here are still, within a distance of sixteen miles of Manchester, many delightful walks, by pleasant streams and through green woods.[17]

During the early years, Buxton's botanical excursions were typically lone affairs, but he increasingly came to associate with other similarly motivated working men. John Dewhurst, a fustian-cutter, was instrumental in bringing together some of the naturalists in collective activities at a time when any form of combination by working people could still be a dangerous business. Some of these 'botanical rambles' were recorded by Buxton, who stressed the pleasure to the participants of walking in the countryside: 'Hundreds of miles did we wander agreeably over the country together.'[18] Buxton was to develop a reputation in the Manchester area, where his botanical expertise was much sought-after. He impressed the Bishop of Manchester with his wealth of information, and he was regularly called upon to advise natural historians from all walks of life. A letter to the *Manchester City News* in the 1920s recalled Buxton's renown in the 1850s:

> In the summer of 1857 or 1858 I went on a walking tour to Cornwall, when I made a pretty large collection of plants, many of which when I got home, I could not find names for, so I went to interview Buxton and see if he could help me. He knew every one of course, and could tell me all about them ...[19]

For many of the peripatetic natural historians, the first contact with others of similar persuasion was the Manchester Mechanics' Institute, an appropriate venue for scientifically minded self-improvers. It was here, in the late 1820s, that Richard Buxton first met John Horsfield, who introduced him to meetings of the Prestwich Botanical Society. The Institute introduced a course of natural history classes from 1839. Buxton again emphasized the rambling aspect of the activity: 'In their company too, many rambles and expeditions were undertaken; most of them were working men and their enthusiasm knew no bounds, though their excursions were mainly perforce on foot.'[20] Buxton also referred regularly to the substantial numbers of working-class natural historians in his widening circle of acquaintances. They included John Mellor of Royton, the 'so-called father of Lancashire working-class botanists ... [who] ... tramped over the hills and dales of Scotland'.[21] Another 'intimate and kindred spirit'[22] was John Nowell of the Todmorden Botanical Society, a handloom weaver who became a twister during the increasing mechanization of the weaving sector. As a native of a small industrial town, Nowell was less typical of the early botanical rambler, although the Todmorden area presented the ideal combination of environmental conditions to stimulate such interests. The same criteria would later influence the formation of associations of naturalists in other small, but expanding, sub-Pennine communities. Abraham Stansfield's description of the Todmorden area, written in 1881, romantically evoked the essential stark contrasts:

> The town is the dullest, the prosiest of the prosy – a cottony town, the neighbourhood pure poetry! In the town itself, if the time be summer, amid the clash and clatter of looms, whirr of wheels, and whizz of spindless [sic], ... walk but a few paces, and you will find yourself on the first step of a ladder of green hills ... It is a place where the lungs can dilate, the mind expand, the spirit soar! ... [there is] much attraction to the geologist and the plant-hunter.[23]

The later associational formation which occurred amongst natural historians on the Yorkshire side of the Pennines was also rooted in the culture generated by earlier individual working men who roamed the local countryside. Notable amongst these naturalists were Gibson of Hebden Bridge, King and Bolton from Halifax, and three Keighley men, the weavers Jesse and John Miller and the printer Abraham Shackleton.

Further north, during the latter part of the eighteenth century, members of a well-established Newcastle commercial and merchant class developed an interest in the study of natural history and the collection of specimens, which would lay the foundations for a more middle-class recreational interest in field study in that district. John Hancock worked in his father's saddlery and ironmongery business in the city, but: 'Whenever business was slack he set off with one or two congenial friends upon pedestrian tours through various parts of the northern counties in search of plants, insects and shells.'[24] Hancock's collection inspired his children, male and female, towards similar ventures. In 1829, Albany Hancock, with a group of naturalist friends, founded the Natural History Society in Newcastle, an association which continues to flourish through its organization of field trips, lectures, and the maintenance of nature reserves in the north-east of England. One of the founders of the society was Joshua Alder, who in 1846 helped to form the Tyneside Naturalists' Field Club. 'The gentle and retiring Alder'[25] joined his parents' provision business in 1807, but his primary interest in natural history stimulated him increasingly towards an exploration of the countryside. The walking excursions which he and his friends undertook were initially confined to the country around Tyneside, but the 'pedestrian tours' were later expanded into Scotland and the Lake District.[26] Nearby, in 1848, the *Sunderland and Durham County Herald* encouraged local amateur geologists to 'Ramble to Marsden Rocks'; the attractions of such an outing were couched in terms of combining healthy exercise with the study of natural science: 'To the student in the science of geology, it affords a rich field for enquiry; it gives to the invalid new life and vigour; cheers the moody and depressed spirit …'[27]

By the middle of the nineteenth century, the field study of natural history, promoting healthy walks in the countryside, had become a significantly popular pastime, particularly around the expanding industrial towns of Lancashire and West Yorkshire. It was a pursuit which absorbed people of varied social status, such as the Reverend W. Houghton, who had his *Country Walks of a Naturalist with his Children* published in 1869, or Huddersfield Naturalists' Society, whose membership included several self-educated working men, although this association of common interest was sustained also by an element of middle-class patronage. The society at Slaithwaite in the Colne Valley was comprised mainly of 'the sons of poor parents', who joined 'botanical rambles, which extended to Halifax on one side, Woodhead on the other …'[28] The all-male membership, which reached 160 by 1870, participated in a regular syllabus of rambles into the surrounding countryside: 'We used to take our time, range the fields and moors, and call at the nearest public-house to get a gill of beer to a little lunch, which was generally carried in the pocket.'[29] It was, however, more common for middle-class professionals to take the lead, with the Huddersfield-Colne Valley area certainly no exception. Slaithwaite, for example, was 'always blessed with good professional men'.[30]

W. J. C. Miller, professional mathematician, principal of Huddersfield College, and amateur student of botany, expressed the opinion, in his *Essays and Nature Studies. With Lectures*, published in 1899, that the best way to gain knowledge of any district is on foot.

The growth of interest both in natural sciences and in open-air recreation led to a proliferation of societies whose activities, in varying degrees, gave an organizational structure to the collaboration of interests. Almost every town in the industrialized districts of Lancashire sustained at least one group of field naturalists who would organize programmes of summer rambles. Not surprisingly, the most flourishing association was the Manchester Field Naturalists' Society (FNS), founded in 1860 by Leopold Hartley Grindon, who, although not born when many of the early Lancashire naturalists had begun their open-air explorations, also made important contacts with like minds at the Mechanics' Institute. The middle-class Grindon, a member of the local Athenaeum Club, had already been president of the Bristol Botanical Society, before arriving in Manchester at the age of twenty in 1838, where he 'joined the Mechanics' Institute and fell in with an eager group of Lancashire botanists'.[31] His experiences and active participation in Manchester helped to consolidate the inter-class collaboration which this aspect of open-air activity perpetuated. In 1904 his obituary acknowledged the interaction with the artisan naturalists: 'Amongst the members of the natural history class of the Mechanics' Institute he found a company of congenial spirits – Crozier, Horsfield, Crowther etc., amongst others, – and together they enjoyed such instructive rambles ...'[32]

As a keen recreational walker, for whom 'country walks were always a great delight',[33] Grindon's most lasting contribution was the FNS, whose activities he reported for many years in regular columns in the *Manchester Guardian* and the *Manchester City News*. In 1910 an elderly early member of Grindon's rambling groups recalled the naturalists' Saturday afternoon expeditions: 'Under his leadership the rambles were delightful social functions ...'[34] The Manchester FNS was by no means the first of its kind, but its scale, and the extensiveness of its programme of activities, expressed a consolidation of the relationship between natural history and forms of healthy country exercise. The society's first report acknowledged earlier roots in the work of its predecessors: '... prototypes in many parts of England, and especially in the celebrated Botanical Societies which have reflected so much credit and honour upon the working men of South Lancashire, during a period of more than eighty years'.[35] Description of the first Saturday excursions also included tributes to some of the earlier botanists. The trip to Bamford Wood on 25 August 1860 would '... explore ground consecrated by the steps of that fine old band of botanical patriarchs, Hobson, Crozier,

Horsfield, and Dewhurst'.[36] The excursion on 15 September was 'a very pleasant sylvan walk' as far as Ramsbottom.[37] The success of the society can be attributed largely to Grindon, who, first as secretary, then as president, worked energetically over a period of many years to develop and sustain all the club's activities. He was especially involved in the flourishing field trips, which, even during the first year, attracted weekly summer attendances of sixty to seventy people. The close and consistent connection which existed in Lancashire between the study of natural sciences and country walking was embodied in the interests of Grindon, and he was a great publicist for both pursuits. Through advertisements in local newspapers, the Manchester FNS tapped an increasing demand for escape into the fresh air. The publicity certainly proved effective, with 550 people attracted to one excursion, although not all, of course, were ramblers or natural historians. Nevertheless, the response does reflect the depth of local interest, and, importantly for the naturalists, facilitated the hiring of cheap-rate special trains, which presented the opportunity for the substantial hard core of the society to travel further afield. In 1895, the *Manchester Guardian* commented on how the 'scope of excursions had been greatly enlarged' for the FNS through the opening-up by the railways of new districts.[38]

The tradition of the Lancashire autodidactic naturalist contributed in no small way to the establishment of a more general interest in natural history in the county. It was a recreational development which was connected directly to responses to the spread of industrialization, but it was rooted in aspects of the pre-industrial culture of the Lancashire hills. The local tradition continued to produce some remarkable individuals long after the early working-class botanists had begun to associate together. In an article entitled *Half an Hour with a Factory Botanist*, the Reverend J. M. Mather, a keen walker in the uplands of east Lancashire, recorded his own experience of the independent and self-instructed working man who rambled in his native countryside. Mather's acquaintance, to whom he was introduced by a walking companion during a ramble above Rossendale, was a factory hand and 'the leader of a group of students of nature'. During their conversation the mill-hand botanist took down a volume of Ruskin from a shelf. Mather felt that the factory system had 'quickened the instincts of the operative for the beautiful'.[39]

Towards the latter part of the century, this breed of man came to be exemplified by Ernest Evans from the Burnley area, whose life represented the ideal of the independently minded and self-motivated, but community-orientated, individual. Evans is not often remembered in the town, although he rose to a position of prominence and considerable influence. However, at his funeral in 1956 he was eulogized by friend and colleague, W. E. Thornber, as 'possibly the greatest citizen

that Burnley had ever known'.[40] Evans's main claim to fame stemmed
from his rise, against the odds, from carding and weaving in the cotton
mills of the Lancashire Calder Valley to his appointment as the head
of the natural science department of Burnley College, and, eventually,
as organizer of scientific education for the area, responsible for a record
number of successes in the national and royal scholarship examinations,
which enabled a large number of students from the district to gain
entrance to the Royal College of Science. His recreational activities
perpetuated the tradition of Lancashire working men, combining a love
of escape to the hills with a passion for natural history. Even during
his earliest working life as a carder under a particularly repressive
factory regime at Barnoldswick, from 1868 to 1870, Evans managed to
satisfy his love of freedom and the open air: '... the countryside of
Craven, which he explored every Sunday, when he could get away from
church attendance, kept up his spirits and prevented his health
from being undermined'.[41]

Evans's growing reputation resulted in an invitation to teach in night
school at the Walk Mill branch of Burnley Mechanics' Institute while
he was still working as a weaver, and in 1899 he was offered a full-time
post at the main Mechanics' Institute in the town, teaching a range of
natural sciences, including botany and geology, as well as other scientific
subjects. From this invaluable institutional base he organized rambles
and field study courses for the young men of the district, some of whom
would form the backbone of the outdoor movement locally. Evans's
important contribution to the formation of a strong nucleus of enthusiasts of improving outdoor pursuits helped to cultivate and perpetuate
the popularity of rambling in north-east Lancashire. The expansion of
open-air activities within local popular culture was nurtured through
Evans's education and encouragement of receptive minds towards a
more comprehensive enjoyment of the local countryside, including a
considerable understanding of the natural history of the district. The
Burnley Express and News paid tribute to him in 1956: '... he knew every
crag and moor, every hill, valley, and clough around Burnley – and he
knew the home and haunt of every plant and animal in this area of
Lancashire'.[42]

Tom Stephenson, a lifelong rambler and rights-of-way campaigner,
was a product of Evans's vigorous educational legacy. He became one
of the key characters of the outdoor movement for much of the
twentieth century, maintaining strongly the tradition of the Lancashire
autodidact. In the autobiographical *Forbidden Land*, published posthu-
mously in 1989, Stephenson paid tribute to his mentor: 'Evans was a
great rambler and many of his students rambled with him. He was
above all a practical naturalist, making frequent field excursions and
introducing his students to geological features.'[43] Stephenson's account

of his own experiences in the Burnley area before the Great War places great emphasis on the important continuity which Evans engendered through his enthusiastic proselytization amongst local working people of open-air recreation and complementary educational interests. Stephenson recalled a Saturday afternoon ramble in 1912 led by a young Burnley weaver who was a botany student of Evans. The group came across a miner examining a flower on the outskirts of town:

> Soon the young weaver and the collier ... were discussing in learned detail the characteristics of the flower until they were agreed upon its genus and species. 'You are a botanist?' asked the weaver. 'Well a bit of one like,' was the reply. He had studied botany and geology under Evans a dozen years previously. Twenty years later such men were among the founders of North-east Lancashire Federation of Rambling Clubs.[44]

It was Stephenson himself who became the most influential graduate of that alfresco academy.

Across the Pennines, during that same important formative period at the turn of the century, the natural history ramble was being popularized by Samuel Wood, 'a working-man, entirely self-taught',[45] whose collection of accounts of his countryside expeditions was published in 1901 under the title of *Random Notes; Being Prose Sketches of Nature under Various Aspects*, and priced at 1s. Another prolific walker and natural historian to bring those combined activities to more general notice was the Lancashire dialect poet Edwin Waugh, the 'poet of the moorlands'. Waugh was always keen to give to his rambles some definite purpose, which he achieved by investigating local history and folklore, the wealth of Lancashire traditions. He also studied the flora of his district, becoming 'familiar with all the wild flowers of Lancashire'.[46]

Although the recreation of rambling, combined with the study of natural phenomena, transcended commonly ascribed class divisions, it was still more likely that people from less humble origins would have the means, the opportunity and the inclination to encourage others in their chosen pastime. Prosperous middle-class members of natural history societies obviously found it easier to assert an influence in local communities. Mr Earl Binns, a founder member in 1909 of the Colne Natural History Society, was a 'great botanist ... [who was] great company on rambles'; he was noted locally for his skill in placating irate farmers when trespassing on their land, and for possessing an '... expert knowledge of all the footpaths for many miles around this district and also a good knowledge of botany which made him an ideal companion to be out in the country with'.[47]

The active participation of J. W. Puttrell – the first president of the

Derbyshire Pennine Club – in the associational life of the open-air
movement around Sheffield and the south Pennines was founded on a
gospel that promoted a combination of strenuous physical activities
with an interest in natural history and an early form of environmental
campaigning. Puttrell spread the message through a series of popular
lecture tours, articles in the *Sheffield Daily Telegraph* and, during the
1920s, in local broadcasts on rambling in the Peak District. He
presented his 'Natural History' and 'Rambles and Scrambles' talks over
a period of many years to a range of institutions, whose common
denominator was a Christian nonconformist connection. Puttrell's
bookings included scientific societies, the Wesleyan Literary Society,
the Presbyterian Church Guild, the Mechanics' Institutes at Bradford
and Hunslet, Meersbrook Park and Netherfield Congregational Churches, Hillsborough Wesleyan Chapel, Glossop Road Baptist Church,
Derby CHA and HF Rambling Club, and at the Temperance Hall and
YMCA in Sheffield. In an article in the *Telegrap*h in 1912, Puttrell
called on 'all readers who are interested in rambling, preservation of
footpaths, and the cultivation of a love of natural beauty' to attend
a meeting to consider the formation of a federation of Sheffield
ramblers.[48]

Such individuals, from differing social backgrounds, but imbued with
a common culture, were the mainstay of institutional organization,
which consolidated the natural history strand as a key element in an
emerging movement founded on open-air interests. Study of the natural
sciences was combined with country walks and rural excursions in
organizations which ranged from Mechanics' Institutes and local scientific associations, with their natural history classes, to the rambling
clubs which proliferated towards the latter part of the nineteenth
century and beyond. The very earliest associations of naturalists had
often been informally based on a mutually convenient public house,
where participants would discuss their interests and arrange further
trips. However, as this recreational phenomenon crystallized during
the second half of the nineteenth century, the growing trend was
towards formal societies, consistent with the contemporaneous spread
of scientific associations and educational institutions, which owed much
to the patronage of middle-class professionals or amateur dilettanti. In
north-east Lancashire, for example, the 'scientific ramble' flourished
as one strand within that diverse local cultural milieu of educational
and related interests which had evolved hand in hand with the industrial
and urban expansion of the area to produce associations such as the
Burnley Literary and Scientific Club and the Padiham Scientific Association – both of which contained natural history sections – the Burnley
Natural History Society (NHS), Calder Vale FNS and Blackburn
Field Naturalists' Association. Nonetheless, the temperance and gravity

of such associations should not be overstated, as the activities of the Calder Vale society demonstrate: disputing with gamekeepers, for example, and enjoying a sing-song at the Red Pump at Whitewell. All these associations incorporated scientific rambles within their itineraries, some of which were recorded in printed reports. During 1884 the *Burnley Express* ran a series describing such rambles, which were obviously the accounts of well-heeled middle-class naturalists who had walked as far afield as Glencoe. They helped to inspire fellow members of the naturalist and scientific associations who were less well endowed with either the means or the time required to cover such distances; these included men in the tradition of the uneducated Burnley weaver William Dugdale, who, 'utilising time after a hard day's work, battled successfully with many of the different problems of science until he became a leading geologist in the neighbourhood'.[49] Prominent in the Burnley Literary and Scientific Club was newspaper editor and writer Henry Houlding, the 'Bard of the Brun' and 'Poet of Pendle'. Houlding encouraged local open-air pursuits through his articles on geology and natural history, which appeared in the published transactions of the Literary and Scientific Club. Publications of the Burnley NHS and minutes of the Padiham Scientific Association also described rambles on field trips, while the Burnley group reported on the participation in the weekly summer season rambles by members of similar societies from Nelson, Accrington and Bacup. The Burnley NHS, which was attached to the town's Mechanics' Institute, stated its objects explicitly, on an undated poster: 'The society has been formed to stimulate and encourage the study of the natural characteristics of the Burnley District, and to arrange RAMBLES and EXCURSIONS to the beautiful, healthy and interesting places of the neighbourhood.'[50]

Such sentiments were echoed on many occasions by other associations, including those rambling clubs whose programmes incorporated elements of botanical study. Leeds Co-operative Field Naturalists' Club, founded in 1882, featured weekly summer rambles in their syllabus, and the Crosshills NHS from Airedale collaborated with Colne NHS just over the hill in Lancashire. Naturalists from Ovenden and Cragg Vale organized a joint ramble in Bellhouse Clough and on Erringden Moor in May 1905. The member who reported the Ovenden group's Midsummer's Day celebration ramble to Ogden Clough of that year resorted to the poetry of Emerson to evoke the delights of nature rambles: 'Give me health and a day with Nature and I will make the pomp of emperors look ridiculous.'[51] Obviously believing in an early inculcation of the joys of nature, Ovenden naturalists took a party of poor children on a ramble through the woods at Hardcastle Crags in 1905. In October 1910 the Crosshills NHS combined with forty Keighley naturalists on a ramble to Howden Woods. The Keighley association had been founded as early as 1868 as the Keighley Botanic Society, and was then 'composed chiefly of working men'.[52] By 1913 the eighty-five members included a significant number of professionals, including teachers, historians and journalists. The Keighley Literary and Scientific Association, formed in 1881, also included activities for naturalists, as did the flourishing natural history section of the Bradford Scientific Association, which became Bradford Natural History and Microscopal Society in 1881, and which was instrumental in a developing collaboration in the district between associations such as Upper Airedale Natural Scientific Association, Craven Naturalists' Association and Frizinghall Naturalists' Association. These Yorkshire societies were affiliated to the Yorkshire Naturalists' Union, which organized a full programme of summer rambles, often assisted by reduced rail fares. Other activities on Bradford's scientific rambling syllabus included an excursion to the Ruskin Museum at Meersbrook Park, Sheffield on 28 June 1890. The formation of the Bradford Scientific Association in 1875 was a reflection of the upsurge of improving institutions in that town. A centenary history of the association attributes the intellectual phenomenon to an 'influx of refugees from the continent',[53] although that claim is not substantiated. From 1883 the *Practical Naturalist*, edited in Bradford by H. S. Ward and H. J. Riley, described the activities of the local natural history associations, including an account of 'botanical rambles' undertaken by the Reverend D. D. Waters.[54] This Bradford quarterly was one of a range of similar contemporary publications, whose titles included *The Birmingham Naturalists' Gazette*, *Cheetham Natural History Magazine*, and *The Young Naturalist*. The *Practical Naturalist* also included B. Illingworth's 'Notes By An Occasional Rambler', and numerous references to Saturday afternoon and holiday rambles, such as that undertaken by 'The Gleaner' (James Firth), rambling in the 'Knockmeledown Mountains' *(sic)*.[55] The first issue of *Practical Naturalist* reported on a conference of natural history societies held at Keighley in 1883.

The rise of the field naturalists' societies and the natural history sections of more general scientific associations in the nineteenth century has given rise to questions relating to the interaction between patronage, culturally constructed hegemony and social control. Investigation of the complexities of class formation are certainly pertinent to this area of recreational development. However, it is clear that within the the ideological and ethical foundations of these associations, which did generate a good deal of cooperation across generally accepted class demarcations, there can be detected an evolving movement based on a culturally delineated echelon of a social model, distinguished by vertical as much as horizontal divisions. It is particularly difficult to make generalizations about the motivation underlying the mediation of common culture, as it manifested itself through the natural history and open-air connection. This dimension to the construction of a collaborative social stratum was undoubtedly influenced by a significant degree of patronage, characterized by enlightened self-interest, but it depended equally on the simple motive of escape from the physical and psychological drawbacks of everyday life by an intelligent but largely apolitical sector of workers. Patronage is always a problematic concept; there were numerous instances of a high-minded belief in helping the deserving and worthy to achieve some degree of fulfilment. An affinity of interests stimulated genuine comradeship, generated through relationships between influential, wealthy patrons and naturalists from humble backgrounds, which differed from either the traditional organic form of patronage which relied on the mutual interdependence of unequal members of a hierarchical structure, or a newer form of patronage rooted in the ulterior motive of social manipulation. What is certain is that working-class naturalists were unlikely to travel far from their own district without the encouragement that often resulted from membership of the various societies which gave impetus to nineteenth-century inter-class cooperation.

Richard Buxton, for example, travelled further afield under the sponsorship of an anonymous gentleman, who was almost certainly Edward William Binney FRS, noted for his work in geology and palaeobotany, whom Buxton first met at the Mechanics' Institute natural history classes. The weaver John Nowell 'rambled and botanised ... over no inconsiderable portion of England, Wales, and Ireland' with the president of the Todmorden Botanical Society.[56] Nowell engaged in correspondence with botanists and specimen collectors from several areas of the country – 'his correspondents being men in every station and condition of life, from the peer to the peasant'[57] – and his reputation spread to Sir William Hooker at Kew. Acceptance into the largely upper-middle-class, highly respectable mainstream of the nineteenth-century British natural science establishment, came with the naming of a moss, a liverwort and a fern after Nowell, thus bestowing the same type of immortality with which the likes of Hooker, Banks and Farrer had been honoured.[58] As a member of the prestigious Yorkshire Ramblers' Club, Farrer, a graduate of Balliol and owner of the Ingleborough Estate at Clapham in north-west Yorkshire, despite an obviously different social background from Nowell, combined the same range of open-air interests and activities.[59] The large Huddersfield Naturalists' Society, which met in pubs, and bought beer wholesale for resale to a membership which included a substantial number of working-class men, received establishment approval, including the patronage of a member of the local gentry and the town's MP. Higher up the valley, the

Slaithwaite naturalists were said to 'have worked themselves up by study and perseverance'.[60]

In *The Heyday of Natural History*, Lynn Barber subscribes to the theory that social control was the main underlying motive for the support given to the nineteenth-century artisan natural historians, and to the societies that encouraged them to explore the countryside in their spare time. This view parallels the contemporary concern for the provision of public walks for urban workers: 'It was a form not only of rational, but, more importantly, of innocent amusement. It was better for the working-classes to spend their spare time chasing butterflies than drinking or fighting or gambling or whatever other iniquities they usually got up to.'[61] This prevailing orthodoxy, consistent with the wider range of theory pertaining to the construction, institutionalization, and consequent consolidation of the respectable middle-class ethos,[62] ignores the complexity of social relationships, and gives insufficient weight to any sustained independent interest amongst the different sections of the working classes. Popular scientific rambling was consistent with the rationalizing forces of nineteenth-century society, but it is a misleading condescension to assume that such pursuits, and their underlying values, belonged exclusively in the domain of the monied classes, and that participants from the working classes were social climbers: '... the general middle class approbation for this type of amusement meant that any working man who did take up the study of natural history could be sure of encouragement from all the local do-gooders'.[63] Barber's generalization does in fact refer to the naturalists of the earlier part of the nineteenth century, but such motives, in a more developed and organized form, are often also ascribed to the later period. The activities and experiences of some of the natural history associations contradict much of the simplistic theory. The Slaithwaite Naturalists' Society represented only a minority interest in their West Riding community, but they were also part of a broader, thriving, progressive social and political scene in the Colne Valley, which promoted overall community improvement through a range of channels. In their rambles over the moors the 'earnest and determined' members often included a visit to local public houses, where they involved themselves in political discussion, which differentiates them from the general pattern of apolitical natural historians during the earlier period: 'If there was anyone at the inn ready to argue on any point under the sun, these men were ready. Politics was a great theme then, because there were so many things to adjust, wrongs to redress, and reforms to make.'[64] Partly expressed through particular forms of recreation, a significant urge to betterment of both self and community was integrated into a sensible and respectable doctrine of civic improvement, which, by the turn of the century, informed the policies of a 'wise

Urban District Council'[65] which provided community leisure facilities such as the Slaithwaite public baths, and encouraged the use of open-air amenities such as local footpaths. Slaithwaite's position at the heart of the Colne Valley made it a hub of the forces of political progress which, by the end of the nineteenth century, were gradually overcoming some of the conservative barriers to certain aspects of community improvement. The battle for Sunday trams was won, making it easier for people to spend their leisure time in the open air, after riding from the towns to the various termini. Bands and choirs constituted the main recreational focus in the Colne Valley, but the rambling naturalists belonged within that overall milieu of an independently motivated creed of general civic improvement.

The Clarion socialist principle of individual fulfilment through recreation and an appreciation of the natural world[66] was encapsulated in the ideals and the activities of the Clarion Field Club (CFC), which was formed in 1895 to give practical expression to Robert Blatchford's *Merrie England* notion. The Blatchfordian doctrine certainly depended on an interpretation of existing thought, notably that of Ruskin and Morris, but the underlying philosophy was also consistent with the cultural and sporting, mind and body concept of the classical Olympian ideal, which was contemporaneously revived as a western cultural icon, suggesting a deeper-rooted reaction against the values of commercial modernity. Blatchford, and his colleagues at the *Clarion* and its affiliated publications, promulgated a creed which combined physical exercise and social intercourse with educational and cultural activity, in a simple life communion with the natural environment which rejected the march of urban industrialism.

As offshoot of the larger Clarion movement, the CFC was in itself a relatively insignificant organization. In 1896 it had just over seven hundred members in thirty-eight branches, many of which maintained close connections with the left-wing political associations of their locality, usually the ILP, sometimes the Cooperative movement, and, in Burnley, the SDF. The CFC's founder, Harry Lowerison, son of a Durham miner and disciple of Ruskin and Morris, actively promoted the value of fresh air and the belief in the superiority of the countryside over the town. It was a vision that was fundamentally Arcadian, thereby connecting with contemporary simple and back-to-nature models, such as that espoused by Edward Carpenter. However, the ideology of the CFC was shaped by primarily progressive notions of social development, which placed the greatest emphasis on companionship, cooperation, education and personal improvement. Recreation, health and 'individual regeneration' were essential components of the projected socialist commonwealth.[67] Notwithstanding its small membership, the CFC exerted a significant influence, and its principles were circulated widely, particularly through the columns of *Clarion*. Although numerically small, through the activities of its various branches it added its influence to the consolidation of a connection between field studies and country rambles. There was frequent collaboration between different branches of the club, and joint open-air excursions in conjunction with other Clarion associations, including the cycling clubs and the vocal unions. Cyclists and naturalists from Hull, for example, combined on a boat trip up the Yorkshire Ouse in 1898, while the Potteries CCC affiliated its members to the North Staffordshire CFC: 'We have also decided to arrange our runs in conjunction with the Field Club rambles ...'[68] Turn-of-the-century rambles around Hardcastle Crags in Yorkshire, organized by Robert Blatchford's brother, Montague ('Mont Blong'), brought together a 'couple of hundred well-behaved and happy people' from Clarion field clubs, cycling clubs, and vocal unions.[69]

Even these politically affiliated Clarion naturalists were, not surprisingly, often more interested in the recreational and social focus of the group than in any high-minded ideals. The great majority of nineteenth-century naturalists, particularly from the earlier period, were basically apolitical escapees from urban conditions and from the mundane, who were pursuing a harmless, but intelligent, form of amusement, which was increasingly enjoying a widespread popularity beyond the confines of the culture of a single social class. This general political quietude did not, however, necessarily signify assimilation into an alien ideology. The self-taught naturalists were, in the main, simply following their inclinations towards their own all-absorbing leisure interests, which, by their very nature, automatically removed them from the frequent bouts of urban turmoil. James Cash's retrospective analysis of the activities of the Lancashire botanists of the first half of the nineteenth century would seem to lend weight to Barber's thesis:

> Whilst the operatives of Middleton were sacking and burning the cotton mills which had ceased to yield them employment, and whilst soldiers were shooting down the rioters without mercy, Dewhurst, Hobson, Horsefield [*sic*] Mellor, Crowther, and a host of others – all worthy men – were pursuing their harmless and ennobling pleasures upon the Lancashire hillsides ...[70]

However, independent escapism should not be conflated with forms of social control. In 1834, William Swainson described a pastime which was 'as much in reach of the cottager as of the professor'.[71] Barber indeed supports the notion of independent involvement, by stressing that two hours' walking from even the largest urban area would give access to the specimens which the naturalists required, and that later in the century cheap rail excursions enabled continued access to the natural environment. Naturalists from the lower social classes were, nevertheless, rarely able to travel as readily or as far afield as were their more leisured counterparts, and any form of assistance would thus have been welcome to the autodidactic botanist.

Barber also cites the advice of the Scottish stonemason Hugh Miller, a geologist who advocated study, the cultivation of the mind and the avoidance of Chartism. Such advice ignored the fact that most of the aims of the Chartists were maintained as much by prosperous middle-class advocates of civic reform and general community improvement – such as the members of the Burnley liberal radical coterie in the 1850s – as by purportedly revolutionary working-class groups. Indeed, British radical politics has never been confined to a single economic group. Moreover, although hindered by a minimum formal education, working people were not always naturally inclined towards trivial leisure pursuits, being quite capable of aspiring towards their own forms of intellectual, sensual, and physical fulfilment. Such motivation, and its accompanying set of values, did, nevertheless, supply ample ammunition for the ide- ologues of rationalism. Buxton, Horsfield, *et alii* were unwittingly exploited by establishment proselytizers as examples of what could be achieved by self-improvement and rational forms of recreation. In 1849, *The Economist*, in an article entitled *Have Working Men Time to Improve*, highlighted the study of nature as a route to self-betterment. It was an article with a highly topical motive, inveighing against political activists who sought to improve the lot of the majority of working people through radical political and social reform: '... those who trade not with their hands but with their tongues. The loom and the plough know them not; yet they always affect to speak in the name of the working classes.'[72] Answering complaints that working men had no time to improve, *The Economist* showed its colours as a voice of the proponents of utilitarian political economy, by adopting a line that was typically self-righteous and condescending: 'If there a were will [*sic*], the way would be found. They have many holidays – many days when work is suspended or slack – many evenings to dispose of, and now, in all great towns, many opportunities to self-improvement.'[73] The small but significant minority who roamed the countryside to study natural history during the first half of the nineteenth century were being enlisted into the utilitarian camp. They were cited as the paragons of what could be achieved by the diligent, thereby inadvertently lending support to the overall scheme of those who envisaged and planned an ordered society based on their own model. The early botanists were never likely to challenge seriously the prevailing orthodoxy, but, how- ever much they may have fitted conveniently into the pattern, it was never a simple question of the inculcation of those who were, in reality, self-motivated men, who had developed their own interests before they had ever become subject to adoption and patronage by a rational and improving element of the middle class. The code of values expressed in the introduction to Richard Buxton's *Botanical Guide* promoted an ideal which seems particularly appropriate to the 1840s, combining aspects of a stereotypical pre-industrial organic model of society, belonging to the Tory nostalgic tradition of opposition to industrialization and commercialism, with the increasingly dominant rational and utilitarian concerns of mid-century society. In the 1850s Buxton made an appeal to the landowners, which contained a strong measure of respectful pleading, but which would certainly have had no chance of consideration if couched in aggressive and demanding terms:

> ... the lords of the soil will yet allow the pent-up dwellers in the crowded city to walk about and view the beauties of creation – yes, not only permit it, but derive much true pleasure from seeing the sons of toil rationally enjoying themselves in rambling through their domains, and exploring the wonders of nature ... I therefore would venture to request the landowners, at least to preserve the old footpaths which cross their fields and woods, if they should decline to allow fresh ones to be made, like their forefathers of old.[74]

The general demeanour of the rambler-naturalist has always tended towards the philosophic and the pacific. The breed was typified by John Nowell, who was said to be 'the very spirit of tranquillity' and exuded an 'atmosphere of love and peace'.[75] In respectable and responsible vein, Buxton appealed to his 'fellow workmen living in the back streets and narrow alleys' to avoid 'any annoyance or injury to the property of the owners of the land near the footpaths ... and thus show that the working man can not only admire the beauties of nature, but also thoroughly respect the rights of property'.[76] John Horsfield's brief flirtation with radicalism certainly influenced his incorporation into the sphere of generally politically undemanding self-improvers. Writing in the *Manchester Guardian* in March 1850, Horsfield recalled a narrow escape from the authorities when attending the Peterloo demonstration in 1819, and how he had learned from that episode the lesson of steering clear of the dangers of political involvement. At a later period, Ammon Wrigley, a Saddleworth mill worker, who 'ever loved the quiet ways of life ... [and had] ... no worries about creeds or politics, and cared nothing for isms, cults or ologies ...', belonged to a local fellowship in the 1930s which rambled in the local hills; his abiding interest was in 'hills, moors and all little things that live in the open air'.[77] Such views as these have sustained a politically quiescent strand, which has mollified the more strident and activist dimension of an outdoor movement.

Apoliticism was less evident towards the end of the century, and there were plenty of rambler-naturalists who were overtly political. Among the more notable was Ernest Evans, who combined country walks, attendance at Mrs Stroyan's botany classes and work for the Burnley NHS with the trade-union work which gained him the reputation as an agitator who was consequently blacked by most of the mills between Colne and Burnley. The influence of Evans on the popularity of rambling and natural history in north-east Lancashire was consistent with the perpetuation of a political dimension established on a broadly anti-Tory, free-thinking tradition, challenging, if only in a usually restrained or rhetorical fashion, the existing land system and the local restrictions which it sanctioned. Although never really a naturalist, Tom Stephenson emerged from the same tradition as a strongly motivated and politically active countryside campaigner, whose initial challenge to accepted doctrine was as a conscientious objector to the Great War. The Evans brand of the open-air, educational, and improving creed was, of course, the product of an era when progress for the majority was beginning to appear a realistic proposition, and when individual self-amelioration could quite readily be combined with a wider cooper-ative concern, which promoted more and more the concept of general community improvement. Assimilation into the local establishment was consistent with justifiably optimistic support for the municipal route to a peaceful social revolution, creating better opportunities for the majority through a range of local institutions and associations. By the end of the nineteenth century the activities of numerous natural history societies were reinforcing the wider expression of that municipal and community creed.

The natural historians were at the forefront of a significant, intelli-gent, inquisitive contribution to the construction of a larger movement. A strong measure of *gravitas* is evident, expressed, for example, in the importance that Richard Buxton attached to teaching himself to read and write, and he 'soon acquired a taste for good literature'.[78] John Horsfield, too, 'became immoderately fond of books'; he recalled how, earlier in his life: 'Reading, writing, and arithmetic had hereto furnished me with ample materials for amusement, during the greater portion of my leisure hours ...' and how he soon became interested in botany.[79] L. H. Grindon's diverse interests, apart from 'his abiding monument' the Manchester FNS,[80] included literary studies as a member of the Athenaeum. Study and a profound belief in educational opportunities for all were inextricably linked with Ernest Evans's open-air and natu-ralist activities in the Burnley area. Such serious-minded, educationally improving motivation demanded something more than fresh air, physi-cal exercise and social recreation. The associational collaboration with other mentally stimulating or serious-minded activities confirmed the ethical foundation which characterized this developing strand. The Blackburn Field Naturalists' Association was formed in connection with the Literary Club in 1866, the same year that the local footpath society came into being to protect an essential amenity for the naturalist and the country walker. Lectures and talks describing scientific rambles featured prominently on the winter programmes of many of the natural history groups. This pursuit of high-minded cross-cultural diversity informed the programme of events of associations such as the Leeds Co-operative Field Naturalists' Club, which included rambles, excursions, exhibitions, lectures, and conversazioni. A joint ramble by members of the clubs at Bolton and Darwen in May 1907 resulted in a talk on botany, a Ruskin lecture and 'a brief organ recital terminated the intellectual feast'.[81]

These ethical underpinnings do suggest the wider respectable and responsible function of the associations. They made a point, for example, of stressing to members that trespassing was generally to be discouraged and property rights respected. There is further evidence of the form of élitism which has been an influence on responses to the growth of general tourism. Inter-class cooperation enabled considerable access to private and normally restricted land: Ovenden naturalists were given permits to Ogden Clough and adjoining moorland, while the Huddersfield NHS obtained permission for members to enter private estates. However, the fact that relations with the landed hierarchy were not always amicable is attested by the experience of a party from the Calder Vale Naturalists' Society in 1872, which was watched and shepherded by gamekeepers during a botanical excursion to Whitewell: '... their pleasure and success was somewhat spoiled by the presence of keepers in the wood, who accompanied the party "en chaperone", and who allowed no divergence from the path, for fear of disturbing the game'.[82] The imposition of a perceived respectability was ensured by the process of vetting membership applicants, which was common to most such institutions. The image of serious-minded respectability can be overstated. Motives tended towards the sensible, rational, and reasonable, rather than the puritan and prudish, or to unnecessary deferential compliance with unreasonably obstructive elements in contemporary society. An article by naturalist and outdoor man James Sugden of Slaithwaite, originally published in the *Huddersfield Examiner*, objected to the unreasonableness of the narrow-minded Sabbatarians, who were attempting to curtail Sunday leisure activities and stop the running of Sunday trams:

If advocates of temperance and religion would go out into the highways and hedges, and meet the people in the open air, and arrange services at the various termini, they would do more good than Paul Prying to see how many of the passengers enter public houses.[83]

A characteristic trait of the British outdoor movement has been a healthy suspicion of zealous dogma.

A commitment to environmental protection has informed the natural historians' influence on the character of the more widely motivated outdoor movement. It is an obvious thread of continuity connecting the early formative years with a present-day concern with green politics. The history of this environmental campaigning is punctuated by instances of conservationist campaigns, whose anti-commercial sentiment suggests a conservative motif. However, protection of the natural environment stemmed more from an optimistic and progressive desire for a better future for the majority than from nostalgic ruralism. Contrasting the northern Peak District to nearby Sheffield in 1915, Charles Chandler produced a timeless summing-up of the type of attitudes against which nature lovers reacted:

> We are a reckless, extravagant people. We have had – and still have – one of the most beautiful countries in the world. But we have never troubled as a nation about keeping it beautiful. The commercial spirit which gets into our very blood as soon as the town fixes its grip upon us drives all the sentiment out of us.[84]

J. W. Puttrell, himself a keen naturalist, organized a campaign from the same city in the 1930s against the dumping of refuse at Eyam in the Peak District. The continuity in the evolution of that environmental strand is, nevertheless, complicated by the measure of ambiguity contained in the motives and perceptions of early naturalists, which differentiates their role from that of later conservationists. The primary objective of most nineteenth-century naturalists was the collection of specimens, which meant that any legislation aimed at protecting flora and fauna would be considered by some to be a hindrance. An example of this paradox was the Huddersfield Naturalists' Society's petitioning of Parliament in 1887 against a bill which would protect 'Sea- or Wild-Birds'. Nonetheless, the general tenor remained unambiguously preservationist, in keeping with the late-Victorian formation of associations such as the Society for the Protection of Birds, and the Selborne Society, which perpetuated the inspiration of Gilbert White.

The formation of a rambler-naturalist strand within the evolution of the outdoor movement is strongly embedded in 'regional *mentalités*'.[85] Building on the traditions of autodidactic botanists who escaped to the countryside during the early period of industrialization, such recreational pursuits became a significant contribution to the heterogeneous popular culture of Lancashire industrial towns. In the Calder Valley, for example, around the turn of the century, Saturday rambles in pursuance of nature study – and sometimes incorporating botanical instruction – were regular features of the programmes of Colne Literary and Scientific Association and the natural history societies in Burnley, Colne, Padiham and Nelson, the latter attracting sixty people to a ramble to Salterforth in May 1908. As an important feature of the community recreational culture, these activities were popularized by columns in the local press, such as the series of 'Rambles Round and About Nelson' by A. Wilmore B. Sc., FGS in the *Nelson Leader* in 1908. Wilmore suggested the use of trams to get into the country beyond Colne, pointed to 'a rich hunting ground for the botanist', and advertised the activities of the Nelson NHS.[86] The development of the rambler-naturalist strand was consistent with the growth of a specific local popular culture, whose nature was shaped by the involvement of local ILP and SDF branches, the Cooperative movement, and the Weavers' Institute in Nelson. From 1900, the Nelson ILP branch was promoting its own contribution to local culture, combining the study of sociology, history, grammar and Esperanto with 'Field Days' for those 'who desire to get away from the never ending vista of bricks and mortar ...'[87] The naturalists' field trips can be contrasted with the popular workmen's excursions of the same period, which also involved an escape to the countryside, but which lacked both the mental and physical stimuli of their more serious-minded, improving counterpart.

A similar popular cultural mainstay evolved within the comparable socio-economic milieu of the West Riding of Yorkshire. As in Lancashire, associations such as the Huddersfield Naturalists' Society, retrospectively referred to as the Working Man's Society,[88] represented a form of recreation which was built on to aspects of established local cultural traditions that had survived the process of migration to urban settlements. Contrasting experiences can be identified in the development of other urban-industrial areas. The regional identity of Tyneside was generated out of a more homogeneous popular culture, in which professional rowing and, subsequently, association football became the cornerstones of the gregarious unity on which a chauvinistic pride in local identity was firmly established.[89] Potentially self-improving open-air recreation had little popular tradition on which to build, and natural history societies sustained their position as overwhelmingly middle-class institutions; the membership of the Tyneside Naturalists' Field Club, for example, was dominated in the 1870s by reverends and doctors, with 'field meetings' retaining an exclusive flavour. This particular dimension to the generation of a leisure-based aspect to diverse regional cultures both contributed to and reflected localized social attitudes and the related nuances of political consciousness.

The development of the natural history societies, which connected an interest in the study and appreciation of nature with an enjoyment of open-air leisure, represented the most obvious expression of a particularly influential dimension to the growth of the British outdoor movement. The orderly, educative, and broadly improving motif inherent in such uses of leisure did suit certain ulterior social and political motives, and lent itself to cultural hegemony. For Christian social and moral reformers, proximity to nature was conducive with closeness to its creator, in a pastoral response which was a reaction against physical and spiritual pollution by industrial commercialism. That anti-capitalist impulse gave meaning to the Utopian socialist adherence to the principles and practice of nature-study in pleasant and healthy environments. However, this scientific-orientated strand needs to be separated both from ruralism and from notions of idealized pre-industrial social relations. Emerging associational collaboration evolved from the early autodidactic tradition, which continued to impart its influence as an element in an active culture that was infused with a predominantly progressive ideology and a rational ethos. This evolving structure depended upon the role of intelligent, independent and self-motivated individuals, who, consistent with other strands in the movement's development, combined together in areas of common interest to contribute to the creation of its tangible existence.

Notes

1. Yorkshire Ramblers' Club, 'Looking Forward', Paper No. 5, 3 March 1894, Leeds Local Studies Library.
2. Pateman, T.W., *Dunshaw. A Lancashire Background* (London, 1948), p. 145.
3. Thomas, K., *Man and the Natural World. Changing Attitudes in England, 1500–1800* (London, 1983).
4. Stansfield, A., *Essays and Sketches* (Manchester, 1897), p. 36.
5. Phillips, G. S., *Ebenezer Elliott* (Sheffield, 1852), p. 114.
6. Hobkirk, C. P., *Huddersfield: Its History and Natural History* (London, 1859), p. 44.
7. Charles Kingsley (1846), quoted in Allen, D. E., *The Naturalist in Britain* (London, 1976), p. 166.
8. Plomer, W., ed., *Kilvert's Diary* (London, 1938).
9. *Nelson Chronicle*, 27 August 1897, p. 5.
10. Chancellor, V., ed., *Master and Artisan in Victorian England* (New York and London, 1969).
11. *Dictionary of National Biography* XII, p. 497.
12. *Burnley Express*, 22 May 1990. Newspaper cutting received from local historian Mr K. Spencer, author of the article.

13. Gaskell, E., *Mary Barton: A Tale of Manchester Life* (London, 1848), p. 75.
14. Percy, J., 'Scientists in humble life: the artisan naturalists of south Lancashire', *Manchester Region History Review* V, 1 (Spring/Summer 1991), pp. 3–10.
15. Cash, J., *Where There's a Will There's a Way! or Science in the Cottage* (London, 1873), p. 18.
16. Buxton, R., *A Botanical Guide to the Flowering Plants, Ferns, Mosses, and Algae found indigenous within sixteen miles of Manchester* (London and Manchester, 1859), p. xii.
17. *Ibid.*, p. xiii.
18. *Ibid.*, pp. 6, 9.
19. *Manchester City News*, 20 March 1920, in collection of newspaper cuttings relating to Richard Buxton. Manchester Local Studies Library.
20. Garnett, H., 'Richard Buxton. An old-time Manchester botanist', *North West Naturalist* 6 (Manchester, 1931), p. 18.
21. Stansfield, *Essays and Sketches*, p. 44.
22. *Ibid.*, p. 41.
23. *Ibid.*, p. 37.
24. Goddard, T. R., *History of the Natural History Society of Northumberland, Durham, and Newcastle upon Tyne, 1829–1929* (Newcastle, 1929), p. 167.
25. *Ibid.*, p. 160.
26. *Ibid.*, p. 158.
27. *Local Tracts, Durham*, p. 48. Newcastle Local Studies Library.
28. Sugden, J., *Slaithwaite Notes of the Past and Present* (3rd edn; Manchester,1905), p. 39.
29. *Ibid.*, p. 40.
30. *Ibid.*, p. 39.
31. Sykes, M., *In the Steps of Leo Grindon* (Manchester Local Studies Library, n.d.).
32. *Manchester Guardian*, 21 November 1904, p. 12.
33. *North West Naturalist* 5 (1930), p. 17.
34. *Manchester Evening News*, 29 December 1910, in newspaper cuttings relating to L. H. Grindon. Manchester Local Studies Library.
35. Manchester Field Naturalists' Society, *Report* (1860), p. 4.
36. *Ibid.*, pp. 6–7.
37. *Ibid.*, p. 17.
38. *Manchester Guardian*, 11 January 1895, p. 9.
39. Mather, Rev. J. M., *Rambles Round Rossendale*, vol. 2 (Rawtenstall, 1894), p. 155.
40. *Burnley Express and News*, 28 April 1956, p. 6.
41. *Ibid.*, 14 April 1956, p. 6.
42. *Ibid.*, 28 April 1956, p. 6.
43. Stephenson, T., *Forbidden Land* (Manchester, 1989), p. 67.
44. *Ibid.*, pp. 68–9.
45. *Sheffield Daily Telegraph*, 24 April 1901, p. 3.
46. Waugh, E., *Lancashire Sketches* (London and Manchester, 1892), p. xii.
47. Hodgson, J. H., 'An Appreciation of Mr. Earl Binns', in Binns, E., *Colne Naturalist Rambles, 1926–1953* (Colne,1953), Introduction.

48. *Sheffield Daily Telegraph*, 22 June 1912, in Putrell, J.W., Newspaper Cuttings, Sheffield Local Studies Library.

49. *Burnley Express*, 13 September 1884, p. 6.

50. Burnley Natural History Society (poster, n.d.), Burnley Local Studies Library.

51. *Halifax Courier*, 1 July 1905, p. 3.

52. Ogden, J., *Keighley Naturalists' One Hundred Years, 1868–1968* (Bradford, 1968), p. 2.

53. Bradford Scientific Association, *One Hundred Years Old, 1875–1975* (Bradford, 1975), Bradford Local Studies Library.

54. *Practical Naturalist* 1, 1 (January 1883).

55. *Ibid.*, 1, 5 (January 1884), p. 1.

56. Stansfield, *Essays and Sketches*, p. 39.

57. *Ibid.*, p. 40.

58. *Ibid.*, p. 42.

59. Illingworth, J. and Routh, J., eds, *Reginald Farrer. Dalesman, Planthunter, Gardener* (Lancaster, 1991).

60. Sugden, *Slaithwaite Notes*, p. 39.

61. Barber, L., *The Heyday of Natural History* (London, 1980), p. 34.

62. Thompson, F.M.L., *The Rise of Respectable Society. A Social History of Victorian Britain* (London, 1988).

63. Barber, *Heyday of Natural History*, p. 37.

64. Sugden, *Slaithwaite Notes*, p. 41.

65. *Ibid.*, p. 106.

66. See Chapter 5.

67. London Clarion Field Club (leaflet, n.d.), NMLH, Manchester.

68. *Clarion Cyclists' Journal* 5 (March 1897), p. 7.

69. *Clarion*, 13 July 1901, p. 222.

70. Cash, *Where There's a Will*, p. 18.

71. Swainson, W., *A Preliminary Discourse on the Study of Natural History* (London, 1834), p. 130.

72. *The Economist* 7 (1849), p. 405.

73. *Ibid.*

74. Buxton, *Botanical Guide*, pp. xiii–xvi.

75. Stansfield, *Essays and Sketches*, p. 46.

76. Buxton, *Botanical Guide*, p. xvi.

77. Wrigley, A., *Rakings Up. An Autobiography* (Rochdale, 1949), p. 13.

78. Garnett, 'Richard Buxton', pp. 18–21.

79. *Manchester Guardian*, 2 March 1850, p. 9.

80. *Ibid.*, 21 November 1904, p. 12.

81. *Bolton Journal and Guardian*, 17 May 1907, p. 7.

82. *Burnley Advertiser*, 15 June 1872, p. 3.

83. Sugden, *Slaithwaite Notes*, p. 106.

84. Chandler, C.H., *More Rambles Round Sheffield* (Sheffield, 1915), p. 8.

85. Langton, J. v. Gregory, D., 'Debate. The production of regions in England's Industrial Revolution', *Journal of Historical Geography* 14 (1988), pp. 170–6.

86. *Nelson Leader*, 31 July 1908, p. 9.

87. *Ibid.*, 15 March 1907, p. 8.
88. Graham, F., *The History of a Society* (Huddersfield, 1968).
89. See Taylor, H., 'Sporting Heroes', in Colls, R. and Lancaster, B., eds, *Geordies. Roots of Regionalism* (Edinburgh, 1992).

Chapter 4

A Developing Campaign for Access

From the later nineteenth century the attention of open-air recreational campaigners focused increasingly on the issue of reasonable access to uncultivated land. This campaign was a natural extension of the work of the early footpath protection societies, but the emergence of a lobby promoting practical implementation of a revolutionary principle needs to be distinguished clearly from the defence of traditional rights of way. Customary rights of way permit access only along predetermined and regularly used linear routes, whereas the concept of open access establishes the right to wander at will on uncultivated areas, effectively broadening the agenda of the open-air recreation lobby. The prominent campaigner Tom Stephenson commented in 1981 on the continuing practice of confining country walkers to 'pedestrian tramlines'.[1] The issue was always complicated by the fact that 'open countryside' was not defined officially until the drawing up of the 1949 National Parks and Access to Countryside Act: '... any area ... to consist wholly or predominantly of mountain, moor, heath, down cliff or foreshore'.[2]

The stated objectives of access campaigners has contributed to problems of definition. For example, the 1888 Mountains, Rivers and Pathways (Wales) Bill claimed customary Welsh rights of open access to uncultivated mountain land, and to the use of rivers and lakes, but simultaneously aimed at reinstating regular rights of way. Opening the debate on the second reading of his bill, T. E. Ellis, the member for Merionethshire, restated the object of his initial bill:

> ... to secure public right of access to the mountains and waste lands in Wales, and also to rivers, lakes, and streams. It provided that any pathway that had been used for any five successive years during the last 49 years should be again used by the public ... From and after the passing of this Act, the public shall have free right to enter upon, and access to, mountain land, moor, or waste land, and access to any walk along the bed or bank of any river or lake for the purpose of recreation, or winberry [sic] gathering, or scientific research.[3]

Accounts of the development of a countryside lobby have also generally perpetuated the confusion by conflating the two concepts. Recurring confusion over whether particular disputes were concerned with open access or merely with maintaining an age-old right to walk along a clearly defined footpath has added to the ambiguity. For example, the Winter Hill episode at Bolton had been concerned with reopening a route over the moors (see Chapter 1), although a more radical element, led by local socialists, sought to expand the dispute to unrestricted access to uncultivated land. They hoped to emulate the success of the people of nearby Darwen, who were, during the same year, celebrating their moor 'being now and for ever the property of the Darwen people'.[4] Attempts to escalate the Winter Hill conflict into the topical area of wider access stimulated the exaggerated local conservative propaganda: 'The Social Democratic Federation, who have taken the matter up, declare their intentions not only of fighting the case in the law courts as regards the road, but of disputing Colonel Ainsworth's title to any of the surrounding moors.'[5]

The practice of confusing these two separately evolving concepts, with their differing origins and objectives, remains common, although they are distinguished and discussed as separate entities in, for example, Marion Shoard's *This Land is Our Land*.[6] James Bryce, author of the earliest access bills, made the important distinction between open access or the 'right to roam' and mere linear traversal of private land by way of clearly defined footpaths when he spoke of 'interfere[nce] with the right of the people to walk over uncultivated ground'; he added: 'I am not to be prevented from going to that loch because it happens to be in a deer forest and off the footpath.'[7] Even Bryce, however, fused the issue of rights of way with the form of freer access to the uplands of which he was the most important early advocate. For instance, when opening the parliamentary debate on the second reading of his Access to Mountains (Scotland) Bill in May 1892, he stated that: 'Footpaths on the Kilpatrick Hills, on the Clyde, near Bowling, have been closed by proprietors ...'[8]

Countryside campaigners at the end of the twentieth century liberally apply the term access in its broadest sense, although their predominant concern, manifested in annual days of action organized by the highly respectable Ramblers' Association (RA), is the reopening of restricted footpaths in pastoral and woodland areas of the Home Counties. This conflict continues to be fought between landowners and predominantly middle-class suburban-based ramblers, in a updated version of the underlying town versus country dispute over land use, and the availability of rural recreation for sections of the urban populace. The conflation of the campaign to defend rights of way and a broader concern for access continues:

A campaign that will take place next Sunday aims to highlight the problems the public has in gaining access to the British countryside and enjoying our common heritage ... These include not being allowed to walk on private land. Even where there are footpaths or common land, owners may still prevent walkers from gaining access.[9]

A clear definition of objectives is also necessary in order to avoid damaging connotations, which opponents of improved access use to sustain their justification of the dominant policy of general exclusion. The evolving mainstream countryside access campaign has never sanctioned inconsiderate or wholly unrestricted access to walk wherever any individual might choose.

The failure to establish an unambiguous agenda has been accentuated by a propensity to compromise by way of informal, voluntary and localized agreements, which in many instances have been even more restrictive than limited seasonal agreements with the game-shooting and stalking interests. Particular interpretations of respectability and reasonableness have aggravated the tactical disunity of the broad outdoor lobby. The question of what constitutes reasonable access, and the means of pursuing that objective, continue to fuel disharmony in the movement. The more radical ramblers criticize the compromising element of the movement:

'With friends like that who needs enemies?' I wonder whether these people have ever studied the leaflet containing the membership application form. Under the heading 'Private – Keep Out' it states: 'Ramblers insist that there are still many areas where the public is barred for no good reason. We want to see not only hill and moor, but woodland, riverside, heathland and coastline opened up for quiet enjoyment.' ... If the critics do not accept our policy, why do they join? [10]

Considering the degree of influential support that the access lobby enjoyed, and the persistence with which the issue was pursued in Parliament, the continuing failure bears witness to the impotence of radical forces when confronted by the persistence of pre-industrial prerogatives within rural society.[11] Hazlitt reflected on the apparent British propensity to defend jealously the exclusiveness of private property well before newer pressures on land use had exerted themselves fully:

The motto of the English nation is 'exclusion'. In this consists our happiness and our pride. If you come to a gentleman's park and pleasure-grounds , you see written up, 'Man-traps and steel-guns set here' – as if he had no pleasure in walking in them, except in the

idea of keeping other people out ... Everything resolves itself into
an idea of property, that is, of something that our neighbours dare
not touch, and that we have not the heart to enjoy.[12]

The momentum which the access debate picked up through the turn
of the century, and the measure of respectability that it maintained, is
attributable to an influential Liberal parliamentary lobby, which introduced access bills on nine occasions between 1884 and 1909. James
Bryce's original bill, which applied only to Scotland, was dismissed
without debate, but served the dual purpose of setting the agenda for
subsequent debates and feeling out the strength of the various interested
forces. Bryce introduced an identical bill in February 1888, which
received a second reading before being dropped. In April of the same
year T. E. Ellis's Mountains, Rivers and Pathways (Wales) Bill was
rejected after opponents insisted that the claimed tradition of open
access to mountains in Wales was false. Bryce did succeed in having
his bill debated in March 1892, and, despite a rallying of the landed
and sporting lobby, led by the representatives of Cairngorm deer-forest
owners, the principle of the bill was accepted by Parliament. However,
tactical obstruction and more pressing political concerns intervened to
halt further progress.[13] The 1892 bill was supported by such diverse
and influential individuals as Winston Churchill and Arthur Henderson,
and at the division it was the 'ayes' which prevailed by 190 to 61.
However, stalling tactics during the committee stages, in a busy election
year, led to its being dropped at the recess. The Liberal election victory
contributed paradoxically to the subsequent weakness of the parliamentary lobby. Bryce's appointment to the Cabinet deflected him towards
the more pressing business of a particularly busy government; he was
later appointed Ambassador to the United States. Bryce was, in fact,
always the ideal party man, following faithfully the line of Liberal
orthodoxy.[14] Although his energies were diverted towards other political
business, he did make one further attempt in February 1898, but the
bill was again rejected without debate. In 1900 Bryce's brother Annan,
the MP for Inverness Burghs, took on the mantle of his older brother,
presenting the same bill without success. He tried again in 1906, 1908
and 1909, which effectively meant that James Bryce's original Access
to Mountains (Scotland) Bill had been submitted and rejected eight
times. When the Bryce bill was presented in 1908 there was another
access bill on the order paper, submitted by Charles Trevelyan, who
was at that time MP for Elland in the West Riding. Trevelyan's bill
extended the parliamentary access campaign beyond its original Scottish
focus to include England, Wales and Ireland, although the Lake District
Defence Society had already attempted to draft a bill in 1888, which
would provide access to land over 800 feet high and to lake shores.[15]

Trevelyan's first national access bill was defeated largely on the strength of an opposition case, which emphasized the perceived effects on lucrative sporting estates of an influx of tourists.

The parliamentary campaign helped to ensure that the issue began to receive serious consideration in the 1880s, at the same time giving an air of respectable authority to the access lobby. However, this newer concern with recreational amenity, impelled by the significant expansion of open-air leisure activities, was rooted in a longer-standing discourse over the loss of commons and public open spaces. Responses to the consequences of the continuing enclosure of common land were given an uncheckable momentum by the emergence from the 1830s of the same rational and utilitarian concern with the uses of leisure time that had heightened awareness about the erosion of rights of way. A growing concern with the necessity of healthy exercise for urban workers was reinforced, at least up to the 1850s, by a continuing belief in the miasmic origins of frequent epidemics, and was the driving force behind the first real defence of open spaces. Bills aimed at protecting commons in the interests of recreation for urban populations culminated in an act of 1837, which stipulated that all enclosure legislation should allow for the provision of public open spaces. During the debate a motion was introduced by Joseph Hume, which stated: 'That in all Inclosure Bills provision be made for leaving an open space sufficient for the purposes of exercise and recreation of the neighbouring population.' [16] By instituting grants to local authorities to purchase areas of common land, Peel expressed approbation for this amendment, which reversed the trend towards the confiscation of land. This was early evidence that the narrow self-interest of the landed classes could not be guaranteed by the more flexible and generally progressive ideology of the leader of the Tory party.[17] In recommending restraints on unbridled enclosure, Peel also expressed the same concern with moral and physical improvement that had stimulated the debate over the provision of public walks in proximity to towns and urban areas. Again, the focus of attention was switched increasingly to the needs of the expanding manufacturing districts:

> Such an arrangement would have a most beneficial effect, not alone on their health, but also on their morals, by gradually withdrawing them from scenes where their time was more likely to be much less innocently employed ... [N]o person objected to the improvements that had been made in our parks in and near the metropolis, and no one grudged the money expended in that way; but he feared that we were too much disposed to confine ourselves to the metropolis in these improvements, and too apt to forget the wants of the manufacturing and other towns, all of which required places of recreation as much as the metropolis.[18]

Of course Peel's stance also reflected his own particular regional and economic areas of interests.

Notwithstanding the volume of support from the establishment for open-air recreational amenities, the practice of enclosure continued to exert pressure on public access to common land. Opposing the Improvement of Common Fields Bill in 1838, Sir E. Sugden claimed that it 'would authorise the enclosure of every common in England, even Hampstead Heath'.[19] Further legislative restriction on uncontrolled enclosure was contained in the General Inclosure Act of 1845, which stipulated that, in the case of commons within five miles of large towns, the necessity of enclosure had to be proved, and that allotments must be provided when the common was close to a town with a population of 10,000 or more. However, such restrictions proved virtually ineffective, and an additional 500,000 acres were enclosed during the following twenty years, with only minimal provision made for recreation. In highlighting some of the dangers inherent in the 1845 bill, William Sharman Crawford MP invoked the usual defence of the rights of the people, and extended the argument to stress that they were not restricted to a single generation: 'The provisions of the Bill would offer a bribe to those who had the present use of those rights to sell that which they had no power to dispose of, namely, the rights of future generations.'[20]

At that time, the attack on traditional common land rights did, of course, depend upon an economic nexus. However, the reference to future generations was prophetic, foreshadowing the switch to demands for healthy recreation, rather than the original *raison d'être* of customary rights founded on medieval precepts. Nevertheless, the earliest defence of commons for the use of the people did contain its own identifiable impulse towards the promotion of forms of open-air recreation. Demands for access to open spaces for leisure activities owed at least as much to utilitarian motives as they did to poetic Romanticism or to new urban nostalgia for interpretations of the rural idyll. The alacrity with which images of the past were employed as a means to invoke the appeal to tradition did, nevertheless, represent a common denominator between defenders of commons, footpath campaigners and the later lobby in favour of open countryside access.

The same concern for recreational space was later translated into the construction of public parks. In some instances the provision of such amenities was seen as a function of urban local government – a public fund provided parks in Manchester and Salford as early as the 1840s[21] – but recreational open space was also facilitated by such individuals as the Earl of Bradford, who provided Bradford Park for the people of Bolton, 'to give Health and happiness to the laborious classes'.[22] Wealthy industrialists also provided public parks: men such as Strutt, whose public arboretum was opened in Derby as early as 1840; Lister in Bradford; and Armstrong in Newcastle.[23] These facilities were part of a wider provision of the public amenities which developed as a central strand in the optimistic philosophy of high-Victorian municipal development. They have been associated generally with a planned and more large-scale promotion of rational recreation, and with such notions as social control or progression towards a common culture.[24]

Although situated partly within that broad context of 'improving' notions of increased leisure, the pursuit of access was motivated further by other, more radical aspirations. The voice of the outdoor recreation lobby was in unison with that of the often more radical ideologues, who proffered a range of solutions to the wider problems raised by the land question. The generation of a highly respectable campaigning lobby became embedded in the mainstream of reformist politics, with prominent Liberals such as James Bryce and Charles Trevelyan in the vanguard. Access proponents have always compared unfavourably the British propensity for exclusion with the more liberal attitudes taken in some other countries towards the recreational potential of unculti- vated land. Presenting his access bill in 1892, James Bryce related the issue to his own experience abroad:

I have climbed mountains in almost every country – I have travelled in almost every country where mountains are found, and I have made inquiries but I have never heard of a single instance in which the pedestrian, the artist, or the man of science has been prevented from freely walking where he wished, not even in those countries where the pursuit of game is most actively followed.[25]

Both as a prominent access campaigner and as the owner of extensive estates which included grouse moors, Trevelyan's stance on the function and responsibility of the country landlord is a particularly interesting one. His democratic social reforming objectives underpinned the rec- onciliation of two potentially conflictual roles. He adopted a uniquely reasoned approach and conciliatory tone, which were reflected in a speech made in 1908 referring both to recreational users of the moors and to the workers who crossed his land on the way to the site of a new reservoir being constructed to supply Tyneside:

... he would not be such a selfish and sulky curmudgeon as to give orders to gamekeepers that they were to exclude tourists or make these men go four miles round in order to get to their work in future ... The real walker and the climber was not going to do very much harm.[26]

Consistent with the compromising tendency, there was provision in Clause 4 of Trevelyan's bill to legislate against interference with shooting parties. He also categorized walkers into three classes, and claimed that it was only his small third group which wanted to walk at will over uncultivated hills and moors. Trevelyan's radical credentials as a landowner with a keen lifelong interest in the development of open-air leisure opportunities for all are beyond question. Nonetheless, the recreational demands on either rural Northumberland or the uncultivated areas of continental countries cannot be compared meaningfully with the diverse pressures exerted on the Scottish Highlands or the South Pennine uplands.

Notwithstanding the radical approach to access adopted by such highly respectable establishment figures as Bryce and Trevelyan, the broader outdoor lobby has always been divided over the degree to which the prevailing system should be changed, and has consequently been equivocal about its ultimate aims. The important distinction between footpath protection and open access again becomes apparent. To many advocates of the defence of traditional rights of way, the principle of the exclusive use of all private property remained sacrosanct. Among the most vociferous opponents of early bills concerning access to mountains was J. Parker-Smith, MP for the Partick division of Glasgow, and a member of both the SMC and the Scottish Rights of Way Society. In an article published in *Blackwood's Magazine* in 1890, Parker-Smith opposed legislative regulation, adopting the give-and-take collaborative stance, which has characterized relations between select groups of mountaineers and Highland landlords. It was a line which gained the official sanction of the conservative, Edinburgh-based SMC, particularly the first editor of the club's journal, Joseph Gibson Stott. It is interesting to note that the SMC's first honorary presidents were the major Highland landowners, Cameron of Lochiel and the Marquis of Breadalbane. The first *SMC Journal*, published in 1891, toed the conservative line: '... amongst right-thinking persons there will be a disposition readily to agree with Mr. Parker-Smith ...'[27] An apparently contradictory view was, nonetheless, expressed in the inaugural address given by the president of the SMC, which seemed to imply support for the principle of unrestricted rambling in open country, although it was stressed also that the permission of landowners should be sought before the respectable members of the SMC could 'roam over the untrammeled country, far from smoke and din, drinking in draughts of air as it rolls to us over a hundred hills ...'[28] Parker-Smith also spoke in the Commons against Bryce's 1892 access bill, a stance which, given his known position as a mountaineer and supporter of the principles of rights of way, gave obvious succour to defenders of the *status quo*. The dominant conservative anti-access line related directly to the character of the SMC. Club membership was made up overwhelmingly of well-to-do mountaineers, whose main open-air activities required only footpath access to craggy west-Highland areas, where shooting and stalking, in their organized, commercialized and larger-scale forms, were relatively impractical. As upper-middle-class alpinists, they spent a significant proportion of the restricted season in such areas as the Alps, the Pyrenees, or the Dolomites. Elitism and a degree of group self-interest can be detected in an article in the club journal in May 1896 by Professor G. G. Ramsay, who was referred to in a 1975 edition of the journal as 'the bourgeois academic':[29]

> We did not desire the Club to become a *stravaging* [*sic*] or marauding Club, insisting on going everywhere at every season, with or without leave, and indifferent to the rights and the enjoyment of farmers, proprietors, and sportsmen ... Deer-stalking is a rare and noble sport, identified for centuries with the Highlands ... [W]e know nothing of the theory which assumes that proprietors form the only class whose rights and wishes as to the disposal of land should be disregarded.[30]

The ideological and tactical differences within the turn-of-the-century Scottish mountaineering and hillwalking mainstream were perpetuated by personal enmity and rivalry. Ramsay of the SMC and Bryce of the Cairngorm Club carried on a broader-based dispute as Oxford academic contemporaries, both of whom had gained Trinity College fellowships. Ramsay referred to Bryce as 'that awful Scotch fellow who outwrote everybody'.[31]

It was certainly not by chance that the first really serious consideration of the question of access to open country emanated from Scotland, where the British access lobby had its earliest direct origins. A separate tradition of customary rights had established the nominal freedom to walk on private land. However, new demands imposed by the larger-scale commercial sporting interests had led to a serious depletion in customary practice. In the Highlands in particular there were great tracts of moor and mountain and open space, whose main function had, in the century preceding Bryce's first Scottish access bill, been redefined increasingly towards the exclusive exploitation and enjoyment of a small landed minority. Further acquisitions were made by the granting of the common land to the Highland estates during the late eighteenth and early nineteenth centuries. In the north of Scotland such structural change would generate one of the greatest of all rural socio-economic upheavals, and a backcloth to the protracted struggle to obtain greater recreational opportunities in Britain's extensive areas of open space. The Highland clearances were originally carried out in order to accommodate the commercial opportunities of sheep-rearing.[32] However, changes in the upland economy, making the commercial exploitation of game a more attractive proposition, increasingly created conflict, with growing demands from town-dwellers for countryside recreation amenities. An inexorable decline in the economy of the far north interacted with the industrial and commercial boom further south to create circumstances favourable to extensive deer-forest development; by the 1880s there were 2 million acres of deer forest in Scotland, a figure that had risen less than a decade later to 3.5 million acres. It has been argued that the deer forest and other sporting developments of the second half of the nineteenth century would have proceeded regardless of the fortunes of the sheep-based economy.[33] Disturbance to cattle and sheep was, in fact, used as an argument against access bills. It was employed, for example, during the 1892 debate by Colonel Malcolm, MP for Argyllshire, who also insisted that increased access was effectively a licence to walk anywhere. Such propaganda was maintained by the anti-access lobby right through to the passage of the 1949 act, and often descended to the realms of ludicrous scaremongering by agencies of social conservatism, such as the *Daily Mail* during the 1930s.[34]

It is abundantly evident that in the century and a half between the final suppression of the Highlands in 1746 and the consolidation of old landed and parvenu sporting interests at the end of the nineteenth century, the weight of authority was allowed to come down strongly in favour of commercial exploitation of the upland economy by a minority, at the expense of the well-being of the majority. The ideological confrontation engendered by these developments in the upland rural economy depended largely on the aspirations of the various formative elements in the early growth of a British outdoor movement, but was also complicated by nationalistic references. Hunting for sport did have undoubted value to some ailing local economies, but could also be defined in a radical frame of reference as an expression of frivolous and antisocial aristocratic culture. Such criticism was encapsulated in the 1920s by the Scottish Labour politician Tom Johnston: 'Land run to waste, land misused, land devoted to anti-social practices, yields more rent to private owners than land tilled by peasants. And so, say the lairds, the peasants must go.'[35]

Game had not always been commercially exploitated, and deer-stalking in particular had for centuries contributed to the maintenance of a more interdependent, organic Highland economy. In 1773 James Boswell recorded in his journal the ease with which anyone could go off and hunt deer at will: 'A red coat [*sic*] of the 15th regiment, whether officer, or only serjeant, I could not be sure, came to the house, in his way to the mountains to shoot deer, which it seems the Laird of

Glenmorison does not hinder any body to do.'[36] Boswell's journal entry
for the previous day serves both to illustrate the emerging problems of
the Highland economy and to emphasize the fact that the influence of
some lairds extended only to the immediate locality of their clan. Seventy
men had already emigrated from the glen to America; under the pressure
of rent, which had risen in twenty years from £5 to £20 per annum, the
laird was planning to follow them during the following year. It was all
part of the process by which much of the Highlands was converted first
to large-scale commercial sheep-rearing, and later into a playground
for conflicting recreational pursuits. Aspects of a pre-commercial age
of deer-stalking are described in Osgood Hanbury Mackenzie's accounts
of clan life on the Inverewe estate in the western Highlands. Mackenzie's
narrative is based on material contained in ten manuscript volumes of
'Highland Memories', covering the period 1803 to 1860, which he
inherited from an uncle, Dr John Mackenzie. Deer-hunting is portrayed
as an integral element of a community-based local culture. A certain
tolerance of, and even respect for, local poachers is implied. There are
also, however, indications that irreversible change was imminent. Mackenzie related his own youthful experiences in the 1850s:

> Knowing me to be very keen on deer-stalking ... he [Hector Mac-
> Kenzie of Taagan] remarked that he wondered why I did not try to
> ingratiate myself with my eccentric old English neighbour, who
> owned some seventy thousand acres, forty-five or fifty thousand of
> which were the most famous stag ground in the country. It was all
> then still under sheep, but notwithstanding this, it had a good stock
> of its original breed of deer on it ... which had never been regularly
> stalked, and where the deer had only occasionally been killed by
> poaching shepherds ... I told the old gentleman that I had no money
> of my own except a little pocket-money. He asked what I could give
> him, and I told him I could afford only five pounds. Marvellous to
> say, though almost a millionaire himself, he agreed to take that.[37]

The introduction of new plutocratic wealth into the western Highlands gave rise to one of the most celebrated of nineteenth-century
access disputes. In 1882 W. L. Winans, an American millionaire, took
out a long-term lease on a 25,000-acre estate in the Kintail district of
Wester Ross, and, with the intention of creating a vast and exclusive
sporting reserve stretching eastwards over some 200,000 acres to Beauly
Forest, succeeded in forcing the majority of the local crofters off the
estate. The Winans policy of total exclusion extended to interference
with cattle-droves and preventing a Glasgow naturalist from pursuing
entomological field study. In a desperate attempt to overcome unco-
operative tenants, Winans, through his agent, claimed that any crofter

who stepped out of his cottage door was automatically trespassing. The issue was brought to a head when a pet lamb owned by Murdoch Macrae, a shoemaker from a long-established family on the Kintail estate, was subject to an interdict in July 1884 because it had strayed onto Winan's domain. An apparently trivial incident then escalated into a major dispute with much wider implications. It was a manifestation of the deep-seated problems that were rooted in the emerging threats to the established life of the local community.

In keeping with the traditions of his trade, Macrae was a small-time local activist for the cause of the crofters in his capacity as member of the Land League, which agitated on behalf of the dispossessed. The so-called 'Pet Lamb Case' in many ways represented a turning point in the exploitation of the indigenous population. Attention had been increasingly focused on the issue of the recreational use of the uplands, and the arguments of the access campaigners were fuelled by the Winans–Macrae episode, which was regularly cited as an example of exploitation, highlighting the sort of extreme measures that landowners were willing to employ in order to establish exclusion zones in the Highlands.[38] The dispute was conducted against a background of inquiries by the Napier Commission, set up in 1883 to investigate the plight of the Highland and Island crofters, whose case was articulated in an increasingly convincing fashion by the newly formed Highland Land Law Reform Association. Winans was defeated eventually in the courts of law in 1885, by a combination of sound organization, radical liberal elements in the legal profession and local solidarity; funding for the Macrae defence was thought to have come from a Highlander who had made money after emigrating. Clannish Highland solidarity proved to be a telling influence. It found expression through the anti-access position adopted in the 1892 parliamentary debate by the MP for Bute, Mr Graham Murray, Solicitor-General for Scotland and successful council in the 'Pet Lamb Case', whose speech echoed the obvious sympathy for indigenous Highlanders and their threatened lifestyle. Along with other opponents of legislation in favour of easier access, he presented the popular and convincing, but generally spurious economic argument: 'But, Sir, we cannot touch sport without also touching a much larger question, and that is the economic value of the Highlands.'[39] The moral and ethical aspects of local economic sufficiency have been invoked persistently against expansion of rural access for urban populations.

It was predominantly in the eastern Highlands that the main attention of the early access campaign was concentrated. In these wild, but relatively less rugged districts, dominated by the high plateau of the Cairngorms, the large landed estates were well suited to the husbanding of deer and grouse in commercial-scale enterprises. But this was also the area best suited to the purposes of the increasing numbers of hillwalkers, who sought the freedom of the open spaces. The consequent conflict of interests was pursued ardently on the expanding estates of the Dukes of Atholl. The Atholl lands, dominating the south-western Cairngorms, were consolidated by the enclosure of the 'Common of Glentilt' [40] [sic] in 1808, when, in a legalized land-grab by the local establishment, 30 acres went to the minister of Blair Atholl, 590 acres to General Robertson of Lude, and 1,290 acres to the Duke of Atholl. The Glen Tilt common was a linear strip of the poorer and higher land, which had previously split the Atholl estates in two. The expansion of Atholl proprietorship was the signal for the eviction of eight hundred people from the immediate area of Glen Tilt. By the first decade of the twentieth century, the Duke of Atholl owned 91,700 acres of sporting land in Perthshire, by which time great areas of the northern half of Scotland were consigned to the same purpose, including approximately half of the huge county of Inverness-shire.

It was against such a background that the Cairngorm Club, founded in 1893, attempted to walk without hindrance in the hills that comprised the hinterland of their Aberdeen base. Members of the club formed the nucleus of the access lobby. Bryce's inaugural address, published in the club journal, highlighted another facet of the character of a man who had a reputation as the epitome of the conscientious and highly respectable establishment Liberal MP: 'Perhaps I ought to add a further charm of Scotch mountaineering – the risk of encountering a brand of hostile ghillies, or having an interdict applied for at the instance of Mr. Winans.' Bryce continued his address in an optimistic vein, which retrospectively appears foolish: 'But as this source of excitement is threatened with extinction, I pass it by for the present.' [41]

Distinctive and openly expressed fundamental ideological differences certainly existed between the two main Scottish mountaineering and hillwalking associations at the end of the nineteenth century. Nonetheless, several members of the SMC campaigned with equal enthusiasm for improved access. Members of both clubs were involved in the stravaiging and marauding which have characterized direct action in Scotland in defence of rights of way as well as access to the open spaces:

> These were the advocates and exponents of Rights of Way and Access to Mountains, the deer disturbers and signpost-erectors who walked out with the pale of SMC constitutional precept: '... respect proprietory and sporting rights, and endeavour to obtain the co-operation of proprietors.' These bolshies of the Golden Age, the heyday of the deer forest, as well as of early mountaineering in Scotland, have rested largely in obscurity ever since. [42]

The stravaigers amongst the SMC membership were predominantly from the substantial and influential Edinburgh professional middle class, and shared many common characteristics with other early stalwarts of the nascent outdoor movement, including Bryce, but also with the English academics Sir Leslie Stephen and A. H. Sidgwick:

> ... a relationship has always existed between the SMC and the *stravaging* [*sic*] faction, however little acknowledged it may have been; the Club may have done its best to ignore them, but they have patently not gone away, though the radical passions of the last century have subsided.[43]

Stravaiging, or wandering at will, has generally been linked exclusively with noted nineteenth-century Scottish rights-of-way campaigns, but its true definition is more indicative of the wider Scottish customary right to roam on uncultivated land. It is a term which evokes a wayfaring tradition in Scottish popular culture. The main associational focus of the stravaigers was the Scottish Rights of Way Society, some of whose members joined parties which toured the Highlands to challenge abuses by landowners. They included Professor J. S. Blackie, who had been issued with a writ in 1867 to prevent him from seeking access to Buachaille Etive Mor above Glencoe; C. E. W. McPherson, secretary of the society; and, contrarily, J. Parker Smith, parliamentary opponent of Bryce's Access to Mountains (Scotland) Bill. The popular stravaiging open-air tradition in Scotland could, however, never be associated with the mainstream development of the SMC. In an article published in the club journal in 1975, B. S. Fraser highlighted the social and cultural chasm separating the establishment-based SMC from a more popular outdoor movement. Fraser's narrative records his own pre-1914 days in the Scottish hills. He acknowledges the influence of his father, a working-class outdoor man who, although he spent much of his spare time climbing, walking, fishing and camping in the Highlands, and made several trips to continental mountains – including climbing in the Pyrenees in 1909, inspired by Hilaire Belloc's guide – would never think of joining the SMC, even after moving to Edinburgh for work: 'Grannie's revealing and uncomplaining phrase "no for the likes o' us." Dad could never have afforded the hotels from which the SMC members often set off for the hills.'[44]

The leadership of the Cairngorm Club proved more radical and adventurous, encouraging stravaiging activities by its members. Access campaigners included A. I. McConnochie (M'Connochie in Highland references), the editor of the *Cairngorm Club Journal* and producer of numerous Cairngorm and Deeside guides. The hill men of the Cairngorm Club deliberately challenged stalkers, landowners and their ghillies, publicizing the cause through the club journal. The huge

expansion of Cairngorm deer forests became the big threat to the old
established drove-road rights of way, but it also served to stimulate a
more radical movement for access by the hillwalkers, whose own outdoor activity coincided with the stalking season.

Access proved to be less of an issue in England in the nineteenth
century, although Canon Rawnsley led a group from within the Lake
District Defence Society (1883) which was keen to incorporate the issue
of improved fellside access into the broad agenda of the society. The
parliamentary access lobby was never really established into a wider
British context until the introduction of Trevelyan's bill in 1908. Questions about the uplands in England were, nevertheless, raised on several
occasions during debates on access to Scottish mountains. The English
campaign stemmed from a more specifically focused lobby, which sought
to re-establish public rights of free access to common land. The highly
respectable Commons Preservation Society had been formed in 1865
as a product of liberal philanthropic concern about the threat to urban
commons. Meanwhile, the popular campaign for access to moors and
mountains in England was generated in the sub-Pennine areas, where
the pressures of urban-industrial development coincided with an ever-
increasing exclusion from the moors: 'Future generations had to pay
dearly for the generosity of Parliament in handing over gratis large
tracts of territory frequently on the outskirts of rising industrial towns.'[45]
For example, Kinder Scout and its adjoining uplands, the venue for
mass trespasses in the 1930s, had been crown land until 1830, open to
the public to roam at will. However, this vast expanse of moorland,
comprising an area of approximately 20,000 acres, was subsequently
allocated to the owners of contiguous properties. Public exclusion from
much of the predominantly uncultivated land in the more elevated areas
of the Pennines contrasted with the situation which pertained in the
mountains of the Lake District, where substantial common rights had
been retained, and, crucially, where grouse were a rarity. Introducing
his bill in 1908, Trevelyan cited the example of Sheffield, where the
open moors to the south and west of the city were closed almost entirely
to the people of the city. Supporting Bryce in 1892, Mr Roby, the MP
for Eccles in the Manchester-Salford conurbation, gave voice to a
popular desire to legislate for English grouse moors as well as the
Highland deer forests that had been the focus for the original lobby.

Campaigning outdoor organizations did, nonetheless, lend considerable support to the cause of commons defence, although they carefully
qualified the expansion of their role with warnings about responsible
behaviour and a need to avoid trespass. Around the extended urban
fringes, any remaining area of common land that had survived un-
enclosed became more and more important as a recreational amenity,
to be defended vigorously. Two of the most notable cases of struggles

to maintain or regain public access to moors were initiated on either side of the Pennines in the 1870s. The sporting interest had no part in triggering the campaign to save Hunslet Moor, one of several areas of common land on the fringes of the expanding industrial city of Leeds. The offenders in this instance were industrial capitalist speculators in the shape of the Middleton Coal Company, although the origin of this commercial enterprise was as an offshoot of the landed estate of Middleton, which had enclosed the common to facilitate more efficient and expansive mineral exploitation. Mining on Hunslet Moor was nothing new, with restriction dating back to an Act of Parliament of 1758, authorizing the construction of a railway across the moor from Middleton colliery. The company received full corporation support, founded on an agreement to deliver 23,000 tons of coal per annum at a fixed price to a staithe on the south bank of the River Aire in central Leeds. A growing demand to regain open access to the moor generated a campaign which became focused in October 1877, when the prominent commons defence activist John De Morgan addressed 4,000 people at a public meeting. De Morgan's brand of radical populism was rooted in a tradition which connected the Chartist era to emerging socialist solutions. He was a 'red republican, associate of Bradlaugh, anti-Vaccinationist, and tyro of the Magna Carta Associations'.[46] Later in the same year placards were posted on the walls of Hunslet inviting people to attend a meeting at 3 p. m. on Saturday 8 December. The invitation was signed by John De Morgan of the 'Commons Protection League': 'Let 50,000 men of Leeds assemble legally, peaceably, and in order ... There must be no rioting, and·I shall give the first man into custody who attempts to provoke a breach of the peace.'[47] During a demonstration with an estimated attendance of between 20,000 and 40,000, De Morgan carried out his threat to pull up one of the railway lines which the company had constructed across the moor. Despite a strong police presence led by the Chief Constable, De Morgan was not interfered with on this occasion, although he had been imprisoned previously, following his active leadership of a dispute during which his inflammatory speeches were said to have 'led to the pulling down of fences at Selston Common in Nottinghamshire, extending over eight miles of land ...'[48]

Rumours of De Morgan's arrest proved to be unfounded when he addressed a further meeting on the following Saturday. An important consequence of the mass demonstrations was the formation of the Hunslet Moor Defence Committee, which met at the town's Mechanics' Institute. The committee represented an organized and respectable negotiating and fund-raising body, with the capacity to provide the essential backing during the subsequent dispute. They appointed a deputation to confer with the Corporate Property Committee of Leeds

Corporation with regard to formal negotiations with the Middleton estate. An injunction was brought by the local lords of the manor to restrain Messrs De Morgan, Gilston, Margerison and Howes from going on to the moor. In February the case against De Morgan, who described himself as a commoners' agent, was brought before the Court of Chancery in London, which removed the injunction. The *Leeds Mercury* reported on De Morgan's use of a writ of habeus corpus. The removal of the injunction was, nevertheless, considered to be the end of the matter: 'The first legal skirmish has taken place, and has resulted in a gain to the Commoners, of course the great battle has still to be fought, and I believe will result in a victory for our cause.'[49] In April 1878 a meeting of the freeholders of Hunslet produced a fighting fund, which got off to an auspicious start when Mr Barran MP and the Reverend E. Wilson, Vicar of Hunslet, each donated £20. Popular pressure from Hunslet for the restitution of public access to the moor, including an emphasis on the recreational needs of this industrial suburb, persuaded the authorities to institute their civic responsibility through the Leeds Corporation Act of 1879, which was, amongst other things: 'An Act to confer further Powers on the Corporation of Leeds with reference to Hunslet Moor.'[50] Chapter 8 of this act emphasized the importance of retaining public recreational amenities: 'And whereas there are within the borough certain waste lands known respectively as Hunslet Moor and Woodhouse Ridge, and it is desirable that the same should be preserved as open spaces for public use or recreation.'[51]

At Darwen in central Lancashire it was the municipal government that was largely responsible for gaining for local people the right to take recreation on nearby moorland, although the changing attitude of the landowning family, albeit under substantial pressure, afforded the opportunity for a negotiated settlement. The campaign developed into a *cause célèbre* in and around the town. The liberal radical civic triumphalism which accompanied the gaining of free access did not go unchallenged. Local socialists, supported by the SDF's newspaper *Justice*, sought to gain credit and grass-roots prestige by publicizing and overstating their own role in the episode. At the time when public exclusion from the moorland was first brought out into the open in 1878, Darwen Moors was being used as a grouse-breeding ground and shoot. The dispute, which simmered for eighteen years, was triggered by a trespass prosecution against five Darwen men, heard in the Court of Chancery on 2 August 1878, less than six months after the Hunslet hearing:

... writs were issued by Edmund Ashton the younger, who owned the shooting rights over the moor, and the Reverend W. A. Duckworth, Lord of the Manor, against Richard Ainsworth, Joseph Kay,

James Fish, Ellis Gibson and John Oldman, all inhabitants of Darwen, for trespass ...[52]

A perpetual injunction was awarded to restrain the defendants, although rights of highway were excluded, and the corporation was ordered to map all the rights of way over the moor, which totalled 26 miles 7 furlongs and 5 yards of road and pathway. The local municipal oligarchy, however, adhered to their original objective of gaining open access for the citizens of the Darwen district.

The eventual takeover of the common by the corporation was really enabled by changing circumstances in a landowning family which had remained stubbornly resistant for sixteen years. When the main landowner, W. T. Ashton, died in September 1894, his three sons were more amenable to the overtures of the town council, and proved willing to negotiate a settlement. This does not deny that there was a continued need for pressure and persuasion, but satisfactory settlement was the likely outcome following the demise of the old intransigent order. Open access to Darwen Moors for the recreation of the people was achieved late in the summer of 1896. The victory gave rise to triumphant acclaim by both the locally dominant liberals and their socialist opponents, both of whom claimed a progressive victory over the conservative regressive forces that had obstructed the rights of the people. The new generation of Ashtons, also keen to be well thought of in the district, adopted a philanthropic role. H. D. Ashton was one of the speakers on Saturday 5 September at the celebratory demonstration, when he was cheered and applauded. He spoke of his family's mutual interest with the people of Darwen, and of how he was 'exceedingly proud that the agitation and struggle, that had endured for so long a time, had ended in this peaceful and successful demonstration ... it would be a source of real good fellowship one towards another'.[53] The extensive reportage of Ashton's speech in the *Darwen News* highlighted essential factors which had contributed to the mutually satisfactory conclusion to the dispute:

> ... gentlemen who were proud of their native place and who thought well of their town's folk. They could only hope that the people would assist and do their best to preserve the Common from injury ... He trusted that parents – fathers and mothers – would bring their children to the Common, not only for the health that could be derived from it; but to see the beauties of the country around. Let those parents teach their children to love a quiet walk in the country ...[54]

The social improvement themes of respectability and rational recreation, more commonly associated with a liberal philanthropic agenda, were here promoted by a former representative of a more generally obstructive and exclusive landed social stratum. Speeches by the town's MP, by councillors and the mayor all expressed gratitude to the Ashtons, while he himself confirmed this general cooperation between the old landed interest and the emerging power of municipalism when he praised the role of the local liberal radical press: '... the proprietors of local newspapers who so well and ably served the town through the Press'.[55] The collaboration and mutual back-slapping did not moderate the tone of triumphalism or diminish the strong political dimension to the cause. In a celebratory supplement, the *Darwen News* reported 'The Town en Fete': 'Everybody and his wife in Darwen turned out on Saturday last to take some part in the monstre [*sic*] demonstration which had been organized to celebrate the freedom of Darwen Moor Common.'[56] The victory celebration was a major event, reflecting optimistic civic pride in a 'rising, vigorous, and prosperous town'; there was a 'triumphal march ... flourish of trumpets ... [and] nine brass bands', as well as fireworks, a bonfire, and a mayor's banquet; tradespeople flew flags and bunting from their premises, and it was reported that:

> ... the celebration of the incorporation of Darwen Moor will be an event memorable in local history. Preparations on a scale even lavish and grand have been made by the respective friendly and trades societies, which have backed up the Mayor and Corporation in a manner redounding to their credit.[57]

The *Darwen News* included a programme of events, and maps were made available showing the boundaries of the common as well as its various footpaths. The *Lancashire Daily Post* reported 'Public Rejoicing'.[58] The collaboration between a landed proprietor and a municipal government, and the acclamation of free and open public access, did not, however, save John Ramsden from a 2*s*. 6*d*. (12½ p) fine for trespass later in the year, following his arrest for poaching.[59]

The scale of the celebration in Darwen, and the publicity which it attracted, gave ample opportunity for political in-fighting and point-scoring, consistent with the intricate grass-roots development of complex Lancashire politics. One dimension to local popular Toryism was deliberately snubbed through a tactical exclusion of the local Orange Order: 'The refusal of the Orangemen to join the procession simply because the Catholic brethren were to have the precedence in the order of walking, need excite no surprise, for it is just what might have been expected' – there was talk of 'dire consequences' if the Orangemen had taken part.[60] By contrast, the socialists were particularly keen to play a major part in the celebration, and thereby assert their position as the most vociferous and active campaigners. It was a further

instance of the SDF in Lancashire seizing every opportunity to adopt
a high profile in grass-roots issues. *Justice* took up the banner, claiming
the bulk of the credit for the socialists, encouraging SDF comrades
from nearby towns to take a prominent position in the procession, and
highlighting the opportunity for proselytization. On the morning of
the events in Darwen, *Justice* reported on the intention of the Burnley
and district branches of the SDF to organize a demonstration, and
condemned the way in which the Darwen oligarchy, backed by the
local institutional infrastructure, planned to take all the credit:

> ... to celebrate the acquisition of such public rights. Bands, friendly
> societies, municipal magnates, and others will attend the demonstra-
> tion. The press seem to have forgotten who took the first step and
> are now heaping the whole credit on the shoulders of a few middle-
> class men. The number of people that is likely to be on the Moor on
> September 5th is likely to beat the record, so we Social-Democrats
> intend to take advantage of this and propagate our principles on
> this moor.[61]

Justice considered the Darwen Moor episode not as a victory for the
people in gaining free access to an excellent recreational facility, but
as a further assertion by the town's Liberals of their ideological, political, and economic control over the district: 'Darwen Moor is now
practically under the control of Darwen Corporation.'[62] In seeking to
regain some of the initiative, the SDF encouraged attendance at the
rally of comrades from branches at Blackburn, Chorley, and Great
Harwood. Tom Glossop, a leading SDF man in London, came up to
speak. *Justice* favoured a highly visible presence on the day, urging
socialists to 'bring your banners and red flags ... get there early and
form the nucleus of the meeting'.[63] Nonetheless, the Darwen celebrations, with mutual back-slapping between landowner and the urban
liberal oligarchy, and toasts to the Queen, were a triumphant assertion
of progress which effectively nullified socialist attempts to expand their
local political influence.

Agrarian crisis, coupled to a growing demand for country 'sport' in
the later nineteenth century, stimulated the further commercialization
of the rural economy, bringing a greater proportion of marginal, and
therefore largely uncultivated land into the exclusion zone. Justification
for landowners' changing perceptions of the value of land, and the
concomitant desire to exclude the public, was legitimized in a political
ideology, evolved during the seventeenth and eighteenth centuries,
which identified the primary function of government as the protection
of private property. Liberals too subscribed to this notion of the sacro-
sanctity of property, but balanced it against a basically philanthropic

defence of the recreational aspect of open spaces, founded on the rights of the people. More and more proprietors of hill country turned to the opportunities presented by the increasing demands of the *nouveaux riches* for shooting and stalking, rather than compete in a market whose commercial openings were depleted severely by cheap refrigerated imports of Argentinian and Australasian meat products, wool and hides. The issue of access came to prominence during a period when the increasingly anomalous peculiarities of the British land system were generating a wide-ranging high-profile debate. Many liberals challenged the value of land and the level of rents, whereas socialists suspected a transfer of obligation from exploitative landowners to state-sanctioned capitalism, which was rapidly revising its essential *laissez-faire* principle: '... reduction of rents would benefit only the railway monopolist, grain speculator, and middleman'.[64] It was in this context that new commercial and traditional landowning philosophy and practice coalesced and became strengthened even more by parvenu aspirations, which contributed to a consolidation of the landed class's position, ensuring the maintenance of the sort of cultural rituals that conflicted with an urban desire for country leisure activities. Towards the end of the nineteenth century the politics of the land question and the defence of the landed *status quo* was complicated further by the increasingly liberal membership of the expanding hunting fraternity. Nonetheless, it was urban liberals who comprised the mainstay of the general lobby in favour of land reform, an issue which ramified into concern with the recreational use of upland areas. One example of this dominance was the strong liberal tradition in the Aberdeen area, which underpinned the formation of the Cairngorm Club, ensuring a concerted challenge to landed interests in the eastern Highlands. The pursuit of access to the mountains was, in fact, written into the constitution of the club: 'Rule II (3). To consider the right of access to Scottish mountains, and to adopt such measures in regard thereto as the club may deem advisable.'[65]

The relationship between the 'sporting' estates and local economies has generated widespread conjecture and produced some spurious justification. Detailed attempts at economic vindication figured prominently in the parliamentary arguments against access bills. Lord Elcho, for example, stressed the employment opportunities presented by the deer forests, while also claiming that an influx of visitors would be detrimental to the overall well-being of local economies: 'It was shown that deer forests employed a large number of people, who, if there were no deer forests, would not be employed at all.'[66] Advocates of exclusion from much of Scotland's uncultivated upland set out their impressive array of statistical evidence. Figures provided by the MP for Bute showed that of 445 grouse moors in Perthshire, 225 were let out at a rental of no less than £32,000 per annum, while deer forests in the county raised £110,000 per annum. Conveniently excluded from the equation were the potential alternatives, which were frustrated by such a narrow and deliberately preferential economic base. Land values and incomes from rents were compared with those obtaining to the ailing sheep-farming economy. During the parliamentary debate of Trevelyan's 1908 access bill, Mr Mason, MP for Windsor, cited two comparative examples of deer forests:

a)   current rental for deer stalking, £3,000 p. a.; previous rental as sheep run, £700 p.a.

b)   deer stalking, £3,100 p.a.; previous rental as sheep run, £400 p.a. + £600 p.a. for seasonal grouse shooting.

It was also stated that, in the second example, sheep farming employed four permanent shepherds, while the sporting estate employed twenty-eight ghillies, although it was not made clear how much of the latter's work was seasonal. Such arguments suggest that countryside access campaigners were defending some mythical 'golden age' of the sheep. The economic case for exclusion was, paradoxically, connected to a notion of progress, through which commercialized country sports would, it was claimed, facilitate the general improvement of local communities.

The case for a shooting-based economy for the upland areas was never subject to any objective appraisal of alternative economic models which might present the greatest long-term benefit to such rural communities, and thereby provide the best counter to the debilitating effects of continuing depopulation. Early debates on the proper use of uncultivated open spaces were characterized by a high level of support for planned approaches, which would facilitate a more rational assessment of all relevant factors. The destruction of a balanced crofting economy had already produced mass migration to a marginal existence on the coast, to urban and industrial life in the Glasgow area and the coal and iron district of Lanarkshire, or, more famously, to Canada, New Zealand or Australia. Some depopulation was the inevitable consequence of continuing general urbanization, but the potential for a mixed, planned, and viable Highland economy, including provision for various types of recreational activity, was frustrated by policies geared to the needs of the upland sporting interests. As part of the negative response to increased demands for more varied and expansive rural recreation, cottagers were forbidden even to take in tourists to supplement income, while landlords forced some hotels to close down.

Unobtrusive recreational access could be denied even for the purpose of serious field study. During the 1908 parliamentary debate Charles Trevelyan raised the case of a botanical survey, whose organizer, seeking access to Scottish mountains at a convenient time to the landlords, wrote to all deer-forest owners, but received less than a dozen replies, all of which were negative. Several landed Scottish MPs rose to deny any knowledge of such a communication, failing to mention that such business matters were invariably placed in the hands of agents, who were given *carte blanche* to administer independently the general policy of an estate. Speaking in support of Bryce's 1892 bill, Mr Mather, member for the Gorton division of Manchester, relating his own experience of exclusion from the mountains near Braemar in the autumn of 1891, added an interesting dimension to the economic aspect of the debate, providing an example of how an artificial imbalance had been created in the Highland economy. Mather was: '... struck by the fact that Braemar villagers had to use Swiss milk because the valley pastures were used to grow fodder for winter feed for deer'.[67] Economic arguments against access also ignored the seasonality of much of the work for the predominantly sporting estates, which grafted a competitive market philosophy onto the traditional agrarian model characterized by older problems of insecurity rooted in dependence.

Annan Bryce, in support of Trevelyan's 1908 bill, invoked long-established Highland custom when claiming that the whole population of Scotland would be better off with a reduction in the number of deer forests: 'Why should they be compelled to keep to a footpath when the lands originally belonged to their clan who had a free right to roam over them?'[68] In 1892 James Bryce had also framed his argument in customary sanction:

> Eighty years ago everybody could go freely wherever he desired over the mountains and moors of Scotland ... I am informed by friends familiar with Scottish law that there is no case in our law books of an attempt to interdict any person from walking over open moors and mountain, except of recent date ...[69]

The Scottish appeal to the long-established principle and practice of access to uncultivated tracts of land was confronted with the problem that such rights had never been clearly defined, depending only on their customary status. Of course, just as the big commercial sporting interests were a recent development, so was the influx of visitors in search of recreation and open space. Any right to roam had always been *de facto* rather than legally stipulated. When applied to practical circumstances, the principle of the rights of property have generally taken preference over the principle of the rights of the people. The weight of Scottish opinion which James Bryce claimed in support of his bill depended more on a nationalistic local solidarity than on any real support for visitors in pursuit of healthy recreation. It was also emphasized that the power of exclusion was granted originally (a) for cultivation of the soil, and (b) to allow privacy in the immediate proximity of a residence – rather than for the creation of expansive upland exclusion zones, maintained purely for the amusement of land-owners and guests.

The emerging lobby in north-east Scotland was also confronted by a particularly difficult adversary. There has been no area where the large-scale utilization of marginal land, and consequent exclusion of the public, has been as strongly underpinned by the dubious authority of invented tradition as the Scottish Highlands in general, and the Cairngorms in particular.[70] Victorian Balmoral, and the whole cultural milieu of which it is a prominent emblem, has provided the apparently unimpeachable approbation of royal patronage for sporting interests in Britain's upland areas. Such an endorsement for the maintenance of the landed *status quo* permeates from its eastern Highland base into other areas where similar interests have been paramount; shooting party sorties from Balmoral to, for example, the North Yorkshire moors continue to perpetuate that influence. In the case of the Cairngorms, the later nineteenth-century quest for improved access was confronted by a system which took much of its strength from a created Victorian tartan culture, backed by such noble and romantically evocative images as 'The Monarch of the Glen'.

Nonetheless, the largely successful defence of that system has been founded on much more than straightforward deference or the romantic appeal of contrived tradition. What was created from the middle of the nineteenth century was a reconstructed economic framework which has been essential to the survival of the remaining community. During the second half of the twentieth century the character of this local economy has switched more and more towards catering for the huge tourist industry, which depends on an intimate relationship between magnificent scenery and an idealized local culture. Defenders of the rural *status quo* have constructed a plausible case in order to demonstrate that the substantial sums which elements of the socially aspiring *nouveaux riches* invested during the second half of the nineteenth century supplied the lifeblood of an ailing rural economy, providing employment and arresting the destructive fall in land values. Income from rents could be portayed as essential to the investment needed to rescue the ailing local infrastructure, thus reinvigorating the communities which it supported. In reality, the new monied ownership of land in upland areas added substantial impetus to the exclusion of visitors: 'The tendency on the part of old landowners to exclude the people has led to a similar tendency on the part of the *nouveaux riches* ...'[71] In seeking legitimation through custom, the Scottish access lobby effectively broadened its appeal. The connection with the rights of the people equated the campaign with a nationalist agenda, which challenged the right of foreigners, particularly if they were English, to exclude the indigenous population from their native heath: 'The time has come when we must assert what we believe to be the paramount rights of the nation.'[72] James Bryce was particularly keen to stress the connection between an influx of English commercial-industrial wealth and the demise of a flourishing organic, clan-based community of earlier times: 'They had no value for sporting purposes 70 or 80 years ago. Why have they now? ... [B]ecause railways and steamboats have made it easy to get to these happy hunting grounds – made it easy for the wealth of England to get to the moorlands of Scotland.'[73] Nonetheless, the campaign remained consistent in its support of urban demands for greater opportunity for rural recreation:

> The scenery of our country has been filched away from us just when we have begun to prize it more than ever before. It coincided with the greatest change that ever passed over our people – the growth of huge cities and dense populations in many places outside those cities – and this change has made far greater the need for the opportunity of enjoying nature and places where health may be regained by bracing air and exercise, and where the jaded mind can rest in silence and in solitude.[74]

The growing trend towards more and more exclusive control over vast areas of largely uncultivated open space continued to frustrate attempts to introduce a greater measure of democracy into solutions to the problem of utilizing land in the best interests of a wider, modernizing society. The survival of anachronistic socio-economic structures has been ascribed to the adaptability of a landed order, whose own apparent modernizing response to increased economic competition concealed a fundamentally regressive socio-political function. It is fool-ish to deny that conscientious landowners are particularly adept at countryside conservation, but that role is overstated in many instances in order to justify continuing exclusion. Moreover, there are many who remain sceptical of the motives of those who conserve an artificially created environment for the specific purposes of hunting and shooting. The access campaigners' sustained attack on the rural conservation case can be seen, for example, in an article in the *Observer* newspaper: 'Conservation is a favourite argument used by grouse moor owners as a reason for not opening up their land to the public. However, there is no reliable scientific evidence to support this argument.'[75] The pressure on upland areas – in the form of reinforced demands created by greater mobility for the majority – has also come into conflict with an urgent need to conserve the threatened natural heritage. Concern for the conservation of wilder areas of countryside has meant that even the concept of the national park has become open to reinterpretation, so that the Park Management Committee in the Peak District, the country's first and most frequented national park, is now forced to consider a policy of exclusion from certain areas.[76]

At the time when the agenda was being established for an ongoing access debate, the antagonists sought to swing the argument in their favour by recourse to emotive references that might generate further support for their camp. Trevelyan and other access proponents followed Bryce's lead by condoning radical reform in terms of a socially unifying progressive notion of healthy exercise for all:

> ... there was a growing feeling in all classes of society that in order to live a thoroughly healthy life in town, and in order that vigour might be properly maintained, it was necessary that the population should have country air, exercise, and pursuits, at any rate during the holiday periods of the year.[77]

The willingness of access campaigners to accommodate the demands of alternative interests – most notably and most lastingly those of the country sports minority – helps to explain the depth of support which this group attracted during that formative period. Further sympathy was based on an increased acceptance of the need, and indeed the right of urban populations to seek physical and mental renewal in the open countryside. That agenda was laid down from the outset by James Bryce and his numerous and often influential parliamentary and extra-parliamentary supporters, many of whom were themselves active in open-air pursuits of all types:

> It is not against sporting interests I direct the Resolution, and neither has it anything to do with the general policy of the deer forests ... All I ask to-night is to bring forward the grievance and suffering caused to the people of Scotland, and in a lesser degree to the people of other parts of the United Kingdom, by their exclusion from their right to enjoy the scenery of their own country, and to seek healthy recreation and exercise on their own mountains and moors.[78]

Physical fitness was given full play in attracting a wider body of support to the interwar access lobby, which was instrumental in consolidating a substantive outdoor movement: 'The main object of the outdoors [sic] movement, in all its various forms, has always been, and still remains, the right to wander at will over uncultivated land.'[79]

Opponents of open access deliberately played up the image of indisciplined urban trippers. Lord Elcho, MP for Ipswich, but also a member of a Scottish Tory landed family which owned coalmines in Fife, took a close interest in Bryce's access bills. He claimed that no advantage would accrue to local economies from the incursion of tourists, who would only destroy the natural environment: 'They would bring nothing with them and they would leave nothing behind them. The family paper and broken ginger beer bottles are the only traces that are left behind them.'[80] The blight of the ginger-beer bottles was invoked again sixteen years later by the MP for Barkston Ash, Mr Lane Fox: 'They knew what was left in the track of the tourist traffic in this country in the shape of orange peel and ginger beer and whiskey bottles [sic].'[81] James Bryce's desire to protect the Highlands and other wild areas from potential pollution was less contrived. Contained within his broad countryside interests is evidence of an early expression of the nascent environmentalism which contributed to the generation of an outdoor movement. His concern with the protection of natural environments typified the sort of motivation that reconciled conservative antipathy to developments such as railways and hydro-electric schemes with an advocacy of the progressive concept of constructing a rigid system of controls, foreshadowing the onset of the twentieth-century implementation of planned solutions. Bryce, who had previously invoked the spirit of the Tory Romantics, Scott and Wordsworth, spoke of the effects of Nature on the thoughts and imagination of men, and of 'chasing away cares and the dull monotony of every-day life'.[82] The quest for rational progress within the construction of the outdoor movement was tempered with a form of romantic anti-utilitarianism that was suggestive of Ruskin. Bryce appealed on behalf of 'people in whom education, expanding every year, stimulates the taste for poetry and beauty. Man does not live by bread alone.'[83]

The roots of a campaigning access lobby flourished as a result of its importance to an emerging and revised liberal orthodoxy, in which nineteenth-century philanthropic principles and motives, mediated by the enduring influence of the Romantic Movement, were merged with social democratic reformism. The genesis of the access lobby was only one expression of the more general late nineteenth-century radical milieu of ideas that were founded on the search for solutions to the land question, although strong roots had already been established in the earlier rearguard action to defend common land against the encroachment of enclosure. As the campaign for better recreational access developed in the twentieth century, new landowners, such as the water companies and the military, entered the fray to complicate the issue, but the intrinsic rationality and reasonableness of the campaigning lobby had already been established firmly on its reforming ideological and political foundation.

The recurrent unwillingness to distinguish open access from the defence of traditional linear rights of way has depended partly on the fact that the freedom to roam is more difficult to legitimize in customary rights. Except in the realm of commons preservation, any claim to the sanction of common law has been much less easy to substantiate than that of other radical causes prosecuted with reference to older rights. Failure to achieve satisfactory compromise solutions has led occasionally to a more aggressive promotion of access. This more challenging radical agenda was constructed most notably within left-wing political challenges to the legitimacy of obstructive privilege. Towards the end of the nineteenth century, the attack on 'the grim castle of landlordism'[84] came increasingly from the evangelized radical voice of socialism, which was raised, for example, in the Clarion publication, *Scout*, in an article entitled 'On the Gentle Art of Stealing Commons': '... striving to comprehend the moral make-up of a landlord ... generically a contemptible thief'.[85] A small-scale involvement in local disputes by SDF branches and the Clarion movement in the 1890s developed into a national response in the 1920s and 1930s, orchestrated by the British Workers' Sports Federation (BWSF), although this communist-affiliated leisure organization was confined largely to its Sheffield and Manchester strongholds.[86] Notwithstanding this significant input from a more radical form of political activism, a generally highly respectable and compromising tactical approach dominated the formation of a campaigning movement, whose character was shaped by the interaction between parliamentary and extra-parliamentary agitation to improve recreational amenity for the urban majority.

Appendix

James Bryce

The major formative influence which James Bryce exerted on the generation and development of an access campaign was founded on his close affinity with the interests of mountaineers and hillwalkers. Throughout his busy and pressurized adult life in public affairs, he was sustained by a keen pursuit of various forms of outdoor recreation. His love of open spaces had been stimulated originally by the encouragement he received during his youth. He had developed a love of mountains at the age of eleven while staying at Cushendall, Co. Antrim on a trip to his native Ulster from the new family home in Glasgow. That initial impression was consolidated in the following year on a holiday visit to an uncle in Kendal: 'The beauties of the Lake Country made a profound impression on me ...'[87] Interest in the natural environment was sustained through other outdoor expeditions, such as geological excursions into the Mourne Mountains in 1852. At the age of twenty-one Bryce wrote a flora of the Isle of Arran. His Glasgow base was convenient for picking up mountaineering skills in the Arrochar

Alps in the rugged area of Argyll to the west of Loch Lomond. From the 1860s the mountaineering trips became more expansive, taking in the Alps, the Pyrenees, the Dolomites and as far afield as the Transylvanian Carpathians. Bryce's empathy with the open-air recreationist was extended beyond his interest in climbing and walking, when he was bitten by the cycling craze of the 1890s. Continental tours were undertaken, including a spring holiday in Normandy and the Touraine in 1897, or the tours in the company of Bowen, a master at Harrow school, which took them to the south of France, and to the Hanau, Jena, Weimar and Black Forest districts of Germany. A range of mutual interests produced a friendship with another great advocate of the outdoors, Sir Leslie Stephen, who proposed Bryce for the presidency of the Alpine Club in 1898. In the following year Bryce was elected to the élite position of president of the Athenaeum Club. His friendship with Stephen, founded on a common reforming liberal ideology, was tempered by a spiritual discord, as he repudiated the secularism of Stephen and others. Bryce's undenominational Christianity, although rooted in a staunch Ulster Presbyterian background, was, nonetheless, critical of restrictive, narrow dogma: 'He was a man of facts and feelings rather than of fine-spun arguments about the Absolute, of active rather than of speculative energies ... a strong and serious moral purpose ...' [88]

After a career in the legal profession, Bryce was elected to Parliament in 1880 as the member for Tower Hamlets. However, it was as MP for South Aberdeen, from 1885, that he really became involved in the emerging campaign against the restriction of access to the countryside. This activity was consolidated through his presidency of the Cairngorm Club. Experience in the United States had given Bryce an insight into the concept of national parks as a planned approach to the recreational use of the wilder uncultivated areas: 'This most respectable of radicals remains a prophet without honour in his own country; the conservation scenery he urged so strongly is now an accepted objective, but the problems he sought to avoid still await solution.' [89] Bryce's citation of the American example came from a radical liberal perspective. However, it was equally pertinent to socialist responses, such as that constructed by Arthur Ransome in 1908 in an article in *The Worker*:

Instead of the herditary [sic] owner, I imagined the People. Instead of a private park, I imagined that I was walking through and enjoying a National park, a kind of English 'Yosemite'. Why not? If we, under our present miserable economic system, can afford to allow one man to own and to use such a park, surely the People who owned all the land, nationally and not individually, could afford to indulge in such a luxury.[90]

James Bryce's prominent role in the early parliamentary campaign for country access was augmented by his major contribution, in collaboration with colleagues in the Cairngorm Club, to the first real extra-parliamentary challenge to the practice of preventing walkers and others from roaming freely in the Scottish hills. Those original eastern Highland objectives were escalated during the latter part of the nineteenth century into the wider British campaigning lobby that has been such a central feature of the outdoor movement in the twentieth century.

Notes

1. Quoted by Ramblers' Association director, Alan Mattingly, in *Rambling Today* (Spring 1993), p. 62.
2. National Parks and Access to Countryside Act, 1949, Part V, Section 59 (2).
3. *PD*, 3rd Series, 324 (1888), cols. 1287–8.
4. *Darwen News*, 12 September 1896, p. 4.
5. *Rossendale Free Press*, 19 September 1896, p. 2.
6. Shoard, M., *This Land is Our Land* (London, 1983), Chs. 7–8.
7. *PD*, 4th Series, 2 (1892), col. 94.
8. *Ibid.*, col. 101.
9. *The Guardian*, Education Supplement, 22 September 1992, p. 1.
10. *Rambling Today* 6 (Autumn 1992), p. 11.
11. For the continuing dominance of pre-industrial social structures, see Mayer, A. J., *The Persistence of the Old Regime* (Beckenham, 1981).
12. Cook, J., ed., *William Hazlitt: Selected Writings* (Oxford, 1991), p. 155.
13. See Roberts, J. M., *Europe, 1880–1945* (2nd edn; London, 1989), p. 139, for the influence on Liberal politics of the Irish Home Rule Bill.
14. Fisher, H. A. L., *James Bryce*, vol. 1 (London, 1927), p. 191.
15. McGloin, P., 'The impact of the railway on the development of Keswick as a tourist resort, 1860–1914', unpublished MA thesis, University of Lancaster, 1977.
16. *PD*, 3rd Series, 37 (1837), col. 162.
17. Shaw-Lefevre, G. J. (Lord Eversley), *Commons, Forests, and Footpaths* (London, 1910), p. 22.
18. *PD*, 3rd Series, 37 (1837), col. 163.
19. *Ibid.*, 41 (1838), col. 1123.
20. *Ibid.*, 82 (1845), col. 15.
21. Wyborn, T., 'Parks for the people: the development of public parks in Victorian Manchester', *Manchester Region History Review* IX (1995), pp. 3–14.
22. Whittle, P. A., *Bolton-le-Moors, and the Townships in the Parish* (Bolton, 1855), p. 198.
23. Porter, B., 'Cragside. Arms and the man', *History Today* 45, 1 (January 1995), pp. 46–52; Armstrong donated Jesmond Dene to the city of Newcastle.

24. Walker, H., 'The Outdoor Movement in England and Wales, 1900–1939', unpublished Ph.D. thesis, University of Sussex, 1988, Ch. 1; Wyborn, 'Parks for the people'.

25. *PD*, 4th Series, 2 (1892), col. 94.

26. *Ibid.*, 188 (1908), col. 1444.

27. *Scottish Mountaineering Club Journal* 1 (Edinburgh, 1891), p. 328.

28. *Ibid.*, p. 3.

29. Aitken, R., 'Stravagers and marauders', *SMC Journal* XXX, 166 (1975), p. 351.

30. *SMC Journal* IV (1896–7), pp. 88–9.

31. Aitken, 'Stravagers and marauders', p. 355.

32. Craig, D., *On the Crofters' Trail. In Search of the Clearance Highlanders* (London, 1990); Johnston, T., *The History of the Working Classes in Scotland* (2nd edn; Glasgow, 1929), pp. 154–81; Prebble, J., *The Highland Clearances* (London, 1963); Richards, E., *A History of the Highland Clearances, 1746–1886* (London, 1982); Shoard, *This Land is Our Land*, pp. 69ff.; Smout, T. C., *A Century of the Scottish People, 1830–1950* (London, 1987), pp. 59ff. A revisionist interpretation, suggesting that the Scottish Highlands would eventually have depopulated to a similar extent without forced eviction of tenants, is given some credence by Smout (pp. 59–60) and by Richards (pp. 474–5).

33. Orr, W., *Deer Forests, Landlords, and Crofters. The West Highlands in Victorian and Edwardian Times* (Edinburgh, 1982), ch. 1.

34. *Daily Mail*, 3 July 1931, p. 9.

35. Johnston, *Working Classes in Scotland*, p. 210.

36. Boswell, J., 'The Journal of a Tour to the Hebrides.', in Johnson, S., and Boswell, J., *A Journey to the Western Islands and the Journal of a Tour to the Hebrides* (London, 1984), p. 236.

37. Mackenzie, O. H., *A Hundred Years in the Highlands* (London, 1921), p. 119.

38. Mackay, I. R., 'The Pet Lamb Case', *Transactions of the Gaelic Society of Inverness* 48 (1972–4), pp. 188–200, provides a detailed account of this episode.

39. *PD*, 4th Series, 2 (1892), col. 122.

40. Buist, D. (Land Surveyor of Perth), 'Plan of the Common of Glentilt. As Divided 1808', EPL.

41. *Cairngorm Club Journal* 1 (July 1893), p. 6.

42. Aitken, 'Stravagers and marauders', p. 351.

43. *Ibid.*, p. 357.

44. Fraser, B. S., 'Prentice Days', *SMC Journal* XXX, 166 (1975), p. 358.

45. Sugden, J., *Slaithwaite Notes of the Past and Present* (3rd. edn; Manchester 1905), p. 419.

46. Joyce P., *Visions of the People* (Cambridge, 1991), p. 75.

47. *The Yorkshire Post and Leeds Intelligencer*, 6 December 1877, p. 4.

48. *Ibid.*, 8 December 1877, p. 5.

49. De Morgan, J., *Report of Chancery Proceedings in the Hunslet Moor Case, 22nd February 1878* (London and Leeds, 1878), p. 3. Leeds Local Studies Library.

50. Leeds Local Acts, 1842–1901, p. 456. Leeds Local Studies Library.
51. *Ibid.*, p. 457.
52. *Darwen News, Supplement*, 12 September 1896, p. 1.
53. *Ibid.*
54. *Ibid.*
55. *Ibid.*
56. *Ibid.*
57. *Ibid.*, 5 September 1896, p. 4.
58. *Lancashire Daily Post*, 7 September 1896, p. 2.
59. *Ibid.*, 2 October 1896, p. 2.
60. *Darwen News, Supplement*, 12 September 1896, p. 4.
61. *Justice*, 5 September 1896, p. 2.
62. *Ibid.*
63. *Ibid.*
64. *Ibid.*, 16 May 1896, p. 3.
65. *Cairngorm Club Journal* II (July 1896), p. x.
66. *PD*, 4th Series, 2 (1892), col. 116.
67. *Ibid.*, col. 127.
68. *Ibid.*, 188 (1908), col. 1464.
69. *Ibid.*, 2 (1892), col. 95.
70. Trevor Roper, H., 'The invention of tradition: the Highland tradition in Scotland', in Hobsbawm, E. J. and Ranger, T., *The Invention of Tradition* (Cambridge, 1983).
71. *PD*, 4th Series, 2 (1892), col. 127.
72. *Ibid.*, col. 100.
73. *Ibid.*
74. *Ibid.*, cols. 102–3.
75. Beskine, D. (Ramblers' Association), quoted in *The Observer*, 21 July 1991, p. 4.
76. *Guardian*, 17 August 1993, p. 5.
77. *PD*, 4th Series, 188 (1908), col. 1440.
78. *Ibid.*, 2 (1892), col. 103.
79. Sheffield Campaign for Access to Moorland, *Freedom of the Moors* (Sheffield, 1988), p. 2.
80. *PD*, 4th Series, 2 (1892), col. 92.
81. *Ibid.*, 188 (1908), col. 1453.
82. *Ibid.*, 2 (1892), col. 103.
83. *Ibid.*, col. 92.
84. *Labour Prophet* (January 1985), p. 7.
85. *Scout* 8 (November 1895), p. 228.
86. Rothman, B., *The 1932 Kinder Trespass* (Timperley, 1982); also see below, Ch. 7.
87. Fisher, *James Bryce*, pp. 28–9.
88. *Ibid.*, p. 303.
89. Aitken, 'Stravagers and marauders', p. 357.
90. *The Worker* (Huddersfield), 5 September 1908, p. 2.

Chapter 5

The Outdoor Movement on Wheels, 1878–1914

Three significant dates mark the growing importance of the bicycle in the development of the outdoor movement. In 1878 a national institutional focus and campaigning lobby was established for leisure cyclists with the formation of the Bicycle Touring Club, which later became the Cyclists' Touring Club (CTC). From 1885 the replacement of the 'ordinary' or 'penny-farthing' by the 'safety' bicycle made the pastime more generally accessible. Thirdly, when John Boyd Dunlop, a Scottish veterinary surgeon domiciled in Belfast, produced the prototype of the pneumatic tyre in 1888 the bicycle advanced from being a technological novelty to a practical form of individual transport, which would be adopted for a range of reasons, including pleasant exercise in the fresh air in the open countryside. Cycling really took off as a popular pastime during the period which spanned the turn of the century. Its contribution to the outdoor movement was in many ways typified by the fellowship of Clarion cycling clubs (CCC), notwithstanding their stated primary objective of furthering the socialist cause.

The mentality and underlying philosophy of the tourer does need to be distinguished from that of the racing fraternity, and from the large numbers of 'scorchers' and 'speed worms'.[1] These latter upset the authorities and were the cause of conflict, such as during the police crusade against cycling at Southport in 1896, or when the police took action at Epsom in the same year against 'scorchers' who included groups of Aldershot soldiers. In his *Essays and Sketches*, published in 1897, Abraham Stansfield gives a flavour of the contemporary perception of cycling as a menace. Stansfield spoke extravagantly of a 'prevalent craving for delirious excitement' and of 'hecatombs of victims'.[2] The growing fellowship of leisurely, country-loving cyclists generally disowned the irresponsible element. Speakers at club AGMs, as well as newspaper cycling columnists during the early heyday of the pastime, led the way in warning against the dangerous and speed-obsessed riding that brought widespread opprobrium on the activity.

The initial division in attitude and ethos amongst cyclists set the agenda for a dichotomy that continues to divide the British cycling fraternity into two distinct interest groups, tentatively drawn together by aspects of a common interest. In the period before the Great War the differing interests can be generally and conveniently circumscribed by the separate objectives of the CTC and the National Cyclists' Union (NCU), an organization established to administer the needs of the racing and record-breaking athletes, whose creed conformed with the contemporary cult of athleticism. However, with significant numbers of cyclists spanning both aspects of the popular pastime, such a convenient division demands qualification. Many of the thousands of people who enjoyed fresh air, countryside and convivial company on the weekend cycle club runs which proliferated from the 1890s were among those who competed in time-trials and record attempts. Almost all of the numerous cycling clubs participated in competitive events and at the popular annual race meetings, such as that held every Whitsuntide at Barnard Castle in Co. Durham – the 'Barney Meet'. The clubs also sustained a thriving social scene, with dances, dinners, smoking concerts, and conversazioni included in their programmes. Club runs into the country consolidated the social function, with dinner and tea at a local hostelry providing the convivial focus, where non-cycling members would often arrive by wagonette or brake. Many club members, however, were attracted solely by the touring and country-loving side of a healthy recreation. Countryside events were often organized, such as the annual picnic of the Newcastle-based Brunswick club, held during Tyneside's race week holiday in June, which had been developed as a festival with strong temperance undertones in the 1880s, when the annual race meeting was moved from the Town Moor to Gosforth Park. Apart from the national CTC, there were also local clubs which concentrated on touring. They included Bishop Auckland Star Cycling and Touring Club, with 126 members in 1897, and Holywell Touring Cycling Club, which was based on the mining villages around Seaton Delaval in south-east Northumberland. Nonetheless, the distinction between the leisurely, if often energetic, tourist, and the dyed-in-the-wool racing man became more definite from the later 1960s.

The touring cycling fellowship developed as a specific movement in its own right, but led the way in campaigning for the common good of all cyclists. S. Dawson, a prominent member of the Lancaster club, typified those who were instrumental in setting the agenda for cycling campaigns which have united keen cyclists in the motor age of the twentieth century. Motor traffic was, of course, the major stimulus to the road improvements for which Dawson and others campaigned, but it was also a growing source of friction with the leisure cyclist. As touring cyclists ventured further into wilder countryside, the demand for routes to the more attractive areas escalated. A letter to the *Sheffield Daily Telegraph* expressed the benefits to the cyclist of new roads into the Peak District.³ The correspondent asked for the support of the *Telegraph* for a proposed road from Huddersfield and Holmfirth to Ashopton and Grindleford, and for the upgrading of a track from Langsett.

Cycling publications and the press covered all aspects of late nineteenth- and early twentieth-century cycling. *The Northern Cyclists' Pocket Guide*, first published in 1897, confirmed the fundamental difference between the two types of recreational cycling by catering for the racer and the tourist in separate sections. The *Bradford Daily Argus* included a brief factual report of a tour in the south of England by members of Saltaire CC in August 1898,⁴ while the *Bolton Journal and Guardian* gave a more typical fuller coverage of Bolton cyclists touring Wales at Easter 1907 with the assistance of a 6s. 10d. (34p) rail ticket from Manchester to Shrewsbury, returning from Oswestry – 'Taking advantage of facilities offered to cyclists and walkers.'⁵ *The Northern Cyclists' Pocket Guide* had earlier encouraged the use of the railways as a means of reaching more varied cycle routes, and published lists of North Eastern Railway tourist fares from Newcastle.⁶ Many of the touring cyclists also pursued the similarly motivated recreational activities of rambling, mountaineering and the study of natural history. The writing of the nature-loving, rambling and cycling socialist journalist Allen Clarke gives a taste of that combination of open-air interests, as it developed into a flourishing aspect of the popular culture of the industrial towns of turn-of-the-century Lancashire.⁷ That culture is also reflected in Fred Balshaw's weekly outdoor articles in the *Bolton Journal and Guardian*, typical of a genre that included in its scope a range of open-air activities, but highlighted in particular the cyclist who best fitted the model of the intelligent, independent, and inquisitive individual, who might be seen as characteristic of the emergent outdoor movement. Balshaw's descriptions of walks and cycling tours incorporated articles on those topics which often stimulated the interest of the outdoor fraternity, such as landscape, natural history, local history and architecture.

The cycling craze of the 1890s was established on the new popularity of the bicycle amongst freedom-seeking, athletic, young middle-class men. Women too took to cycling on a significant scale, and this liberating pastime became a symbol of a struggle for emancipation which recognized links between leisure and independence. Cycling's popularity was reflected in the large number of publications which covered every aspect of the pastime, in local newspapers – 'the enormous and ever-growing bicycle traffic'⁸ – and in other contemporary literature; H. G. Wells's Hoopdriver, hero of *The Wheels of Chance*, and Mr Polly both represented one stratum of the class of person in contemporary society who was beginning to discover liberation from the city. An article in *King of the Road*, one of the numerous short-lived turn-of-the-century cycling periodicals, illustrated the impact of the craze: 'The man of the day is the Cyclist. The press, the public, the pulpit, the faculty, all discuss him. They discuss his health, his feet, his shoes, his speed, his cap, his knickers.'[9] Whatever the main motives of the participants, there is no doubting the scale of the late nineteenth-century vogue for cycling; from within this social phenomenon there emerged a large body of keen outdoor people who came to represent an important dimension to the growth of an open-air movement. In the period following the formation of the CTC, cycling clubs proliferated in all parts of the country, but especially in the cities and the industrial towns, as part of a widespread desire to get out into the fresh air.

The activities of one of the early clubs were recorded by S. Dawson in his *Incidents in the Course of a Long Cycling Career*. The Vale of Lune CC, founded in 1879 and disbanded in 1882, and its successor Lancaster CC, formed in 1887, organized club runs, tours, a road race up the Lune Valley to Hornby and attendance at the annual North of England Meet at Harrogate. Lancashire featured prominently from the middle-class-dominated earlier stages of the cycling boom. Burnley and Colne, for example, both had clubs in the early 1880s; Colne Bicycle Club's first annual ball in the Cloth Hall was attended by '80 ladies and gentlemen'.[10] Cycling achieved such popularity in that district during the 1880s that an annual meet was organized at Whalley, and by 1892 Burnley Victoria CC had emulated Burnley CC in setting up a rural social base as a focus for their outdoor orientated and convivial club life: 'Burnley Victoria Cycling Club ... following the example set by Burnley Cycling Club ... have selected a "country residence" where they can spend a weekend, and which will serve them as headquarters' – twenty pounds was spent on furnishing and decorating this 'romantic spot' at Hurst Green.[11] In May 1896, the official opening of the 'Burnley Wheelers' Cottage' at Pendleton was attended by more than a hundred cyclists.[12] Included in the inaugural speech was advice to younger members not to participate in 'scorching'.

By the 1890s – the decade which Alex M. Thompson ('Dangle') of the *Clarion* termed ambiguously the '*Fin de Cycle*'[13] – cycling had become so popular that scores of clubs each contained around a hundred members; Bradford Wheelers CC, for example, gained seventy new members in 1899 after the main popularity of the pastime had supposedly waned. The *Burnley Gazette* reported in 1896 on the 'immense popularity of the cycle and the universality of its use',[14] an impression which the *Rossendale Free Press* confirmed ostentatiously in the same month: 'So large had the patronage of the cycle become that it had been reported many businesses were menaced, notably the tobacco trade, the pianoforte business, and the hatters and tailors were crying out.' The same article highlighted some of the attractions of cycling: 'In the interests of health cycling had already made for itself a reputation, but another thing it was specially adapted to do was to create in cyclists a greater love of nature.' [15] Outdoor columns in the urban local press were full of encouragement to cyclists, typically expressed in a romantic idiom. The theme was perpetuated strongly in sports and outdoor periodicals, like *Bicycling News and Sport and Play*, published in Birmingham, whose 'Whirligig' column, written by 'Itinerant', gave the full flavour of a genre which paralleled other contemporaneous open-air literature, such as the ubiquitous reports of countryside rambles: '... let's get off into the country in this beautiful weather, for spring is coming quickly up this way, and it is as well to be out and about when things are looking so fresh and fair'. This correspondent reported watching and listening to the birds, and eulogized the physical and aesthetic joys of the open road: 'No work, no worry, but just sit quiet and pedal swiftly as the jigger sped along with a swish and a hum, and the musical clink of gravel against the rims, while the birds sang ...' [16] On another occasion 'Itinerant' contrasted Birmingham with the peace, quiet, and relaxation of the rural areas, which in springtime were 'a perfect paradise ... springing freshness and delight', and described cycling along quiet lanes in beautiful weather and meeting 'a huge company of cyclists' at Berkswell, which included the Sociable CC.[17]

During the early cycling years particularly popular destinations became established as weekend venues for hundreds of cyclists, who congregated to refresh themselves during club runs and to socialize with other groups. These social focal points contributed to a consolidation of the fellowship of the cycling world, linking leisure cyclists over a century. The popular venues developed as common ground for the racing set, for the more leisurely tourists, as well as those who combined both activities. Ripley in Surrey, for instance, with its public houses and tearooms, attracted cyclists from the south-east of England, especially the numerous south London fraternity: 'Ripley is to Londoners what High Leigh, Knutsford, Halewood, Cranage, Holmes Chapel etc. are to Liverpool and Manchester cyclists.' [18]

The pretty village of Ponteland, eight miles to the north-west of Newcastle, and convenient to the industrial districts of Tyneside and south-east Northumberland, was typical of the rural venue invaded by urban-based cyclists, who brought a flourishing trade in lunches and teas to the three local inns on weekends and holidays. The *Newcastle Daily Chronicle* reported the size of the phenomenon on Good Friday 1898: the Seven Stars Hotel was host to seventy members of the Heaton CC and forty from the Bellegrove CC; a hundred yards down the road there were forty members of Arthur's Hill CC and thirty from Elswick Ordnance CC at the Diamond Inn; around the corner, the Blackbird

Inn played host to sixty-six cyclists; and three miles up the road a further ninety-five lunched at the Highlander Inn. Sociability as an end in itself can certainly be seen to have contributed to the popularity of the cycling clubs, as well as the attractions of fresh air and exercise in the countryside. Some north-east cyclists also ventured further afield, taking advantage of weekend and ten-day tickets of the North Eastern Railway, whose 'tourist programme' contained 'full details of the cycling and walking, and the circular tours'.[19]

The annual handbook of the CTC provided a useful source of information for the touring cyclist, with guides to tours and routes, to tea- and coffee-houses, approved hotels and inns, repairers, and other essential services. The price of the handbook – 1s. 6d. (7½p) – and the club subscriptions – 2s. 6d. (12½p) – were, nonetheless, somewhat prohibitive to many lower-middle-class and working-class cyclists. There were also numerous complaints, particularly during the first decade of the twentieth century, that several of the CTC-recommended hostelries were beyond the means of many of the less prosperous weekend escapees from the towns.

Temperance hotels featured prominently in the venues frequented by the early cyclists, establishing a consistent strand in the philosophy of the leisure cycling fraternity, which continued at least up to the 1950s. Tyneside cyclists patronized temperance hotels at Belsay, Matfen, and Alnwick in Northumberland, for example, while Burnley CC rounded off their first season with a club dinner at Cronkshaw's Temperance Hotel in November 1884. The choice was, of course, a natural one amongst active and generally health-conscious open-air recreationists, but was also the product of a distinct tendency towards an ethos perceived as rational and respectable, influenced not just by a belief in sobriety *per se*, but also in a particular attitude to the proper use of expendable income. The temperance issue was an important factor, contributing to the formation of the culturally defined social substratum in which many of the developing outdoor fellowships can be located. Drink and increasingly trivial and commercialized forms of recreation can again be seen to be largely rejected, and, although this tendency should not be overstated in a movement which has rarely been zealous in its attitudes, similar preferences can be detected during the cycling and general outdoor boom of the 1930s. Temperance cycling clubs were commonplace, including five in the Tyneside area alone in the 1900s: Jarrow Grange Temperance CC, Jarrow Loyal Temperance CC, Hebburn Temperance CC, Lily Temperance CC of New Hartley Colliery, and Wallsend Temperance CC. Brierfield Temperance CC in Lancashire, had a 'membership ... confined to total abstainers'.[20]

The early cycling boom of the 1890s was certainly partly dependent on the adoption of the pastime by the upper echelons of society, through which it also gained a measure of social acceptance. However, the order and formal discipline with which the plethora of cycling clubs were imbued stemmed from their dominant middle-class social basis. Each club run was controlled by a club captain, a sub-captain, and a bugler who conveyed the captain's instructions to what were often extremely large groups. Neat uniform was *de rigueur* for these officers. The clubs did in many ways serve as an energetic outdoor extension of ordered Victorian middle-class etiquette, and their popularity hinged around this important social function, but they also contained within them the nucleus of the self-motivated, independent, country-loving cyclists whose interests and ethos gave impetus to the twentieth-century outdoor movement. By 1900 cycling had become overwhelmingly a recreation for the less well off: 'Cycling became associated with the lower middle class and working class – and it still is.' [21] C. E. B. Russell's account of the leisure activities of young working-class men in Edwardian Manchester presents further evidence of the increasing use of the bicycle by clerical and manual workers, as a means to pleasant, but energetic recreation, away from the urban environment: 'Numbers of working class lads possess bicycles, and regularly make use of them on Saturday afternoons.' [22]

One of the more significant contributions to the first popular cycling boom came from the socialist Clarion clubs, whose influence on the construction of an outdoor movement was disproportionate to their numerical strength. The CCCs formed the largest and the most active element of a general movement, which was formed in 1894 as a recreation-based, but politically motivated offshoot of the *Clarion* newspaper, established by Robert Blatchford in 1891 as an alternative socialist platform. As one of the main disseminators of a brand of socialist philosophy that rejected the ugliness of industrial capitalism, Blatchford was less an original thinker than an interpreter for popular consumption of the often romantic and Utopian visions of Ruskin and, especially, William Morris. This interpretive proselytizing role of *Clarion*, and the recreation-based publications which it spawned, should not be underestimated in attracting a wider audience to the otherwise esoteric intellectual presentation of anti-capitalist solutions to the intrinsic problems of the prevailing system. A major function of the CCCs was to carry the message to the wider community.

Although the guiding principles of the Clarion movement, exemplified by the fellowship of cyclists, were often scorned by many people with apparently similar sets of beliefs, they in many ways typified the general philosophy underlying the growth of a movement. Despite the prevailing aversion to, and fear of, the promotion of socialist doctrine, much of the activity organized by the CCCs succeeded in establishing their popularity as the archetypal expression of cordial and benign outdoor fellowship, pursuing the underlying objective of a fairer society. The ethical input of the Clarion cycling fraternity into the ideology of the broader outdoor movement during the crucial period in its development around the turn of the century was based on a version of nonconformist dissent, which challenged the inherent conservatism and cant of institutionalized convention. Escape from the town and the increasing artificiality of urban life, and a love of the countryside and the revitalizing properties of nature, have been persistently common themes. There was a strong strain of nostalgia for idealized aspects of an earlier age, but it remained consistent with the retrospective radical creed which reconciled conservative references with the generally reformist and improving objectives. The ideology of the Clarion cycling fellowship had its roots in a desire to enrich an impoverished popular culture that was more and more the victim of capitalist commercial exploitation. The CCCs espoused a creed that saw human fulfilment through leisure as an achievable proposition, in what *Justice* referred to as the 'revolutionary use of joyfulness'.[23] The appeal of the natural environment, simplicity and good fellowship were important dimensions to a vision of a better future. It was not, however, an ideology which constituted a dogmatic or truly formal creed, but it offered an open and flexible alternative, which absorbed a set of loosely interrelated ideas and interests.

It was the *Clarion* message that first stimulated Tom Groom and six fellow Birmingham socialists to initiate the parent CCC at a national level, as well as its regional offspring. Groom had been an early member of the SDF, who later joined the Fabians and became one of the first members of the ILP. At an inaugural meeting on 26 February 1894 the seven men from Birmingham founded the Birmingham Socialist CC, which, as a result of a common interest in the Clarion movement, became the Clarion Cycling Club on 7 March 1894. The Clarion cycling philosophy, which combined communion with nature with fellowship in the pursuit of socialism, was outlined in a *Clarion* report by a Birmingham member in 1894 on a run to Rugeley to meet the newly formed Hanley CCC: '... bringing us into touch with green fields and blue skies, it also enables us to fraternise with Clarionettes of other towns'.[24] This correspondent proceeded to encourage the proselytizing role of the clubs, demonstrating that the much publicized evangelical *raison d'être* of the CCCs often only came as an afterthought to an association of cyclists for whom the new doctrine obviously had differing degrees of attraction: 'How about a cycling corps of Clarion Scouts. A pocketful of leaflets and an extra copy or two of the Clarion carefully left at different stopping places may have good results.'[25] In the same edition of *Clarion*, 'Swiftsure' suggested that Manchester ILP Wheelers should change their name to Clarion Wheelers. It was a change that created the strongest and most active CCC, achieving a membership of 150 as early as 1895, and 300 by the end of 1897. As Clarion cycling burgeoned during the period up to the end of the century, Lancashire and north Cheshire proved to be the key areas. From the huge following in the Manchester district, to the CCCs in smaller towns such as Hyde, Farnworth, Horwich, Tyldesley, and Newton-le-Willows, a socialist cycling movement gained momentum amongst the working populations of the mill towns and other industrial and commercial communities that lay in close proximity to the fresh air and freedom of some exhilarating open country. Nelson CCC attracted more than 100 people to its December social in 1897, and in the same year Bolton CCC, which had 'every prospect of being the largest cycling club in Bolton', had a membership of 145.[26] In July of the following year the Bolton club's picnic at Anglezarke attracted 150 people. The formation of the Manchester Union of CCCs in 1903 affiliated 19 sections from Macclesfield to Bolton.

The appeal of the CCCs was far from confined to the urban areas of north-west England. The number of clubs rose steadily 'from Edinborough [sic] to Plymouth, and from Hull to Bristol'[27] during 1897, the year in which the early popularity of cycling peaked, and as the general socialist movement became more established before being diluted and further factionalized. Bradford claimed 112 members and the membership of the Nottingham CCC rose from 40 to 140 in the two years of its existence. By the end of 1897, the national total of Clarion cyclists topped the 2,000 mark, representing 75 clubs from places as diverse as Gloucester, Glasgow, Keighley, Newport, Farsley (Yorkshire), and Newcastle. Of these, only Coventry failed to increase its membership during 1897. In August of that year *Clarion* claimed that: 'It would be difficult to tour around England or Wales to-day without dropping on to a Clarion cyclist.'[28] Although the general cycling vogue then began to wane, membership of the CCCs continued to grow. The number of clubs increased annually during the 1900s, to 120 in 1905, 182 in 1908, 230 by the end of 1909, leading to the 1913 zenith, when overall CCC membership peaked at something over 8,000; by 1915 the movement had declined to 5,000 cyclists in 150 clubs. It was the end of the first and most important period of the Clarion cycling phenomenon. During the 1930's response to unemployment, bad conditions, and the rise of fascism in Europe, the national CCC blossomed again, with membership rising to 7,000 in 1936 on the back of the interwar leisure boom.

In terms of late-Victorian and Edwardian popular recreational and culture-based political movements, the Clarion was dwarfed inevitably by the Primrose League. As Martin Pugh demonstrates, 'the late

Victorian cycling boom encompassed more than hardy Fabians and Clarion Cycling Clubs'.[29] The Primrose League Cycling Corps was particularly popular amongst young women, who were afforded the opportunity of participating in a fashionable pastime, free from a fear of molestation; these did not generally include the more emancipated women, who adopted rational dress. There were certainly marked similarities between Clarion and Primrose League calendars, although the socialist cycling clubs tended towards the more serious and intellectually stimulating type of activity. *Clarion* responded to the growth of the cycling wing of the Tory popular propaganda machine by urging its followers to greater efforts. The CCCs' outdoor philosophy represented something more than intellectually-undemanding popular politics garnished with social events; it developed beyond mere social fun to generate the popular rural meets and camps. The unifying fellowship, which was consolidated at these events, was expressed by a Rochdale Clarionette in *Clarion Cyclists' Journal* in 1896: 'The common happiness of our kinship with nature brings us nearer to a common sense of humanity ... Closeness to nature leads to nearness to man, to an intimate pervasive consciousness of human fraternity.'[30]

The main activities on the CCCs' itineraries were fully in accordance with a contribution to the generation of an outdoor movement, although there was also a tendency towards some of the more marginal, unconventional activities, which contributed to the sometimes eccentric admixture with which contemporary radical movements on the left of the political spectrum were flavoured. R. C. K. Ensor described the diverse mishmash of ideals and interests that influenced the nature of British socialism during the formative years of the Clarion movement: '... cycling, literature, music, arts and crafts, rational dress, feminism, vegetarianism, and back-to-the-land – all gaily jostling one another in a generous and utopian atmosphere of socialist enthusiasm'.[31] Reporting a cycling 'pilgrimage to Epping' to *King of the Road* readers in 1897, J. Cartmel described one of the participants, Jobson, in a presumably sarcastic vein, as 'an Anarchist, member of the Smoke-abatement Society, member of the Expeditious Burial Society, member of the Balloon Society, member of the Pre-historic Society', as well as a few other societies for good measure.[32] It would, though, be wrong to assume that Clarion cyclists were merely unconventional misfits, combining together in a common love of cycling and contempt for the established order. The main impetus behind the creation of the movement, and its continuing expansion once the initial bicycle boom of the 1890s had receded, was a new breed of cyclist, which sympathized with the fundamental Clarion principles, but was attracted particularly to the movement's energetic outdoor fellowship. A substantial proportion of the membership was drawn from that stratum of society that adopted the tag of respectability, and which had expanded significantly around the turn of the century, particularly in the urban areas, in response to the changing demands of a developing national economy, which depended upon new skills and a rationalized commercial and bureaucratic organization.

By and large, the mentality of touring and leisure cyclists was rooted in the type of social critique presented by the Liberal MP C. F. G. Masterman in *The Condition of England*, published in 1909, which condemned the trivial, commercialized utilization of increasing leisure time, including the vicarious pleasures offered by spectator sports and entertainments. Masterman's conservative organic response articulated the fairly commonly held sentiment that identified the origins of a social and moral degeneration in the general imposition of modern commercial urban existence:

Divorced from the ancient sanities of manual or skilful labour, of exercise in the open air, absorbed for the bulk of his day in crowded offices adding sums or writing letters, each a unit in a crowd which has drifted away from the realities of life in a complex, artificial city civilisation, he comes to see no other universe than this – the rejoicing over hired sportsmen who play before him, the ingenuities of sedantary [*sic*] guessing competitions, the huge frivolity and ignorance of the world of the music hall and the Yellow newspaper.[33]

Many of the late-Victorian and Edwardian cyclists rejected aspects of this commercially dominated world by utilizing the simple technology of the bicycle to seek alternative recreation, as a means of regeneration in healthy and attractive environments. They belonged most commonly to the sort of urban and suburban social stratum whose progressive and independent philosophy articulated a widespread dissatisfaction with the prevailing *modus vivendi*. Masterman's general pessimism was qualified by his recognition of hope for the future being engendered from within this particular class. The current predicament, he believed, was an aberration, rectifiable through a loosening of the hold of the city and its dominant commercial culture:

It probably represents but a passing phase in a progress towards intelligence and a real sense of values. That progress would be aided by any loosening of the city texture by which, and through improved means of transit, something of the large sanities of rural existence could be mingled with the quickness and agility of the town.[34]

The urban clerical and artisanal classes featured prominently in the turn-of-the-century adoption of countryside cycling as a popular alternative open-air pursuit; the respectable working-class Heaton area of Newcastle, with its abundance of churches and dearth of public houses, was the type of place where the activity flourished. The local cycling club was among the most popular in the district, while residents of Heaton also figured prominently among the elected officers of other cycling clubs in Newcastle. The real 'suburbans' of Masterman's social analysis were the lower middle classes, who helped to sustain the cycling boom, and who, 'in conjunction with the artisan class below', were identified by Masterman as 'the healthiest and most hopeful promise for the future of modern England'.[35]

Judith Fincher has highlighted the difficulty of defining accurately the social composition of the Clarion movement, and most of the evidence is based on contemporary impressions.[36] The clerks, the shop assistants and the skilled manual workers of the industrial and commercial centres, who took readily to self-motivated but gregarious pastimes such as cycling, were a product of a structural change in the pattern of employment. Ensor saw the Clarion movement as: 'appealing primarily to the young thinking men and women in the clerk and artisan classes of Lancashire and the West Riding'.[37] Theodore Rothstein's contemporaneous impression of those groups in society who were most attracted to the broad principles of British socialism can also serve as a rough indicator of the social composition of the CCCs:

> It is the better paid artisan, the skilled labourer, the earnest trade unionist, who is decently clad and fed, who enjoys a home and a friendly circle, who knows how to respect himself and be respected by others, who constitutes the really progressive element in every community.[38]

This was an analysis that also stressed a consciousness of rights and duties. The Ensor and Rothstein models are, of course, generalized and impressionistic, but they do concur with the dominant trend in the membership of CCCs. A regular *Clarion* cycling columnist, Frederick Leeming, was himself a clerk, while one of the irregular freelance contributors, the Scots Mancunian Clarion activist Charles Reekie from Ancoats, was a railway clerk. A poem composed by 'Saga Monger' for *King of the Road* appealed to the young man, and suggested what drove him to cycle in the country during leisure time:

> I'm a junior city clerk,
> I scribble and scratch all day,
> In an office dingy and dark,
> At the usual rate of pay.[39]

For many of the numerous commercial clerks of Manchester and Liverpool, membership of a CCC afforded the opportunity to combine an exhilarating and sociable outdoor pastime with the radical political activism through which many of them responded against their poor working conditions and low pay and status.[40] This reputation was confirmed in a Clarion pamphlet written by H. H. Elvin, a socialist clerk, who also stressed their potential power in the contemporary economy: '... wherever we go, we are sure to find a clerk in the van of the movement. The key to the industrial world is in our hands. If we decided to throw down our pens and walk out of the office, industry would be paralysed.'[41]

Other typical rank-and-file Clarionettes were mentioned in the movement's press: the first issue of *King of the Road* described Widgerson, a Clarion cyclist who worked in a draper's shop, and who joined CCC runs in order to escape into the countryside; James Pybus, a Stretford (Manchester) metal-planer was mentioned in *Clarion* in 1897. The Clarionettes were unified by a prevailing ethos and by a shared attitude to changing leisure patterns. Their guiding principles referred back to an earlier working-class autodidactic tradition, which had been effectively marginalized by a remoulding of popular culture as part of a consolidated capitalist economic base.

In contrasting the rural idyll with the dominance of overpowering commerce, Clarion cycling writers were pursuing a theme common to the generation of the wider nascent cycling movement. A sentimental verse contained in *King of the Road* in 1897 was typical of a prolific, and unfortunately hackneyed genre:

> A fig for the wealth of a swelt'ring town,
> Where merchants chaffer and deal.
> Give me cool glades with cool moss grown,
> Where streamlet murmurs o'er pebble and stone,
> And the hum of my steed of steel.[42]

However, the messages that were frequently contained in such romantic descriptive writings confirmed the constancy of the political edge which differentiated the Clarionettes from the main body of touring and leisure cyclists. This ideological *gravitas* equips the Clarion cyclists with a more readily discernible identity as a campaigning element in the growth of the outdoor movement. The politics were founded on the obvious general objective of promoting the cause of socialism, but focused also on a number of issues germane to the common interests of outdoor people. There was, for example, the sustained attack on the landed hierarchy, which was a natural ramification of diametrically opposed interests. To the Clarion cyclist, who was escaping from industry and commerce into a countryside dominated by the will of the landowners, socialist opposition to both capitalism and feudalism seemed a particularly felicitous creed. The autocratic parochial power of the landed proprietors was indicated, for instance, in a touring report in *Clarion Cyclists' Journal*, complaining of the Duke of Beaufort's exaction of tolls from scenic viewpoints in the Wye Valley. The correspondent also stressed the rejuvenating properties of the cycle tour: 'The memory of that scene, and of many others I have viewed in my cycling perigrinations, will long remain with me, to lighten the burden of monotony in these dreary Lancashire towns.'[43] Another Lancastrian, who called himself 'Old Chappie', interjected into his description of a cycling tour in Wales his own criticism of the profit-motivated effects of unbridled capitalism. He was reacting to the despoliation by lead-mining of a fine natural landscape around Cwmystwyth on the mountain road from Devil's Bridge to Rhayader in the hills of mid-Wales: 'This eyesore is the public's share of the profits, like the smoke from our mill chimneys and the fumes from our chemical works of some of our Lancashire towns.'[44] The Clarion cycling fellowship's critique of capitalism, distaste at pollution and sympathy with nature contributed to the construction of a conservationist strand in the countryside campaigning function of the outdoor movement.

Romantic and practical campaigning dimensions to the Clarion cycling ethos combined to produce a form of activism that was stimulated by an absorption of humane and sympathetic principles. Empathy with the minority cause found expression in *Clarion*'s 'Cycling Notes', which expounded on campaigning issues ranging from the caging of birds to the eviction of gypsies. These were, of course, obvious areas of sympathy for active lovers of natural history and the freedom of the open air. Regular columnist Haydon Perry adopted a particular case, in which gypsies were evicted from Epping Forest by police, forest-keepers, and local residents. Perry shrewdly identified faults in gypsies, before pointing out that they were far from being alone in their imperfection. Common ground was identified with the open-air recreationist: 'Our dusky friend is not only picturesque, which any villain may be; he is a kind and open-hearted fellow, and not seldom a poet and naturalist to boot ... [S]hould not every cyclist who is a lover of nature be sorry for a gipsy's misfortune.'[45] The writer was picking up a Bohemian thread in the contemporary reaction against the bonds of a restrictive conventionality, which was itself a social manifestation of a smoothly functioning capitalist economy, and therefore an appropriate focus for the critical attention of the Clarion movement. The eclectic sympathies expressed by members of the Clarion clubs suggest a measure of romantic *naïveté*, but also an optimistic humaneness. As a fashionable symbol of freedom and of harmonious communion with nature, the gypsy was the subject for the sort of idealization that was epitomized in the work of George Borrow, and which gave succour to those who in some measure clung to a romantic, Arcadian vision of the countryside.[46] The majority of Clarion cyclists may not have subscribed fully to this form of sentimentality, but the implied underlying values of affinity with nature and hint of alternative living were compatible with characteristic aspects of the movement's model for a better future. A certain degree of sympathy for that mode of living added impetus to such communal events as the CCC camps and summer meets.[47] Several members backed up their interest in natural history and substantial knowledge of flora and fauna with membership of Clarion Field Clubs (CFC).

The Clarion's intermingling of outdoor pursuits was instrumental in the construction of a wider movement. The cyclists also enjoyed walks and rambles, especially during the winter months when many roads would be either snow- and ice-bound or impassable quagmires, at a time when most country roads consisted of loosely bound aggregates of rolled stone, gravel, sand and dirt. For CCC members who did not succumb wholly to the temptations of the social season, when the majority of cycling clubs embarked on their winter programmes of dinners, dances, concerts and 'smokers', walking presented an obvious alternative to the bicycle. Some rambles were organized in collaboration with the outdoor activities of other Clarion clubs, such as the rural walks in Yorkshire in conjunction with the vocal unions, described in *Clarion* by Montague Blatchford ('Mont Blong'). In 1901 Clarionettes were among the Lancashire and Yorkshire socialists who walked in bad weather in the vicinity of Hardcastle Crags with 'Mont Blong', 'a Pantheist by nature', who commented on 'a couple of hundred well-behaved, happy people'.[48] The cyclists' camp itineraries also included rambles. Among a range of activities available at the summer camp of 1896, for example, was 'a programme of rambles and rides'.[49] *Clarion* commented in September 1897 on the idea of 'winter rambling from the station to the clubhouse' as an alternative to cycling, and in the same issue reported that 'Saturday afternoon rambles are being organized by some of the clubs'.[50] During the same year the Cheadle and District CCC from north Cheshire combined the two activities by cycling to the Peak District and climbing Kinder Scout on foot.

Whether on foot or by bicycle, healthy exercise in pursuit of fresh air and freedom has been a common objective that has united the diverse elements within the the outdoor movement. The efficacious benefits of open-air leisure activities were at least as important to the main body of CCC membership as were the initial political function of their organization, or the varied social and educational attractions. The purely physical benefits were stressed at an early stage by

'Swiftsure' in his 'Cycling Notes': 'Yet it's wonderful what benefit cycling is to one's health. Whether one is employed at the bench or the desk.'[51] This physical aspect remained largely free of any of the puritanical inferences with which it is often associated. These open-air recreationists were responding positively to what Masterman described simplistically as a 'secular change ... from the life of the fields to the life of the city'.[52] They sought renewal in a natural environment with which the majority had lost touch, seemingly irreparably. However, despite the often dogmatic rhetoric uttered by the Clarion leadership at all levels, the average CCC member fitted equally uncomfortably into the model defined by the histrionic Victor Grayson, who might have been indulging in self-parody:

> ... the Clarionette with red tie, flannel shirt, and bicycle, who has been moved to continuous anger by the vision of trampled women and starving children in the cities of poverty. Such men see the world transfigured in the light of a great crusade. They are convinced that by demonstration and violence to-day, or (at latest) to-morrow, 'the people' will rise in their millions and their might, pluck down the oppressors who are 'sucking their blood', and inaugurate the golden age of the Socialist millennium.[53]

The main body of Clarion cyclists did maintain strong ideals with a varying degree of intensity, and contributed conscientiously to the struggle for a better future in response to the all too common evidence of social injustice, but bloody revolutionaries they were not. Their 'golden age' was a progressive goal, but was as much rooted in ideas of pre-capitalist Arcadia as it was the product of visions of a revolutionary 'millennium'.

The problem for Robert Blatchford, and other prophets of utopia, such as John Trevor, was that in trying to attract a mass following to their cultural and ethical alternatives they could never compete with either the more entrenched or the newer and larger cultural forces. In a critique of popular cultural poverty which was rooted in Morris, the ideologues of the Clarion movement were addressing their appeal to paragons of the tradition of self-improvement. Theirs was an attractive ideal to many, and yet only appealing to a minority constituency. Notwithstanding the emphasis on recreation *en route* to a socialist commonwealth, the all-pervading mistrust of an ideologically debilitating commercialized culture situated the left's attempts to construct an alternative social model in the liberal paternalist tradition. The philanthropic activity of the Clarion clubs stemmed from the pragmatic objective of gaining converts and positive publicity, but bore a close resemblance to the existing improving and moralizing message, propounded by establishment rational recreationists, which alienated a majority of working people. While Robert Blatchford was invoking images of 'Merrie England' and the 'cakes and ale' tradition of urban Lancashire,[54] other elements of the Clarion movement sought to raise the moral and intellectual awareness of the workers by offering counter-attractions that were consistent with the elevating intentions of the mainstream of nascent British socialism. However, Blatchford's own philosophy was inconsistent, often displaying a more puritanical facet.[55] In a recent work, Chris Waters illustrates some of the ideological dilemmas which confronted the early socialists.[56]

The philanthropic dimension to the Clarion cycling movement found practical expression in a hire-purchase scheme that made bicycles more easily available to poorer members. Bicycles were relatively expensive items, beyond the means of many working people, although the second-hand cast-offs from the initial cycling craze would have widened the market. Charles Booth commented on the availability of cycles to some working-class Londoners through a system of hire purchase.[57] The original financial backers of the Clarion project were two prosperous stalwarts of the movement in the Manchester area, J. D. Sutcliffe and William Ranstead. A scheme to assist any Clarionette who could not afford the necessary initial investment was first mooted by 'Swiftsure' in *Clarion* in 1894, when he advocated a '... system of purchasing cycles by the aid of the hire system'.[58] The suggested figure of five shillings (25p) per week still represented a heavy demand on the clerk's or skilled worker's weekly wage, which averaged in the region of twenty-five shillings (£1. 25), and suggests a general propensity to thrift and temperance. In September 1894, 'Swiftsure' again promoted the system of hire purchase 'to give the poor the opportunity', and suggested that '... men at a Labour Club or works form a club and pay subscriptions to buy second hand bikes – then as funds build up purchase new ones'.[59] The scheme was administered by Ranstead at his Gandy Belt Works at Seacombe in Cheshire, to where contributions to the fund were sent. The Clarion-affiliated journal, *Scout*, joined in the effort to raise funds, and wrote of the need to buy in quantity and to supply women's machines: 'Will the Clarion cyclist who lent the National Committee £200 increase his offer to £2,000 or £2,000,000.'[60] In 1897 Ranstead and Sutcliffe contributed £100 and £200 respectively to supply bicycles which were to be made available through a hire-purchase scheme. Forty machines were initially provided for the clubs in the region, but the weight of applications meant that an additional supply had to be bought. This original stock made up the solid foundation for what *King of the Road* called 'The New Clarion Scheme' to make bicycles available on easy terms; the periodical reported that 'the Clarion Board is prepared to finance the scheme, and on a much larger scale', and a plan was devised to 'supply one hundred machines for a start'.[61]

Although they had a fundamental mistrust of the motives of contemporary philanthropic institutions, the cyclists in the vanguard of the Clarion movement were themselves involved regularly in charitable action. Such activity was devised as an important dimension to socialist evangelism. Local CCCs were always strongly represented and extremely active in 'Cycling Charity Parades', such as those at Liverpool and on the Manchester racecourse, which became a feature of the cycling boom, and which gained prestige and positive publicity for the Clarion clubs. The central concern was with the condition of children in urban slums. This was the 'Cinderella' work, founded on three primary practical objectives: firstly, catching them young, and thereby inculcating malleable recruits to the socialist cause; secondly, attracting to the movement a number of people who were impressed by the good work – 'Our Cinderella work is bound to attract sympathisers'; [62] and thirdly, consistent with the Clarion cyclists' belief in the efficacy of exercise and fresh air, the 'Cinderella' activities aimed specifically at offering such opportunities to the children, and enabling them to experience the joys of nature, giving a practical expression to the underlying Clarion doctrine, which promoted healthy recreation as an aid to individual fulfilment and wider social improvement. Various schemes emerged from the original Clarion 'Cinderella' work. The Nottingham section helped the children of men affected by a lock-out, while the Potteries cyclists hired a large room for a party given for 120 children. The emphasis was on trips into the countryside, including visits to Clarion camps: 'Sixty-one children from the slums of Manchester and Salford were taken in sections of ten ... for four days into the beautiful country.' [63]

The Clarion literature indicates clearly that cycling itself and related social activities were the abiding obsession, and that the message of socialism, although conscientiously disseminated, was often peripheral. In 1897 *Clarion Cyclists' Journal*, acclaiming their organization as a national institution 'from the Surrey Downs to Edinboro's [*sic*] Castle Rock', suggested what the Clarion cyclist represented:

In politics he will stand for good roads and plenty of 'em; in religion he is for such cycles as will give rise to the least suffering; his general policy is 'keep your own side', and while endeavouring to bring the Clarion Cycling Clubs into closer communication with each other, he will minister to the taste of the student, the lover of the beautiful, the tourist, the social reformer, and all those seeking good fellowship.[64]

This was a singular and idiosyncratic assessment of Clarion priorities, but is indicative of why the movement was subject to the charge that it was trivializing socialism and thereby contributing to a dangerous measure of dilution and resultant weakness. However, to the eclectic and apparently inconsistent Blatchford and his allies the important thing was to broaden the appeal, and thus prevent socialism from stagnating within the confines of a narrow intellectual caucus. In its ideal form, Clarion was to be of the people, for the people, with everyone enjoying a good time, while creating the new commonwealth. The business of spreading the 'New Gospel'[65] was incorporated into the pursuit of a whole range of broadly rational pleasures. The Clarion approach to socialism was summed up by James Bartley, writing in *Clarion* in 1901. The open-air activities of the CCCs fitted comfortably within the precepts of this model:

> Socialism, or a knowledge of Socialism, will not be brought about solely by learned treatises on 'economic rent', or by the most efficient expositions of 'theories of value', whether Marxian or Jevonian ... [T]here are thousands who can be touched by the friendly glance, the handshake, the cheery greeting, the genial smile. These are more potent 'saviours of society' than the political economists, and the Fellowship is more likely to prove a more powerful instrument for creating converts than the most eloquent orator who ever thumped a table or hammered a tub.[66]

The message which the Clarionettes promulgated actively represented an essential component in the struggle to mould a new order, in which there would be equal opportunity for everyone to work together towards a brighter and healthier world where creativity and broadly educational pursuits would give some meaning to leisure. The CCCs were prominent in the promotion of secular models for social elevation through cultural regeneration. Their self-reliance and optimistic cooperation offered counter-attractions to commercialism and the nascent leisure industry. Despite the obvious concordance with the goals of traditional social reformers, this was, nonetheless, a *sui generis* creed, founded on the notion that each individual could transform himself if given sufficient opportunity, and thus effectively rejecting the condescending attitudes of establishment moralizers, although a more sympathetic response to philanthropy is evident in *Clarion* than in more stridently political organs such as *Justice*, which fronted the SDF's condemnation of philanthropists.

What was significantly absent from the message that the CCCs themselves disseminated was the puritan dimension which British socialism absorbed from its strong Christian nonconformist influences. The espousal of a freer and more liberal interpretation of underlying principles widened the existing gulf between the Clarion movement and their more serious-minded and dogmatic socialist comrades over tactical and ideological differences. At the heart of the dispute was a clash of personalities between Clarionettes and supposedly puritanical ILP members, who were exemplified by the dour and painstakingly conscientious Keir Hardie. The conflict has, however, been overstated. There was much common membership of ILP and CCC, while open collaboration and mutual interest were features of the relationship, especially during the earlier and most optimistically idealistic years of Clarion cycling.[67] For example, Keir Hardie himself was present at the second of the annual camps which the CCC organized as a practical focus for the aim of energetic open-air fellowship. He was received warmly by the campers with hearty greetings. In addition, the SDF's supposedly dogmatic politicking was qualified regularly in the pages of *Justice*, for instance in an article entitled *Socialism and Sport* in 1891: 'That a love of sport is consistent with and necessary to the intellectual and moral development of human character I firmly believe.'[68] The SDF also formed their own cycling corps in 1896, attending such events as the cyclists' parade in conjunction with the International Socialist Congress Sunday demonstration on 26 July 1896. The objectives of the SDF corps were strictly propagandist, although they did combine pleasure with the essential business, for example on a run from London to Tonbridge in August 1896.

Reports from local CCC sections highlight the strong amiable links with more exclusively political organizations. Bolton CCC was founded at the West Ward ILP clubroom in Prince Street in February 1896 – this recently resurrected CCC is still based at the Wood Street headquarters of the Bolton Socialist Party and Club. Soon after its inception, Manchester CCC planned its headquarters in conjunction with Elvington Street ILP, South Manchester ILP, and Moss Side Socialist Society, as well as the local Labour Church, while the Oldham section moved its HQ to the local Socialist Club in 1899. The venue chosen for the Scottish Clarion meet in the summer of 1899 was Dunfermline Socialist Society and Cooperative Hall. Section reports which the CCCs sent to the Clarion press stressed the attendance of members at ILP meetings. In September 1897, *Clarion* reported on the large numbers of CCC members who attended meetings of the TUC, the Labour Church, the ILP, School Boards and 'Cinderella' committees. In July 1897 the proceeds of a 'smoker' organized by West Bromwich CCC went into local ILP branch funds. ILP fund-raising was in fact a regular feature of the activities of the CCCs. Although the connection between associations sharing the same constituency in the wider struggle to introduce socialist solutions was a natural one, it was the strongly politically motivated stalwarts of the clubs who really established and maintained the links with political associations.

The localized complexities and nuances which helped to shape the emergence of British socialism undermine any facile general perceptions of the ILP and the SDF as either wholly dry and dogmatic, or as totally sceptical of the function of leisure activities as part of the social basis of a movement that was courting more popular appeal. There is a certain irony in the fact that by the early years of the twentieth century some Clarion members were coming to view the specifically political associations as being themselves the diluters of socialism, with particular reference to the ILP's increasing collaboration with the gradualist vein of left-wing politics in the pragmatic pursuit of labour representation. It was an issue which triggered the resignation from Halifax ILP of Montague Blatchford, the *Clarion* journalist, and energetic but headstrong CCC member. In 1893, in an article concerned with the necessity of attracting the young, *Justice* called for 'more joy and fun – we are too serious'.[69] The *Blackburn Labour Journal*, voice of the local ILP, pursued the same theme, and also retained a countryside and nature correspondent.

Although the failure of the Labour Churches, and consequently their politically aware interpretation of the Christian creed, has been partly attributed to the success of the CCCs,[70] the optimistic and energetic missionaries on bicycles were in fact disseminating a doctrine whose language and imagery were those of Christian revolutionaries, in keeping with their widespread adoption of the 'Religion of Socialism':[71]

> Then, behold, there arose certain young men who possessed bicycles, and they said to the bearer of the message: 'Lo, behold, here we are! Strong, healthy, young, energetic, and intelligent! We will take the Message of Peace to the uttermost parts of the country, and, that the messengers shall be identified with the message, we will call our organizations Clarion cycling clubs.' [72]

Despite the apparent divergence from both the Labour Church and other elements in early British socialism, the Clarion movement shared with them a common fundamental ethos, which was firmly grounded on undogmatic and non-sectarian nonconformist Christianity. The religious connection was never far from the surface during the development of the CCCs, but it was a particular interpretation of Christian principles, which rejected the conventions and constraints of mainstream doctrine and practice. The morality expressed in the columns of *Clarion* and its associated cycling journals was not only a guiding light for Clarionettes, but also formed an integral part of the message which CCC propagandists carried on their forays into the rural districts.

It gave ethical direction to their cooperative fellowship: 'Every man on this earth is more or less his brother's keeper. No man is born or can live for himself alone. The man who is strong is harnessed morally to the one who is weak, and should take his share of the weak one's burden of life.'[73] To many secular socialists, such sentiments were fully commensurate with the duties inherent in a humanist doctrine, but secularism held only limited appeal to the adherents to the philosophy of the Clarion movement. A nonconformist connection was especially apposite in a movement which, in effect, was seeking to fill a similar role to community churches and chapels, in providing an ethical base for recreational activity. It depended on the adoption of a form of socialism which continued to express deep-seated traditions of local nonconformist religious culture. That continuity was typified in the idealistic, humanitarian creed which underpinned the formation of the flourishing CCCs of the Lancashire industrial towns, and in the language and imagery through which it was sustained. Robert Blatchford certainly saw the Clarion movement in terms of religious conversion, referring, for example, to 'The New Religion'[74] in 1892, in one of the widely circulated pamphlets published by Clarion press, which sold at 1d. each, rising to 1½d. by 1904, and which included titles appropriate to a countryside-orientated and religiously influenced socialist organization: for instance, 'Land Lessons for Town Folk', 'Land Nationalisation', 'Land, Labour, and Liberty', and 'Christian Socialism; Practical Christianity'. Blatchford's friend and biographer, N. A. Lyons, stressed the irreverential aspect of that creed:

> ... no other religion has dared like Socialism, to argue with police inspectors and to laugh at kings ... The priest says: 'Order yourself humbly and reverently towards your betters; be contented; be sober; be industrious; never hit back.' Socialism says: 'Work, laugh, love, and don't forget the sparrows.'[75]

In the promotion of his 'new religion', Blatchford was particularly scathing of the establishment version:

> This is a Christian country. What would Christ think of Park Lane, and the slums, and the hooligans? What would He think of the Stock Exchange, and the Merchant Hall, and the racecourse? What would He think of our national ideals? What would He think of the House of Peers, and the Bench of Bishops, and the Yellow Press? ... you are Christian in name, but I discern little of Christ in your ideals, or your daily lives. You are a mercenary, self-indulgent, frivolous, boastful, blood-guilty mob of heathen. I like you very much, but that is what you are like.[76]

The diatribe against established values was typical of Blatchford's right-eous hyperbole, although the underlying sentiments certainly appealed to adherents of his version of socialism who were disaffected by much of what professed to be Christianity. The founder of the Clarion movement was also, however, wholly inconsistent in his doctrine. Claims made in 1904 in *God and My Neighbour*, which combined vitriolic criticism of the *status quo* and an exposition of his own professed humanist philosophy, appear ludicrous in the light of his increasing espousal of nationalist and imperialist notions: 'Rightly or wrongly, I am opposed to Imperialism, Militarism, and conquest. Rightly or wrongly, I am for universal brotherhood and universal freedom.' This was a creed that he stressed more than once: 'My Christian friends, I am a Socialist, and as such believe in, and work for, universal freedom, and universal brotherhood, and universal peace.'[77] Despite these asser-tions, Blatchford had, in fact, fallen in with the cause of the imperialists during the South African war, triggering an ILP boycott of *Clarion* publications. He advocated vigorously the arms race with Germany, and his wholehearted support for the First World War was to include addresses to recruiting meetings. Clarion and social democratic cyclists were as susceptible as anyone to the inculcation of the imperial idea which accompanied an increasingly competitive period of European colonial expansion and consolidation. The sentiments of 'Merrie Eng-land' were easily translated into the idea of 'England for the English'. The corrosion of high ideals by nationalism and jingoism largely depended on the collective paranoia which was sustained by blanket propaganda. Blatchford's apostasy both undermined his own movement and gave the impression of a buffoon.

Love of native country was, of course, an important motivation to the formation of an outdoor movement, and those sentiments are easily perverted into forms of nationalism which can be either bellicose or pacific, depending on prevailing circumstances. The strange ideology of Robert Blatchford cannot be taken as an accurate reflection of the predominant philosophy of the CCCs, although he remained a major influence on grass-roots membership. The national CCC founder, and lifelong organizer and campaigner, Tom Groom, remained a strong advocate of a creed of cooperation and pacifism, which helped to sustain non-chauvinistic internationalism as a constant factor in CCC ideology. Groom attended international socialist sports events, such as that at Ghent in 1913, and was instrumental in the setting up of the Interna-tional Socialist Sports Association, with its slogan of 'Peace through Sport', which became the British Workers' Sports Association (BWSA) in 1923. The BWSA was taken over by the Communist Party in 1928 and renamed the British Workers' Sports Federation (BWSF). In the 1930s Groom helped to re-form the overwhelmingly Clarion cyclist-

dominated BWSA, which was accused by the BWSF of being bourgeois.[78]

At the local level the core ideology of the CCCs depended upon a
transformation of sound and consistent, fundamentally Christian principles into a humanist doctrine. It was a creed that depended heavily
on the unifying focus of the Labour Church, which John Trevor had
founded in Manchester in 1891, as a response to frustration with his
own impotence in attempting to break the stranglehold of the cant and
conservatism which gripped established Christian religion, and to offer
guiding principles with which the majority of working people could
identify.[79] The idea spread throughout the urban areas of the country
in the 1890s as an affirmation of the Christian characteristics of British
socialism. In most areas it was a short-lived phenomenon, but proved
more durable in the industrial communities of Lancashire and the West
Riding; it is no coincidence that these were the heartlands of Clarion
cycling – CCC members maintained close ties with the Labour Church.
The inaugural meeting of Birmingham CCC was held at the Bond
Street Labour Church, a former Methodist chapel, setting the agenda
for a continuing collaboration based on a common ethos. The Potteries
CCC participated in events organized by Hanley Labour Church, such
as their 'Religion and Intellect Meeting' in April 1895. From 1896
Manchester Clarion cyclists used the Labour Church in Booth Street
East. *King of the Road* reported on Bradford CCC's 'connection with
Bradford Labour Church'.[80] In November 1897, for example, the Bradford Clarionettes 'took part in two parades in connection with the
Bradford Labour Church and provided speakers'.[81] During the same
month the CCC in Nottingham threw in its lot with the local Labour
Church. Elsewhere, many individuals within the Clarion movement,
including some of the cyclists, were also members of Labour Churches,
underlining the opposition to the prevailing orthodoxy and its frequent
hypocrisy: 'There is a class of professed Christians who seem at times
to be every thing that Christ was not. He taught tolerance, love, and
pity. They practice bigotry, hatred and persecution.'[82]

More tolerant interpretations of the Christian gospel underpinned
the cycling movement's regularly recurring conflict with beleaguered
conventions of the establishment and its institutions. Many of the
dominant values were accepted, but only as far as the point where they
began to interfere with reasonable leisure pursuits. John Lowerson has
seen the corruption of the Victorian Sunday by the early cycling craze
in terms of 'middle-class apostasy'.[83] The challenge to the more extreme
socially imposed restrictions was most prominently manifested in the
continuing controversy over Sabbath observance. As with the walkers,
the cyclists were keen to make the best use of the only full day away
from work, without challenging fundamental Christian principles. The

Newcastle Daily Chronicle was among those to comment on the increasing use of Sunday: 'Cycling on Sundays is increasing very much in this country.'[84] On one Sunday in 1904 an observer from the Lord's Day Observance Society counted 1,922 cyclists passing through Croydon in a two-hour period. The whole conflict cannot be separated from the wider context of a growing popular rejection of conventional restraint. Legislative prescription was no longer a realistic proposition for the tenacious authoritarian strain in society. The renewed vehemence of the Sabbatarians was partly induced by frustration at an inability to impose legislation such as that which had been applied earlier to undesirable Sunday pursuits like gambling (1845) and Sunday Fairs (1850). Compulsion had become largely displaced by institutionally underpinned social convention, through which persuasion and coercion were combined in defence of the tenets of rigid orthodoxy.[85] A rising demand for freedom, and a greater degree of independent choice, inexorably added weight to the challenge to the *status quo* as part of a larger ideological struggle, fought out at the highest political level. It was the very topicality of the deeper underlying issues which explains the publicity given to the Sabbath debate during the 1890s and 1900s. More than any other group, the turn-of-the-century cyclists transferred a predominantly urban-based conflict to the relatively stagnant hierarchical rural community. Their large-scale intrusion often offended rural sensibilities, and indeed helped to sustain the ever-present tension between town and country, which has been a constant feature of the growth of the outdoor movement.

The growing concern with the preservation of the sanctity of the Sabbath was founded on both ethical and practical motives. Evangelical Sabbatarians sought to combat what they perceived as the sinfulness of any form of Sunday recreation. An important factor in the equation was the partly self-interested motives of many of the clergy, who applied themselves to the crisis of falling church attendances, which belie the supposed importance of organized religion as a dominant institution of contemporary society. Apathy was, most certainly, the major factor. However, the dynamic intellectual climate, which increasingly questioned many of the old certainties and the conventions of the established religions, including restrictive and oppressive forms of Sabbath observance, stimulated the emergence of the secularism, rationalism, and agnosticism that combined to challenge seriously the immutability of existing belief.

During the development of the cycling trend in the formation of an outdoor movement, social-class considerations were transcended by the mutually agreed values and interests that fuelled a conflict with organized religion. It was an extension of what Brian Harrison, in his assessment of 'Religion and Recreation in Nineteenth Century England', has seen in terms of 'culture-conflict' rather than 'class-conflict'.[86] Concern with the consolidation of improving forms of recreation was an integral part of the debate. Healthy open-air pursuits such as cycling contained a measure of ambiguity in their motives, which makes them difficult to categorize in terms such as rational or improving, but the important touchstone is their undoubted foundation on self-dependent and respectable notions of freedom, which served to confirm rather than deny a belief in the spiritual dimension to human nature. What was challenged was the central role of church and chapel attendance.

Lines of a poem printed in *Truth* confirmed the topicality of the issue of Sunday cycling:

> They're complaining from the pulpit, with an energy undue,
> That the craze for Sunday cycling is emptying the pew.[87]

T. C. Smout points to anxiety in the Church of Scotland in the 1890s about the threat posed to church attendance by leisure cycling.[88] Notwithstanding the obvious fact that large numbers of cyclists saw Sunday merely as an opportunity to enjoy their chosen leisure pursuit, accusations of religious apathy or agnosticism need to be weighed against substantial contrary evidence. During the earliest period of the cycling boom, the main platform of the enthusiasts, the BTC (CTC), had 'recommended Sunday cyclists to attend "Divine Worship at least once during the day"',[89] although the challenge to the conventions of the Sabbath never really materialized until the popularity of cycling had expanded more fully. It was also evident that the clergy were themselves split over the issue of the proper function of the Sabbath. In 1902 the Bishop of Manchester cited the invention of the bicycle as a major contributor to the reduction in religious observance. But a significant proportion of the clergy did, of course, subscribe to the belief in beneficent, healthy, open-air recreation, particularly where it encouraged greater appreciation of the wonders of God's world, and a consequent affirmation and strengthening of man's spiritual awareness. Views relating to the spiritual function of nature fuelled the incessant controversy over the pros and cons of Sunday cycling, and even found its way into verse. This poetic proponent of the activity made the telling point that the pastime attracted far more young people away from potentially much more damaging and time-wasting uses of leisure time, while promoting the benefits of health and of physical and mental refreshment to cope with the working week:

> ... doesn't take them from the Church but from the pot-house
> from the street
> As it bears them off rejoicing to the country fresh and sweet.

White-faced office boys it carries to the woods where throstles
    sing

Care-worn city clerks it hurries off to nature's fairest scenes
Flower-decked and trellised hop grounds; babbling brooks and
    village greens.
Round-backed artisans it bears, too, from the small and stuffy
    room

No, it seems by far more likely that the cyclists thus may learn
From the fairest sights of Nature to that Nature's God to turn.
Moved to thought and to reflection by the wonders that they
    see. [90]

The verse is trite and sentimental, but does indicate an important
element in the inevitable clash between increasing demands for reasonable leisure and the formal practice of organized religion.

The issue was expressed ambivalently in comments in the *Newcastle
Daily Chronicle*, whose correspondent witnessed an exodus of cyclists
from Tyneside at Easter 1898: 'Even clergymen are willing to admit
that so long as the religious duties of the day are not neglected cycles
may be ridden with much less offence than is to be found in riding or
driving horses on that day.' [91] The more liberal type of response from
within the theological establishment was firmly rooted in a clerical
propensity for countryside exercise. Such attitudes did, nonetheless,
conform with a particular type of spiritual practice, founded on quietist
and informal traditions of religious observance, which were often
integrated with open-air activities. The Quaker and Unitarian involvement is one such example, contributing to the middle-class
nonconformist dimension of the theological response.

The church parade for cyclists became a popular feature of club
syllabuses. In August 1890 three hundred cyclists attended a church
parade at Weeton near Leeds, where the vicar – himself a cyclist –
spoke in favour of Sunday cycling, provided that religious duties were
not neglected. The following week a church parade at Knotty Ash on
the outskirts of Liverpool attracted members from several cycling clubs.
The vicar again gave his blessing to cycling on Sunday. The converse
position was stated, for example, in the *Halifax Comet* in 1898, in which
the Reverend Todd preached that 'no one ought to cycle on Sunday'. [92]
During a big 'Cyclists' Church Parade' at Blagdon in Northumberland
in May 1898, which was an annual fixture on the Tyneside cyclists'
calendar on the first Sunday in May, the Reverend J. Reynolds Parkin
expressed a more ambiguous attitude, combining guarded approval with
qualified criticism. He praised a 'gathering that represented and ex-

pressed the healthy, joyous life of the body', but issued severe warnings against the neglect of the spirit; the audience were left in no doubt as to the primacy of the spiritual 'higher' over the athletic 'lower aspects of human life'.[93] The Reverend Parkin's speech demonstrated the complexity of the relationship between recreation and national institutions and ideology. He topically connected outdoor exercise with national fitness and the Empire, while simultaneously emphasizing the dominant spiritual aspect of the nature of the men who, in his estimation, had made England great. There was no mistaking the intended message conveyed to the cyclists gathered to hear this nationalistic open-air sermon, with its high-minded appeal to character-building through a form of muscular Christianity that gave precedence to the spiritual dimension.

The fundamentally anti-establishment creed of the CCCs, as well as their emphasis on active recreation, placed them at the forefront of the conflict over Sunday cycling, with *Clarion* taking the lead in the attack on Sabbatarianism: '... sombre and horrible, dark and nameless nightmare of sabbatarian doctrines and those who regard mirth as sinful'.[94] The half-day Saturday afforded insufficient leisure time in which to escape the bonds of the capitalist-imposed time discipline: 'Five and a half days victims of Capital, and the seventh the slaves of cant; one short half day per week is all the time they can spare ...'[95] E. B. Fay ('The Bounder') maintained the attack on the Sabbatarians in his regular *Clarion* column on 'Sabbath Observance'. Clarion movement writers used the issue as an opportunity to attack the establishment generally. *King of the Road* responded to the claim of the Reverend Hugh Price Hughes:

> [Hughes asserts that] '... the young men who spent their Sunday mornings on cycles and evenings at sacred concerts, will never write their names in the history of their nation.' This won't trouble the Sunday cyclist much. The moral character of many of those whose names loom large in the text books of history might have been cleaner if they had been erased a little by the rubber of the wheel.[96]

The exponents of Utopian socialism easily reconciled their roots in nonconformist dissent with the political dimension that gave the Clarion cyclists their most visible role as socialist evangelists. *Clarion* and its associated cycling press regularly reminded the membership of the importance of spreading the word. The inflated language and the dominant symbols topically combined religious and military images. *Clarion Cyclists' Journal* called for a renewed effort leading up to the municipal elections of 1896: 'In these elections our members as a Clarion cyclist force, fresh from camp life, can do splendid work. A band of such cyclists animated by the socialist spirit and energetically engaged in electioneering becomes a great arm of power. To Arms, then, Clarion cyclists.'[97] Despite the high profile of the cycling corps, the political activism of the leadership was rarely matched within the rank and file of the fellowship, for whom the social side offered the main attractions. In 1901 Julia Dawson carried out a survey of Clarion members, which attempted to determine the main motivation for belonging to an ostensibly proselytizing socialist association. There is no doubt that some importance was attached to the movement's core ideology by the majority of its members, with 'socialist lectures' among the prime attractions, but the results of the survey indicated the predominantly social and recreational motives of the Clarionettes. What was also firmly established, however, was the overwhelmingly serious and rational nature of the activities, which were organized into seventeen categories, and selected in order of preference as shown:

1. Social evenings.
2. Literature study.
3. Music.
4. Socialist lectures.
5. Literature distribution.
6. Cinderella.
7. Arts and crafts.
8. Science (field clubs etc.).
9. Athletics.
10. Political propaganda.
11. Gardening.
12. Debates.
13. House to house visiting.
14. Sunday schools.
15. Pushing the Clarion.
16. Organizing women workers.
17. Writing to the press.[98]

The importance attached by the popular membership of CCCs to the main political *raison d'être* of the movement is difficult to determine accurately. The descriptions of club activities, in their diverse forms, came, of course, almost exclusively from the politically active organizers and administrators. Activity also varied significantly from section to section, notwithstanding regular cooperation and collaboration between areas. Bradford CCC, one of the larger clubs, was among the most

active politically, in keeping with the nature and prominence of Bradford socialist politics in the 1890s.[99] Formed at Bradford East Labour
Club in September 1894, with Ben Tillett as president, the Bradford
section immediately proceeded to contact other Labour clubs to offer
them assistance, and threw itself wholeheartedly into the task of propaganda: 'Bradford C.C.C. turned out the village [Wyke] with the bugle
and distributed leaflets.'[100] The following month they 'roused Barn-
sley'.[101] Neighbouring Leeds, by contrast, was said to be apathetic, to
the frustration of *Clarion* correspondents, who were obviously disappointed at the poor reception of the ILP in the city: 'The amount of
apathy we have to contend with in this belated city of ours ... is indeed
appalling, and beyond comparison' – this Leeds correspondent compared his own branch with that in Bradford, and also railed against
'cyclists who are individuals'.[102] The Liverpool section adopted auda-
cious tactics, supplying the Earl of Derby's tenants with copies of
Clarion and leaflets at Knowsley, and even attempting to subvert the
local constabulary: 'We also called at the Police Station, and left some
tracts for the edification of the gentlemen in blue.'[103] A Clarion cycle
run to Hovingham in 1895 was met by 200 policemen, and *Scout*
reported that one cyclist discovered a pile of rifles with fixed bayonets.[104]
In July 1899 Clarion cyclists were ordered off land at Calderbrook.

The evangelical work in conjunction with the Clarion 'Vans' gave
the cyclists a certain notoriety amongst other less politicized elements
in the broader cycling fellowship. The 'Vans' toured the country with
their orators, spreading the word by way of impromptu political meetings in town squares and on village greens. The first 'Van' was used
as the focus for the inaugural Clarion camp, and was initially employed
as a platform for political agitation when Clarion Scouts set up in the
centre of Liverpool during a period of high unemployment, to distribute
food and to offer socialist solutions. It was the Liverpool Clarion cyclists
who first followed the 'Van' and distributed literature on sorties into
the towns and villages. The idea was seen as a great success within the
movement, and other 'Vans' with their cycling outriders were soon on
the road. London eventually had three such groups, while the Midlands
produced the first motorized 'Van'. The 'Vanners' became a common
sight throughout the country, attracting noted orators and political
figures, such as Victor Grayson, Fred Bramley, Secretary of the TUC,
and Tom Kennedy, MP for Kirkcaldy, to the vigorous and optimistic
front line of the movement. The Clarion's political activities were, of
course, countered by the more popular Primrose League's similar
proselytizing tactics.

An important function of the CCCs' keen, but often light-hearted,
promotion of a version of the socialist gospel was its success in bonding
together, in common purpose, Clarion cyclists from all areas of the

country. The objectives of 'Socialism and Good Fellowship', and the National CCC motto, 'Socialism the Hope of the World' were never wholly submerged under the club's recreational side, which attracted so many young people into local sections. Wigan CCC adopted the more realistic motto of 'Pleasure and Business'. Much of the reputation of the CCCs as a political organization stemmed from the activities of a number of members in each district who cooperated with local socialists from other organizations in pursuit of the envisaged commonwealth. In 1944 Tom Groom referred back to the importance of politically active Clarion cyclists to successful local collaboration during the early years of socialism:

> There was not a Socialist organization in Birmingham that had not one or more Clarion cyclists on its committee, or a Socialist subscription list without its item from the C.C.C. So taking it by and large, the Birmingham C.C.C. outlined from the beginning, the duties and observances of every well-conducted Clarion C.C.[105]

The liberal interpretation of the notion of respectability adopted by the majority of touring and leisure cyclists was no real obstacle against challenges to areas of social convention. The pastime has in fact been attributed a major role in a significant social revolution; from Galsworthy in the 1890s to David Rubinstein in the 1970s, the first cycling boom has been credited as a major influence in the emancipation of women.[106] In his portrayal of Jessie, Hoopdriver's chance acquaintance in *The Wheels of Chance*, H. G. Wells gave a flavour of that newly discovered expression of freedom, and of a desire amongst young women for modernity. The bicycle was a symbol of liberation in the fight to break the shackles forged by Victorian convention. In the vanguard of women's cycling were members of the relatively influential upper middle class and even some aristocratic ladies, such as the particularly active campaigner Lady Harberton, Lady O'Hagan, first president of Burnley Ladies' CC, Lady Norreys from Belgravia and Lady Cairns from Windsor. The broader struggle embraced a number of crucial subsidiary causes, such as the admission of women to Oxbridge degrees. Underlying this highly visible and well-recorded social conflict was a more subtle and widespread revolution, represented by the substantial numbers of women who were very active in cycling clubs throughout the country. Women cyclists continued to be the subject of controversy and abuse, and consequently were emblematic of the larger gender struggle, at least up to the 1930s. They encountered problems with motorists as early as 1898. The *Newcastle Daily Chronicle* commented on 'Sunday excursionists, who also ridiculed women cyclists'.[107]

As women adopted these physically active forms of recreation, a number of social conventions were threatened. Some male as well as female cyclists rallied together in a common cause, founded on a mutual belief in the absurdity and regressive character of much of the existing etiquette. The 'Cycling Notes' column of Bolton's obviously male-orientated sporting weekly, *Cricket and Football Field*, apparently viewed the emergence of a liberating leisure pursuit for women as progressive: 'Certainly it has opened up a new pleasure for ladies, who are able to enjoy an outdoor exercise, with ease and freedom to themselves, and which a little while since was outside the range of probability even.'[108] *Bicycling News and Sport and Play* commented on the large numbers of women who were cycling in the countryside by the mid-1890s, and mentioned the practice of 'escorting ladies', but also expressed in verse a favourable reaction to their participation in the pastime:

> Here come the fresh cycling lasses,
> Out for a health-giving run –
> We'll toast them with full-brimming glasses,
> And welcome them every one.[109]

A number of upper-class women cyclists took the initiative from 1896, in organizing and conducting women's cycle trips and tours through a Chaperone Cyclists' Association. Entrenched attitudes did, nonetheless, ensure that the participation of unescorted women in this healthy open-air activity remained socially unacceptable for many, right into the 1930s. It would be a gross oversimplification to attribute the popularity of women's cycling wholly to a nascent women's movement, but it must have represented a refreshing and unprecedented release from their hitherto very restricted recreational opportunities.

The connection between leisure cycling and women's emancipation came fully to the fore over the much-debated question of proper female attire. Cycling presented the main focus for persistent agitation by the Rational Dress Society. Bloomers, in increasingly *risqué* forms, were the specific symbol of the agitation, particularly amongst the more daring young women who participated in the mid-1890s cycling boom. Sections of the establishment were so outraged by the issue that in 1894 the *Birmingham Daily Post* reported that an MP had even determined to introduce a parliamentary bill, 'to forbid the wearing of the "rational" dress costume by women cyclists'.[110] A Mrs Fenwick Miller wrote to the *Birmingham Chronicle* to point out that a woman was as much a biped as a man. Harassment of all cyclists was a general problem, especially during the 1890s, but women were targeted particularly; for instance, in October 1896, the *Burnley Gazette* reported on 'lady cyclists [being] assaulted, insulted, and blackmailed'.[111] As an affront to the social mores imposed by dominant Victorian sexual hypocrisy, women's rational dress represented an especially controversial affront to convention, but in many ways it was also representative of a more general challenge presented by elements of a formative outdoor movement, which, in adopting attire suitable to the pursuit of energetic open-air recreation, stood out as fundamentally unconventional in attitude. A famous test case in 1899 brought legal defeat – but moral victory and important publicity – when Lady Harberton, founder of the Rational Dress Society and a member of the CTC, challenged the right of the landlady of the Hautboy Hotel at Ockham in Surrey to refuse to admit her.[112]

Any examination of the social consequences of the expansion of certain types of open-air recreation contains a danger of overestimating the potential liberating effect for substantial numbers of women. Experiences varied widely, depending upon the associations involved, while true equality can be discerned only rarely in an overwhelmingly patriarchal culture. Not surprisingly, the issue attained the greatest prominence on the agenda of the CCCs, motivated as they were by radical activism, and with a relatively high proportion of independent women in their ranks right from the early years.[113] For example, in 1897 the Bolton section included seventeen women in an overall membership of ninety, while Bradford had thirteen out of seventy-seven. Women were actively involved in every aspect of the running of the clubs. Bolton CCC provided an important formative influence for radical women in the town such as Elsie Bocock, Helen Wright and Alice Foley, all of whom later became involved in local campaigning politics. Foley's autobiographical *A Bolton Childhood* recalls how the cyclists followed 'in the wake of the missionary Clarion Van', but also points to the importance of the social fellowship and the drawing power of the recreational dimension to the Bolton CCC: '... and a new era of fun and comradeship opened out'.[114] The experiences of these particular women belong to the period after the Great War, but they followed in the politically and socially challenging tradition of 'the lasses in the Bolton Clarion Cycling Club', who were praised in *Clarion* in 1897.[115] Much of the success of the Clarion movement's proselytizing peripatetic 'Van' can be ascribed to the work of Julia Dawson, a cyclist who made full use of a significant degree of independence and responsibility, asserting her influence as a regular contributor to *Clarion* on a range of issues, which included various recreational activities, socialist solutions to prevailing problems, and the role of women in contemporary society.

In keeping with its general stance on the liberating potential of healthy open-air recreation, *Clarion* consistently lent support to women's cycling: '... the bicycle is one of the most beneficent epochs in the history of woman's emancipation, and is bound to have far-reaching consequences'.[116] Several aspects of the cause were also picked up in the *Clarion Cyclists' Journal* and *King of the Road*. A measure of female emancipation was actively pursued by the CCCs, even if there is a discernible patronizing flavour evident in some of the attitudes. It was always highly likely that the phenomenon, which by its very nature challenged and indeed overthrew some of the restrictions imposed by dominant convention, should enjoy a good measure of sympathy and active support from a radical and progressive movement, especially from within its flourishing affiliated cycling clubs. In its 'Women on Wheels' page, composed by 'Queen of the Road', *King of the Road* catered specifically for the large female membership. As well as campaigning for free movement and greater opportunities for recreation, women shared the same motives with men for escape into the countryside:

> Out into the country! Away from the smoke and the smother of the town: away from the shrieking of Ship Canal 'Sirens', and the never-ending rattle of laden lorries: away from the sight of mill chimneys and factory windows, and soot-grimed Manchester streets. The autumn air is crisp and tingling as we speed along the white Cheshire roads ...[117]

'Queen of the Road' highlighted the antagonism felt towards cyclists in general, and to women in particular, condemning the 'evilly disposed persons' who strew the path of cyclists with glass and tacks.[118] Another regular feature was a cartoon of a female cyclist, which generally satirized entrenched topical attitudes: 'Mrs. Spence Blifkins: "What a horrid sight! This cycling is becoming dreadfully democratic. I shall never permit you to ride Sybil."'[119] The issue of rational dress was adopted wholeheartedly by the Clarion movement. *King of the Road*, for example, took up the case of a young teacher, who had been 'called to resign either her position or her bloomers ... but she refused to bow down to the fetish of Unsuitability'; the reporter stressed the sensible and progressive attitudes that gave common cause to socialists and most cyclists: 'Let us show the young lady that in her vigorous and spirited defence of the right of a woman to dress as she pleases, she has the sympathy and respect of all reasonable people.'[120] The wearing of rational dress to allow unrestricted movement was consistent with a sensible, and particularly practical approach. To *King of the Road*, the struggle took on universal significance, requiring 'single-minded efforts to emancipate the human race from a convention which clogs the free movement of woman towards a larger and wider sphere of influence'.[121] However, there was a disparity between the campaigning ideal and reality. Stella Davies's account of Clarion women cyclists in the Manchester area suggests that rational dress was not the norm even in 1914, and that Clarion women shared conservative characteristics with Primrose League ladies:

> Either we were too modest or too hard-up to buy special clothes, not sufficiently go-ahead sartorially or maybe we instinctively fore-stalled Bernard Shaw's advice; 'If you advocate unconventional ideas, do so in unconventional clothes.' No eccentricity in clothing was noticeable among Clarion Women though the men occasionally indulged a fancy.[122]

Justice's campaign in support of rational dress in 1899 was critical of women cyclists for succumbing to the pressures of convention: 'Of course, women themselves are to blame for this. If all cycling women had worn the rational dress and stuck to it, in spite of a little ridicule, all opposition to it would have died down a long time before this.'[123]

The socialist involvement in the popular pastime of cycling and in related issues was in keeping with their general publicity-seeking tactic of energetic grass-roots involvement. Every opportunity was taken to challenge the establishment. However, what is also evident is a strong bond of common interest between CCCs and other elements in a developing cycling movement, which they in many ways epitomized, collaborating over open-air concerns, and expressing much of the prevalent philosophy of a movement which offered respectable alternatives to restrictive aspects of *status quo* social convention. The politically motivated challenge to the prevailing orthodoxy ramified into concern over some of the most salient contemporary social issues.

The first cycling boom coincided with a period during which a particular concern with aspects of recreation contributed to a distinguishable transformation of popular culture. Cycling added an important dimension to the construction of a nascent outdoor movement, whose development was impelled by an expansion of leisure time. This popular phenomenon also emerged concurrently with a Utopian socialist creed which emphasized the potential attractions of human fellowship constructed through particular forms of recreation. Clarion's ideologically underpinned contribution to the cycling movement catered specifically for a disenchanted stratum of society which felt uncomfortable with popular culture, while simultaneously rejecting mainstream liberal philanthropic solutions. Chris Waters identifies those who were attracted to such socialist organizations as the CCCs as 'lonely and isolated, uncomfortable amidst the conviviality of pub-centred working-class culture'.[124] The alienation of the worker whose cultural and recreational preferences differ from prevailing popular orthodoxy is timeless. What was unique about those who sought wholesome and convivial fellowship with kindred spirits around the turn of the century was that they were afforded the opportunity to combine an alternative culture with the added ingredient of an optimistic and improving political agenda. Simply to equate the CCCs and similar associations with a short-lived rejection of dominant cultural configurations is also to ignore the longer-term implications, and therefore their wider significance to developments in open-air leisure. The emphasis on individual fulfilment through social and cultural fellowship, social amelioration, community politics, dissatisfaction with the dehumanizing effects of large-scale industrial capitalism, and, of course, the environmental concern stemming from a love of the countryside and nature, all suggest a nascent ideology consistent in its basic objectives with the broad political philosophy of present-day 'green' thinking.[125] Elements of that same ideology, incorporating values associated with a broader improving culture, informed and sustained the development of the wider associational collaboration of country-loving cyclists into a contributory element in the growth of the outdoor movement.

An idealized version of the early touring cyclist who associated with others of similar interests was represented in an obituary of a popular CCC member, which was published in *Clarion* in 1897:

> [He combined] a well of enthusiasm [with] the gift of curiosity ... repository of curious knowledge ... His own convenience was always a trifle when weighed against that of others ... he knew all the flowers and birds. The world was so full of interest for him ... [He was] skilled as a roadside doctor and mechanic.[126]

It is a picture of the energetic, inquisitive, unselfish, and intelligent practical person, but with romantic and optimistic facets, motivated by a love of nature and of human fellowship. Although this is an uncritical eulogistic depiction, the reader was presented with an ideal to which to aspire, an ideal that was just as appropriate to the membership of the larger outdoor movement.

Notes

1. *Halifax Courier*, 25 April 1908, p. 3.
2. Stansfield, A., *Essays and Sketches* (Manchester, 1897), pp. 49, 55.
3. *Sheffield Daily Telegraph*, 7 May 1907, p. 3.
4. *Bradford Daily Argus*, 24 August 1898, p. 6.
5. *Bolton Journal and Guardian*, 19 April 1907, p. 8.
6. Morrison, J. H., ed., *The Northern Cyclists' Pocket Guide* (Newcastle, 1897).
7. See Chapter 3.

8. *Cricket and Football Field* (Bolton), 29 August 1896, p. 3.

9. *King of the Road* (October 1897), p. 6.

10. *Burnley Express*, 5 January 1884, p. 7.

11. *Burnley Gazette*, 14 November 1892, p. 3.

12. *Ibid.*, 16 May 1896, p. 5.

13. *Clarion Cyclists' Journal* 5 (March 1897), p. 1.

14. *Burnley Gazette*, 7 October 1896, p. 3.

15. *Rossendale Free Press*, 10 October 1896, p. 2.

16. *Bicycle News and Sport and Play* (Birmingham), 23 April 1895, p. 16.

17. *Ibid.*, 14 May 1895, p. 16.

18. *Cricket and Football Field*, 2 January 1897, p. 3.

19. *Newcastle Daily Chronicle*, 28 April 1898, p. 3.

20. *Burnley News*, 22 March 1913, p. 10.

21. Roberts, D., *This Veteran Business* (Southern Veteran Cycling Club, 1984), p. 9.

22. Russell, C. E. B., *Manchester Boys. Sketches of Manchester Lads at Work and Play* (Manchester, 1905), p. 113.

23. *Justice*, 6 May 1893, p. 2.

24. *Clarion*, 21 July 1894, p. 6.

25. *Ibid.*

26. *Clarion Cyclists' Journal* 6 (April 1897), p. 7.

27. *King of the Road* (April 1897), p. 12.

28. *Clarion*, 14 August 1897, p. 263.

29. Pugh, M., *The Tories and the People, 1880–1935* (Oxford, 1985), pp. 30–1.

30. *Clarion Cyclists' Journal* 2 (September 1896), p. 3.

31. Ensor, R. C. K., *England 1870–1914* (Oxford, 1941), p. 334.

32. *King of the Road* (April 1897), p. 3.

33. Masterman, C. F. G., *The Condition of England* (new edn; London, 1960), pp. 75–6.

34. *Ibid.*, p. 76.

35. *Ibid.*, pp. 56, 76.

36. Fincher, J. A., 'The Clarion Movement: A Study of a Socialist Attempt to Implement the Co-operative Commonwealth in England, 1891–1944', unpublished MA thesis, University of Manchester, 1971.

37. Ensor, *England, 1870–1914*, p. 334.

38. Rothstein, T., 'Why is Socialism in England at a Discount?', *Social Democrat* II, 3 (March 1898), pp. 69–70.

39. *King of the Road* (May 1897), p. 3.

40. Cf. Anderson, G. L., *Victorian Clerks* (Manchester, 1976).

41. Elvin, H. H., *Socialism for Clerks* (pass on pamphlet, 26; London, n.d.).

42. *King of the Road* (May 1897), p. 9.

43. *Clarion Cyclists' Journal* 5 (March 1897), p. 5.

44. *Ibid.*, 6 (April 1897), p. 4.

45. *Clarion*, 28 August 1897, p. 279.

46. Mayall, D., *Gypsy-Travellers in Nineteenth Century Society* (Cambridge, 1988).

47. See Chapter 6.

48. *Clarion*, 13 July 1901, p. 222.

49. *Clarion Cyclists' Journal* 1 (August 1896), p. 5.
50. *Clarion*, 11 September 1897, p. 295.
51. *Ibid.*, 21 July 1894, p. 6.
52. Masterman, *Condition of England*, p. 77.
53. Quoted in *ibid.*, pp. 143–4.
54. Howell, D., *British Workers and the ILP, 1885–1906* (Manchester, 1983).
55. Lyons, N. A., *Robert Blatchford – The Sketch of a Personality* (London, 1910).
56. Waters, C., *British Socialists and the Politics of Popular Culture, 1884–1914* (Manchester, 1990), ch. 3.
57. Booth, C., ed., *Life and Labour of the People in London* (London, 1897), pp. 423–4.
58. *Clarion*, 4 August 1894, p. 7.
59. *Ibid.*, 8 September 1894, p. 6.
60. *Scout* 4 (July 1895), p. 100.
61. *King of the Road* (May 1897), p. 15.
62. *Ibid.* (November 1897), p. 20.
63. *Clarion Cyclists' Journal* 3 (October 1896), p. 4.
64. *Ibid.*, 6 (April 1897), p. 1.
65. *Ibid.*, 2 (September 1896), p. 6.
66. *Clarion*, 13 July 1901, p. 1.
67. Howell, *British Workers*, pp. 223–6.
68. *Justice*, 26 December 1891, p. 4.
69. *Ibid.*, 6 May 1893, p. 6.
70. Pelling, H., *The Origins of the Labour Party, 1880–1900* (2nd edn; Oxford, 1965), p. 138.
71. Bax, E. B., *The Religion of Socialism* (London, 1885); Yeo, S., 'A new life: the religion of socialism in Britain, 1883–1896', *History Workshop Journal* 4 (Autumn 1977), pp. 5–49.
72. *Clarion Cyclists' Journal* 1 (August 1896), p. 7.
73. *Clarion*, 3 December 1893, p. 387.
74. Blatchford, R., *The New Religion* (Clarion pamphlet 9; London, 1892).
75. Lyons, *Robert Blatchford*, p. 107.
76. Blatchford, R., *God and My Neighbour* (London, 1904), p. xi.
77. *Ibid.*, pp. 195, x.
78. Jones, S. G., 'Sport, Politics and the Labour Movement: the BWSF, 1923–35', *British Journal of Sports History* 2, 2 (September 1985), p. 154.
79. Yeo 'A new life'; McLeod, H., *Religion and the Working Class in Nineteenth Century Britain* (London, 1984).
80. *King of the Road* (April 1897), p. 13.
81. *Ibid.* (November 1897), p. 20.
82. *Clarion*, 3 December 1898, p. 387.
83. Lowerson, J., 'Sport and the Victorian Sunday: the beginnings of middle-class apostasy', *British Journal of Sports History* 1, 2 (September 1984), pp. 202–20.
84. *Newcastle Daily Chronicle*, 20 April 1948, p. 4.
85. Wigley, J., *The Rise and Fall of the Victorian Sunday* (Manchester, 1980).
86. Harrison, B., 'Religion and recreation in nineteenth century England', *Past and Present* 38 (December 1967), p. 121.

87. *Cricket and Football Field*, 11 July 1896, p. 7.
88. Smout, T. C., *A History of the Scottish People, 1830–1950* (London, 1987), pp. 157–8.
89. Lightwood, J. T., *Romance of the CTC* (London, 1928), p. 58.
90. *Cricket and Football Field*, 11 July 1896, p. 7.
91. *Newcastle Daily Chronicle*, 20 April 1898, p. 4.
92. *Halifax Comet*, 12 March 1898, p. 13.
93. *Newcastle Daily Chronicle*, 9 May 1898, p. 7.
94. *Clarion*, 3 December 1898, p. 387.
95. *Ibid.*, 29 February 1896, p. 72.
96. *King of the Road* (December 1897), p. 6.
97. *Clarion Cyclists' Journal* 3 (October 1896), p. 9.
98. *Clarion*, 23 November 1901, p. 2.
99. See James, D., *Bradford* (Halifax, 1990), pp. 74–9; Laybourn, K., *The British Labour Party, 1881–1951* (Gloucester, 1988), pp. 19–36 *passim*; Laybourn, K., *The British Labour Party 1890–1979* (London, 1988), pp. 20–1; Reynolds, J. and Laybourn, K., 'The emergence of the Independent Labour Party in Britain', *International Review of Social History* XX (1975), pp. 313–46.
100. *Clarion*, 29 September 1894, p. 7.
101. *Ibid.*, 6 October 1894, p. 7.
102. *Clarion Cyclists' Journal* 6 (April 1897), p. 7.
103. *Clarion*, 6 October 1894, p. 7.
104. *Scout*, July 1895, p. 9.
105. Groom, T., *National Clarion Cycling Club, 1894–1944* (Halifax, 1944), p. 3.
106. Rubinstein, D., 'Cycling in the 1890s', *Victorian Studies* 21 (Autumn 1977), pp. 47–71.
107. *Newcastle Daily Chronicle*, 9 May 1898, p. 7.
108. *Cricket and Football Field*, 2 January 1897, p. 3.
109. *Bicycle News and Sport and Play*, 14 May 1895, p. 16.
110. *Birmingham Daily Post*, 16 August 1894, p. 8.
111. *Burnley Gazette*, 31 October 1896, p. 6.
112. See Watson, R. and Gray, M., *The Penguin Book of the Bicycle* (London, 1978), pp. 136–9.
113. See Davies, C. S., *North Country Bred. A Working Class Family Chronicle* (London, 1963); Nield Chew, D., *The Life and Writings of Ada Nield Chew* (London, 1982), ch. 19.
114. Foley, A., *A Bolton Childhood* (Manchester, 1973), p. 72.
115. *Clarion*, 9 October 1897, p. 328.
116. *Ibid.*, 2 October 1897, p. 319.
117. *King of the Road* (Novenber 1897), p. 12.
118. *Ibid.*, p. 13.
119. *Ibid.* (November 1897), p. 1.
120. *Ibid.*, p. 9.
121. *Ibid.*
122. Davies, *North Country Bred*, p. 120.
123. *Justice*, 15 April 1899, p. 5.
124. Waters, *British Socialists*, p. 158.

125. See Gould, P. C., *Early Green Politics* (Brighton, 1988).
126. *Clarion*, 14 August 1897, p. 263.

Chapter 6

Rational Holidays

The concept of rational holidays developed into a significant practical expression of the late nineteenth-century reaction against the trivial and commercially exploited utilization of increased leisure time. The provision of cheap and simple accommodation sustained the growing popularity of active open-air recreation, giving momentum and a further institutional focus to the construction of the outdoor movement. It catered for a basic need of walkers, mountaineers and touring cyclists from the urban areas, who were in the forefront during all stages in the development of this facility. The fellowship which initiated the provision of simple accommodation and healthy and rational holidays came to represent one of the most readily identifiable and directly influential manifestations of an outdoor ideology. It was sustained by cooperative principles, a communion of interests and the necessary collective discipline that was established right from the outset; in the early 1890s the Co-operative Holidays Association's (CHA) centre at Newlands near Keswick established such disciplines as lights out at 11.00 p. m. and rising and breakfast bells. These routines have always of course been something of a practical necessity for those whose interests were active and outdoor, such as those described by cooperative holiday pioneer T. A. Leonard: 'We believe in spending long days in the open exploring the wildest and most interesting places in the neighbourhood of our centres.'[1]

The development of a network of accommodation for those inclined towards simple and economical forms of open-air recreation was rooted in the same Christian nonconformist ethos that helped to shape the nature of the larger outdoor movement. The influence of a fusion of liberal philanthropic and Utopian socialist principles was again strongly in evidence, although that hybrid ideology was more obviously directly nourished by the common roots in Christian morality than were other dimensions to the nascent outdoor movement. It was a doctrine in which the ideal of social reconstruction through radical structural changes in patterns of employment was combined with ideas emphasizing the increasingly important social role of leisure. Some socialist writers integrated critiques of prevailing attitudes to both work and leisure. We can find such a juxtaposition on consecutive pages of one publication:

> So long as working men can be persuaded to believe that their interest lies in this country continuing to be the world's manufactory, to the prejudice of more healthful and natural occupations, capital will stick with the tenacity of a leech.[2]

> ... opportunities should be given for the young to meet together on leaving school for healthy recreation. Social clubs should be formed, where, in addition to games, means should be provided for the development of the cardinal virtues.[3]

There was a consistency with Morris's comprehensive philosophy of life, which incorporated ideas on healthy natural leisure as an undeniable human right into a fundamental concern with the function and value of work:

> ... first of all I claim good health; and I say that a vast proportion of people in civilisation scarcely even know what that means. To feel mere life a pleasure; to enjoy the moving of one's limbs and exercising one's bodily powers, to play, as it were, with sun and wind and rain; to rejoice in satisfying the due bodily appetites of a human animal without fear of degradation or sense of wrong-doing ...[4]

Earlier intellectual roots can be discerned in Ruskin's wide-ranging social criticism, which included a warning against the consequences of misguided recreation and a perceived abuse of the new-found measure of freedom:

> A healthy manner of play is necessary ... to a healthy manner of work ... [T]he choice of our recreation is, in most cases, left to ourselves, while the nature of our work is as generally fixed by necessity or authority. It may well be doubted whether more distressful consequences may not have resulted from mistaken choice in play than from mistaken direction in labour.[5]

Contributions to the recreation debate came from differing ideological angles. The *Contemporary Review*, for example, adopted a condescending tone. In an article entitled 'The Physiology of Recreation', Charles Roberts felt that the great mass of the working population 'have but vague notions of their own on the subject'.[6] In a somewhat inconsistent article, Roberts did, however, also recommend that recreation should represent a change from working conditions, and suggested that 'recreation is a subject deserving study and organization'.[7]

The debate stimulated by the 'leisure problem' generated ideas which offered practical alternatives to facile uses of increased leisure time, including more fulfilling ways of spending the annual holiday. The commercialization of holidays was an uneven process, influenced by regional cultural and economic factors. Manchester was the pioneer of the Saturday half-day, followed by other Lancashire textile communities: 'By the 1870s many cotton towns enjoyed agreed (though unpaid) summer holidays of three days beyond the weekend, and twenty years later further extensions brought about a full-scale "Wakes Week" ...'[8] Excursions and longer holidays away from home during the Wakes Weeks, were enabled by a proliferation of savings clubs and other sources such as membership of the Cooperative Society, which formed essential ingredients of the collective self-help structure in industrial communities. A good railway network and relatively high family incomes based on multiple contributions were additional reasons why Lancashire led the way in the field of popular holidays. Blackpool became both the big draw, and consequently the main focus of attention for the reformers of popular leisure.[9]

The popularity of Blackpool as a resort was firmly established as the Mecca of the northern working classes well before its great period of expansion from the 1870s.[10] The earlier years were dominated by the better off, pursuing more staid and sedate forms of leisure. The statistics were, nonetheless, still impressive. As early as 1864, towards the end of north-east Lancashire's main period of urban expansion, the *Blackburn Times* reported that '15,000 passengers passed through Preston on Saturday, *en route* for Blackpool'.[11] A report from the same period in the same publication indicated one of the motives for the escape to the coast away from the unhealthy mill towns, although it is unlikely that many of the early excursionists would have lived in the area of east Blackburn described: '... the unfortunate wretches born in this locality cannot but feel the horrid neglect of nature'.[12] It would be some time before the 'seaside holiday habit percolated downwards through the increasingly complex social strata'.[13]

As the seaside holiday became a fixture in the calendar of many working-class families, it was Blackpool, convenient to those Lancashire industrial communities that enjoyed relatively high levels of disposable income and free time, which came to epitomize the popular resort. As such, Blackpool became the main focus for the critical attention of reforming proponents of rational recreation of varying political persuasion, including founders of popular educational schemes and cooperative country holiday ventures. The numbers of visitors increased in leaps and bounds in the last three decades of the nineteenth century.

In the early 1870s, a town of some 6,000 inhabitants was already inundated by more than half a million visitors annually. The social level and the tone of the attractions, however, continued to be dominated by the middle class until the 1880s: 'The last quarter of the nineteenth century saw the holiday habit spread to the better-off skilled workers, and in some parts of the country, especially the Lancashire textile district, it became almost universal by the turn of the century.' [14] In his social history of the English seaside resort, John Walton illustrates the volume of the annual exodus from the cotton towns; in 1889 13,000 people booked out of Darwen for Blackpool; in the same year 21,800 left Burnley, a figure which rose to 70,000 in 1899; by 1905 15,000 Accrington people stayed away for a week; and by 1919 '10,000 Nelson people stayed at Blackpool for at least four days', while a further 1,000 stayed at Southport.[15] *Rochdale Labour News* reported critically on the mill town escape to the seaside resort in 1899:

> With about £2 10s. saved out of their bodily needs, in some going-off club, they will betake themselves, some of them, to the farthest place for the least money, while others will besport themselves at Blackpool or some other equally convenient watering place, loitering on the sands by day and at night stewing in some almost suffocating place of amusement. And this is a workingman's holiday! [16]

The popular expansion of Blackpool illustrated the primary characteristics required for a successful commercialization of recreation and popular culture. It depended upon a collaboration in mutual interest between private enterprise and the collectivism of municipal government in a 'philistine pragmatism',[17] which identified a new route to personal and civic prosperity based on the unique position of their town.[18] To the entrepreneurs, Blackpool represented a new form of civic progress, simultaneously providing the urban masses with brief respite from the mundane. To many of philanthropic or socialist reforming inclinations the commercial phenomenon was anathema. Katherine St John Conway, for example, related her own impressions for the readers of *Workman's Times* in 1893: 'Blackpool was to me hideous – a place where many men and women gather together who know not what is or what might be, who think Socialists idle dreamers, and England a glorious country so long as she keeps the cotton trade, ...' [19] Conway concentrated on the women in the crowd, articulating the concern of socialist women with the betterment of their own gender, but her testimony also reflects the relative level of independence enjoyed by Lancashire working women:

> ... the weary-full garish crowd of which we formed a part. In long

rows stood the Cheap Jack stalls, a nightmare of stripes and stars. On the grey sea wall were grouped the sunshades and frocks of the lasses who learn to shriek instead of laugh, to chatter instead of talk, and to parade instead of stroll in the dull blankness of brick walls and in the close confinement of a factory prison.[20]

'The Cobweb', writing in *Rochdale Labour News*, offered a romantic version of why the open countryside was preferable to the popular resort and the bustle of the pleasure-seeking crowd as an escape from the industrial town:

We are often questioned why we seek the woodlands and the fields in preference to Blackpool! Liverpool! Hartlepool! or any other 'pool' where trippers jostle and scramble after pleasure, and we have to naively answer: There are different sorts of pleasure; to hearken the throstle, the cuckoo, the rock pigeon, and the songsters of the grove is more to our ear than the snort of the engine, the roar of street traffic, or the incessant thunder of the mill.[21]

Nonetheless, socialists were by no means averse to proselytizing amongst the frivolous crowd jostling at the seaside. ILP propaganda meetings were held on summer Sundays on Blackpool sands, expounding on subjects such as 'The Religion of the Labour Movement'.[22] Another organization to recognize the potential benefits of making a sally into the territory of the opposition was the National Home Reading Union (NHRU), an association which would exert considerable influence on the development of provision for holidays spent in keeping with the tenets of rational recreation. From 16 to 20 July 1889 the NHRU held their summer assembly at Blackpool, and returned during the following summer. The choice of venue would undoubtedly have been influenced by the practical considerations of plentiful and cheap accommodation and excellent rail links from the urban centres. These assemblies were based on holiday instruction courses, which promoted a pleasurable pursuit of enlightenment of the intellect and the soul, as well as encouraging attention to physical health. The original assembly had been held at Oxford in August 1887, following a suggestion from committee member Charles Rowley, an experienced organizer of intellectual and open-air recreational activities for the workers in his capacity as the founder and leader of the Ancoats Brotherhood, another Lancashire-based organization concerned with the sort of working-class elevation that went beyond mere palliatives and strove for fundamental cultural transformation.[23] It was in fact the NHRU that was the real progenitor of the concept of rational and improving holidays at prices within the range of working people. Their ideological and ethical *raison d'être* underpinned the function of this vital aspect of the movement. The trigger to the practical implementation of the idea of the rational holiday was a decision taken at the 1890 Blackpool Summer Assembly to open centres for educational and outdoor activities at a number of localities. The NHRU's monthly journal had already laid out the main objectives in April 1890:

> To organize summer assemblies at convenient centres, when lectures will be delivered by experienced teachers, social gatherings held, and excursions arranged ... [S]ocial intercourse and rational enjoyment ... make our Union a centre of life and light for thousands of earnest workers. We desire to utilise the summer holiday of our members for such purposes as these.[24]

The 1889 assembly at Blackpool had introduced eminent lecturers, organized social evenings, and, consistent with Congregationalist roots, preached sermons in support of the NHRU in many of the resort's places of worship. The course of lectures ranged from literature, history and geography, to music and folk lore. The fee for the full week's assembly was 10s. (50p).

It was as a member of the NHRU that T. A. Leonard was encouraged to work out a larger scheme for rural holiday centres, offering appropriate recreational opportunities to such organizations as the Pleasant Sunday Associations and Working Men's Bible Classes in the north of England. In an article in *Labour Prophet* in 1895, Leonard recalled how he persuaded 'thirty young Lancashire millhands' to participate in the prototype of the cooperative open-air holiday, invoking the rural-based Utopian socialist influence by quoting Robert Blatchford, while commending the formative role played by the NHRU:

> 'The fact is, the people don't know what you mean by the word England, and you have to show them that God has made other and more beautiful things than machines and factories.' ... That is a Socialist's work, and I want readers of the LABOUR PROPHET to know of an organization that is leading the way in good style.[25]

The article went on to describe the NHRU's programme of 'ideal holidays'.[26] The association gave its name, financial assistance, and organizational experience to the centres in which Leonard was involved, the first of which were officially opened in August 1892 at Ambleside and Keswick. This initial venture led to the formation of the CHA in 1893. The first parties of men and women spent a week in the Lake District, exchanging centres mid-week after a rendezvous on the summit of Helvellyn. These pioneers of organized rational holidays set the agenda for subsequent similar groups, each of which was led by a host and hostess, and a professional or university lecturer, who talked on the literary associations of the area, or the local flora or geology: 'Canon Rawnsley talked on literary and historical associations of the district ... which set many to read Wordsworth and Ruskin.' [27] Each party aimed at a social and denominational mix, and a prototype scheme was implemented, which offered free holidays, funded from collections at services, to convalescent workmen and deprived groups such as washer-women and other worn-out women workers.

The CHA was a direct product of the broad recreational concerns of the NHRU, and not simply a spontaneous local expansion of the activities of a Congregationalist rambling group in the Lancashire textile town of Colne, where it was originally based.[28] What evolved was a give-and-take collaboration between those associations that emphasized different aspects of the same core philosophy, consistent with the Congregationalist creed that encouraged both cooperation and spiritual independence in the nonconformist tradition. The CHA encouraged members to participate in NHRU educational activities and to read their recommended literature, while promoting the formation of local NHRU groups, 'especially in Manchester, where they met at College House, Brunswick Street'.[29] General education did continue to form one of the main objectives of the CHA, although Leonard, while favouring the university extension lectures and the reading circles, chose to emphasize the primacy of the physical function of his association; the spiritual dimension often remained unstated, but was taken for granted as a vital motive:

> The cultivation of the habit of going out on tramps at all seasons and in all weathers should be the duty of all loyal C.H.A. folk who want to keep young and preserve physical efficiency in these days, when the tendency seems to be all in the direction of developing brains at the expense of bodies.[30]

The NHRU continued to encourage their members to take holidays with the CHA, once the latter organization had taken over the travel and accommodation elements of the original enterprise. The two associations maintained a close collaboration, which included common membership and the sharing of officers. John Brown Paton, founder of the NHRU and a mentor of Leonard, held the presidency of the CHA.

The NHRU's influence disseminated a potent mixture of self-help, cooperation, philanthropy, socialism, Christian moralizing, conservative nostalgia for an imagined past, and a progressive pursuit of vigorous social action. It had strong middle-class establishment philanthropic roots, which nurtured a belief in the general efficacy of expanding the capacity for the educational and rational recreational improvement of the working classes. Emphasis on that characteristic of the NHRU identifies it as one of the agencies contributing to the permeation of the tacit principle of a common culture. The NHRU was founded at Grosvenor Square, Mayfair. Its founders included a number of clerics, including the Bishop of London, but also officials of the cooperative movement and George Howell MP. The original idea had been intro- duced to Paton during a visit to Switzerland, when he met two American ministers who had founded a scheme for summer holiday instruction courses. The educational base for the British expression of this ideal grew into a network of literary and scientific circles, which provided courses in home reading for 150,000 people. Paton initially intended a collaboration with the university extension movement, but found the scheme to be too narrow. The resultant reading circles developed an integrated learning format, which combined the recommended reading with exercises in the comprehension of pertinent ideas, and also put together the courses of instruction that were the central focus of summer assemblies. The reading lists were published and the issues raised in the Union's *Monthly Journal*, which included a section on 'Answers to Difficulties' raised by readers. Membership fees in 1890 were 3*s*. (15p) for general readers, 1*s*. 6*d*. (7½ p) for 'artizans' and 1*s*. for 'young people'.[31] Certificates were issued for the completion of courses. The *Bolton Journal and Guardian* publicized the work of the NHRU summer schools in 1904, extolling the benefits of the 'study of natural history and geology in the country', and 'the idea that knowledge must be related to experience – NOT reading of books by the light of midnight oil'.[32] A number of branches were established in Lancashire and Yorkshire, and a meeting in support of the NHRU was a feature of the Co-operative Congress held in Glasgow at Whitsuntide 1890. By 1895 the union claimed 6,500 members, with 70,000 school-children in the reading circles.

Paton was a Scottish Congregationalist, who worked in Sheffield before setting up the Congregational Institute in Nottingham. His version of the Christian creed synthesized ideas pertaining both to personal salvation and to overall social improvement. Like other later Victorian conscientious reformers, his doctrine stemmed from a belief that much of Christian religion was stagnant, deprived of the oxygen of ideas that would promote actively the pursuit of positive social change. Quoting Abraham Lincoln, he referred to the Church as 'a stationary engine'.[33] The essence of Paton's reforming doctrine is ident- ifiable in the institutions in which he became involved, as well as in his significant and sweeping contributions to the construction of active solutions to a range of contemporary problems, encouraging individual improvement, but, consistent with contemporary ideological trends, emphasizing the necessity of state intervention. Paton lectured at Manchester University in November 1909 on the subject of 'Poverty and the State', and produced articles on the same topic for the CHA's *Comradeship* magazine. Appalled by the numbers of paupers in Edwardian Britain, he expounded on the inadequacy of the existing Poor Law. At the heart of this political concern with the multiple effects of widespread poverty was a dominant belief that reformers should devote a substantial proportion of their energies to the highly topical problems of education and the land, which were selected specifically as crucial factors determining the level of vitality of a civilized and progressive society.

During summers spent at Newtonmore on Speyside in 1886 and 1887 Paton developed an interest in the plight of the crofters. It was a concern that echoed Ruskin, Morris and Carpenter in its identification of a lack of independence resulting from the destruction of cottage industries by shoddy mass-produced articles, and the perpetuation of the prevailing regressive system of land ownership. Nostalgia for an imagined rural past was reflected in a sympathy for H. Rider Haggard's belief that a residue of yokels was being left on the land by the inevitable migration of the more enterprising and intelligent element of the rural population. The underlying concern was with the loss to the rural structure of yeoman stock and the idealized liberty that they represented. Paton studied solutions to rural problems which had been implemented in Denmark, Switzerland and Bavaria. He had also investigated agricultural banks in Europe as the means to investment in rural training and to the creation of a resurgence of the cultural and moral life of country communities. The outcome was the Agricultural Banks Association, set up in 1899 with the cooperation of the Toynbee Bank Association. In August 1893 he founded the English Land Colonisation Society, intended to offer a centralized administration to cooperative agriculture. The system was put into practice at Alburgh in Norfolk, where a committee of cooperative smallholders paid 40s. (£2) per annum per acre, with any surplus going towards improvement and development. The introduction of copyhold tenure was indicative of the practical nostalgia which informed the scheme.

The whole Christian-based concern with the development of appropriate opportunities to regenerate a society under stress had wide-reaching and often divergent ramifications, which are indicative of the nature of the formative ethos. It was a contribution that contained both the germ of a philosophy and the physical energy that would generate the formation and consolidation of this important dimension to the institutional development of the outdoor movement. The neuroses and moral instability that were seen to be so much in evidence in the expanding urban areas were to be the subject for Paton's application of schemes constructed from his rural-based solutions to the perceived malaise of predominantly urban society. Rural colonies and training farms were manifestations of a practical version of the contemporaneously popular back-to-the-land philosophy. Land colonies and rural training for the urban unemployed always arouse suspicion of dubious motives, linked, for example, to the practical rationalism of Bismarckian social policy; a model for the British schemes was, indeed, a colony at Bethel in Westphalia, described in 1893 by Julie Sutter in *A Colony of Mercy, or Social Christianity at Work*. 'Social Christianity' was the key to the guiding principles of such schemes, promoting the somewhat patronizing, but nevertheless conscientiously conceived aims of individual independence, physical and mental health, and moral character. Leadership was to be by example rather than as a result of preaching or moralizing. The whole ethos was that of a nascent social service, intended to generate improvement rather than impose control. It is anachronistic to challenge too vigorously the soundness of the moral principles that gave the impetus to these schemes. The most famous colony was that at Lingfield in Surrey, set up in 1895 on 268 acres purchased with money guaranteed by Paton. Lingfield took able-bodied men from the London unemployed, and trained them for productive work on the land. Meanwhile, the Starnthwaite Colony near Kendal offered to epileptics the opportunity for genuine employment, as a more acceptable alternative to consignment to the ranks of the unemployable, swollen by a substantial residual social stratum.

Paton's moralizing zeal aimed especially at an inculcation of young males with a particular set of values, which would set them on the right road for life. Suspicious of the Boys' Brigade, and its role as nursery for the army, he founded the Life Brigade, whose prime function was to save life. The high Victorian principles which are normally associated with the public school were strongly in evidence, but moderated significantly by a fundamentally pacific and more benign philosophy. Supplementary to the interest in the training of youth were Paton's suggested programmes of talks, which, for example, prepared Sunday school pupils for a half-holiday ramble, or described what might be seen on a summer holiday in Epping Forest. The moral value of games was underlined, instilling fair play, self-discipline, and *esprit de corps*, thereby associating Christianity with moral and physical perceptions of manliness and nobility. In a letter to C. E. B. Russell of Manchester, Paton spoke of: '... instincts native to every boy which ought to be awakened and nurtured and strengthened – the heroic, courageous, loyal, self-command, chivalry ...'[34] The Life Brigade incorporated drill and parades, uniform and discipline, as the means to a form of solidarity. The exercises had a purpose; recruits were instructed, for instance, in fire-drill, ambulance-drill, and aquatic life-saving drill. The values echoed those of W. T. Stead's 'War Against War' peace campaign. A similar movement was started by Liverpool Quakers in 1898, and in 1897 T. A. Leonard started a corps of boys' lifeguards in connection with his Sunday school.

The same concern with youth informed much of the activity of the NHRU, whose aim was not just to encourage reading *per se*, but to wean the newly educated majority away from the pernicious influence of cheap and sensationalist literature. Paton expressed this aspect of the work of the 'People's University':

> The Home Reading Union was chiefly formed in order that it might, before children left school, train them to the right use, the healthful use, of the gift of reading, so fateful, so perilous, and thus train them in the beauty of our literature, so that they may be elevated beyond the reach of pernicious writings.[35]

The 1870 Education Act created a wonderful opportunity for popular cultural improvement, but was also seen by some as presenting every child with a potential Pandora's box. Essential guidance was seen as a necessary function of the NHRU. One of Paton's primary aims was to bring a decent level of education to the people's homes, '... to help the people to think for themselves ... all nature is an open book to the man who thinks'.[36] It was a sentiment in keeping with his strong belief in the need for independence for each individual.

Although there was an obvious compatibility with the new orthodoxy of a turn-of-the-century radical liberal creed, the NHRU's dissemination of an improving culture displayed a high level of consistency with the Christian moralist roots of a particular version of socialism, with which so many establishment reformers were perfectly happy to be associated. Paton himself identified the protean or 'chameleonic' nature of that creed:

> There is a kind of Socialism which pervades the N.H.R.U. in which I delight. Socialism has become a chameleonic word, having many aspects and colours ... Here, verily, we have the true Socialism which should pervade all life – the highest stooping to the humblest; the strong giving their strength to the feeble; the wise giving their knowledge to the ignorant.[37]

Labour Church support for the socially improving purpose of NHRU and CHA holiday schemes confirmed the sympathetic relationship that existed between the variety of institutions united by social objectives which incorporated aspects of popular cultural reform. John Trevor was in a group which visited Barmouth in 1894, reporting on 'the beauties of Nature and social intercourse [and] the happiest and healthiest of holidays' to readers of *Labour Prophet*, in an article entitled 'Co-operative Holidays'.[38] John Brandwood, a member of the same party, also described the excellence of the Barmouth centre and its range of activities. The Reverends T. A. Leonard and T. H. Mark acted as guides, while the Reverend Z. Mather of Barmouth, a geologist, contributed to a programme of events, which included bathing, boating, discussions and music. Brandwood reported that a visit would be made to 'the Isle of Erin [presumably the Portrush holiday centre] this year during Ramsbottom Wakes'.[39] This same ideology underpinned Paton's formation of social institutes, the first of which was set up in London in 1894. The institutes, which spread to Nottingham, Glasgow, Birmingham and Leicester, combined physical exercise with educational classes. Before returning to his pastorate at Colne, Leonard, a former Nottingham Congregationalist Institute student, was put in charge of the Islington Social Institute, adding a further dimension to his training for the leadership of the cooperative holidays movement. The Social Institutes Union later united with the Federation of Working Men's Clubs.

Leonard's pastoral work in Colne, adopted and suitably adapted from its origins in liberal philanthropic nonconformism, was informed by a Christian socialist ethos, coloured by the type of moralistic tone that was characteristic of a turn-of-the-century reforming intellectual milieu, which envisaged social progress through cultural reconstruction. His Congregationalist nonconformism was 'based on individualism and spiritual autonomy ... [and] ... wider religious liberty',[40] but also shared much common ground with the philosophy that had engendered the doctrine of social action that underpinned the foundation of the Labour Church: 'The "Rev." need frighten no one ... a Christian and a Socialist of the finest type – strong, tender, and light-hearted.'[41] The ethical and moral roots and continuing common interests of that broad-based ideology stimulated and sustained what John Walton has called '... idealistic circles where open-minded Nonconformity overlapped with Blatchfordian socialism'.[42] A movement that was steeped in orthodox Protestant Christian morality enjoyed the overt support of socialists in *Clarion* and other publications of the political left, giving valuable publicity to the cooperative holiday principle. Active support from the Labour Church, coordinated in *Labour Prophet*, was wholly consistent with the common ground shared as practical expressions of the same hybrid doctrine. Through the important influence of Leonard, and the circle that he represented, the symbiosis of Christian and socialist principles produced a cooperative creed, whose associational expression aimed at the fulfilment of the specific objective of minimizing the deteriorative effects of what were perceived as inane and trivial leisure pursuits. The Wakes Week at the seaside, taken up with wasteful amusements and vacuous pleasure, took the brunt of Leonard's attack on the dangers that accompanied the expansion of popular recreation. The moralizing tone of philanthropic and socialist attempts to refine popular culture are again in evidence in his affirmation of the frequently recurring contemporary theme of the guidance of the general populace towards better ways:

> Such is the spirit of these ideal holidays, as yet alas! out of reach of myriads of our toiling brothers and sisters, but within that of many who, for lack of the knowledge how to do things better, will go and fritter away their money and strength over the shady delights of some popular seaside town, with its niggers, switchbacks, and dancing saloons ... [43]

The subject had risen to prominence in Colne after Leonard had preached a sermon on holidays at the Congregational Church in August 1891: 'The devil weilds [sic] no small influence over holiday times in particular, and there is therefore the greater need to bring the influence of Christ as an antagonistic force.' In encouraging the congregation, and indeed the local population at large by way of press coverage, to 'Take Holidays Sensibly', a specific reference was made to Blackpool, which also incorporated a quotation from the Book of Job: '"Speak to the earth and it shall speak to thee". One thinks that when the race grows wiser, Blackpool, with its brass bands and bluster will be deserted.' Leonard's appeal for alternative uses of limited leisure, linked to his belief that the joys of nature were hidden from the majority of mill-town inhabitants, often made recourse to the common nonconformist idiom of Old Testament references, such as 'Moses in the wilderness'.[44] As a result of the sermon, when Leonard raised the question of recreational opportunity, the Young Men's Guild in the town organized the raising of a fund 'for the purposes of sending poor people to the sea-side during Colne holidays'.[45] Presumably, Blackpool was not the intended venue. In June 1893 the *Colne Times* was the vehicle for Leonard's proselytization of the rational enjoyment of the local holiday. Writing from his new position as honorary secretary to 'the promoters of a scheme which embodies a new ideal of summer holidays', he asserted that 'English summer resorts often do more harm than good both physically and morally'; he went on to explain how health and recreation could be obtained from holidays: 'And how can this be done in a better way than by taking exercise in the bracing and invigorating air of the country.'[46] The concern with both the physical and the spiritual elements of human development was manifested on cooperative holidays through a combination of brisk rambles and mountain ascents with open-air religious services. This health-promoting doctrine was consistent with the contemporary philosophy of physical, mental and spiritual development, and it attracted support from differing ideological standpoints. *Rochdale Labour News* quoted Ruskin on the subject: 'No physical error can be more profound, no moral error more dangerous, than that involved in the monkish doctrine of the opposition of the body to the soul. No soul can be perfect in an imperfect body. No body perfect without a perfect soul.' [47]

The genesis and development of the CHA, and its role in the vanguard of the formation of a popular national movement, has generally been ascribed simplistically to an evangelical crusade, in which Leonard single-handedly drew the misled industrial toilers of Colne away from the demoralizing temptations of worthless amusement towards a prototype movement, which subsequently spread the gospel of rational holidays to the rest of the country. Leonard was in fact conscientiously and energetically carrying out his brief from the NHRU to develop the notion of rational holidays into an associational formation in his own area of industrial Lancashire. The original germ bore fruit in the establishment of the two Lakeland centres, visited initially by parties drawn from 'members of our Adult Classes and Pleasant Sunday Associations, and other men's societies'.[48] An obituary in the *Colne Times* in 1948 lauded the 'Pioneer of [a] Movement Which Started in Colne' and 'attracted 100s of 1,000s to a new form of holiday', and which was 'so popular that Leonard had to call on the help of friends Dr. Paton of Nottingham, J. L. Paton, master at Rugby, then High Master of the Manchester Grammar School, Canon Rawnsley of Keswick, and Alderman James Johnston of Manchester'.[49] Leonard was the main mover of this particular aspect of the broader movement, and it was his philosophy that provided its most influential current; the CHA and the later Holiday Fellowship (HF) were his associations. Nonetheless, it is inaccurate to identify a movement as the brainchild of one man or as the consequence of one inspirational sermon; the emergence of a practical basis for rational holidays and appropriate accommodation was carefully constructed on a deeper foundation. It is also unlikely that many of the followers of this new direction in leisure came originally from those who were readily attracted to the delights of the coastal resort. Substantial numbers were certainly eventually persuaded to appreciate alternatives to existing recreational options, but in the early days Leonard and colleagues were preaching to the converted, providing a much wanted leisure facility for those who already appreciated the joys of the open-air countryside holiday, like the members of the church rambling groups in the district. Such schemes presented the opportunity to many less well-off urban lovers of the outdoors to enjoy an extended period in the most attractive areas, while also meeting their desire for more rewarding pastimes, educational interests and a social fellowship founded on common interests: 'We explored the northern part of the Lake District and then went south to the wild country of North Wales with ever increasing numbers and deepening love of our holiday fellowship.'[50] The fellowship that was engendered in the holiday centres contributed to a consolidation of already existing subdivisions into partially culturally defined social groupings. The facilities offered by the CHA helped to sustain this cultural delineation as much as they were instrumental in 'elevating the masses'.[51] Subsequent expansion and publicity did, nonetheless, implant the rational recreational idea into the national consciousness, raising awareness of the potential scope of leisure, as well as providing choice for those who identified naturally with particular areas of interest. The country holiday centres matched most of the requirements of these people:

> ... among the mountains and the beautiful and interesting scenery of the Lake District ... periods of really healthful bodily recreation and bodily and mental enjoyment ... conducted on the co-operative plan ... comparatively inexpensive ... on tramp in groups of a dozen ... evenings in social intercourse, with music and chatty lecturettes upon the geological wonders of the neighbourhood and the fair souls who made that fair region alike the scene and inspiration of their toils.[52]

Leonard himself never claimed the cooperative holiday movement as his own, but he did act as its main publicist:

> I want the readers of Labour Prophet to know of an organization that is leading the way in good style. The National Home Reading Union have issued a programme of some ideal holidays that are to be held this and next month in four of the loveliest spots in the kingdom – Keswick, Barmouth, Portrush, and Tavistock. We communise and organize on these holidays.[53]

The same article in *Labour Prophet* described an open-air creed which reconciled Christian and Utopian socialist principles, quoting the verse of Edward Carpenter and claiming 'a new reverence for God, a new conception of happiness, and a deeper realisation of the joys of living'.[54] In 1895 Leonard picked up the anti-Blackpool theme in *Clarion*, stressing the benefits of nature to the urban worker:

> Better than all the whirligig holidays spent by the average north-

country toiler at Blackpool and Douglas is a week spent with nature, ... A few hours since I passed through Ancoats, and saw the wizened faces of the little dwellers in Shantytown. Now, man's inhumanity to man is thrust out of sight, and Nature's loveliness is all that is visible.[55]

This was part of a report to *Clarion* readers on a cooperative holiday at Barmouth, run by the NHRU, which was by then also administering centres at Tavistock and at Portrush in Co. Antrim, in addition to the original Lake District venues. For 31s. 6d. (£1.57½) inclusive, the centres offered 'everything that helps to make a real holiday', including bathing, excursions, 'rambles led by guides [and] field talks on rocks, plants, birds, antiquities'. Leonard also suggested the cooperative holiday centres to Clarion cyclists, extending 'a welcome to all Clarionettes, women as well as men'.[56]

CHA membership and attendance at the holiday centres did, in fact, include large numbers of women, despite the prime function of the early NHRU as a guiding influence on young working men and boys, the inclusion on CHA book lists of such titles as *Healthy Boyhood*, and the stated aim of 'winning back the love of men for the simple ways of country life'.[57] H. Hill has described the CHA as 'one of the first movements to offer young Victorians of both sexes opportunities outside of churches and chapels for meeting each other on a footing of equality and goodwill'.[58] Photographs of late-Victorian and Edwardian CHA groups are notable for the numbers of women present – there were twenty out of forty-eight in a party from the Keld centre in Swaledale, for example. An article in the December 1912 issue of *Comradeship*, discussing a reported loss of male membership of the association due to excessive discipline and restraint – 'overmasterfulness of some of our officials' – claimed a ratio of around three to two in favour of women at some of the centres – 'nearly 60% women'.[59] In 1910 a 'Free Holiday Memorial Fund' was established in memory of Fanny Pringle, a CHA stalwart from Birmingham, who had participated in one of the first Lakeland holidays in the summer of 1893. The healthy gender mix and apparent lack of discrimination sustained the important social function of the CHA, and its offshoot HF, and contributed to the popularity of their affiliated rambling clubs. The role of social fellowship extended to an invitation to 'lonely folk who have not homes of their own' to spend Christmas at certain of the centres.[60] The unintentional sexual angle to the fellowship was, nevertheless, contained strictly within the limits of prevailing respectable norms. Writing in *Comradeship*, Leonard reiterated this keystone of his association's overarching morality when reacting to one of the inevitable consequences of the CHA's increasing popularity amongst young people: 'When comradeship between men and women passes into flirtation, and young people forget to respect each other, they perjure not only themselves, but the whole party, and the holiday movement generally.'[61] *Comradeship* also offered an opinion on the subject of rational dress for women involved in active open-air pursuits. A compromise was suggested between sensible comfort and practicality, and the desirable measure of respectability: '... suitable apparel for women in the mountains ... skirts three inches below the knee, of strong material'.[62]

Membership of the CHA and other similarly motivated associations was increasingly drawn from the younger section of a social stratum to whom spiritual independence and cultural and recreational individuality were central to personal fulfilment, but whose aspirations were, in the main, frustrated by continuing economic dependence:

> ... the majority of us to whom the ideals of the Association appeal, belong to that class of workers who are dependent upon the goodwill of our employers for our daily sustenance. For fifty weeks of the year we often have to suppress any personal views and ideas we have just because we realise that our employers have the power of taking our bread and butter away from us. We tend to grow machine-like, and in time a good many of us become mere machines with no views of our own. The C.H.A. offers to us an atmosphere in which we can keep alive our truest nature.[63]

The appeal of the annual escape to freedom from the grind of economic necessity was a major factor in the impressive expansion of the association by consistent annual increments, from a membership of 268 in 1893 to 13,719 in 1911; CHA holiday centres received approximately 20,000 guests in 1913. During the same period the number of holiday centres rose from the original two in the Lake District to forty-two, including five on the Continent and five in Ireland. The British centres ranged geographically from the Gareloch in the west of Scotland, to Addiscombe in Surrey and Boscastle in Cornwall. There were thirty local groups in 1911, of which eleven were in Lancashire and nine in Yorkshire. The number of groups continued to expand after the outbreak of war, reaching forty-one in 1917.

The emphasis on Lancashire and Yorkshire was further reflected in the formation of two smaller holiday associations, organized by local groups of Unitarians. They provided facilities and activities for the significant minority from the industrial towns who were motivated by the same individually improving and cooperative ethos as members of the CHA, although tending more towards middle-class philanthropy in their sponsorship and organization. From 1894, Unitarians in Halifax devised a scheme which would provide inexpensive rational holidays 'aimed at those who labour by hand and brain'.[64] The Unitarians were very much involved in the creation of an institutional structure in Halifax which would encourage the working class towards improving activities. Northgate End Unitarian Church impressed its own influence on local community activity through the formation of Halifax's Orchestral Society, Literary and Philosophical Society, the Thespians, and scout and guide troops. Unitarian holiday provision was based on the hire of a private boarding school at Mylngarth in the Windermere area during the summer break, which accommodated thirty people at a time for a week, at a cost of 30s. (£1.50), plus 5s. (25p) for the 'carriage fund': 'Miss Tagart, of London, well known in philanthropic circles, arranged the cheap accommodation.'[65] The Reverend F. Summers of London and Mr H. V. Mills, one of the founders of the Starnthwaite colony, were among the guides. The activities followed the familiar pattern of other serious-minded, outdoor-orientated recreational schemes. They included lectures, music, social evenings, visits to the haunts of the Lake poets, and, of course, mountain rambles, such as that up the valley of Kentmere in 1894, described in the *Halifax Evening Courier*: 'Professor Marr, of Cambridge, accompanied the party, and addressed the company during the "rests" on the agents which had been at work in sculpturing the valleys, and shaping the hills as we found them.'[66] Marr was a Fellow of St John's College, Oxford, and a leading authority on the geology of the Lake District. The Halifax Unitarians also organized holiday trips further afield during the 1890s, to venues such as the Isle of Wight and Paris.

A larger scheme was initiated in 1901, under the guidance of the Bolton-based British Holidays Association (BHA). It was another Unitarian organization, which was motivated by the reforming liberal philanthropic ideology that flourished in the town, alongside a complex network of grass-roots socialist cultural associations of varying degrees of size and influence, as well as the hugely influential Tory populism that nourished a flourishing membership of the Primrose League, which in Bolton in 1900 equalled the national membership of the ILP.[67] Its first holiday venue was at Lingholme, near Grange-over-Sands, and further centres were opened at Ramsey, Llandudno, Scarborough, Chepstow and Ben Rhydding, serving a total capacity of 345 guests. Again, the activities were in the rational holiday mould, and the ideology was cooperative, with financial gain forbidden by the constitution of the association. The *Bolton Journal and Guardian* praised the BHA, and reported on the attractions to the urban Lancastrian of the Lingholme centre:

> ... luxuriant countryside refreshing to the eye of Lancashire town-bird ... living evidence of the Brotherhood of Man. The gregarious

instinct of human nature is easily provided for: the seeker after companions for walks, drives, cycle rides, journeys o'er highway and byeway, by mountain and moor and wood, is sure of boon friends at these houses.[68]

Guests at Grange rambled and cycled in the quiet local countryside, and the reporter from the *Journal* was particularly impressed by the damson blossom, a feature of the south Lakeland area which has always attracted outdoor people north from the Lancashire mill towns. The BHA, 'a movement that provides healthy holidays and bright companions',[69] attracted the patronage of several of the local worthies in the Bolton district, including vice-presidents W. H. Lever, Dr Macnamara and J. H. Yoxall MP. Branches were opened in Bury, Manchester, Halifax and Bradford. CHA members also used the BHA centres.

The philanthropic character of the BHA was reflected in its provision of free and assisted holidays for 'recommended deserving people', who were deliberately not identified as such at the holiday centres: 'only the committee knows who they are'.[70] In 1906 the financial balance of the BHA was devoted to fifty-four free and thirty assisted holidays. Such assistance was a feature of the cooperative and rational holidays movement from the early days of the NHRU guest-houses, when those receiving financial support were asked to contribute 6s. (30p) towards the cost of their week. The CHA held regular collections which in 1909, for example, raised a total of £437 0s. 3d., enabling 395 free and 34 assisted holidays. A further example of a philanthropic promotion among the urban poor of rational uses of leisure can be seen in the actions of W. P. Paton, a son of the NHRU founder, who, while serving as one of the guides at the Barmouth holiday centre, brought Liverpool slum children to stay at his seaside lodgings, from where he took them on healthy and educational excursions.

The CHA's expansion abroad expressed in practical terms the internationalism that was shared with a number of outdoor associations, particularly during periods of general international disharmony, notably leading up to 1914 and during the campaigning zenith of the outdoor movement during the 1930s. Foreign travel, with concomitant broadening of the mind, was a common theme amongst promoters of rational recreation of varying political persuasion. *The Worker* latched on to the highly topical concept of 'Entente Cordial' (*sic*) in 1905, relating the idea of 'cementing the bonds of international fraternity' to their own brand of anti-Blackpool socialism: '... anyone who can go to Blackpool or the Isle of Man for 10 or 14 days can have 7 or 8 days in visiting all the principal cities in Belgium or Holland at the same cost'.[71] The estimate of that cost included 26s. (£1.30) from Huddersfield to Rotterdam or Antwerp via Grimsby. The promotion of friendship through travel, aimed at furthering an 'International Brotherhood of Man',[72] stimulated a pioneering trip by CHA members to the Taunus Mountains of Germany at Whitsuntide 1910, among the objects of which was the mediation of deteriorating relations. *Comradeship* connected the German trip to a fundamental objective of their own movement: 'The holiday "spirit" and the ethical basis of the Association fits it for a grand international work. Our movement is not a commercial but a brotherly one ...'[73] As well as the German base, the CHA established holiday centres at Dinan in Brittany and in the Swiss Valaise during 1910. A return visit later in the year by some fifty Germans included tea with Ramsay MacDonald on its itinerary. *Comradeship* marked the occasion by extolling the cause of international fraternity.

> Nation with nation, land with land,
> Unarmed shall live as comrades free;
> In every heart and brain shall throb
> The pulse of one fraternity.[74]

In addition to the obviously topical pursuit of international harmony, an expansion into foreign travel manifested the CHA commitment to the educational priority which it had inheriteed from the NHRU, and which was expressed most typically through the practical educational dimension to the active holiday programmes. Internationalism stimulated an interest in Esperanto and in the study of foreign languages, which was promoted in various editions of *Comradeship*. One dimension to this ethical legacy were the reading circles, such as the one formed by Manchester CHA members in December 1912 in conjunction with the local NHRU, which charged 1s. (5p) per annum subscription to defray expenses. Their first meeting discussed Ruskin's *Sesame and Lilies*. The programme of the reading circle organized by the London CHA Rambling Club also included the works of Ruskin, as well as travel and science subjects. In apparent contradiction of his own protests about a prevailing overemphasis on the cerebral at the expense of physically healthy activity, Leonard gave his blessing to the wider cultural function of the cooperative holidays movement, and commended readers to the NHRU list: 'Part of our C. H. A. ideal is to create a fellowship of readers as well as a fellowship of trampers ...'[75] One of the authors reviewed in *Comradeship* was George Borrow. Recommended books for the CHA reading courses included Carlyle's *Past and Present*, Balmforth's *Social and Political Pioneers*, a variety of nature studies, and publications produced by the Fabian Society; it was an ideologically eclectic literary mix, which even included Richard Jefferies's *oeuvre* of romantic ruralism.

In keeping with the foundation of a wide cultural base on which the outdoor movement in Britain was constructed, the CHA collaborated with or lent support to other associations that contributed to the growth of a rational and serious-minded dimension to popular cultural evolution. Members were encouraged to support the work of the Workers' Education Association and other educational organizations, including language groups. There was also an involvement with the Home Music Study Union, which originated in 1907 at Whitby, and which published its own magazine, *The Music Student*. 'Open-air singing' became a feature of the activities at some of the CHA centres.[76] It was a culture in accordance with the underlying creed of individual and cooperative improvement, or what Leonard referred to as 'that wonderful discovery of potentialities in both men and movements'.[77]

Unsurprisingly, the cooperative holiday movement also lent its influence in matters of direct practical concern to open-air recreationists. Problems of access to the countryside and the loss of rights of way stimulated a campaigning spirit, which was added to the evangelical approach to the question of leisure and popular culture. The CHA was directly affected by footpath closures during 1910 in the vicinity of their Newlands and Wharfedale holiday centres. *Comradeship* urged support for the Commons Open Spaces and Footpaths Preservation Society (COSFPS), and expressed frustration at the failure of countryside access bills in 1907 and 1908. An article on 'Public Rights of Way' claimed that it had become 'increasingly difficult to substantiate a Right of Way on behalf of the public'.[78] There was also a nascent environmentalism beginning to be expressed through the pages of the magazine. Support was given, for example, to Canon Rawnsley's protests in 1910–11 against the removal at Launchy Ghyll in the Lake District of ancient trees which had constituted part of a primeval oak forest. *Comradeship* railed against the dominant values that sanctioned such acts of official vandalism as those perpetrated at Thirlmere by the Manchester water authority: 'A sense of commercialism infects the air ... servants of twentieth century utilitarianism ...'[79] In addition to support for access and environmental issues, endorsing the trend towards a more collectivist, planned approach to the use of national resources, *Comradeship* expounded on the topical issue of town planning. There was, nevertheless, some ambivalence contained within the fundamental creed, which meant that cooperative motives and a general concurrence with the need for planning had to be reconciled with those individualistic principles which helped to shape the holiday movement. The general growth in 'officialdom' was criticized in *Comradeship* in 1912: '... smothering of individuality goes on apace, and we all tend to become mechanical, sophisticated, conventional and perhaps vapid'.[80] Such notions were, of course, consistent with the weight of contemporary feeling against statism and the much-reviled socialism. Contemporary libertarianism proved to be a common denominator between political ideologies of both left and right.

Interpretation of the concept of individual freedom took on a particular significance in the history of the development of the CHA, and the advancement of the rational recreational principles which it propagated. For the leadership and a majority of the association's members, freedom was never equated with licence. The fine dividing line that exists between individual taste and interpretation and the question of the responsibilities that are so essential to any system of democratic cooperation, engendered a crisis which produced a split in the rational holiday movement. The rift, which occurred over basic questions of principle, serves to reaffirm the 'rough' and 'respectable' dichotomy in the process of social stratification, and emphasizes further some of the primary precepts guiding the ethos of the outdoor movement. The general assumption has been that Leonard resigned from his holiday association as a personal rejection of a gradual middle-class takeover, the influence of creeping conservatism, and the subversion of the original principles of simplicity and economy. But this is somewhat misleading, although Leonard himself added credence to such a version of events, when he wrote that 'despite our working-class origins we were becoming middle-class in spirit and conservative in our ideas. Our centres tended to be of the conventional order, and the adventurous centre of simple, economical ways was not popular.'[81] There was certainly an element of all of these factors contributing to Leonard's disillusionment with the direction in which the CHA was moving, and in his desire to reinvigorate a movement whose original dynamism was endangered increasingly by stagnant convention. However, the main underlying influence on the parting of the ways was, ironically, the very popularity of CHA holiday provision, rather than the exclusiveness suggested by a middle-class takeover. The controversy of 1912–13 was prompted by problems of rowdyism and the growing incursion of what strict adherents to CHA principles defined as a hooligan element.

Reporting on the twentieth anniversary AGM of the CHA, the February 1913 issue of *Comradeship* broke the news of Leonard's departure; the meeting, it reported, had been 'overshadowed by a cryptic and puzzling announcement in the agenda concerning the departure of our General Secretary and the formation of a daughter organization'.[82] Concern had been mounting for some time over the question of the degree of discipline that was essential for the maintenance of standards of behaviour, consistent with the philosophy of a movement which was confronted increasingly with 'a growing tendency to rowdyism at certain of the centres ... [and] senseless vulgar practical joking that frequently takes place in bedrooms ...'[83] The exuberant, selfish, but generally relatively harmless type of behaviour that has consistently caused conflict within the outdoor movement constituted a threat to the initial purpose and the cohesion of the CHA. The zest of young working people, celebrating freedom from restraint in their own way, weakened the original function of this strand in the movement, while severely damaging the desired public image. The CHA was becoming a victim of its own success, weaning some people away from Blackpool to more energetic and healthy recreation in the hills, but also absorbing characteristics of a more gregarious popular culture:

> ... unmannerly forcing of ourselves upon the attention of the public by singing and rocketting at large railway stations; and in the uncontrolled way we let ourselves go on mountain tops and other quiet sanctuaries of natural beauty, to our own loss and to the unspeakable annoyance of strangers who may be there ... worse if abroad – bringing discredit on our nation.[84]

The social attractions of the movement certainly contributed significantly to its cohesion and expanded its popularity. But at the same time they developed in ways that threatened any chance of a gregarious fellowship successfully coexisting with the quietism of an association that was founded as a counter to the noisier and more trivial use of recreation. Conviviality and communal singing were perfectly in accordance with the foundation of friendship and a group spirit, but, again, it became a question of where the fine dividing line was drawn, and at what point it was crossed:

> It seems as if we are getting into a rowdy way of singing songs ... Macnamara's band was yelled morning, noon and night, indoors and out, among the silent hills by day, and along country lanes at night, to the exasperation of quiet folk, until all but the noise-lovers were tired out.[85]

By the end of 1912 the dispute had come to a head, thoroughly undermining the principles of cooperation based on collective self-discipline: 'Unfortunately there is a rough and rowdy element among our fellows ...'[86] A young working-class cooperative holidaymaker supported the need for discipline, but blamed the problems on 'certain childish persons in the week's party who ought still to be at boarding school under its discipline'.[87] It is unclear whether, in his reference to the boarding school, this correspondent was alluding to a more middle-class background, or to the rowdy element of his own experience. In an association founded on the notion of individual improvement, indiscipline was automatically equated with a poor and untrained mind, although it was stressed that youthful high spirits were perfectly com-

mensurate with the spirit of the movement: 'We must clearly differentiate between the hilarity and breeziness that should be the possession
of noble-minded youth, and the rowdyism of the uncontrolled and
weedy mind ...'[88] *Comradeship* pointed out that letters of complaint
about 'rowdyism at night', 'practical jokes', and 'horseplay' came 'not
from crabbed, old-fashioned folk, but young, healthy and jolly members
of our fellowship'. Correspondents insisted that good sleep was an
essential requirement of the healthy holiday, and that an alternative
popular philosophy of leisure was under threat from behaviour that
was 'selfish, irrational, and contrary to the spirit of active goodwill that
is the chief constituent of what has been called the C.H.A. spirit'.[89]

The growing intrusion of rowdy behaviour represented the most
patent example of the subversion of the objectives of the rational holiday
movement. The initial *raison d'être* of the CHA and similar organizations
– as suppliers of alternatives to popular recreation – was vulnerable to
other forces which, while adding momentum to desired expansion,
simultaneously contributed to a corruption of the stated aims, by
inevitably going beyond the original intended simplicity. The development of the sort of sophistication and urbanity that Leonard and his
first rambling and holiday groups could never have envisaged was
epitomized by the largest and most influential of the CHA rambling
clubs, which proliferated around the turn of the century – by 1913
there were thirty-five such clubs. The London CHA Rambling Club
was formed at Gatti's Restaurant in the Strand in November 1901. In
the chair was one of J. B. Paton's sons, J. L. Paton, who was at that time
head of University College School, Gower Street, Bloomsbury. Membership was open to 'members of the C.H.A., the National Home
Reading Union and their friends'.[90] Numbers rose to 292 in 1905 and
to 405 in 1909. The annual subscription rose from an initial 1s. 6d.
(7½ p) to a 1911 figure of 2s. (10p).

From its highly respectable metropolitan base, the London CHA
fulfilled most of the original functions of the association, as delineated
by its northern counterparts during the developments of the 1890s.
The social side was of particular importance to the popularity of the
group. It was founded on a cultural mix, which blended popular events
such as dances and teas with sorties into the fringes of high culture, such
as promenade concerts and assisting Henry Wood to 'improve musical
tastes in London'.[91] Other cultural activities included the language
classes which started in 1908, and the Dramatic Society, formed in
1911. In 1918 the London CHA helped to form the Kelmscott
Fellowship in commemoration of William Morris. From 1904 club
nights, dances, and teas were held at Furnival Hall in Holborn, which
was replaced in 1906 by a clubhouse at Croydon; in September 1910
the headquarters were moved to Red Lion Square. These were open

daily, and their basic function was more akin to that of the London clubs frequented by the establishment and the metropolitan intelligentsia. The earlier Holborn venue had replaced a venture at Twickenham, where a guesthouse had been opened in April 1903; River House, set in grounds that stretched for a quarter of a mile along the Thames, was also used for regular Thursday club nights, but had failed through a lack of visitors. Despite its somewhat select social and cultural tendencies, the London CHA in many ways remained faithful to the guiding principles on which the national association was founded. It persisted with schemes for the provision of basic accommodation and rational holidays, organizing long weekends, such as those in 1903, at Bexhill at Easter, and at Cambridge at Whitsuntide, which cost 23s. 6d. (£1.17½), inclusive of rail travel. At Whitsuntide 1909 a large group of CHA ramblers were accommodated in a marquee at Passfield in Surrey. In May 1911 a guesthouse was established at Clapham Common. Adherence to the idea of simple accommodation was demonstrated by weekends at Betchworth Camp on Box Hill, where sleeping was on sacking on the floor. By 1921, a bungalow had been built on the site, able to accommodate eight people.

The problems that increasingly hindered the smooth functioning of the CHA, and prompted Leonard's departure to found the HF, were never really stated openly. The split was explained by a series of platitudes, aimed at a diplomatic separation which would ensure that the movement as a whole would continue to flourish financially. The CHA had certainly become distended, too popular to sustain accurately its original ideals. In an article in *Comradeship*, in which there were detectable signs of his pending departure, Leonard claimed that the organization had become too big for one man. However, in the subsequent edition of the magazine he tellingly reiterated the theme of discipline and 'rational behaviour':

> We want to enlist the sympathy and example of our members on the side of order and rational behaviour, and to prevent the recurrence of those happenings which led the Reference Committee after last season, very reluctantly to take the extreme measure of requesting certain guests not to apply for admission to our centres again.[92]

An amicable working relationship existed between the CHA and its progeny right from the inception of the HF in September 1913. Leonard set the conciliatory tone from the outset: 'There is no thought of competition between the old and the new movements ... [We must] respect each other's "spheres of influence".'[93] Such coexistence was established in a number of practical ways. *Comradeship* adopted an expanded role as the voice of the HF, featuring Leonard's regular column, 'Concerning the Fellowship', until the HF introduced its own magazine, *Over the Hills*, in 1924. The HF took over the Newlands centre near Keswick as its initial holiday base, and adopted the German side of the operation, concomitant with Leonard's special interest in the international aspect of the movement. The goal of international harmony sustained a pacifism that survived into the Great War, unlike many other early twentieth-century claims to internationalism, which had succumbed to all-embracing xenophobic nationalism by 1914. The HF had printed cards, headed 'The Fellowship Resolve. New Year 1915', the text of which appeared in the December 1914 issue of *Comradeship*:

> I resolve that I will work every day of this New Year to destroy in men's minds the idea of war. War is the devil that has crossed all the purposes of God since the beginning of the world. Peace in the message of the angels. Fellowship is the spirit of life. Without Peace and Fellowship nations cannot evolve, and men cannot become Supermen.[94]

An HF leaflet publicized the formation of the new organization and stated its aims clearly: 'To organize holiday making, to provide for the healthy enjoyment of leisure, to encourage the love of the open air, and to promote social and international friendship.'[95] Thus, the original agenda was re-established, again providing simple and inexpensive opportunities for working people to participate in a basically improving use of leisure time, avoiding the unwanted intrusion of the rowdy element, and reinvigorating the earliest spiritual motives of a movement founded on nonconformism:

> We want to bring our holidays within the reach of poorer folk, and to this end to keep the arrangements as simple as possible ... We propose to set ourselves to solve the problem of how, in spite of rising prices, to supply cheap holidays, and at the same time to deepen their physical and moral value to those who take part in them.[96]

A new scheme offering free holidays was adopted as a further confirmation of primary objectives. The HF registered under the Industrial and Provident Societies Act, and set up headquarters at its first year-round permanent centre at Bryn Corach, Conway. The so-called 'tent-house centres' made truly simple holidays available in more inaccessible areas, encouraging the 'freedom and camaraderie of camp life'.[97] HF membership was on the basis of a one pound share to be purchased in eight annual instalments, reaffirming the founding co-operative principles of this particular philosophy of leisure. Leonard encouraged CHA members to take a share in the HF. By the end of 1913 the fellowship had attracted 120 members, and was justifiably optimistic about future expansion. Both the CHA and HF developed into flourishing purveyors of physically and mentally active holidays in the open-air recreation boom of the interwar period.

A Utopian socialist version of the provision of simple and inexpensive countryside accommodation to facilitate outdoor rational recreation was contemporaneously developed by enthusiasts within the Clarion movement. Clarion clubhouses provided cyclists with simple accommodation consistent with the movement's fundamental concept of cooperative open-air fellowship. The origins of this particular form of provision had been in the spring and summer meets and camps, through which *esprit de corps* and communal bonding in a common interest were established during the 1890s. They continued as important focuses for the open-air and social fellowship of the Clarion cycling movement right up to the Second World War. The clubhouses were a development which had more to do with reducing the costs incurred by members of the CCC than with offering, in themselves, serious-minded alternatives to the seaside resort. However, in accordance with the role that the CHA had adopted, it was again a case of providing a facility which a certain class of people required, rather than leading significant numbers away from the popular culture of beer and skittles. The introduction of this alternative facility was partly stimulated by the regular concern expressed in the Clarion press about the price of refreshment and accommodation encountered on cycle runs into the rural districts. As *Clarion* reported: 'The C.T.C. houses are often too expensive for us',[98] while *Clarion Cyclists' Journal* declared: 'We have in all our clubs a great number of members who cannot run out with the club owing to the high prices charged for meals at the places we visit.'[99] The founder of the national CCC, Tom Groom, claimed in the 1940s that the Clarion clubhouses were the precursors of the youth hostels, which were opened as a practical response to the interwar open-air boom:[100] 'And so sprang up in England the first chain of Youth Hostels.'[101] Retrospective accounts have unquestioningly perpetuated such uncritical observation.[102] Similarities and common objectives are certainly clearly discernible; there was significant consistency in the fundamental principles of the two associations. Both were intent on providing simple, but comfortable overnight shelter, affordable to lovers of countryside leisure activities, who sought independently an alternative to the prevailing conditions in the industrial towns and conurbations. Cyclists of all ages were prominent in the energetic cooperative fellowship which sustained Clarion clubhouses and youth hostels alike, not only through regular use, but also in the voluntary contribution to the general upkeep of property, an aspect that added substance to the growth and consolidation of the outdoor movement. But although the two institutions did share many basic principles, important qualifications need to be made. Firstly, liberal philanthropic origins set the Youth Hostels Association (YHA) apart from the socialist commonwealth of the Clarion, although a fundamental ethical concurrence cannot be ignored. Secondly, the Clarion clubhouses owed little to the mildly puritanical side of the ethos that informed the development of the YHA. A drink and a smoke were part of the convivial atmosphere of the Clarion fellowship, while the collective discipline and the idea of a mutually beneficial curfew situated the development of the YHA more within the ideological realm of the early CHA and the HF.

The idea of active open-air recreationists gathering together in an area of attractive countryside gave rise to the first CCC meet in 1895, the year after the formation of the first club in Birmingham, setting in motion a process that would lead to the recognition of a demand for cheap rural accommodation. More than a hundred Clarionettes converged on the Peak District town of Ashbourne to attend the gathering which was organized by the Birmingham section, but which attracted cyclists from other areas, including a substantial contingent from the Manchester area. In 1896 the Easter meet drew more than two hundred Clarion cyclists to Bakewell, travelling from as far afield as Bristol and Edinburgh. The importance of the geographical centrality of the Peak District, and its proximity to urban-industrial areas, is again in evidence. Political propaganda was prominent on the agenda of these early events, but it was good fun, friendship, and a love of fresh air which dominated affairs. Local fears that the arrival in Bakewell of hundreds of rabid revolutionary socialists for an Easter meet would trigger serious disorder did, of course, prove to be wholly unfounded. The thoroughly rational behaviour, manifest respectability and good spirit displayed by the Clarion cyclists proved frustrating to the journalists who had turned up in the hope of more exciting copy. Even so, when the Easter meet was held at Chester in 1898, the local authorities thought it necessary to call up the police reserve, and to have plain-clothes policemen follow the cyclists around. By 1897 this type of gathering had already gained a momentum that reflected the first cycling boom and the concomitant burgeoning of the CCCs, and between four and five hundred turned up for the main event at Leek. The Bolton based *Cricket and Football Field* reported on the 'Easter Meet spoiled by Leek-y weather'.[103] Again, the emphasis was on good fun, although apparently leaning towards the more trivial, since it seemed that 'irresponsible leg-pulling, rather than business, was the order of the day'.[104] In May 1897 the *Manchester Guardian* reported on the forty-nine Manchester Clarion cyclists who attended a meet at Knutsford, Cheshire. A camp in July of the same year at Woodborough in Nottinghamshire was joined by an outing of the Labour Church. Scottish Clarionettes organized their own meets, such as that at Falkirk during the summer of 1897, or at Dunfermline in September 1899; these two venues suggest less emphasis on the importance of pleasant rural surroundings and more on mutually convenient rallying points for CCCs in Scotland, but the objective of bonding an active fellowship based on healthy rational pursuits remained the same. The Easter meet became an increasingly popular feature of CCC activity before the First World War. Among the cyclists who contributed to an 'Invasion of Chester'122 in 1910 were contingents from Paisley and Glasgow, King's Lynn and Lincoln, and from London, although the majority of the 1,362 signatories of the attendance roll were from Lancashire and Yorkshire. Cycling and enjoyment in the fresh air again played a big part in the proceedings, although the political function of the Clarion movement was strongly in evidence; Robert Blatchford and Victor Grayson were present at a big socialist demonstration, and a number of the cyclists 'rode through the villages singing a few of the best-known socialist songs'.[105]

The Clarion propaganda 'Van' was the nucleus around which the popular summer camps grew. In 1895 it was parked at Tabley Brook in Cheshire, where the addition of three bell tents and a marquee provided accommodation for 80 *Clarion* readers. This prototype camp was partly funded by the Manchester Clarion stalwarts Ranstead and Sutcliffe, and furnished from Gorton ILP headquarters. It was the beginning of the organization and funding of annual camps by the strong Manchester CCC. The varied programme, offering events ranging from cycle rides and walks to suppers and evening sing-songs and a Labour Church service, reflected again the nature of a fellowship which encompassed the philosophy of both the Clarion movement and of the larger expression of rational recreation, to whose expansion it contributed. Catering for hungry outdoor people was a vital function of the organization. Breakfast or tea were provided for 9d. (3½p), while dinner cost 1s. (5p) and supper 4d. (1½p). The charge for a bed for the night was 6d. (2½p). The motivation of many Clarion cyclists can be detected in accounts of the 1896 camp. *Clarion Cyclists' Journal* highlighted the combination of 'universal brotherhood' with 'Living according to Nature'.[106] A correspondent from Rochdale CCC, indicating the friendly and homely atmosphere of the camps, employed archaic constructions in language with biblical overtones, confirming the deep-seated nonconformist influence: 'Having drunk in the sights, longing eyes were cast towards the place of refreshment, where we did rest ourselves and did drink and smoke and sing sweet songs.'[107]

It was an idea first mooted by the editor of *Clarion Cyclists' Journal* in the October 1896 edition that led to the convocation of a meeting on 31 January 1897 to discuss the possibility of opening a 'club-house': 'A country club-house for Liverpool, Manchester, and South Lancashire clubs.'[108] The initial plan was that volunteers would establish a permanent facility to accommodate twenty-four people in bunks and to provide 'good homely meals for 6d. [2½p]'.[109] Charlie Reekie of Ancoats stressed the importance of these envisaged premises as a means of obtaining relief from industrial squalor. He illustrated his message by referring to places that he had experienced personally, such as Ancoats, Wolverhampton, Tipton, Warrington, Rochdale and 'Bowton' [sic]: '... and if the Clarion cyclists do nothing more than promote opportunities for men to get away as much as possible from these places, out into the country, then they will have done some good'. Reekie suggested less talk and more action, urging the CCCs to 'DO SUMMUT'.[110] The Lancashire cyclists did, indeed, almost immediately put the plan into action, as *Cricket and Football Field* reported: 'The cycling clubs connected with that great body [The Clarion] all over Lancashire are in the throes of a country-house scheme ... to have sleeping and dining accommodation ...'[111] From the summer of 1897, CCCs in the Manchester district set out to raise the funds to purchase and convert a house at Bucklow Hill near Knutsford in Cheshire, which would provide not only accommodation and refreshment, but also recreational and social facilities, and activities in keeping with the Clarion movement's brief of fellowship and individual improvement. Two thousand – each worth 5s. (25p) – shares were issued, with further financial backing coming from prominent figures in the movement, including Robert and Montague Blatchford, William Ranstead, and Emmeline Pankhurst. The scheme was put into operation with what *Cricket and Football Field* called 'that enthusiasm which seems to fire every Clarionite'.[112] An emphasis on the social aspect and fellowship contributed to the immediate popularity of the project. *Clarion* praised the 'joys and comforts',[113] which attracted, for example, 150 people for tea and 60 to stay the night on Saturday 24 July 1897. On the following day there were 140 for dinner and 180 for tea. The friendly atmosphere impressed the correspondent of *Cricket and Football Field*, who, although writing for what was the sports and recreation edition of the Liberal *Bolton Journal and Guardian*, was eager in his praise of the spirit encountered at a venue run by a movement whose nominal primary function was the proselytization of a socialist message: '... much as one may disagree with socialist principles, a visit to the clubhouse at Bucklow Hill at any time affords evidence of the brotherly feeling which exists between them as cyclists'.[114] The same publication reported on the popularity and the spirit of the clubhouse during 1898: 'I learn that from 150 to 200 Clarionettes are visiting the house each week-end, and right merrily goes the time when these comrades in arms get the music a-rolling.'[115] *Cricket and Football Field's* regular focus on the activities of the movement stemmed from the popularity of Clarion cycling in the Bolton area. The local CCC, supported by breakaway sections at nearby Horwich and Farnworth, were involved strongly in the original club-house venture, and in 1898 opened their own premises at Rivington in the upland country to the north-west of Bolton.

During the autumn of 1897 the clubhouse at Bucklow Hill was extended to include a pavilion. However, it could only be retained until the expiry of the lease in June 1902, when Manchester CCC relocated its headquarters to a site at nearby Handforth. This new clubhouse was maintained by a steward and his wife, but the daily running of the establishment was on a cooperative basis, where everyone helped with meal preparation, washing-up, making beds and other essential chores, confirming at least a measure of continuity through to the later youth hostel movement; a connection with which Stella Davies has also concurred: 'The organization was similar to that of the present Youth Hostels of which it was an early example.'[116] Davies came from a Methodist background in Rossendale, before moving to the Blackley area of Manchester, the city where she was to work a ten-hour day as a telephonist in Ancoats. After being introduced to Clarion cycling in 1914, she became a regular visitor to the Handforth clubhouse. She described the substantial development of the venue, as well as the type of social activity carried out there which continued to bond the Clarion fellowship:

> The club-house had been a Tudor farmer's home; the large kitchen was panelled in oak and there were mullions in some of the windows. The undivided bedroom which spanned the lower rooms was used as a women's dormitory. The men were accommodated in a hut in the garden ... a large hall with stage for meals, concerts, dramatics.[117]

The annual subscription to the scheme was 5s. (25p), and £1 shares were issued, although fractions of shares were also made available. During the period of the First World War, the charge for meals was 9d. (3½p), or 6d. (2½p) without ham.

From its original enterprise in the north-west, the clubhouse concept expanded into other areas of the country, most numerously and most lastingly in Lancashire and Yorkshire. Their popularity as the providers of wide-ranging recreational opportunities to meet the increasing de-mand of a particular class of people contributed substantially to the continuing general expansion of the Clarion cycling movement up to the outbreak of war. A maximum membership in excess of five hundred was attracted to Handforth, where: 'Merry multitudes saluted the May sun last week-end at the clubhouse. The newly-arrived billiard table proved a great attraction.'[118] The same article heralded the construction of a tennis-court. Similar facilities were later made available at one of the most popular Clarion clubhouses, which was situated in the Ribble Valley near Clayton-le-Dale. Another venue which became particularly popular was that at Chevin End, Menston, to the north of Bradford. It was this type of facility which contributed in no small way to the renewed vitality of Clarion cycling in the interwar period. The club-houses incresingly became sports and social centres, and by the 1930s the role of providing simple inexpensive accommodation for outdoor people of all ages had been filled adequately by the national organiz-ations of the YHA and SYHA.

The range of facilities provided by the CHA, HF and CCCs – and to a lesser extent the smaller Unitarian contributions – met a significant area of recreational need in the period before 1914. It represented an independent and specific expression of a wider response to the expansion of leisure, as well as being a reaction against the hugely increased commercialization of recreational amenities, which was generating sim-ultaneously a popular cultural transformation. The common ground shared by nominally ideologically diverse organizations like the Con-gregationalist CHA and the utopian socialist CCCs gave a firm foundation for the construction of this important dimension of the outdoor movement. Leonard and his fundamentally liberal philan-thropic movement exuded a strong flavour of socialism, which attracted support and positive publicity from both the Labour Church and *Clarion*. Such areas of mutual interest made it easy for people such as the Manchester ILP alderman James Johnston to become involved both with the schemes of the Clarion cyclists, and with the CHA, to which he was invited to add his energy and intellect – as well as his practical experience of philanthropic and outdoor affairs – to that of Leonard and J. B. and J. L. Paton. All these organizations, whatever political principles they espoused, and whatever the social background or motives of their founders and principal characters, presented a much-needed recreational facility. What they provided would appeal in particular to that element of late nineteenth- and early twentieth-century British society, which Chris Waters has defined as 'artisans already attuned to the message of self-help'.[119] This stratum had, however, already become more ideologically expansive and socially diverse by the latter part of the nineteenth century.

Notes

1. *Colne Times*, 11 August 1911, p. 8.
2. *The Worker* (Huddersfield), 21 July 1905, p. 2.
3. *Ibid.*, p. 3.

4. Morris, W., 'How we live and how we might live', *Commonweal*, 18 June 1887, p. 195
5. Ruskin, J., *The Stones of Venice*, vol. III, in Cook, E. T., and Wedderburn, A., eds, *The Works of John Ruskin*, vol. II (London, 1904), pp. 151–2.
6. *Contemporary Review* LXVIII (July 1895), p. 103.
7. *Ibid.*, p. 104.
8. Walton, J. K., *Lancashire* (Manchester, 1987), p. 295.
9. *Idem, The English Seaside Resort* (Leicester, 1983); and 'Residential Amenity, Respectable Morality and the Rise of the Entertainment Industry; the case of Blackpool, 1860–1914', in Bennett T. *et al.*, eds, *Popular Culture: Past and Present* (London, 1982).
10. Walton, *English Seaside Resort*.
11. *Blackburn Times*, 24 August 1864, p. 3.
12. *Ibid.*, 14 April 1866, p. 5.
13. Walton, *English Seaside Resort*, p. 5.
14. *Ibid.*, p. 2.
15. Bennett, W., *The History of Marsden and Nelson* (Nelson, 1957), p. 220.
16. *Rochdale Labour News* (August 1899), p. 2.
17. Walton, J. K., and Walvin, J., eds, *Leisure in Britain, 1780–1939* (Manchester, 1983), p. 182.
18. Walton, *English Seaside Resort*.
19. *The Workman's Times*, 17 June 1893, p. 1.
20. *Ibid.*
21. *Rochdale Labour News* (June 1899), p. 4.
22. *The Workman's Times*, 12 August 1893, p. 2.
23. Pimlott, J. A. R., *Recreations* (London, 1968); Rowley, C., *Fifty Years of Work Without Wages* (London, 1911).
24. National Home Reading Union *Monthly Journal, Artizans' Section* (April 1890), p. 75.
25. *Labour Prophet* (July 1895), p. 102.
26. *Ibid.*
27. Paton, J. L., *John Brown Paton. A Biography* (London, 1914), p. 230.
28. Dalby, A., 'Foundation and First Steps', in Holt, A., ed., *Making Tracks* (London, 1985), p. 11; Stephenson, T., *Forbidden Land* (Manchester, 1989); Walker, H., 'The Outdoor Movement in England and Wales, 1900–1939', unpublished Ph.D thesis, University of Sussex, ch. 5; Waters, C., *British Socialists and the Politics of Popular Culture, 1884–1914* (Manchester, 1990), p. 75.
29. Mrs D. Raulson, Stainland, Halifax; oral source.
30. *Comradeship* (November 1909), p. 17.
31. NHRU *Monthly Journal, Artizans' Section* (October 1889–May 1890).
32. *Bolton Journal and Guardian*, 10 June 1904, p. 6.
33. Paton, *John Brown Paton*, p. xvi.
34. *Ibid.*, p. 330.
35. *Ibid.*, p. 286.
36. *Ibid.*, p. 279.
37. *Ibid.*, p. 290.
38. *Labour Prophet* (July 1895), p. 104.

39. *Ibid.*, p. 103.
40. Selbie, W. B., *Congregationalism* (London, 1927), p. 180.
41. *Labour Prophet* (July 1895), p. 104.
42. Walton, *English Seaside Resort*, p. 40.
43. *Labour Prophet* (July 1895), p. 102.
44. *Colne Times*, 7 August 1891, p. 6.
45. *Ibid.*
46. *Ibid.*, 2 June 1893, p. 4.
47. *Rochdale Labour News* (January 1899), p. 2.
48. *Colne Times*, 2 June 1893, p. 2.
49. *Ibid.*, 23 July 1948, p. 3.
50. *Ibid.*, 11 August 1911, p. 8.
51. Waters, *British Socialists*, p. 75.
52. *Colne Times*, 2 June 1893, p. 4.
53. *Labour Prophet* (July 1895), p. 102.
54. *Ibid.*
55. *Clarion*, 8 June 1895, p. 183.
56. *Ibid.*
57. *Comradeship* (February 1911), p. 63.
58. Hill, H., *Freedom to Roam* (Ashbourne, 1980), p. 27.
59. *Comradeship* (December 1912), p. 35.
60. *Ibid.* (November 1910), p. 17.
61. *Ibid.* (December 1910), p. 35.
62. *Ibid.* (April 1911), p. 69.
63. *Ibid.* (December 1912), p. 35.
64. *Halifax Evening Courier*, 29 September 1894, p. 5.
65. *Ibid.*
66. *Ibid.*
67. Pugh, M., *The Tories and the People, 1880–1935* (Oxford, 1985), p. 2.
68. *Bolton Journal and Guardian*, 17 May 1907, p. 8.
69. *Ibid.*
70. *Ibid.*
71. *The Worker* (Huddersfield), 22 September 1905, p. 9.
72. *Comradeship* (December 1910), p. 37.
73. *Ibid.*
74. *Ibid.*, p. 38.
75. *Ibid.* (September 1910), p. 3.
76. *Ibid.* (November 1910), p. 25.
77. *Colne Times*, 11 August 1911, p. 8.
78. *Comradeship* (February 1910), p. 35.
79. *Ibid.* (February 1911), p. 62.
80. *Ibid.* (December 1912), p. 36.
81. Leonard, T. A., *Adventures in Holiday-Making* (London, 1934), pp. 53–4.
82. *Comradeship*, February 1913, p. 52.
83. *Ibid.* (December 1910), p. 35.
84. *Ibid.*, p. 36.
85. *Ibid.*
86. *Ibid.* (December 1912), p. 35.

87. *Ibid.*
88. *Ibid.*
89. *Ibid.* (February 1913), p. 67.
90. Brown, S., *A History of the London CHA Club From its Inception in 1901 to the Diamond Jubilee in 1961* (London, 1965), p. 2.
91. *Ibid.*, p. 3.
92. *Comradeship* (April 1913), pp. 66–7.
93. *Ibid.* (September 1913), p. 5.
94. *Ibid.* (December 1914), p. 16.
95. Holiday Fellowship, introductory leaflet (September 1913), p. 2.
96. *Ibid.*, pp. 1–2.
97. *Ibid.*, p. 2.
98. *Clarion*, 14 August 1897, p. 263.
99. *Clarion Cyclists' Journal* 5 (March 1897), p. 10.
100. See Chapter 7.
101. Groom, T., *National Clarion Cycling Club. Fifty Years Story of the Club, 1894–1944* (Halifax, 1944), p. 4.
102. Lawson, Z., 'Wheels Within Wheels – the Lancashire Cycling Clubs of the 1880s and '90s', in Crosby, A., ed., *Lancashire Local Studies in Honour of Diana Winterbottom* (Preston, 1993), p. 142.
103. *Cricket and Football Field*, 24 April 1897, p. 3.
104. Groom, *National Clarion Cycling Club*, p. 3.
105. *Cricket and Football Field*, 30 March 1910, p. 3.
106. *Clarion Cyclists' Journal* 2 (September 1896), p. 2.
107. *Ibid.*, p. 4.
108. *Clarion Cyclists' Journal* 5 (March 1897), p. 9.
109. *Ibid.*, p. 10.
110. *Ibid.*, p. 11.
111. *Cricket and Football Field*, 13 March 1897, p. 3.
112. *Ibid.*, 5 June 1897, p. 3.
113. *Clarion*, 31 July 1897, p. 247.
114. *Cricket and Football Field*, 25 March 1898, p. 3.
115. *Ibid.*, 15 May 1898, p. 3.
116. Davies, C. S., *North Country Bred* (London, 1963), p. 84.
117. *Ibid.*, pp. 83–4.
118. *Clarion*, 8 May 1914, p. 12.
119. Waters, *British Socialists*, p. 76.

Chapter 7

A Substantive Interwar Outdoor Movement

A significant expansion in the pursuit of healthy open-air recreation occurred in Britain between the two world wars, particularly in the 1930s. Changes in leisure patterns during that period affected both the scale and, in various aspects, the character of the outdoor movement. This crucial consolidation was a result of the widespread adoption of country walking, cycling, mountaineering, and other related activities such as camping, by a substantial section of the young urban working and lower middle classes. The generation of a substantive outdoor movement has been identified, both contemporaneously by social commentators, and retrospectively by historians, as one of the social phenomena which have helped to characterize the interwar era. Such assumptions do, of course, concur with a stereotypical periodization of history into conveniently packaged eras, an obvious oversimplification that can obscure the assimilation and formative influence of underlying themes and strands of continuity. The huge popularity of open-air pursuits, producing substantial associational expansion, and the consequent growth and consolidation of an outdoor recreational and countryside lobby in Britain at this time, has, nonetheless, certainly contributed to the feeling of separateness which has attached itself to the period.

Helen Walker's exposition of the development of forms of open-air recreation illustrates something of the character and scale of the outdoor movement in the first half of the twentieth century.[1] However, the full significance of such development, with its widespread social and political ramifications, does demand a more detailed examination than has hitherto been carried out. Moreover, insufficient consideration has been afforded to the manifold influences of continuities, in the shape both of pre-1914 generative influences and in the way in which much that had been germinated in the 1930s came to fruition in the postwar period of reconstruction and beyond, while many of the practical objectives of the outdoor movement continued to be frustrated. The development of a broad, popular, but protean movement, founded on diverse approaches to the formulation of solutions to problems arising from a range of open-air issues, has been an evolutionary process, informed and shaped by the persistence of certain enduringly pertinent themes. Investigation of this process, especially during the 1920s and 1930s, also offers useful insights into the wider arena of a period of social, ideological and political transition.

Notwithstanding the importance of a continuity of dominant motifs and influences in the movement, new developments do need to be considered as distinctively interwar phenomena. Retrospective accounts have tended strongly towards largely unsubstantiated impressions, offering only simplistic analyses, and serving to perpetuate myths and misconceptions, as is apparent in the brief and superficial narratives contained in general social histories. Nonetheless, these fleeting accounts have correctly identified a distinct interwar vogue for outdoor recreational pursuits, which was partly stimulated by responses to prevailing conditions and circumstances. We learn that 'Hiking began to enjoy a boom in 1931',[2] that 'There were millions of pedal cyclists. Cycling clubs proliferated',[3] and that 'it was hiking and rambling that caught the mass imagination ...'[4] In *The Uses of Literacy*, Richard Hoggart records the 1930s' craze in the industrial area of Yorkshire where he lived, and the popularity of outdoor activities amongst urban workers:

> In the 'thirties the craze was for 'hiking', and though that seemed to me to affect the lower middle-classes more than others, the working-classes went too, on to the dales and hills and moors, which luckily are not far from most of the large towns. If walking is not markedly typical of working-class people, then cycling is.[5]

The collective effect of the generally superficial narratives of interwar open-air recreation has been to gloss over the full social and political importance of the boom, and to ignore much of its distinctively British cultural significance:

> The enthusiasm for the outdoors was part of a general movement for physical culture which affected much of Europe during the inter-war period and was reflected in Britain by the keep-fit craze, which spilled over into cycling, hiking and rambling, physical training and naturism.[6]

Interpretations of the popularity of outdoor pursuits in Britain between the wars also too readily identify the movement with prevailing motives in continental Europe, and particularly with the German *Wandervogel* and 'Strength through Joy'. A new concern with healthy recreation did indeed pervade the general consciousness, manifested in, for example, the 166,000 membership of the Women's League of

Health and Beauty (founded 1930), or the British observers who travelled to Germany to examine the organic social concept of 'Strength through Joy'. The influence of that wider contemporary milieu cannot be ignored, but does need to be kept in perspective. Arthur Creech Jones, MP for Shipley and author of the 1938 Access to Mountains Bill, pointed to the different nature of the motivation to participate in healthy open-air exercise which pertained in Britain: 'This country did not want the paternalism applied to workers abroad in the "Strength through Joy" movement, which was far too disciplined and not sufficiently individualistic ...'[7] The expansion of outdoor leisure activities in Britain during the 1920s, followed by the open-air boom of the 1930s, was never state-directed, unlike the situation in some other countries where different ideological influences were at play. Nor was the movement imbued with much degree of paternalism. Indeed, 'lack of government policy was a major fact of interwar leisure provision. The great successes lay with voluntary organizations especially in relation to outdoor sports like rambling and cycling.'[8] It was state intransigence, and the inability to adopt a planned approach to national resources and to growing demands in the sphere of leisure, that provided the major stumbling-block to the outdoor enthusiasts' attempts to gain improved access to open spaces.

Most accounts of the growth and consolidation of the movement towards a glib conflation of a new health fanaticism and urges rooted in the Romantic era: 'Concerns for health and the drives of much-distorted belated Romanticism made the "open air" a partial panacea for squalor and the years of depression.'[9] There is certainly a grain of truth contained in such perceptions, which are based on a solid foundation of contemporary evidence, but misleadingly concentrate on only particular aspects of interwar impressions. The emphasis is understandable, given the fact that contemporary literary accounts and subjective eye-witness views have rarely themselves painted the full picture. Recent studies have supplemented the body of evidence, reflecting the scale and significance of this hitherto underinvestigated phenomenon, although often serving to perpetuate the characteristic contemporary lack of specificity: 'Every Sunday during these years tens of thousands of walkers seeking relief from idleness or dull work and dreary surroundings would pour into the Peak District from the neighbouring industrial cities.'[10]

The philosopher and social commentator C. E. M. Joad, who was himself involved in a range of open-air and countryside issues, was one of the most prolific recorders of the effects of the movement, as well as of its undoubted political implications: 'The eyes of the young people of this generation have been opened; they see their towns as they are, and, turning their backs upon them, go in increasing numbers, first in hundreds and now in thousands, for rest and refreshment of the spirit to the country.' Joad's perceptions were based on his witnessing a large-scale escape at weekends by young people from Manchester into the Peak District: '... it might lead one to suppose that that the whole of Manchester was in exodus'; in a less rhetorical vein he noted that 'it cannot be reasonably doubted that the number of walkers is growing and is likely to continue to grow'.[11] J. B. Priestley was another interested party who testified to the escape to the moors from the industrial urban areas. To Priestley, however, the love of recreational walking was nothing new, as references to his pre-First World War boyhood testify:

> The hills and moors and dales are there for you. Nor do they wait in vain. The Bradford folk have always gone streaming out to the moors. In the old days ... this enthusiasm for the neighbouring country had bred a race of mighty pedestrians. Everybody went enormous walks.[12]

The continuity in particular localities is highlighted, but there is also no doubt as to the scale of the post-1918 expansion. Priestley himself commented on the large parties which left Bradford in the early 1930s: '... gangs of either hikers or bikers, twenty or thirty of them together and all dressed for their respective parts'.[13]

As early as 1922, the *Manchester City News* had identified a 'craze'[14] for rambling in its own area. Joad later asserted that 'in recent years rambling clubs have sprung up by the dozen',[15] while 'The Clarion Rambler', in an article in the handbook of the Manchester Federation of Ramblers, described his own impression of the mass exodus of town-dwellers into the southern Pennine uplands, although again acknowledging earlier roots of the popularity of countryside walking: 'Rambling has caught on and the pioneers ... have lived to see a veritable fever of rambling ... During some fine summer week-ends, there are approximately 10,000 ramblers and fresh-air seekers of either sex somewhere in the Derbyshire highlands.'[16] The growing numbers of publications produced by the outdoor associations indicate not only the scale of a popular fashion of the day, but also the collaboration in common interest of an ever-increasing outdoor fellowship. In 1934 the annual report of the Sheffield and District Ramblers' Federation confirmed that 'the rambling movement goes from strength to strength',[17] a fact that was commented on in the handbooks of all the major ramblers' associations: 'The revival of walking is one of the most healthy developments in the last decade.'[18] The popularity of this pastime during the interwar years is also indicated by substantial evidence of an expanding lobby in favour of improving public access to open countryside, and growing support for a corpus of ideas pertaining to the planning of wilder areas for recreational amenities. Proposing a plan for a national park in the Peak District, A. W. Hewitt signified the demand for healthy recreation in the south Pennines: 'It is the desired land of the ramblers ... the growing pursuit expands with amazing rapidity.'[19] The trend was also being remarked upon in parliamentary speeches supporting access bills. Opening the 1930 debate, Graham White, MP for Birkenhead, spoke of an 'increase in the number of societies for climbing, rambling, and camping',[20] and of the possibilities of one million members when six rambling federations in the north of England amalgamated. In the following year, Ellen Wilkinson, at that time MP for Middlesbrough East, supported her appeal for moorland access 'in view of the increased interest in hiking amongst many thousands of young people'.[21] Introducing his access bill in 1938, Creech Jones spoke of the 'great public demand for the passing of this measure [and the] great organizations which are concerned with open-air activity'. He referred to a pageant in the Lord Mayor of London's procession, at which 'we all saw how remarkable has been the growth of interest in recent years in athletic and open-air activities'.[22] Supporting Creech Jones's bill, the South Shields MP James Chuter Ede related his own experience of the huge numbers of ramblers that left the towns and cities at weekends, indicating the gregarious nature of the open-air fellowship:

> I frequently go out on the Sunday rambles organized by the Southern Railway and I know of nothing more exhilarating even when there are 700 or 800 people on these rambles. On one occasion, I recall, there were 1,600 people who went on one of these downland rambles.[23]

Lieutenant-Commander R. T. H. Fletcher, MP for Nuneaton, suggested that walking had recently become the 'great national recreation, rechristened "hiking" ...'[24] The increasing use of the term 'hiking' in contemporary observations on the outdoor boom is, in a way, indicative of the perceived newness of the popularity of a particular type of leisure walking. The term become quite voguish, and the press reflected the popular fashion, although it was not an entirely new usage; Robert Spence Watson, for example, referred to hiking in Scotland in correspondence to his daughter in 1880.[25]

Media interest in the outdoor leisure phenomenon both reflected and helped to generate the boom, with regular reference made to the availability of cheap transport. The *Manchester Guardian* was at the forefront of press coverage, with its incessant campaigning on issues of importance to the outdoor lobby, and with a regular feature on the second Monday of each month from 1933 on the activities of the ramblers' federations in various parts of the country. The newspaper published numerous other articles on rambling, including what to eat on walks, and, in June 1933, a feature on a sightless ramblers' club. Reports from the regions served to emphasize the interest in outdoor issues, giving something of the flavour of the expanding movement. The *Guardian* reported on rallies in several areas of the country, such as that at Glasgow in 1933, which attracted more than a thousand ramblers. A 'Ramblers' Day' was suggested for the third Sunday in June. At Easter 1933, it was reported from the Birmingham area that scores of young people had to be refused admisssion to youth hostels, which had been overwhelmed with bookings. The *Daily Mail*, despite its rigid anti-access stance, jumped on this fashionable bandwagon in 1931 with its regular feature of 'Hints for Hikers'. At Easter 1938 a correspondent of *The Times* was despatched to join and observe the hiking craze in the Peak District. He joined 'two hundred men and women, youths and girls', who set off in three groups of differing abilities.[26] Such examples of the sheer volume of the walking boom were repeated throughout urban and industrial Britain.

The wireless – the new medium of communication – also expressed regular interest in, and thereby helped to impel, the popular trend to open-air recreation. The writer S. P. B. Mais broadcast a series of talks based on walks he had made during a 15,000-mile journey through Britain early in 1932, consisting of 'seventeen haphazard excursions made at high speed at the request of the B.B.C. for the purpose of stimulating in listeners a desire to explore and rediscover their own island'.[27] These extremely popular programmes, describing the delights of rural Britain, 'earned for him the title of "Ambassador of the Countryside"'.[28] Mais himself stressed the proselytizing objective of his broadcasts: 'If, after each of the talks, listeners did not want to rush off at once and explore the district through which I had just rushed, I had failed entirely in my purpose.'[29]

It cannot be doubted that rambling and walking had by the mid-1930s captured the imagination of a significant proportion of the British public. When the Ramblers' Association (RA) was formed in 1935, it brought together 1,200 ramblers in a national organization, a figure which suggests exaggeration in the estimates of participants in outdoor pursuits. However, such statistics represent only the peak of a pyramid, and make no provision for the rambling clubs that remained outside the umbrella of the national body. The membership figures and level of active participation of just one club in one medium-sized industrial town indicates the widespread popularity of the pastime: throughout the 1930s the Glenfield Rambling Club from Kilmarnock maintained its membership at around 800, with an average of 80 members on rambles, which on special occasions attracted up to 300 people. The rise in membership of the Camping Club to 6,000 in 1933 was directly related to the general expansion of the outdoor movement, and, again, only represents the more visible expression of an overall trend.

By 1930 newspapers were remarking on the growing numbers of cyclists out on the country roads. Backed by a widespread popular adoption of the bicycle as a means of transport and casual leisure, the general sales of cycles far surpassed any previous peak, including that of the first craze of the 1890s. The popular expansion of that earlier era was far exceeded, and it was in Britain between the wars that touring cycling really took off as a popular pastime. Membership of the CTC never surpassed its 1899 peak of 60,449, but nor did the interwar subscriptions ever truly reflect the popularity of the pastime. This may partly be explained by the continuing hint of élitism in the organization, demonstrated by a policy of vetting potential new applicants. In fact, the popular adoption of the bicycle after the First World War happened on a huge scale. In 1924, the CTC claimed that there were six million bicycles in use in Britain, compared to three million in 1912. Annual sales rose from 385,000 in 1920 to a 1935 peak of 1,610,000. These statistics compare with a figure of two million driving licences in 1925. The national boom underpinned a major industry which exported 200,800 cycles in 1924 alone. Touring cyclists represented a major contribution to that general expansion. The genesis of the interwar boom can, in fact, be traced back to well before the end of the war itself. As early as January 1918, the *CTC Gazette* remarked on the rebirth of its own pastime and the optimistic prospects for the postwar period:

> The past twelve months have shown a great increase of cycling throughout the land. Old machines have been refurbished and brought once more into use, while the demand for new machines has so far exceeded the supply that the secondhand market has been well-nigh drained of its resources.[30]

The CTC continued to report increases in numerical strength and consequent prosperity. The April 1933 issue of the *CTC Gazette* reported the birth of the 'National Bicycle Week' movement. It is not possible to gauge accurately the numbers of touring cyclists who were active during the interwar craze, but both the visible statistics and the attention afforded to the pastime by contemporary commentators leaves no doubt as to the significant scale of a recreational phenomenon. By 1938, membership of cycling clubs, including those affiliated to the racing-orientated National Cyclists' Union (NCU), stood at over 60,000. Priestley commented on the large numbers of cyclists in Wharfedale in 1933: 'We saw a good deal of the cyclists, however, passing troops of them all along the road up to Grassington ...'[31] His observations point to the continuing difficulty in distinguishing between the touring and the racing fraternities. He commented critically on the young and energetic propensity to get the head down and go for speed. But the athletic enjoyment of the activity should not be underestimated as one of the motives for many of those who sought fresh air and exercise; it was not necessarily contrary to the desire to stop and stare and appreciate the joys of nature as a pleasant relief from urban conditions and restraints. Nonetheless, Priestley's perception was supported in the postwar period by Richard Hoggart, who confirmed the need to differentiate between the 'tourists' and the 'racers': 'The N.C.U. members may often seem scarcely to know whether the road passes through a town or a National Park; but sightseeing is not their purpose.'[32]

The adoption of countryside leisure pursuits by a substantial section of the urban population during the interwar period was on such a large scale that motivation inevitably ranged from a simple desire to escape and enjoy social fellowship, to high-minded ideals and a reforming political *raison d'être*. Fundamentally essential to the trend was the range of factors that physically facilitated its expansion. One central feature was the increasing availability of paid holidays, a widely debated issue between 1918 and the introduction of the 1938 Holidays with Pay Act. The increase in spare time was, nevertheless, a distinctly evolutionary process. Many of the holiday agreements had been negotiated within particular industries, or backed by institutionalized savings schemes based on the principle of collective self-help going back into the latter part of the nineteenth century. The trend towards paid holidays certainly gained momentum after 1918, providing an important stimulus to the urban workers who were the main beneficiaries. Stephen Jones has argued that the 1938 Act was 'insignificant as compared with the growth of appropriate collective agreements'.[33] A related factor was a gradual reduction in the length of the working week. By 1938 the average male worker spent 48.5 hours at his place of employment, compared to the 54-hour working week of the pre-1914 period. The importance of this change to the genesis of the outdoor movement can be traced to the socio-economic development of Lancashire, and particularly Manchester, where natural history groups had begun to take advantage of the free Saturday afternoon from the middle of the nineteenth century. It is likely that the reduction in working hours meant not only more time, but also more energy to be expended on excursions in the countryside.

Time away from the workplace in the 1920s and 1930s can not always be equated with longer holidays or a shorter working week. Unprecedented levels of unemployment, much of it long term, added a new dimension to the leisure question in many areas of the country. Inactivity and concomitant poverty often produced apathy and despair, but also stimulated positive responses amongst those who sought constructively to minimize the often overbearing depression of the industrial towns and cities. One of the most palpable expressions of this reaction can be seen in the activities of a highly motivated fraternity of climbers, mountaineers and hillwalkers who took every opportunity to escape the conditions of the industrial city of Glasgow.

In the 1930s in Britain a very different kind of mountaineer emerged, men from the industrial cities such as Glasgow. They were men from working-class backgrounds who worked in the shipyards, in shops, or as apprentices, but all had in common the uncertainty of unemployment and the bleak prospect of being young in a large industrial city at a time of dole queues and recession. For many of them getting out of the city was the great escape.[34]

The pull of the hills and the open spaces for young men with time on their hands and with no affinity with urban street life has been described enthusiastically by some of the Glaswegian 'Mountain Men'.[35] Alistair Borthwick's earlier account of this Scottish contribution to the idea of outdoor fellowship stresses youthfulness and unorthodoxy as key influences on a 'mass movement'.[36] The influence of the energetic interwar contribution to the outdoor movement in Scotland can still be felt today, asserted by a class of people who themselves picked up the Scottish stravaiging tradition in their youth, and ensured that subsequent generations were given the opportunity to enjoy the fruits of their legacy. Many of these men remain active today; their accounts of their activities and the kinship that they engendered offer some wonderful insights into the motives of the outdoor fraternity. Bob Grieve of Glasgow, who later became Sir Robert Grieve of Edinburgh, relates how the hills still afforded a form of escape much later in life, despite a considerable change in personal circumstances:

But the escape was a necessity and even to this day at my age, nearly seventy, I still walk on the hills and I still get from them what I got then ... A kind of lowering of the temperature; a falling away of neurosis; an ability to think about problems more easily ... health; and peace.[37]

These were the men who, at every opportunity and by any means available, headed north out of Glasgow, sometimes only as far as the Kilpatrick Hills, or 'up the pipe track'[38] into the Campsie Fells, both within walking distance of the city, although the climbers in particular would get further afield, heading for the Arrochar Alps to the west of Loch Lomond, or for Glencoe. They slept in barns and bothys and caves and camps. In a chapter entitled 'A Taste of Freedom', Ralph Glaser recollects growing up in the crowded Glasgow tenements, and recalls weekends at the Carbeth Muir socialist camp, where regulars maintained a welcoming fire for many years as a focus for open-air fellowship.[39] Jock Nimlin remembers the effects of the big city on the individual, and the joy of getting out of Glasgow: 'And the antidote to this situation was to get away at weekends as we did. A wonderful tonic.'[40] Another area of massive unemployment was Tyneside, where many of those without work were introduced to hiking by the Northumbrian Trampers' Guild, which utilized facilities made available by Sir Charles Trevelyan at his country estate at Wallington Hall. The simple bunk-bed dormitory accommodation adapted from outbuildings at Wallington was later donated to the YHA. Cycling, too, was a relatively inexpensive way of escaping the atrophying effects of urban unemployment:

In the Depression years of the twenties and thirties, many unemployed found relief in cycling away from the dole queues and the disillusioned groups of men who stood on the street corners waiting, not for work for there wasn't much hope of that, but just waiting because there was little else to do.[41]

For the many who could afford it, railway travel was increasingly a means of getting out into the countryside. The interwar expansion of excursions and cheap fares proved as big a boon to ramblers, mountaineers, campers and some cyclists as it did to the wider tourist industry, with the flourishing seaside resorts in the vanguard. Rail travel was available at 1d. per mile in 1932, while walking tour tickets were well publicized and heavily subscribed. In their provision of ramblers' excursions the railway companies were not only responding to a lucrative market, but also stimulating further increases in numbers on organized rambles:

My own earliest contacts with fellow ramblers were by way of the magnificent programme of ramblers' excursion trains which have run from London ever since the Whitsun weekend of 1932. Every weekend of the year they left the central London termini, special trains at special fares ... Such was the golden age of excursion rambling.[42]

Railway 'Mystery Hikes' proved extremely popular. The 'Hikers' Mystery Express', run by the Great Western Railway at Easter 1932, 'drew a record crowd about two thousand strong'.[43] Much of the advertising of the railway and bus companies was aimed specifically at ramblers and hikers, as indeed was that of other commercial concerns, including the tobacco companies, seeking to identify with the outdoor image. Prominent amongst this commercial exploitation of a popular social trend were the posters portraying stylized evocative images of happy people in the countryside. The advertisements produced by the Southern Railway for 'Conducted Rambles' were typical of an artistic genre that flourished in the 1930s. They represented the four seasons, and are now displayed in the National Railway Museum at York.

The main benefit to cyclists from the general transport boom was a large-scale programme of road-building and improvement, producing the practical effect of enabling tourers to travel more easily and further afield. There is some irony in the fact that the cyclists were often at odds with the motorists; the former's representative bodies found themselves campaigning ceaselessly against an increasingly powerful motoring lobby. The majority of the minor country roads, nevertheless, did continue to be of the old composition of rolled stone, dirt and sand, making the extremely popular route through the Trough of Bowland in Lancashire, for example, much more of an adventure than it has since become. Urban cycling, of course, was subject to the discomfort and danger of cobbles, granite setts and greasy tramlines. In his second social survey of York, compiled in 1935, Seebohm Rowntree recognized the general improvement in road surfaces, combined with cheaper bicycles, as factors in the growth of recreational cycling.[44] A comparison of pre-1914 and 1930's prices from the catalogues of Raleigh cycles, or the prices displayed in the reconstructed cooperative hardwear department at Beamish Museum in Co. Durham, would seem to confirm the influence of relatively cheaper models, although cyclists of that era are often sceptical about any such trend. Rowntree also observed an increase in rambling by the residents of York, who could take advantage of bus excursions. The York Co-operative Ramblers, for instance, hired a bus once a month.

Reaction against the Great War gave some impetus to the outdoor movement. One aspect of the new motivation towards healthy open-air pursuits by increasing numbers in the 1920s and 1930s can be detected in a widespread rejection of the old order, and particularly of the regressive eagerness of the establishment to return to the supposed normality of a pre-war world: 'Reaction to the war was a motivation for many in the twenties.'[45] There was an identifiable driving force behind the growth of the movement, constructed from a substantial desire to move forward into a better world for the majority. It encouraged the development of opportunities for improvement which assimilated a need for rational forms of leisure; this largely progressive motif re-emerged in what was predominantly a youth movement. It was founded on a fundamentally new mentality, which emanated out of a broader general rejection of the failures of the past, and an optimistic vision to project into a better future. The anti-war line was prevalent in the continuing Utopian socialist contribution to the development of the movement. The NCCC was particularly vehement in its reaction to the re-emergence of militaristic and nationalistic tendencies in the 1930s: 'If we are to build clean, physical [sic], healthy minds and bodies, we must see to it that "Never Again" will they be torn to pieces on some "foreign field", that they shall be won for Peace and to build that "Merrie England" that the pioneers of our club dreamed of.' [46]

This interwar expansion into a substantive popular movement does need to be qualified. Healthy countryside recreation did become a popular vogue – indeed, it was one of the main contemporary expressions of generally youthful gregariousness and sociability. As such, it became, in effect, a self-generating youth cult, too broad to be identified comfortably with deep-seated principles, or with a central unifying ethos that was rooted any deeper than a gut reaction against the failure of the *status quo* to formulate satisfactory solutions to the prevailing problems of urban-industrial society. It is difficult to identify any all-embracing influence of high-minded ideals amongst the large groups of young, exuberant, predominantly working-class hikers in the Peak District in the 1930s. The comment of a young woman rambler returning from the Peak District to Manchester by train in 1938 gives a flavour of the sociable dimension to the motivation behind the boom: 'I come on these walks because I feel I have missed something when I see the others coming back.' [47] However, notwithstanding the undoubted influence of the desire to follow a fashion, there was far more to the popular participation in healthy open-air exercise than merely following the crowd. Many of the growing numbers of members of outdoor organizations sought independently the measure of freedom largely denied to them by prevailing conditions and conventions. These were the people described by A. W. Hewitt in an article of 1931, proposing a Peak District national park: 'The cramping of people in their monotonous dull rows of houses, cribbed, cabined, and confined to their slag heaps and skyscreening factories, in smoke-ridden areas found nowhere else, has produced the inevitable reaction.' [48] A longing for the freedom of the wide-open spaces had been a central motivating strand throughout the development of the movement, but the momentum which that motivation achieved in the 1920s, and particularly the 1930s, assumed the proportions and zeal of a 'popular crusade'.[49] The escape to the countryside cannot be separated from an overall desire to improve a quality of life that was hampered persistently by a combination of circumstances. New opportunities were obviously a factor feeding the open-air boom, but it was the continuing frustration with the prevailing situation, and the drive to escape, rather than any removal of former restraints, that provided the underlying motivation: 'Most people escaped to the country as a revulsion against the towns, and against working conditions.'[50] Urban conditions featured prominently in the case presented by the supporters of access bills: 'The word "patriotism" is much on people's tongues at the present moment. How can you expect some people to feel patriotic about the rookeries in which they have to live.'[51]

The urban–rural contrast certainly re-emerged in the interwar era as a major influence on the unprecedented growth of open-air pursuits. The juxtaposition of urban ugliness with superb upland scenery was as much a factor stimulating the young working-class exodus from industrial Clydeside in the 1930s, as it had already been for many years in attracting people into the countryside from the sub-Pennine textile districts. Tom Weir recalls the pull of the hills:

> ... from where I lived in Springburn you could see Ben Lomond, Ben Lui, you could see the Arran hills ... the bus to Campsie Glen passed our door, 6d half fare, and for me that was a great discovery because up on the tops of the Campsies there were other ranges of hills and these were my Himalayas. Beyond Ben Lomond the great ranges.[52]

Alistair Borthwick's reflections on his own experience of getting out of Glasgow contrast the grimness of urban depression with the freshness of the discovery of a new world of adventure: 'It was a grim place ... People were on the dole, there was absolutely no hope at all ... Here was an entirely different world where it was alive and things were happening ... It was an explosion, it was a wonderful thing.'[53]

In Britain, this essential environmental contrast has been more extreme over a longer period of time than anywhere else, stimulating the evolution of a particular type of urban-based outdoor movement. Emotional association with certain landscape features was also a factor that drew people to the nearby countryside. It is a feeling expressed in autobiographical accounts produced by lovers of the Pennine Uplands: 'It is, I have no doubt, because I was born on the edge of a Yorkshire moor ... that the call of the hills and the heather has always been welcomed by my soul. No country ever makes the same strong, urgent appeal as my own Pennine country.'[54] In a similar vein, another Yorkshireman, J. Wood, lending support to the concept of the Pennine Way, was of the opinion that proximity to moorland influenced the personality, thereby accentuating the urge to escape from the industrial town: 'And not only the farmer and the shepherd are moulded by the moors. Similarly influenced is the dweller in the grim towns that lie a sixpenny bus ride or less from the fringe of the heath.'[55] However, a contrary view amongst articulate lovers of the uplands also needs to be considered. Natives of the flatlands, such as the prolific writer on the outdoors, W. A. Poucher, were drawn by the lure of the hills as a complete contrast to normality: 'I was brought up in Lincolnshire, that flat and uninteresting county which still appals me ...'[56] Poucher's initial escape was to the south Pennines, before he came to explore hilly regions further afield. The expansive contemporary literature of open-air recreation does give something of the flavour of the interwar need to escape to the countryside, although, in its fairly dominant emphasis on the romantic, the aesthetic and the spiritual, it reflects only the response of a minority, rather than that of the larger, popular outdoor movement. Much of the writing was redolent of nineteenth-century intellectual esoteric ideas relating to the attractions of an unspoiled natural environment. There is a continuity from the earlier ideologues of anti-industrialism. T. L. Tudor typified the genre, invoking both Ruskin and Morris: 'We want the pure and holy hills treated as a link between Heaven and Earth ... I demand that there be left waste spaces and wilds, or romance and poetry, that is Art, will die out amongst us.'[57] Tudor himself expressed the same sentiments, in a similar idiom, to nineteenth-century exponents of hill-walking: '... these tracts of wild country, which are at all times invigorating and sometimes sublime in their barbaric charm'.[58] He also identified the continuing theme of related interests in the motives for country walking, pointing, for instance, to 'the vigorous nature cult' which flourished in the urban-industrial centres.[59] In many ways such observation reflects the importance of a romantic and élitist strand, shaping both the anti-industrial urge and the form of conservationism that the more unified interwar movement shared with intellectual and literary promoters of open-air recreation in the previous century. Association with landscape, often rooted in atavistic notions of the collective memory of a pre-industrial age, was expressed in the writing of those who themselves remained largely aloof from mass participation in the outdoor movement. This prevalent romantic rhetorical idiom was, however, used to describe an integration of the modernizing concept of rational recreation with references to anti-industrial urges. In such a mode J. Wood confirmed a significant popular contribution to the development of open-air responses to urban-industrialism:

Long before rambling became a popular recreation and its distant relation hiking was adopted as a newspaper stunt, decades earlier than the first noisy trams that eased their way over the setts of urban roads, the man of the mills strode upward to the heights and let the wuthering winds clear the soot from his lungs and whip the pallor from his cheeks. His descendants are mostly wedded to the meretricious pleasures of Blackpool and Morecambe when the local tide or feast week comes along, but a minority – and not an insignificant one – is still loyal to the moors on week-ends and bank holidays, and has never quite forgotten that prior to the industrial revolution its ancestry was of the fells.[60]

To interpret much of the expansion of outdoor recreation as a new popular 'stunt' was a patronizing and élitist viewpoint, but it rightly points out an element of discontinuity from earlier origins, suggesting that the hikers of the 1920s and 1930s were in some respects a different breed from the walkers and mountaineers of the nineteenth century. Nonetheless, the ethos and culture that underpinned the earlier genesis and expansion of healthy open-air pursuits remained pertinent to the movement in the post-World War One period: 'Rambling clubs are numerous, directing attention to science and archaeology and bringing special culture into everyday life.'[61]

Criticism that was constructed during the interwar decades expanded into a broader-based, more eclectic reaction against a newer form of general popular cultural formation, which was created from supply-led commercial developments in leisure. The expansion of a more middle-brow movement had the effect of moderating the previously prevalent élitism. It was an intellectual milieu that was expressed appropriately in the writing, broadcasting, and lecture tours of J. B. Priestley, whose social observations encompassed a close interest in the urban exodus to energetic rural pursuits. Priestley's sceptical view of Oxbridge and metropolitan cultural élitism led to accusations that he espoused the burgeoning popular culture in its entirety, and thus sanctioned a level of trivialization. The more democratic and egalitarian 'broadbrow'[62] cultural commentary, however, despite its catholic broad-mindedness, made a point of emphasizing the maintenance of high standards, but, importantly, standards to which the majority could aspire realistically. Priestley helped to promote a form of culture which spurned the more trivial aspects of popular entertainment. He was concerned about the loss of spontaneity that characterized the idealized community culture of his youth: 'Too much of this life is being stamped on from outside, probably by astute financial gentlemen, backed by the Press and their publicity services.'[63] Priestley's attack on uniformity extended to the popular adoption of open-air pursuits, thus echoing, somewhat contradictorily, the more élite viewpoint: 'Even that push towards the open which we have now decided to call "hiking" has something regimented about it.'[64] Nonetheless, his democratic ideal was essential to a contemporary version of an ideology with which many in the outdoor movement could identify. It espoused the associational culture which underpinned community-based social democracy, but disavowed block thinking or any tendency towards dogmatic ideology. The popular crazes for cinema and modern dancing were adopted as enthusiastically by lovers of the open-air as by the rest of the younger generation. It was in the realm of other popular commercial forms of leisure, such as the holiday at the more popular seaside resorts, gambling, drinking, and spectator sports, that the cultural divergence manifested itself.[65]

The rejection of ugliness that underlay the need to escape to the country was formulated within a wider context of contemporary responses which were generally articulated pessimistically. The tone was, however, modified by the enthusiastic adoption of a philosophy of national planning, devised as the most constructive way to counteract both the continuing problems of environmental blight and the growing demands of country leisure. It was no less fervent or articulate in its more popular expression than in the often élite literary response, although it continued to be an intellectual clique, impelled by a purportedly progressive doctrine steeped in selected references to an idealized rural past, whose responses and solutions were more commonly disseminated. The corpus of pertinent ideas, which emanated from influential establishment figures, sought to reconcile élitist perceptions with democratic claims that promoted the perceived better interests of the population at large. It was a doctrine most voluminously expressed by C. E. M. Joad, who combined a criticism of 'The Untutored Townsman's Invasion of the Country'[66] with tireless campaigning for the right of all to ramble in the open spaces, promoting the rights of the people over the rights of the landowner. In his view, 'the people's claim upon the English countryside is paramount ...'[67] The development of this doctrine in the 1930s, and its relationship to the wider context of land use and countryside conservation, was dependent upon a socialistic creed, which adopted what were fundamentally old Tory values of nurturing the land and its traditional rural culture, and adapted them in a symbiosis with the rationalist concept of the importance of educating and encouraging the full potential of the wider community. The paternalistic and condescending aspect to Joad's philosophy of social development was concerned with cultivating both body and mind, and inculcating an appreciation of the beauty and value of natural environments. At the same time, it was strongly redolent of the Clarion socialist open-air creed, which emerged in the 1890s to promulgate and encourage individual fulfilment, aimed ultimately at the improvement of the overall community:

... one of the objects of education is to enable us to develop our latent potentialities, to extend our capacities to the full, to become all that we have it in us to be. In this full development of personality the culture of the body as well as the mind must play its part, and to the culture of the body familiarity with nature in walking and riding, in swimming and climbing, is an essential contribution. Confined in towns we need the country to enable to develop to the full the individualities that ours might be.[68]

Joad, however, also contended that 'the People are Not Yet Ready', and proposed to take their education in hand.[69] The interwar intellectual exponents of countryside recreation and critics of urban industrialism were confronted with a larger-scale invasion of the countryside than ever before, and were at least as scathing about the tripper element as their counterparts had been in the nineteenth century. Joad railed against the popularity of charabanc parties, against such practices as the picking and uprooting of wild flowers, and against the rubbish that was seen as an inevitable consequence of the popularization of rural areas for the recreation of the town dweller: '... the scurf of litter – that grimy visiting card which democracy ... insists on leaving after a visit'.[70] Contemporary perceptions of the dilemmas created by democracy and mass society are evident. But, to Joad and others of his type, such behaviour was explained by the adverse influences on the individual of the brutality, ugliness, and squalor which prevailed in the urban environment. This was basically a social democratic reformist, if somewhat quirkish, stance: 'Citizens educated in rural lore ... will not want to walk through fields of corn or to leave behind them a trail of open gates.'[71]

Notwithstanding the élitism of the literary open-air lobby, the ultimate aim was to assert for the majority of the population the right to make reasonable use of the countryside. It was the interests of the country sportsman and the unemployed *rentier* class which were expected to yield to a planned, more democratic future. Joad's sometimes eccentric plans to assert the paramountcy of the people included the dubious and controversial contention that arable farmers should also yield to their recreational demands, although it remained unclear as to how that ideal should be pursued practically. A counter view was expressed by A. G. Street, who was also a proponent of countryside amenity and improved access, but, as a farmer himself, defended the role of the responsible arable farmer – 'the trustee of our countryside, as regards both its material value and its beauty'[72] – in properly husbanding a valuable resource, which could amply fulfil both working and recreational functions. Reacting against the loss of good land through suburban sprawl and ribbon development, rather than against increasing access for the urban masses, Street supported the principle of land nationalization as the means to preservation and proper management in the interests of all but the speculator and the absentee landlord. As a countryman, he witnessed the increasing despoliation of his surroundings, and felt that the townsman, in trying to enjoy the rural areas, was contributing to their destruction. His idea was that the townsman and the countryman should have a shared interest in the continuing well-being of the countryside.

Despite town and country planning legislation, no really coherent pattern emerged which could satisfactorily facilitate the needs of open-air recreation. Professor Abercrombie stressed the need for more drastic land policy, proposing a national commission for planning, which would set out the essential guidelines. Against the new vogue for planning was set the continuing tendency to formulate land policy in a piecemeal fashion. G. M. Trevelyan, who retained an active interest in open-air activities throughout his life, highlighted the problems of incoherent policy:

> In the matter of the preservation of the beauty of rural England, what we need is a State policy, the support of the Ministry, of Parliament, and of legislation ... The State is Socialist enough to destroy by taxation the classes that used to preserve rural amenity; but it is still too Conservative to interfere in the purposes to which land is put by speculators to whom the land is sold.[73]

Trevelyan was also sceptical of the effectiveness of existing countryside protection bodies, emphasizing the inadequacy of the National Trust, which owned only 60,000 acres in 1937: 'Lay not that flattering unction to your souls that the National Trust is solving the problem of rural amenity.'[74] One of the new bodies was the Council for the Preservation of Rural England (CPRE), set up in 1926 to coordinate the efforts of the various interested parties, to protect country amenities and natural beauty, and to arouse and educate public opinion about its stated objects. The Council for the Preservation of Rural Wales (CPRW) shared the same London address.[75]

The increasing diversity of individuals and groups who contributed to the interwar boom in open-air activities raises legitimate questions as to whether this amounted to a movement in the true sense, or whether we are only concerned with a loose-knit agglomeration of disparate persons, owing little or no allegiance to any unifying body of philosophy or guiding set of values. Some of the somewhat élitist observations made by Joad and others would seem to challenge the notion of a unified movement gelled by a set of common principles: '... this generation has replaced beer by "hiking" as the shortest cut out of Manchester'.[76] This was the outdoor craze witnessed by *The Times* correspondent in 1938. The perception of 'The New Walking' concentrated on the significant change from earlier recreational walking, but also contributed to the submergence of important continuities in the motives for countryside rambling. In referring to Leslie Stephen, Arthur Sidgwick, G. M. Trevelyan and Edward Bowen, *The Times* made the contrast with an earlier élite tradition, effectively and misleadingly ignoring the athletic, competitive and gregarious aspects of that tradition: 'Inevitably it follows that walking has become a social phenomenon. The solitary walker is a rarity; walking with a single companion is not common.' The correspondent appeared to be taken aback by the numbers in the group, by the heavy rucksacks, the lack of guidebooks, maps and compasses, the apparent unwillingness to pause to admire views, and by the pace that was sustained (4 m.p.h.), asserting that 'the walkers marched ahead'. There were comments on the popular fashionable uniform adopted by these young working-class hikers, comprised of 'shorts, corduroy wind jackets, mufflers, and nailed boots'. Their uniformity was persistently stressed, apparently confirming that what was in evidence was indeed a popular fashion of the day, little informed by individuality:

> Not all the walkers are poets, painters, or philosophers, and perhaps that quick mode of walking was best suited to the majority of those in the party, comprising, as they did, mill hands, factory workers, and typists ... [T]he walk was lifted above the level of a mere prison yard exercise by a visit to the church at Eyam, the Derbyshire plague village.[77]

It is undoubtedly necessary to qualify simplistic references to a unified movement. However, certain factors were readily identifiable throughout the interwar years. These included a vigorous and expanding campaigning element, and the associational affiliation into national bodies, which combined to give much of the muscle to lobbies for open access, national parks, long-distance footpaths, countryside conservation and to a general urge to improve rural amenity, in response to vastly increased demand. A substantial proportion of the new generation of lovers of the open air lent their support in various ways to the consolidation of a national campaigning movement. The fact that many may just have gone along for the ride, involved only on the margins, and attracted by a contemporary trend which enabled them to escape their own environment with little thought to related issues, hardly detracts from the expansion and consolidation of a movement underpinned by associational affiliation and collaboration. Whatever the motives of the urban escapees, the nature of their chosen pursuit meant that they would, sooner or later, engage with the question of access to the countryside. As Alun Howkins and John Lowerson point out in *Trends in Leisure, 1919–1939*, the mass pursuit of open-air recreation as an escape from deprivation raised the profile of the access issue to one of growing national importance, while serving also to reinvigorate a debate which had been placed periodically on the agenda since the 1880s. In reacting against one area of deprivation, the burgeoning walking fraternity was unlikely to aquiesce in another form of imposed deprivation for long, without lending its substantial weight to a reforming lobby.

Speakers in support of access bills emphasized regularly the coming together of a broad demand for common action, which was reflected in correspondence from constituents and from interested bodies. Creech Jones, for example, spoke of 'great organizations which are concerned with open air activities'.[78] The National Parks Committee, appointed by Ramsay MacDonald in 1929, and convened under Christopher Addison MP in 1931, brought together a number of interested individuals, as well as organizations such as CPRE, COSFPS and the various regional ramblers' federations. The subsequent Standing Committee on National Parks included representatives from all the outdoor bodies, thereby involving such influential individuals as T. A. Leonard and Edwin Royce, the often outspoken president of the Manchester Ramblers' Federation. Failure to agree on such crucial issues as the correct balance between public amenity and conservation, however, emphasizes the degree of diversity of interests – reflected in the various associations – within the broader movement, which makes it hard to define a clear-cut common ideology.[79] The range of organizations that were either founded or expanded during the interwar period mirrors the scale of a craze that defies generalization. A representative sample of rambling groups taken from London and Yorkshire in 1933 indicates the variety of backgrounds and wider interests, as well as political affiliations, which ranged from socialist to Tory: it includes Bexley Heath Congregational Guild Rambling Club, Park Congregational Ramblers of Sheffield, Sheffield Clarion Ramblers; the rambling sections of Astra Cycling Club, Balham Rotary Club, Battersea Branch Junior Imperial and Constitutional League, and the London Esperanto Club; and those from the junior imperial leagues at Bramley, Leeds, and South Kirby. The clubs were also manifestly socially diverse, ranging, for example, in London, from the Mayfair Rambling Club, based in SW1, to the Fraternal Rambling Club of Islington, the Uleric Rambling Club of Plaistow, and a group from the West Ham Junior Civic Club. The Workers' Education Association had twenty-two rambling sections in London and the Home Counties area, from Twickenham and Dorking to Southwark and Stepney.

In 1933, the Yorkshire Ramblers' Club published a reference book giving details 'concerning the many and varied organizations connected with the open-air movement'.[80] Such diversity, ramifying from the popularity of a contemporary vogue, meant that it was difficult to channel a unified campaigning movement into wielding the sort of influence that the volume of interest truly warranted. But there was a reference in the same publication to 'the force of public opinion' stirring Parliament into action over ramblers' rights.[81] The first *Gazette* of the Ramblers' Council, produced in June 1933, also stressed the weight of public opinion, and called for common action based on common policy. This referred to the sort of measures that were already being carried out on a local basis, such as fundraising for the purchase by public bodies of the Longshaw Estate on the fringes of Sheffield for recreational purposes. The annual report of the Sheffield and District Ramblers' Federation referred to a 'movement [that] is sound and well conducted'.[82] There were several references to constituent organizations within the larger outdoor movement comprising a movement in themselves. It was an epithet most commonly applied to the Youth Hostels Association (YHA), especially by Joad, for example in *A Charter for Ramblers*. The Midland Federation of Ramblers also identified the YHA as a movement, and as an important focus for active outdoor people: '... the Youth Hostel movement seeks to aid and and continue this revival of walking. It includes cyclists – but not motorists – in its scope.'[83] The trend towards closer cooperation between the various open-air interests was, nonetheless, hindered by a diversity of sometimes contradictory priorities and concerns, and was subject constantly to factional differences over tactical issues. However, a positive movement was evolving through associational expansion, consolidation, and regional and national amalgamation.

A particularly active socialist dimension was sustained partly by a resurgence in the fortunes of the NCCC, and its affiliated local sections. Membership topped 7,000 during the summer of 1936, with confident predictions of attaining 10,000, and a hope expressed that a figure of 20,000 could be reached by canvassing the huge numbers of unattached cyclists. The number of Clarion cyclists in fact peaked at around 7,500 in 1937, although *Clarion Cyclist*, the successor to *Clarion Cyclists' Journal*, claimed 8,000 members for the movement in November 1936, and also that the CCCs were 'still enrolling members at the rate of about 100 per week'.[84] The relative failure of the clubs to take full advantage of the new cycling craze can be ascribed in part to the classic marginalizing tactic in which a generally perceived eccentricity was combined with a bad press. However, the Clarionettes did contribute to the strength of the interwar movement, as well as continuing to add weight to its unifying campaigning dimension. The content of *Clarion Cyclist*,

introduced in July 1936, indicated the persistence of the Clarion movement's open-air philosophy, and the way in which recreation and
political involvement continued to combine in a sometimes uneasy
partnership. Recreational and social aspects continued to dominate, to
the occasional despair of political activists and leader writers: 'To make
an exclusive fetish of cycling, with no interest in the realities of life, is
only selfishness.'[85] The often conflictual dual function in the composition of the Clarion fellowship of cyclists was reminiscent of the
pre-1914 dichotomy in the club. 'Kuklos', the author of this article,
went on to re-emphasize the importance of 'political activity and propaganda to make one's native land something to be really proud of'.[86]

The NCCC's consistency in the interwar years with much of its
original campaigning political purpose illustrates an aspect of the split
in the organized and articulate sector of the movement. The political
activists and those who sought to convey the message of socialism
through the agency of open-air fellowship continued to criticize the
cycling clubs, claiming that they were too taken up with the social
attractions of the movement. The debate surfaced from time to time
in the columns of *Clarion*: 'A common taunt of intellectually snobbish
critics is that we propose to cycle or dance ourselves into the socialist
commonwealth.'[87] The Clarion movement also retained anachronistic
characteristics based on ethical influences which had been moulded
during its turn-of-the-century heyday. Even in 1932 *Clarion* could
envisage 'the fellowship spread like a visual flame' by the CCCs: '... the
sacred flame of Jerusalem, carried by enthusiasts to other enthusiasts
from the central altar'.[88] Clarion remained steeped in its Christian
nonconformist ethical origins, but such messages, delivered in a biblical
idiom, carried little weight with a newly secularized British left, which
drew inspiration from a still credible Soviet Union.

The political left of the 1930s certainly viewed the Clarion's outdoor
fellowship of cyclists as an anachronism. T. A. Jackson, a member of
the Communist Party Executive Committee, took issue against Tom
Groom, founder of the NCCC, over the proper role of British socialism. Groom had invoked French revolutionary images in accusing the
Communists of undemocratic practice, at a time when the CCCs'
propaganda campaigns were carrying the message of the established
Labour Party. The social democracy of the CCCs in the 1920s and
1930s was partly in response to the general emergence of totalitarianism.
As the compiler of the *Clarion*'s 'Cyclorama' column, Groom accused
the Communists of 'the contradictory cry of "Dictatorship and Liberty"', and likened their leadership to the Committee of Public Safety:
'Whilst I, as my head drops in the basket, will with my last dying
breath, shout; "Down with T. A. Jackson, Mussolini, Lenin, Trotsky,
and all Dictators".'[89] Nevertheless, Groom also found it necessary to

harangue CCC members into carrying on the propaganda role of the club, indicating the degree of political apathy and the concomitant emphasis on enjoyment and social cycling, consistent with a predominantly apolitical cycling boom. The energetic Groom had always managed to reconcile successfully the business of politics with the pleasure of the recreational aspect to his movement, claiming that he was 'no advocate of all work and no play'. However, he also recognized a need to to remind the membership of the club's original aims and continuing function: 'It is because we are something more than a cycling club that we have lived and shall live. It was the mutual interest in Socialism which brought together the founders of the Clarion Cycling Club.'[90] As T. A. Leonard had discovered previously, Groom realized that founding principles did not necessarily survive wholly intact the wayward and diverse influences asserted by the rising popularity of an organization that promoted recreation and social fellowship. At the very least, a dilution of the initial objectives was inevitable.[91]

Clarion opposition to the National Government underpinned the CCCs' role as prominent activists in the interests of the growing cycling lobby in the 1930s. This campaigning dimension was initiated by the larger and more influential CTC, which set up its Rights and Privileges Committee in 1919 to defend the rights of all bicycle users and to promote their interests. The *CTC Gazette* publicized a number of issues of importance to cyclists, including elements of the sweeping Defence of the Realm Act (DORA), which was reported to have produced a 'noxious press campaign against the users of cycles'.[92] Cycling campaigners increasingly came into conflict with an emerging motor lobby and Ministry of Transport legislation that was perceived as anti-cyclist. Among the threats to the cycling fellowship was a scheme to remove bicycles from the roads onto separate paths. The fact that cycling had become a predominantly working-class pursuit gave a political aspect to the CCCs' strident campaigning. *Clarion Cyclist* stressed the class angle: '... the acts of the present government towards cyclists are definitely "political", and strongly anti-working-class in all their implications. The bicycle is the only vehicle within the means of the workers.'[93]

Minister of Transport Leslie Hore-Belisha, who was likened to tripe and the means test, bore the brunt of the cycling socialists' abuse. Simon Simplelife's regular column in *Clarion Cyclist* picked up the anti-Hore-Belisha and anti-motoring theme: 'Belisha, you're all boloney, you think working class folk ought to stop at home whilst you and your pals turn the countryside into a succession of petrol pumps.'[94] The Clarion movement's Utopian notions were extended to a cyclists' revolution, a fanciful idea cherished by many cyclists right up to the 1960s. An article entitled 'Fifty Years After' envisaged looking back from 1986: the imagined 'anti-motoring revolution' broke out on May Day 1942, when a road-hog sped round the bend in a country village and killed the May Queen. The outcome was that the 'motor menace' became a general election issue, CCC members were elected to the government, and 'slaughter on the roads' was made a capital offence. The revolution produced an outcry 'by those who wish to retain the liberty to kill cyclists and pedestrians'.[95] Such visions, and the more orthodox campaigning which contributed to the unity of the cycling movement, were, of course, stimulated by an apalling road safety record; there were, for example, 7,300 road deaths in 1934 compared to the all-time peacetime peak of 7,700 in 1972, when there were approximately ten times more vehicles on the roads.[96]

Despite its continuing political *raison d'être*, much of the actual agenda of the CCCs differed little from the interests of the predominantly apolitical CTC. *Clarion Cyclist* was dominated by touring articles and romantic rural evocations. The Clarion press also continued to emphasize the social attractions of the movement, with their camp and clubhouse focus. The reopening of the Ribble Valley clubhouse on 24 May 1936 attracted 600 people; its facilities had been improved to include billiards, snooker, table tennis and a putting green. Clarion cycling did, nonetheless, remain true to much of its initial open-air ideology. This consistency is evident in the setting up of an Edward Carpenter Memorial Fellowship, and the raising of funds to purchase Carpenter's house at Millthorpe, as well as the creation of scholarships to Ruskin College, in keeping with the movement's philosophy of improving education. The cycling clubs continued to be by far the most common associations within the Clarion movement as a whole, particularly in Lancashire, Yorkshire, the Birmingham area and Staffordshire, and the London and Essex area.[97]

The Clarion interest in rambling, already manifest before the First World War through the formation of the large Sheffield Clarion Ramblers, and similar associations in Glasgow, Bristol, Bolton and Burnley, was given a national focus by the formation of the Clarion Rambling Club in 1931. The thriving Sheffield-based club in many ways epitomized the nature of the avowedly socialist side of the outdoor movement, invariably coming to the fore in defence of rights of way or the promotion of improved Pennine moorland access.[98] This dimension had been developed at the beginning of the century by G. H. B. Ward and colleagues, and was given additional impetus in 1924 with the formation of the Sheffield Co-operative Ramblers, affiliated to the Co-operative Party, and with a membership drawn chiefly from the metallurgical and engineering industries.

It was immediately after the First World War that a significant level of federation of rambling clubs was begun. In 1919 the Manchester

Ramblers' Council was formed, which became the Ramblers' Federation (Manchester District) in 1922, consisting of thirty-eight clubs, and with individual subscriptions set at 2s. 6d. (12½p). In his inaugural address to the new federation on 21 January 1922, J. Cuming Walters emphasized the importance of the move towards unification:

It brings all ramblers together, and thus it creates – or, if that be already done, it intensifies – the real feeling of fraternity which should prevail among all lovers of the open road. We want pedestrians and climbers – all the tramps and vagabonds of good repute – to be able to greet each other with 'Brother, well met'; and to feel by means of this Federation one bond unites them.[99]

A Liverpool Federation followed at the end of 1922, and eighteen clubs formed the Sheffield Federation in the Spring of 1926, with G. H. B. Ward as chairman, a position he occupied for more than thirty years, sustaining the long-term influence of this socialist on the outdoor movement in Britain. By 1930, federations had been formed in the Midlands, the West Riding, Leicestershire, Lincolnshire, Bolton and north-east Lancashire. A West of England Federation was formed in 1932, the same year as the West Cumberland Ramblers' Federation founded in Whitehaven, which in 1933 became the Lake District federation. Moves to link the emerging federations into a national body had been initiated as early as October 1928 by the strong Manchester, Sheffield and Liverpool groups. At a countryside conference in Hope in Derbyshire in 1930 they were joined by other interested organizations, such as the London Federation, the Peak District and Northern Counties Footpath Preservation Society, the COSFPS and the CPRE. The conference, convened to pursue the notion of forming a national federation, established the nucleus around which a collaborative outdoor movement would consolidate in response to increasingly urgent demands that the ongoing problems of open-air issues should be addressed. The meeting produced a tentative agreement on which the National Council of Ramblers' Federations was established on 26 September the following year at a conference at Longshaw, south-west of Sheffield, attended by delegates from as far afield as London and Glasgow, with T. A. Leonard in the chair. Nonetheless, despite this successful initial collaboration, there was already evidence of potential conflict between open-air and countryside organizations over questions of policy and the proper function of a united lobby. The Manchester delegation, for example, was disappointed at the apparent lack of concern with moorland access.[100] The issue did receive prominence, however, during a national conference held in Manchester the following year. It was effectively the disillusionment of northern ramblers' delegates with the general attitude of the fundamentally establishment countryside bodies that sowed the seeds for the generation of a national organization of ramblers, set up with the stated objectives of pursuing policies which promoted their own specific interests: 'By the early 1930s opinion was growing in the outdoor movement that there was a need for a national body to look after the interests of ramblers, ...' [101] At the council meeting in 1934 it was agreed that the title should be changed to the Ramblers' Association (RA) on 31 January 1935, affiliating more than 300 rambling clubs and enrolling 1,200 individual members. However, it was not until the end of 1939 that the Manchester Federation eventually agreed to join the national organization. The editorial column of the first issue of the national council's journal, *Rambling*, published in June 1933, did, nevertheless, claim a unity of ideals common to all the federations, suggesting the widespread importance of the issues at stake, and the need for a national campaigning body:

> 'Rambling' is to inform you of all ideas, projects, policies and Acts of Parliament which will help or hinder you in your walking: not physical projects, or routes across the country, or rucksacks, or the way to put your legs down, but all national scheme and ideals, all that is common to all the district federations, and all which needs our common action – and that common policy by which, on the right occasion, we can put our foot down. [102]

Both the CHA and HF continued to flourish on their original cooperative principles during the interwar years. These outdoor holiday associations, as well as their affiliated rambling groups which numbered more than 150 in the 1930s, were particularly active in the formation of the RA. In 1926 there were seventy holiday centres administered by either the CHA or the HF. These idealistic organizations were joined by the Workers' Travel Association (WTA), founded in 1921 at Toynbee Hall. The WTA was set up primarily to promote foreign travel aimed at facilitating greater international understanding amongst workers, but it also provided hostel accommodation in the countryside for the less well off, such as that in the Peak District at Hope. Through their quarterly newsletter, *The Travel Log*, the WTA became involved in the organizational and campaigning unity of the outdoor movement, although not exclusively as an out-of-doors organization. [103]

By far the most successful practical manifestation of the desire for cheap and simple accommodation was the YHA, whose formation provided one of the most important collaborative unifying focuses for the national outdoor movement. The nucleus of the hostel movement was created on Merseyside after a special meeting called by the

Liverpool and District Ramblers' Federation in December 1929. A national association was founded in April 1930 following a conference of interested organizations, which included the British Youth Council and the National Council of Social Service. The Scottish Youth Hostels Association (SYHA) was formed in February 1931, with its first hostel at Broadmeadows in the Yarrow Valley, to the west of Selkirk in the border country. The origins of the SYHA can be seen in the mountain bothys which served as important rendezvous for the open-air fellowship, and in the Scottish Young Men's Holiday Fellowship, which provided simple accommodation in lodges with palliasses and blankets for 'trampers' amd mountaineers.

The YHA was an immediate success. The first hostel, opened by the Merseyside group at Pennant Hall in the Conwy Valley on Christmas Eve 1930, was short-lived, but there were 20 hostels in existence by Easter 1931, with 73 open by the end of the year. The YHA had 120 hostels and more than 6,000 members by March 1932, and 180 hostels providing for the needs of 28,000 members by September 1933. In the twenty months to March 1933 the organization enjoyed an increase of 163 per cent in its membership, although obviously from a low base. In the year to September 1931 YHA beds were used 20,000 times, while in the year to September 1933 the equivalent figure was recorded at 157,582. The movement continued to go from strength to strength: '1936, the seventh year of the Y.H.A., was as successful as its predecessors, and at the end of it 60,000 members had been enrolled, 260 hostels were open, and the beds in the hostels had been in use 385,000 times during the year.' [104] By 1939 four separate associations provided 397 hostels in the British Isles for 106,524 members. During a period of large-scale increase in general leisure and travel, the 500,000 overnights in the hostels of England and Wales in 1939 should be compared to the 7 million visitors who stayed in Blackpool, the epitome of the other end of the holiday spectrum. Such a contrast, however, is not really appropriate, given the phenomenal expansion of the popularity of Blackpool in the 1920s and the 1930s; on August Bank Holiday Monday, 1937, for example, 700 trains carried trippers to the resort.[105] It was the opening of hostels that really enabled the large-scale expansion of the outdoor movement in the 1930s, bringing together groups and individuals in holiday and weekend fellowship founded on healthy and energetic exercise in the open air. The Midland Federation of Ramblers identified in the YHA's function something more than a mere social collaboration:

> The Youth Hostel spirit I cannot accurately convey, it has to be experienced. It is social in that it brings together walkers and cyclists in fellowship with a minimum of restriction. But, most of all, it

contributes to the service of beauty – not only the outward beauty of our national heritage, for which we in this generation have to be vigilant trustees, but the inward beauty, which in words 'depends on simplicity – I mean the true simplicity of a rightly and nobly ordered mind and character.' [106]

The Midland Federation also paid tribute to the YHA's contribution to the revival of walking, and commented on the one shilling (5p) overnight fee, which made the accommodation available to almost everyone. The same charge applied to evening meal and to a large breakfast, with a packed lunch available at 6d. (2½p). C. E. M. Joad recognized the importance of the service at such reasonable cost in facilitating the expansion of healthy country holidays and open-air activities for a large section of the population:

Consider what this means to the poor clerk and the young manual worker starting life on 30/– or £2 a week, who wants to see England for himself ... [and who] can plan a week's tramping holiday from one side of the country to the other knowing that total outlay will not exceed 24s 6d. [£1.22½].[107]

An important role played by the new association was that of helping to perpetuate and extend the activities and interests of the existing outdoor organizations. The CTC was quick to praise this crucial new dimension to the expanding movement: 'The simplest accommodation is all that is looked for; no service, but a good, clean sleeping room and somewhere to eat and shelter from the inclement weather.' [108] These simple shelters, shared with others with similar interests, brought opportunities to young people in the 1930s who would continue to use and support the hostels into healthy old age. The *Ramblers' Handbook* of the London Federation also acknowledged the work of the YHA, confirming the benefit to the consolidation of a broader movement:

The Y.H.A. will carry on and extend the work of the Rambling Clubs, it opens the way to the sea and the hills for those who know only the smell of the streets and the noise of the traffic ... It enables a young man or woman to plan and carry out their own escape from the towns.[109]

The YHA's provision of bunk-bed dormitory accommodation and basic self-catering facilities for those who travelled under their own steam, maintained and administered along cooperative lines, epitomized the ethos of simplicity with which the growing popular outdoor movement was imbued. The *Manchester Guardian* saw the new association standing

for 'beauty and companionship with something of hardihood and simplicity'.[110] From the outset, the success of the hostels depended on the
energetic volunteers, who were inspired by the ideals of the movement,
which included the provision of facilities for less well-off country
recreation lovers of all ages: 'Short of funds from the beginning, the
YHA was always a do-it-yourself organization. Volunteers formed
committees, searched for buildings suitable to be converted into hostels, then set about conversion.'[111] It was these voluntary work parties
that sustained the YHA right up until recent times, when a more
commercial doctrine was applied to the management of a financially
ailing movement:

> I was asked to borrow money from each of the various rambling
> clubs in Leicester to pay for the paint and brushes necessary for the
> Eastwell youth hostel. The men's dormitory was in the upper floor
> of a barn and one could see small holes in the roof. The common
> room was a converted fowl house.[112]

Such spartan accommodation typified the hostels, although the buildings that were acquired ranged across the architectural spectrum, from
simple wooden huts, to the finest of country residences, such as the
magnificent Derwent Hall in Derbyshire, now submerged under the
Ladybower Reservoir. The first national office was situated in some
discarded builders' huts at Welwyn Garden City. Much of the early
success of the YHA can be ascribed to the help received both from
other amenity organizations and from sympathetic landowners. The
National Trust and the Forestry Commission, for example, allowed
some of their properties to be used as hostels, while some private
landowners granted the use of buildings and facilities on extended
leases. Patronage and institutionalized respectability were, indeed, hall-
marks of the growing YHA, whose ideals attracted widespread approval
from the establishment. Support and financial assistance came from
such agencies as the Cadbury Trust, the Carnegie Trust, the King
George V Jubilee Trust, and the Board of Education. As a worthy
cause rooted in rational motives beneficial to both mind and body, the
YHA drew on the support of numerous influential individuals, many
of whom contributed throughout their lives to the success and character
of the movement.

Through such a process of affiliation into national organizations,
unified by growing cooperation in a broad and increasingly influential
outdoor lobby, a campaigning movement was shaped. This growing
collaboration expressed itself, for example, through the appointment
in 1932 of a joint committee of open-air organizations, which, following
a meeting in November 1935, developed into the Standing Committee

on National Parks. The associational cooperation that developed in the 1930s set the trend and contributed to the agenda for a period of more positive action during the apotheosis of national planning in the 1940s.[113]

Although there were always differences of opinion, the most pressing concern was with improving countryside access, and the newly articulated lobby provided essential momentum to both parliamentary and extra-parliamentary campaigns. Open access was always going to be a problem, while the question of public rights of way had never been settled satisfactorily. The Rights of Way Act, which entered the statute book in 1933, was designed to simplify the situation, particularly the complex process by which it was necessary to establish footpaths as public highways. The situation had already been complicated by Section 193 of the 1925 Law of Property Act, which established a general public right to take exercise and recreation on moors or commons within the boundaries of an urban area, but not within a rural district. The ambiguity was manifest in the continuing disputes over access to Rombald's Moor in the West Riding. The fact that the open urban moor of Ilkley still produced one of the highest yields of grouse was in fact used by the access lobby to support their case against arguments of disruption and the ruination of a shooting-based economy.[114] Support for the new legislation and a belief in its effectiveness was typified by an article in the *Bradford Telegraph and Argus*:

> The Rights of Way Act of 1933 clarified the situation a good deal, and eliminated many ambiguities. Quite apart from the benefit to ramblers and hikers, it did full justice to landowners by giving them the opportunity to put up prominent notices indicating that it is not their intention to grant dedication of wayright or that they desire to close a path.[115]

In reality, the 1933 act did little to alter existing law, which was weighted strongly in favour of landowners. In the *Telegraph and Argus*'s own area the Yorkshire Ramblers' Club continued to encounter difficulties in establishing rights of way, while the problems of prohibitive red tape were highlighted during attempts made by the West Riding Ramblers' Federation to negotiate the opening of fifty-three footpaths around Langbar in 1938. The revised footpath legislation did remove the old criterion of indefinite use, which generally required the evidence of the oldest inhabitant, but it included the need to prove twenty years' continuous use of the right of way. The landowner could readily circumvent the provisions of the act if he had issued permits and displayed notices to the effect that he did not intend to dedicate a right of way, thus claiming that public access was only granted as a privilege.

By erecting notices before a twenty-year period of use was established, it was also possible for any owner to prevent a footpath from becoming a right of way.

The interwar campaign for access was flavoured inevitably by contemporary ideas relating to the need to plan the use of land as a national resource, as part of the prevailing urge towards town and country planning. Part of the essence of rural planning was the recognition of a need to accommodate the facilitation of recreation of all kinds: '... during the inter-war period, a system of comprehensive Town and Country planning was evolving, designed to ensure the optimal use of each tract of land'.[116] P. Monkhouse's 1932 account of walking in Derbyshire raised the related issue of national planning, demonstrating that the open-air lobby had developed from localized and peripheral dissent into a weighty body of public opinion: '... public opinion, in these last ten years, has swung round round from indifference to an ever increasing interest in the preservation of natural amenities. The "town and country planning" movement is one manifestation of this spirit.'[117] This observation echoed comments made by G. M. Trevelyan in the previous year. One of the obvious problems inherent in this collectivist brief was the reconcilitation of conservation of the countryside with the rising demands of recreation in the open spaces. The need for some measure of regulation was confronted by a widespread desire to increase substantially public access to sensitive natural environments. Obviously, the granting of wider access would also have the effect of taking the pressure off the existing limited areas where access was permitted.

The concept of the planned utilization of land as a resource stimulated a vigorous debate in the 1930s. It was carried out against a background of obsessive balancing of the national budget, with a concomitant unwillingness to spend on the planning of urban and rural environments; a correspondent of *The Times* referred to it as 'Too Much Public Spending'.[118] A letter to *The Times* from Sir Fabian Ware, chairman of the Gloucestershire branch of the CPRE, demonstrated both the ambivalent attitude of that conservationist organization to calls for a planned use of the countryside, and a continuing belief in the efficacy of economic *laissez-faire*. He was referring to perceived problems imposed on the local farming community by an increase of trippers on Minchinhampton Common:

> ... many of them felt that the Town and Country Planning Bill did not provide as statesmanlike a solution of their difficulties as that which they had consistently advocated. It seemed to them to inherit too much of the post-War tendencies to cure public ills by additional public expenditure.[119]

The reverse side of the macroeconomic argument in relation to the question of national planning was stated in a letter from 'Physiocrat' the following week, when he claimed that '*laissez-faire* did not imply that Government should abstain inertly from constructive work'.[120] The trend towards the rational planning of economic, strategic, and public amenity factors did, in fact, in many instances contribute to the diminution of the possibilities of open access in the interwar years. Water authorities and the military both placed restrictions on moorland access, while the Forest Act of 1927, aimed at reducing Britain's dependence on timber imports, granted powers to the Forestry Commission to regulate access and recreation.

At the same time public access to open countryside continued to be dependent upon the attitude and interests of the local landlord. The restrictions faced by people in Scotland are indicated in B. H. Humble's *Tramping in Skye*, in which the more generally prevalent Highland landowning attitude is contrasted with a more liberal stance adopted on the estates of Dunvegan Castle, the ancestral home of the Macleod clan:

> ... instead of the usual vindictive notice 'TRESPASSERS WILL BE PROSECUTED', only the kind sign, 'PLEASE KEEP TO THE PATHS SO AS TO AVOID WALKING ON YOUNG TREES'. Scotland would indeed be a trampers' paradise were other landowners to do likewise.[121]

What is also signified, however, is the developing trend towards the aristocratic commercial exploitation of land in order to maintain the financial viability of estates; this was a continuous factor that contributed to public exclusion. An additional manifestation of highly commercialized estate manangement, and a further threat to access, was the practice of financing new roads and fences in upland areas by selling off sections of commons and moors. The writer W. T. Palmer criticized this tactic in 1934: 'I have known perfervid critics of the "stealing of commons" to be quite unaware of this rather practical point.'[122] Other outdoor literature of the period also expressed the strength of feeling behind an increasingly organized challenge to continuing exclusion. One of the most vehement published attacks on landed privilege in the 1930s was contained in A. J. Brown's *Striding Through Yorkshire*: '... access of any kind is stubbornly denied, and brute force is used to turn the public off the moors. Walkers are treated, not as Englishmen, but like escaped convicts from Dartmoor.'[123] The old radical battle-cry of the free-born Englishman re-emerges persistently. Within the invocation of age-old rights there is also an important emphasis on responsibilities. It was implicit in Brown's plea to landowners to fulfil their obligation to their fellow countrymen:

Men who fought for England (and will probably be called to fight for her again sooner or later) should have at least as much right to explore these uplands as any syndicate has to shoot over them; and they are entitled to at least the same 'protection' as the precious grouse.[124]

To Brown, the arguments in defence of exclusion 'make one gasp'. There was, for instance, the notion that grouse would become virtually extinct if the public were to be allowed on the moors 'after they have survived a century of mass slaughter'.[125] Such simplistic riducule of the stance taken by commercial shooting interests, did, of course, ignore conveniently the fact that the estates themselves carefully husbanded the grouse stocks in order to ensure plentiful supplies during the season. The most contentious area was the Peak District, where in the 1930s more than two hundred square miles of uncultivated moors contained only twelve footpaths of more than two miles in length. The extensive upland of Bleaklow, for example, had no footpaths. There remained thirty-two moors and thirty-two cloughs uncrossed by any public right of way, and twenty-two 'edges' cut off from public access; all this was in an area surrounded by industrial conurbations and smaller urban settlements, in which the open-air craze had attained the largest scale, and had the deepest roots. Similar restrictions in other upland areas, particularly in Yorkshire, Lancashire and Scotland, helped to stimulate the growing national access lobby.

A growing frustration with the continuing exclusion – which the forthright Manchester-based ramblers' spokesman Edwin Royce referred to as 'Paralysis in the Pennines'[126] – led to direct action by more radical elements in the outdoor movement. Mass trespasses, rallies and demonstrations became the best-documented episodes in the history of the British outdoor movement, embedded in the folklore of both open-air and socialist organizations.[127] The dominant reaction to restriction had hitherto been one of mild acceptance, such as that described by Joad in his account of an excursion in 1920 to the Kinder Scout area of the Peak District with a party of Manchester ramblers, who obeyed without protest a gamekeeper's orders to leave the area immediately. Increasingly, however, access activists dismissed the deference and half-hearted protests of the moderate majority, and concerted a campaign of direct action backed by high-profile publicity. Growing sympathy for the campaign was consolidated by such incidents as the offer of a reward of £5 for information leading to the arrest of Peak District trespassers, whose photographs appeared in newspaper advertisements in May 1923. Royce sustained a vociferous campaign against aristocratic and plutocratic intransigence: 'The sporting "fans" will not yield one iota of their unscrupulously obtained "rights", but dare not admit openly their anti-social and unenlightened policy.'[128] He focused a specific attack on the worst offender, the Duke of Atholl, who imputed that political motives were the main driving force behind the introduction of paliamentary access bills.

Since early in the nineteenth century many highly respectable individual country walkers had trespassed where they deemed total exclusion to be morally unjustifiable.[129] The tactic had become increasingly contentious as the pastime expanded, and as outdoor groups were formed which were less willing to defer to the landed *status quo*. In the first two decades of the century the Sheffield Clarion Ramblers, under the determined leadership of G. H. B. Ward, initiated a new trend through their deliberately challenging and publicity-seeking group trespasses.[130] However, although open access became the prominent issue for the outdoor movement, much of Ward's work was concerned with reasserting the age-old principal of right of way on south Pennine paths and bridleways, such as the route from Dore to Hathersage, which was conceded by the landowner in 1928. In the post-1918 open-air recreation boom it was inevitable that the access issue would be brought to a head, and that the main centre of attention for this clash of interests would be the Peak District, where thousands of weekend walkers were denied the right to explore vast areas of uncultivated upland. An important rallying focus for extra-paliamentary campaigning was established when the Clarion-dominated Sheffield and District Ramblers' Federation organized and publicized a mass demonstration in support of the Access to Mountains Bill. This mass rally took place in the natural amphitheatre of Winnats Pass near Castleton on Sunday 28 June 1928, and it subsequently became an annual event: 'Every rambler is expected to be at the annual demonstration in the Winnat Pass at 3 p. m. Sunday June 26th 1932.'[131] Crowds estimated at around three thousand were addressed by influential individuals and prominent figures in the outdoor movement, such as Joad, Ward, Royce and Tom Stephenson, who, in his capacity as open-air correspondent of the *Daily Herald* and editor of *Hiker and Camper*, was able to promote and publicize the cause widely. Despite these shows of solidarity, the camaraderie engendered by the common cause disguised a vehement discord over appropriate tactics. The idea of deliberately inciting direct confrontation remained abhorrent to the majority of ramblers. It would be the socialist open-air organizations that took the lead in the mass trespasses which aimed at raising the profile of the struggle for countryside access.

The famous mass trespass on Kinder Scout was prompted by a group of young ramblers from the Sheffield Clarion, who advertised their intention to assert their right to walk across the area on Sunday 24 April 1932. Leafletting on the day ensured that the event attracted a substantial turnout from the usual large summer Sunday influx of ramblers at Hayfield, who were encouraged to take 'action to open the fine country at present denied us'.[132] The demonstration was dominated by Manchester ramblers affiliated to the British Workers' Sports Federation (BWSF), who led a procession of several hundred in the direction of the summit of Kinder 'singing "the Red Flag" and "the International"'.[133] There was a wide disparity in the estimates of the numbers that took part in the 'raid', but it seems unlikely that more than a hundred actually left the footpath to head for the summit across the open moorland where keepers were posted. During the ensuing confrontation there were minor scuffles, which resulted in the unintentional injury of Edward Beever, a keeper employed by the Stockport Water Authority, who was taken to Stockport Infirmary for treatment. As a consequence of the affray, six Manchester men were arrested on charges of illegal assembly and assault, and remanded on bail until 11 May by New Mills Police Court. The six accused were John Thomas Anderson, 21, a cotton-piecer from Droylsden; a 19-year-old university student, Anthony Walter Gillett; and four young men from Cheetham: Julius Clyne, Harry Mendel, David Nussbaum and Bernard (Benny) Rothman, who remained active for more than sixty years in a continuing campaign to improve access and defend threatened rights of way. Following the hearing at Derby Assizes, before a grand jury consisting of two brigadier-generals, three colonels, two majors, three captains and two aldermen, Gillett was acquitted, but the others received prison sentences ranging from two months to the six months that the Sheffield Clarion Ramblers' *Handbook* referred to as 'the savage sentence on Anderson',[134] the perpetrator of the alleged assault.[135] Sheffield ramblers planned further publicized trespasses in 1932, although only a demonstration at Abbey Brook came to anything.[136] However, Ward and his allies continued to gain concessions for better access to the uplands to the south-west of Sheffield. The effectiveness of mass trespass has never really been determined. Success in raising the national profile of the issue has to be weighed against the bad publicity which could be exploited by the opponents of the principle of access. Such perceptions stimulated scaremongering tactics in sections of the popular press. The *Daily Mail* took the campaign into the realm of the ridiculous in its response to the formation, in 1931, of the Manchester and District section of the BWSF. In an article by Collinson Owen entitled 'The Crimson Ramblers. Communists after the Hikers', the *Mail* claimed that communists were bent on exploiting the hiking craze for their own political ends: 'Our hikers by the ten thousand shoulder their packs and fare forth to discover the beauties of Nature. But the Communists are determined that they shall tramp our footpaths careless of rural charm, musing only on the iniquities of the capitalist system.'[137] The

Mail took the opportunity to defend both commercial and landowning elements of the conservative establishment against the more determined challenge which was being orchestrated by increasingly organized left-wing activists. The BWSF campaign to have private property opened up to responsible ramblers, and to involve public bodies in the provision of overnight accommodation, as well as their exaggerated claims regarding the risk to walkers of being shot at in the countryside, was exploited readily by journalistic sensationalism:

> Thus, if they have their way, it will come to pass that:
>
> 1. Grandmamma, watering her roses, will see the garden gate thrust open and a group of the Manchester and District Ramblers' Section of the British Workers' Sports Federation coming in to see what a private rose garden looks like, and,
>
> 2. A late meeting in the Mayor's Parlour of any Town Hall horridly adjourned because the Crimson Ramblers have come to town, and desire to prepare their evening meal and shakedown generally for the night.[138]

Confrontational tactics also alienated much of the established access lobby, and Tom Stephenson, for example, remained extremely sceptical of BWSF motives.[139] Nonetheless, it could never be doubted that Benny Rothman and his socialist colleagues were keen ramblers, whose objective was to win for urban-based walkers the right to enjoy the countryside; their ulterior motive was not simply to challenge the rural establishment by means of a political stunt.

Respectable political support for countryside access was substantial, underpinning an increasingly vociferous parliamentary lobby, which introduced access bills in 1924, 1930, 1931, 1937 and 1938, culminating in the controversial 1939 Access to Mountains Act. Parliamentary campaigning represented the establishment vanguard of a larger unified national access lobby. The YHA and the rambling organizations passed resolutions proposing that the public demand for an access act should be conceded by Parliament. In a two-way collaboration, several Labour MPs were involved in open-air organizations, and leant support at the Peak District rallies. The debate represented one prominent manifestation of a wider contemporary conflict between two diametrically opposed ideological strands, which had evolved out of the nineteenth-century collision between urban liberal radicalism, reinforced by nascent socialism, and entrenched landed – and predominantly Tory – interests. In the interwar context, the New Liberal influence was transferred into the established Labour Party, promoting a social democratic collectivist ideology that opposed the landed and plutocratic forces, which were often marshalled by the officer class. This new ideological mainstream was in fact epitomized in the work of the landed Sir Charles Trevelyan, and also included prominent access supporter, Lieutenant-Commander R. T. H. ('Rex') Fletcher who later became Baron Winster.

Support for the access bills in the interwar years emphasized the increased urgency of the issue. Reintroducing the bill in 1930, Graham White, who was active in the Liverpool Ramblers' Federation, made reference to its long parliamentary experience, going on to stress that the need was 'still more obvious today'.[140] True to the nineteenth-century rationalist side of its origins, the case was backed by the ideology of utility. Utilitarian arguments were a means of justifying rationally to a Conservative legislature the need for a change in direction to meet new national needs. This perception of rambling and healthy recreation was expressed in four ways. Firstly there was the traditional point of view of the greatest happiness of the greatest number: 'The case for the Bill rests upon the need of securing the greatest amount of health and happiness for the community as a whole.'[141] Beyond this there was the appeal to a recurring obsession with physical fitness as an aid to national efficiency. This had been couched in terms of the topical concern with eugenics in the 1908 debate, but was at least as salient to the bills of 1937 and 1938, when the idea was promulgated that mountaineering and fell-walking were a means of inculcating military skills, especially map-reading. Questions of health, fitness and national efficiency continued to complicate the parliamentary debate over access. There was the same concern with fresh air and physical fitness that had obtained at the turn of the century, although greater emphasis was now placed on the essential outdoor skills. Thus, Colonel Clarke, for example, stressed that 'hiking teaches map reading. Any territorial officer will tell you that it is one of the weakest points in the Territorial Army.'[142] Thirdly there were the always persuasive economic arguments, which, just as in the developing debate before 1914, were backed up by statistics which were bandied about to substantiate the position of both sides. The opposition lobby picked up the earlier theme of threats to finely balanced rural economies. Access opponents continued to stress the potential for damage and disturbance to rural environments. For example, a leading anti-access spokesman, Captain Frank Heilgers, Conservative MP for Bury St. Edmunds, and a substantial landowner in west Suffolk, expressed dissatisfaction with 'the provisions of the Bill for the protection of amenities against damage', and pointed to the 'dangers from fire and litter'.[143] Access campaigners refuted consistently any imputation of damage, disruption or pollution, and their parliamentary supporters emphasized the responsible and knowledgeable behaviour of ramblers and mountaineers who practised a strict code of conduct. Lieutenant-Commander Fletcher, the seconder of the 1938 bill, described the peaceful coexistence between walkers and sheep farmers in the Lake District. Fletcher told the House how he had walked in the area ever since his youth, and emphasized that, after sheep, tourists were its main source of income. Lakeland, of course, was never the habitat of the red grouse. Claims of disruption to the hill-farming economy were also denied by a Conservative supporter of the access bill, Mr Osbert Peake, MP for Leeds North, who lived on the Yorkshire moors: 'Nor are the interests of the sheep farmer and the interests of grazing rights adversely affected if the people behave in a reasonable manner.' [144]

The fourth element in the utilitarian argument was rooted in more fundamental ideological precepts. The line adopted by the landed *status quo*, as expressed by Heilgers and his parliamentary colleagues, was extended to encompass the idea that access legislation would destroy the whole principal of landownership, and would culminate in land nationalization. The access issue had always had wider political implications than merely as a marginal dispute over conflicting leisure interests and recreational amenity. A response in *Progressive Rambler* to the 1939 access act stressed the political dimension: 'The inescapable conclusion was that the access to mountains was a political issue, and ramblers should not shrink from accepting that unpalatable fact.' [145] Eloquent defenders of landed privilege portrayed the provision of access as an unnecessay threat to the long-established rural economic and social system. In the 1930s' context the perceived threat to the old order and stability could appeal to a prominent fear both of socialism and of a totalitarian challenge to the inherent freedom of the British people, a reversal of the old radical reference to the rights of the people. In 1938 Brigadier-General Clifton Brown claimed that 'the prinicples underlying the Bill were to down private property and nationalise the land'. During the same debate Heilgers spoke of the 'nationalisation of property', and gave his own interpretation of the real hidden agenda behind the bill: 'To our minds it also attacks the whole principal of owning land. It would mean that an owner no longer had the right to enjoy his property ... His land would become public property under this Bill.' [146]

The emergence of an interventionist strand within mainstream political thought was portrayed as a threat to fundamental principles of private property ownership. The capacity to taint the access issue with the notion of the nationalization of land was one of the essential strengths of the anti-access lobby. Any potential or suspected threat to the *status quo* was equated readily with revolution, and thereby cast an influence on the negotiation of the compromised dilution of the 1939 access act. When the threads of the issue were picked up again after World War II, the leading campaigner, Arthur Creech Jones, claimed that the pre-war legislation was the best obtainable, short of a minor social revolution. Tom Stephenson's frustrated response was to ask: 'Why are we wasting our time on piffling legislation like this instead of striving for the minor social revolution?' [147] The issue of land ownership in the interwar opposition to increased access was further strengthened by the growing importance of the practical question of water supply, and claims relating to the dangers of pollution of the gathering grounds. This emerging challenge to public access to the moors emphasized the importance of the responsible image presented by the open-air lobby. The strict banning of the public by some water authorities, most notably Manchester, contrasts with their willingness to lease the moors to shooting interests. In the 1930s the open-air lobby, represented by diverse organizations, campaigned to obtain better access to the water gathering grounds, which included some of the finest stretches of uncultivated upland. [148]

The ambiguous nature of a number of the issues that were related to the central question of improved access to the countryside underpinned the irreversible trend towards a compromise settlement between two fundamentally opposed ideologies. That spirit of compromise, reinforced by more pressing international concerns and the prevailing atmosphere of contrived mutuality under the National Government, set the scene for a series of negotiations in which the landed lobby, represented by the Country Landowners' Association and the Land Union, were able to manipulate a highly respectable amenity committee – which consisted largely of members of COSFPS, led by Sir Lawrence Chubb – over the eventual content of the 1939 act. [149] The defenders of the landed *status quo* were keen to portray themselves as reasonable men who could readily find common ground with sensible and rational members of the opposition camp. Praising the spirit of compromise, Lieutenant-Colonel Heneage equated what he identified as a minority of bad country landlords with the less responsible element from the towns who caused damage and left litter: 'We are suffering from what might be called the bad boys on both sides ... but for them there would have been no need for a Bill ... I know that there are many landlords who welcome people on their property and in some cases explain points of interest to them.' [150] Heilgers and Brown were both understandably pleased with the 'reasonable Amendments', which were agreed during the parliamentary debates. Brown claimed that 'a fair compromise has been reached'. After allowing for parliamentary etiquette, there remains a deferential tone to Creech Jones's glib response in which he thanked 'the Honourable Members for the generous things they have said to me', and in his expressing:

... on behalf of the promoters of the Bill our sincere thanks for the co-operation which has been given to us all by all the interests involved ... I wish to add my thanks to the Commons, Open Spaces and Footpaths Preservation Society, and particularly Sir Lawrence Chubb, for the enormous amount of work which they have done.[151]

Creech Jones was also unduly optimistic in summing up the access campaigners' side of the debate: 'This is the end of a fifty years struggle, and marks a definite social advance.'[152] In reality, the enthusiasm and optimism which succeeded the parliamentary passage of the bill in 1938 for royal assent in 1939 gave way to a feeling of betrayal amongst members of the outdoor lobby. Creech Jones's uncomplicated initial agenda had been distorted and complicated beyond recognition. The sell-out from 'a charter for ramblers' to 'a landowners' protection bill'[153] was established by way of a crucial qualifying clause contained in the preamble to the act, which stated that public access to mountain, moor, heath, down or cliff would be 'subject to proper provisions for preventing any abuse of such access'.[154] The principle of unrestricted access to those uncultivated areas for pedestrian exercise was undermined significantly by a set of complex procedures set out in the act. Section 3 stipulated that access orders should be made by application, each of which should be accompanied by copies of the appropriate maps, while the applicant was also required to have had published, at least one month before submission, a notice of intention to apply for an order. Furthermore, applicants were required to 'serve a copy of the notice on the owner of the land to which this Act is proposed to be applied.'[155] As well as several pages of detailed and awkward procedures, the statute also made ample provision for objections, which applicants were required to notify in writing to the Minister of Agriculture and Fisheries. If the Minister did not deem the objection to be frivolous or irrelevant, he would, 'before making an order, cause a public local inquiry to be held with respect to the objection ... and shall consider the report of the person holding the inquiry ...'[156] Landowners were authorized under the act to apply, for various reasons, for suspension of access orders, for instance in dry weather, when they could claim that there was a fire risk. Under Section 5 of the act all access orders could be revoked by a subsequent order made by the Minister. The continuing practice of exclusion, which the 1939 access act effectively sanctioned, was facilitated further by a long list of restrictions that might upset the owner or occupier, relating to damage, litter, unruly behaviour, bathing, and damage to flora and fauna. There was also provision for the revocation of orders by water authorities. The act did not apply to Scotland and Northern Ireland.

The growing influence of the expanding outdoor movement in

Britain between the two world wars was increasingly situated in the larger national political arena, in which demands for change were couched in radical collective terms. Nonetheless, a critique founded on revulsion against the worst effects of urban industrialism inevitably reintroduced and reshaped forms of ruralism. The new rural references of the post-1918 period can be detected in, for instance, the rapid and piecemeal development of garden suburbs, which found expression in a resurgence of a nostalgic vernacular identifiable in much of the architecture of the middle-class housing boom of the 1930s in particular, and also in a style of conservationism, fronted by the CPRE, which was shackled by nostalgia for an idealized earlier era. Such themes do invariably seem to accompany periods of economic and social crisis. However, the recurrent recourse to the rural dream and visions of the free-born Englishman enjoying the freedom of his natural heritage has always been multi-dimensional. As with earlier rural responses to crisis, the practical and active outdoor recreationist needs to be set apart from the realms of nostalgic sentimentality, although backward-looking romanticism did remain as an influence that needs to be incorporated into the wider motivation. Although it would be specious to equate outdoor recreationists from the industrial towns with the intellectual milieu associated with the pessimism of T. S. Eliot or with D. H. Lawrence's literary primitivism, the popular desire to escape to the countryside developed within the same context of deep-seated dissatisfaction with the prevailing system, alienation and environmental ugliness.[157]

It was generally uncomplicated motives that generated the mass outdoor movement of the 1920s and 1930s. The outdoor philosophy of the touring cyclist mirrors that which stimulated so many of the ramblers to get out into the open air. It drew on a form of stoical self-sufficiency which not only endures, but often finds satisfaction in adverse natural conditions – being caught in a storm in some area of wilderness; the brew-up at the roadside; the achievement felt at getting back home through the blizzard; improvised roadside repairs of the cycle. This simple outdoor creed is portrayed in the writing of Albert Winstanley of Bolton, who in many ways typified the new breed of young interwar touring cyclist who sustained the popularity of the pastime into the postwar era of renewed optimism. Winstanley's narratives indicate also some of the additional interests that underpinned the wider outdoor culture of a fellowship comprised of self-motivated individuals. It is a motivation rooted in the past through a love of native landscape and an interest in antiquities encountered *en route*. The new popularity attained by open-air recreation did not undermine the importance of the search for fuller, more fruitful and personally fulfilling uses of increased leisure time by those who were dissatisfied with mass leisure and the growth of spectator entertainments. Autonomous pursuit of broadly defined rational and improving uses of spare time continued to sustain the development of the outdoor movement: 'Some people who walked or cycled were going into the country to follow other interests like natural history or sketching.' [158]

Just as in the earlier formative period of the movement, it is evident that a good proportion of those who took to energetic outdoor recreation in the interwar years were impelled by intelligent and inquiring minds, so often frustrated by a lack of real opportunity for the majority. The generally improving motives of the CCCs, which continued as the mainstay of their guiding ethos during the resurgence of the 1930s, epitomized this aspect of an eclectic philosophy of leisure. In an article in *Clarion Cyclist*, for example, entitled 'Knowledge is Power and Happiness', J. Russell Morris pointed out correctly that 'a great many very intelligent men and women never had a chance to spend long hours poring over difficult subjects.' [159] There is, of course, no reference to the idea that if people wanted more time for study, they should spend less time riding bicycles and socializing with their fellows, although healthy countryside recreation was for many only a part of the larger philosophy, while definitions of rational recreation had altered in the century since they had first been conceived. The Clarion movement introduced the Clarion Education Scheme, which supplied free correspondence courses in various subjects, including English, Esperanto, socialism, history, economics and local government.

The interwar outdoor movement, founded on mass participation by significant numbers of working people from the urban areas, was an important alternative element in a popular culture that was peculiar to that period. However, the expansion of the phenomenon depended strongly on characteristics inherited from nineteenth-century formative influences. Continuity from earlier origins can be detected in, for example, the distinctive motivating principles rooted in the nineteenth-century nonconformist cornerstones of improvement and respectability. There were also more specific areas of consistency, reflected in a continuing challenge to aspects of restrictive convention, which in turn served to highlight the tenacity of earlier social attitudes. Entrenched conservative moralism can be seen most notably in reactions against women's assertion of individuality and freedom. A report in the *CTC Gazette* in 1925 is indicative both of the widespread adoptions of open-air exercise by women and of the continuing convention of chaperoning merely for the sake of appearance: 'Miss L. Juffs led nearly a thousand wheelwomen and their escorts to Wisley Woods.' [160] Women's outdoor recreation apparel, a symbol of the wider struggle for emancipation, continued to excite reaction: 'In those days girls did not wear shorts and we had several people stop their cars and take snaps of us.

We also had abuse hurled at us for being hussies and showing our knees.'[161] While the great movement into the outdoors during the 1920s and 1930s confronted socially conservative attitudes, its campaigning element was at the forefront of evolving challenges to the entrenchment of the landed *status quo*.

Notes

1. Walker, H., 'The Outdoor Movement in England and Wales, 1900–1939', unpublished Ph.D. thesis, University of Sussex, 1988; Walker, H., 'The popularisation of the outdoor movement, 1900–1940', *British Journal of Sports History* 2, 2 (September 1985).
2. Graves, R. and Hodge, A., *The Long Weekend* (New York, 1968), p. 271.
3. Branson, N. and Heinemann, M., *Britain in the Nineteen Thirties* (St Albans, 1973), p. 239.
4. Howkins, A. and Lowerson, J., *Trends in Leisure, 1919–1939* (Sports Council, 1979), p. 49.
5. Hoggart, R., *The Uses of Literacy* (London, 1971), p. 278.
6. Stevenson, J. and Cook, C., *The Slump* (London, 1977), p. 26.
7. *The Times*, 7 April 1938, p. 12.
8. Howkins and Lowerson, *Trends in Leisure*, p. 55.
9. *Ibid*, p. 48.
10. Prynn, D., 'The Clarion clubs, rambling, and the holiday associations in Britain', *Journal of Contemporary History* 11 (July 1976), p. 70.
11. Joad, C. E. M., *A Charter for Ramblers* (London, 1934), pp. 12, 15.
12. Priestley, J. B., *English Journey* (new edn; London, 1984), pp. 166–7.
13. *Ibid*, p. 167.
14. *Manchester City News*, 24 June 1922, p. 7.
15. Joad, *Charter for Ramblers*, p. 15.
16. Manchester Federation of Ramblers, *Handbook* (1931), p. 25.
17. Sheffield and District Ramblers' Federation, Annual Report 1934, in Sheffield Clarion Ramblers, *Handbook* (1933–4), p. 1.
18. Midland Federation of Ramblers, *Handbook* (1932), p. 28.
19. *Ibid*. (1931), p. 14.
20. *PD*, 4th Series, 325 (1930), col. 420.
21. *Ibid*., 5th Series, 252 (1931), col. 1357.
22. *Ibid*., 342 (1938), col. 748.
23. *Ibid*., col. 808.
24. *Ibid*., col. 756.
25. Mabel Spence Watson family letters, Accession No. 213, Tyne and Wear Archive Dept., Newcastle.
26. *The Times*, 1 April 1938, p. 19.
27. Mais, S. P. B., *This Unknown Island* (London, 1932), p. vii.
28. Daily Telegraph critic, quoted in *ibid*., front cover.
29. *Ibid*., p. vii.
30. *CTC Gazette* (January 1918), p. 3.
31. Priestley, *English Journey*, p. 168.

32. Hoggart, *Uses of Literacy*, p. 269.
33. Jones, S. G., 'Trade union policy between the wars. The case of holidays with pay in Britain', *International Review of Social History* 31, 1 (1986), pp. 40–67.
34. MacLean, I., 'Mountain Men', in Kay, B., ed., *Odyssey: Voices from Scotland's Recent Past* (Edinburgh, 1980), p. 79. Also see Borthwick, A., *Always a Little Further* (London, 1939).
35. MacLean, 'Mountain Men', in Kay, ed., *Odyssey*, p. 79.
36. Borthwick, *Always a Little Further*, p. 81.
37. MacLean 'Mountain Men', in Kay, ed., *Odyssey*, p. 80.
38. *Ibid.*, p. 81; part of the track alongside the pipeline carrying water from Loch Katrine in the Trossachs to Glasgow is now incorporated in the West Highland Way long-distance walk.
39. Glasser, R., *Gorbals Boy* (London, 1986), p. 87.
40. MacLean, 'Mountain Men', in Kay, ed., *Odyssey*, p. 87.
41. Whatmore, J., *The CTC Book of Cycling* (Newton Abbot, 1983), p. 38.
42. Sharp, D., 'Southern Area – Pattern of Change', in Holt, A., ed., *Making Tracks* (London, 1985), p. 49.
43. *Manchester Guardian*, 11 April 1932, p. 5.
44. Rowntree, S., *Poverty and Progress* (London, 1941).
45. R. Courtney, oral source.
46. *Clarion Cyclist* 1, 6 (December 1936), p. 87.
47. *The Times*, 1 April, 1938, p. 19.
48. Manchester Federation of Ramblers, *Handbook* (1931), p. 15.
49. Lowerson, J., 'Battles for the Countryside', in Gloversmith, F., ed., *Class, Culture and Social Change* (Brighton, 1980), p. 276.
50. J. Taylor, oral source.
51. *PD*, 5th Series, 342 (1938), col. 762.
52. Tom Weir, quoted in MacLean, 'Mountain Men', in Kay, ed., *Odyssey*, p. 81.
53. Alistair Borthwick, *ibid.*, p. 79.
54. Riley, W., *The Yorkshire Pennines of the North-West. The Open Roads of the Yorkshire Highlands* (London, 1934), p. 13.
55. Wood, J., *Mountain Trail. The Pennine Way from the Peak District to the Cheviots* (London, 1947), p. 15.
56. Poucher, W. A., *Snowdon Holiday* (London, 1943), p. 10.
57. Tudor, T. L., *The High Peak to Sherwood* (London and Philadelphia, 1926), p. 16.
58. *Ibid*, p. 40.
59. *Ibid*, p. 16.
60. Wood, *Mountain Trail*, p. 15.
61. Tudor, *High Peak to Sherwood*, p. 16.
62. Priestley, J. B., quoted in LeMahieu, D. L., *A Culture for Democracy. Mass Communication and the Cultivated Mind in Britain Between the Wars* (Oxford, 1988), p. 324.
63. Priestley, *English Journey*, p. 377.
64. *Ibid*, pp. 377–8.
65. LeMahieu, *Culture for Democracy*.

66. Joad, C. E. M., *The Untutored Townsman's Invasion of the Country* (London, 1946).
67. Joad, C. E. M., 'The People's Claim', in Williams-Ellis, C., ed., *Britain and the Beast* (London, 1937), p. 64.
68. *Ibid*, pp. 64–5.
69. *Ibid*, p. 71.
70. *Ibid*, p. 72.
71. *Ibid*, p. 70.
72. Street, A. G., 'The Countryman's View', in Williams-Ellis, *Britain and the Beast*, pp. 129–30.
73. Trevelyan, G. M., 'Amenities and the State', in Williams-Ellis, *Britain and the Beast*, p. 183.
74. *Ibid.*, p. 186.
75. Williams-Ellis, *Britain and the Beast*, appendix.
76. Joad, *Charter for Ramblers*, p. 12.
77. *The Times*, 1 April 1938, p. 19.
78. *PD*, 5th Series, 342 (1938), col. 748.
79. Stephenson, T., *Forbidden Land* (Manchester, 1989), Ch. 10.
80. Lodge, E., ed., *The Yorkshire Wayfarers' Yearbook* (Leeds, 1933), p. 6.
81. *Ibid*, p. 35.
82. Sheffield Clarion Ramblers, *Handbook* (1933–4), p. 1.
83. Midland Federation of Ramblers, *Handbook* (1932), p. 28.
84. *Clarion Cyclist* 1, 5 (November 1936), p. 68.
85. *Ibid.*, 1, 1 (July 1936), p. 1.
86. *Ibid.*
87. *Clarion*, February 1932, p. 7.
88. *Ibid.*, p. 37.
89. *Ibid.*, 15 April 1927, p. 7.
90. *Ibid.*, p. 11.
91. Kirk, N., 'Traditional working-class culture and the rise of Labour: some preliminary questions and observations', *Social History* 16, 2 (May 1991), pp. 203–16.
92. *CTC Gazette* (October 1919), p. 2.
93. *Clarion Cyclist* 1, 2 (August 1936), p. 23.
94. *Ibid.*, 1, 3 (September 1936), p. 41.
95. *Ibid.*, 1, 2 (August 1936), p. 21.
96. Stevenson, J., *British Society, 1914–1945* (London, 1984) pp. 390–1.
97. Map signifying the location of Clarion clubs, n. d., National Museum of Labour History, Manchester.
98. Walker, 'The Outdoor Movement'.
99. Manchester District Ramblers' Federation, *Handbook* (1923), p. 11.
100. Stephenson, *Forbidden Land*, pp. 83–6.
101. Dalby A., 'Foundation and First Steps', in Holt, *Making Tracks*, p. 12.
102. *Rambling* 1 (June 1933), p. 1.
103. Walker, 'The Outdoor Movement', ch. 6; Walker, H., 'The Workers' Travel Association, 1921–1939', *Bulletin of the Society for the Study of Labour History* 50 (1985), pp. 9–10.
104. *The Lakeland Rambler* (Whitehaven, 1937), p. 101.

105. Stevenson, *British Society*, p. 393.
106. Midland Federation of Ramblers, *Handbook* (1932), p. 28.
107. Joad, *Charter for Ramblers*, p. 15.
108. *CTC Gazette* (January 1930), p. 6.
109. *The Ramblers' Handbook* (London, 1932), p. 29.
110. *Manchester Guardian*, 9 April 1932, p. 8.
111. Youth Hostels Association (England and Wales), *Ah, Happy Days! A Nostalgic Look at the Youth Hostels Association 1930–1980* (St Albans, 1980), p. 2.
112. *Ibid.*, p. 7.
113. Dalby, 'Foundation and First Steps', in Holt, *Making Tracks*; Stephenson, *Forbidden Land*, ch. 10.
114. Ramblers Association documents relating to rights of way in the Wharfedale area. Leeds Reference Library.
115. *Ibid.*, newspaper cutting.
116. Sheail, J., *Rural Conservation in Inter-war Britain* (Oxford, 1981), p. 245.
117. Monkhouse, P., *On Foot in the Peak* (London, 1932), p. 195.
118. *The Times*, 5 April 1932, p. 15.
119. *Ibid.*, 4 April 1932, p. 18.
120. *Ibid.*, 11 April 1932, p. 8.
121. Humble, B. H., *Tramping in Skye* (Edinburgh 1933), p. 51.
122. Palmer, W. T., *Tramping in Derbyshire* (London, 1934), p. 6.
123. Brown, A. J., *Striding Through Yorkshire* (London, 1938), p. 366.
124. *Ibid.*, p. 365.
125. *Ibid.*, p. 364.
126. *Rambling* (June 1933), p. 5.
127. Hill, H., *Freedom to Roam* (Ashbourne, 1980); *Progressive Rambler* 64 (April 1940); Rickwood, P., *The Story of Access in the Peak District* (Bakewell, 1982); Rothman, B., *The 1932 Kinder Trespass* (Timperley, 1982); Rubinstein, D., 'The struggle for ramblers' rights', *New Society*, 15 April 1982, pp. 85–7; Sheffield Campaign, *Freedom of the Moors*; Stephenson, *Forbidden Land*, ch. 7.
128. Manchester Federation of Ramblers, *Handbook* (1932), p. 23.
129. Phillips, G. S., *Walks Round Huddersfield* (Huddersfield, 1848).
130. Hill, *Freedom to Roam*, ch. 2; Walker, 'The Outdoor Movement', ch. 4.
131. Sheffield Clarion Ramblers, *Handbook* (1932), p. 28.
132. *Newcastle Journal*, 25 April 1932, p. 6.
133. *Manchester Guardian*, 25 April 1932, p. 7.
134. Sheffield Clarion Ramblers, *Handbook* (1933–4), p. 35.
135. Hill, *Freedom to Roam*; Rothman, *Kinder Trespass*; Stephenson, *Forbidden Land* – all offer contrasting perspectives on the Kinder Scout episode.
136. Hill, *Freedom to Roam*, ch. 5.
137. *Daily Mail*, 3 July 1931, p. 9.
138. *Ibid.*
139. Stephenson, *Forbidden Land*, ch. 7.
140. *PD*, 5th Series, 325 (1930), col. 149.
141. *Ibid.*
142. *Ibid.*, 342 (1938), col. 771.

143. *Ibid.*, col. 774.
144. *Ibid.*, col. 781.
145. *Progressive Rambler* 1, 69 (September 1940), p. 12.
146. *PD*, 5th Series, 342 (1938), cols. 797, 764.
147. Quoted in Hill, *Freedom to Roam*, p. 79.
148. Stephenson, *Forbidden Land*, ch. 4.
149. *Ibid.*, ch. 8.
150. *PD*, 5th Series, 342 (1938), col. 749.
151. *Ibid.*, cols. 750, 752.
152. Law Reports, Statutes 1939, vol. 1, ch. 30, Access to Mountains Act 1939, Section 3.
153. *Ibid.*, Section 3 (5)a.
154. Stephenson, *Forbidden Land*, p. 165.
155. Law Reports, 1939, vol. 1, Section 3 (4).
156. *Ibid.*, Section 3 (5)a.
157. Williams, R., *The Country and the City* (new edn; London, 1985), ch. 14.
158. R. Courtney, oral source.
159. *Clarion Cyclist* 1, 3 (September 1936), p. 37.
160. *CTC Gazette* (June 1925), p. 14.
161. Miss Joan Beale, quoted in YHA, *Ah, Happy Days!*, p. 3.

Epilogue: The Legacy

A slowly evolving and increasingly interdependent collaboration of open-air interests bequeathed a substantial and influential institutional legacy to the post-1945 world of greater leisure and mobility for the majority, and of planned solutions to problems of recreational amenity. That inheritance depended on the growing cooperation between of national associations, and the adoption of a rational planned approach to countryside amenity. The acceptance of a national planning orthodoxy ramified into legislation concerning the creation of national parks and country access, an aspect which remains topical.[1] The concept of long-distance footpaths, which was first mooted by Tom Stephenson in the *Daily Herald* in 1935, generated the formation of the Pennine Way Association, although the approval of a Pennine Way route was delayed until July 1951, and it was 1965 before Britain's first and most famous long-distance walk was opened officially. Stephenson was only one of many people whose dedication constructed and preserved an open-air recreational legacy for later generations. Essential contributions came from individuals from various backgrounds. Many of the influential, but unsung figures were products of the Lancashire mill-town culture of energetic, nonconformist, social democratic and fundamentally progressive ideals – men such as Tom Tomlinson, who became Britain's first national park chief warden in 1956, responsible for patrolling the key areas of Kinder Scout and Bleaklow in the Peak District, scene of the famous mass trespasses. The sort of guardianship that has perpetuated this legacy can be seen in Tomlinson's appointment in the 1960s as youth liaison officer in the Peak National Park.[2]

Recognition of this distinctive positive legacy, and acclamation of the substantial practical achievements and social and political significance of a British outdoor movement, founded on a locally nuanced progressive core ideology, does not represent a Whiggish or triumphalist affirmation of the irreversible consummation of an ideal. Many of the objectives continue to be frustrated, while gains are often counteracted by losses. Regressive conservative forces within the movement itself, sustained by a strong compromising tendency, have militated persistently against the unified effort needed to pursue the interests of walkers, mountaineers, and touring cyclists. Footpath and access campaigners are fighting much the same battles at the end of the twentieth century as they were in the 1820s – the Manchester liberal radical oligarchy in fact experienced a greater degree of success than many of today's activists in some areas of the country. David Rubinstein's outline of post-1939 developments in access campaigns confirms both the continuing prevalence of exclusion and the fact that much remains to be done.[3] Despite the protests sustained over 150 years by such diverse influential commentators as William Hazlitt, James Bryce, *The Guardian* newspaper,[4] the BBC 'Countryfile' programme, and late twentieth- century chroniclers of the history of countryside access,[5] the British propensity for the exclusion of the majority from the land continues in sharp contrast to examples amongst her European partners of more liberal attitudes to recreational access, such as the Swedish principle of *Allemannsrat*. Behind the green rhetoric and apparent attention to countryside planning, important environmental concerns have been submerged under the weight of the commercial lobby and the still-increasing obeisance to the insatiable demands of motor traffic, a process underpinned by the democratic pretence of the public inquiry system. The principle of the stewardship of nature continues to be of minority, though fluctuating interest to society in general. Idealized and atrophied images of the country sustain an inactive and predominantly regressive sentimental response to the problems of urban society in Britain. An ever-expanding heritage industry is packaged and presented as an entrepreneurial alternative to a properly constructed conservation ethic, as we are gradually reconciled to the realities of the post-industrial age.[6]

A fascinating feature of the active outdoor movement at the end of the twentieth century is its degree of consistency with formative influences. The healthy, rational, recreation-based movement continues to thrive against a multiplicity of counter attractions, which are largely the product of the twentieth-century commercialization of leisure, impelled by rapid technological expansion in that sphere. The movement continues to display many of the characteristics evolved from early origins, thereby confirming the importance of generative impulses and firm roots which have previously been considered only rarely and fleetingly. Open-air recreation organizations are subject increasingly to a process of modernization, but retain a close resemblance to their antecedents in the early associations, through which the local and national institutional structure of the movement was developed. This strong measure of continuity reflects the simplicity of the unchanging motives underlying the relative popularity of healthy, physically and mentally stimulating forms of outdoor leisure pursuits as a respite from urban living. The central unifying focus represented by the movement's campaigning dimension has been sustained by a need to confront continuing restrictions, whose persistence depends largely on the tenacity of landed proprietorship. However, a further crucial factor has been the growing tendency to confine a large proportion of countryside leisure pursuits to officially defined and administered recreation areas, in a controlled extension of the notion of national parks. The planned use of national resources has, of course, produced substantial benefits to outdoor recreational amenity, but it has also, ironically, helped to perpetuate the practice of exclusion from vast tracts of open countryside, as well as the 'stopping-up' of public rights of way, particularly in arable districts and around the urban fringes.

Notes

1. e.g. Access to Commons and Open Country Bill, 1978; Access to Commons and Open Country Bill, 1980; Walkers (Access to the Countryside) Bill, 1982.
2. Tomlinson's contribution to the outdoor movement is outlined in his obituary in *The Guardian*, 6 June 1995, p. 1.
3. Rubinstein, D., 'The struggle for ramblers' rights', *New Society*, 15 April 1982, pp. 85–7.
4. *The Guardian*, Education Supplement, 22 September 1992, pp. 1–3.
5. Hill, H., *Freedom to Roam* (Ashbourne, 1980); Shoard, M., *This Land is Our Land* (London, 1983); Stephenson, T., *Forbidden Land* (Manchester, 1989).
6. See Hewison, R., *The Heritage Industry: Britain in the Age of Decline* (London, 1987); Wright, P., *On Living in an Old Country: The National Past in Contemporary Britain* (London, 1985); *History Today*, January 1995.

Bibliography

Primary Sources

1. Manuscripts

Blackburn Local Studies Library, N19: records of the work of the Blackburn and District Footpath Preservation Society, 1894–1936.

Bolton Local Studies Library, B916. 18 GEN: Bolton County Borough General Purposes Committee, Winter Hill Right of Way (24 January 1902).

British Library, 7912 de. 6 (4), NCU: Rules of the Union (London, 1892).

Burnley Local Studies Library, M97: Burnley Cooperative Society, i) minutes of meetings, 1887–1895; ii) quarterly reports and balance sheets, March 1861–December 1894.

Burnley Local Studies Library, B82: Burnley Natural History Society, i) notice of annual meetings, 1921–1923; ii) list of rambles; iii) poster, inc. objects of the society and list of rambles, n. d.

Burnley Local Studies Library, B82: Padiham Scientific Association, Minute, 1889–98.

EPL: Buist, D. (Land Surveyor of Perth), 'Plan of the Common of Glentilt, As Divided 1808'.

EPL: Wesleyan Methodist Mission, Edinburgh, report, 1896.

House of Lords Archive: COSFPS correspondence relating to commons, National Trust, and Ministry of Agriculture and Fisheries.

House of Lords Archive: COSFPS records and law suits.

Huddersfield Local Studies Library, B570: Huddersfield Naturalists' Society, Rules (Huddersfield, 1886).

LCRO, DDX 1470: Records of Nelson CCC, North Lancashire CCC, Padiham CCC.

Leeds Local Studies Library, LH. 91 (333): De Morgan, J., *Report of Chancery Proceedings in the Hunslet Moor Case, 22nd February 1878* (London and Leeds, 1878).

Leeds Local Studies Library, LP 796. 51. C 78: Leeds CHA Rambling and Social Club, rules, 1930.

Leeds Local Studies Library, LQ 352. L 517: Leeds Corporation Act, 1879, chapter, xxiii – an act to confer further powers on the Corporation of Leeds with reference to Hunslet Moor, in Leeds Local Acts, 1842–1901.

Leeds Local Studies Library, QBX. Y82: papers given to the Yorkshire Ramblers' Club.

Leeds Local Studies Library, Q333. 2. RI4Y: Ramblers' Association, documents relating to rights of way in the Wharfedale area.

MAD, MSC 613. 7: Clarion CC, programme of meet at Clayton-le-Dale, Whitsuntide 1938.

MAD, MSC 796. 6: Clarion Cyclists' Clubhouse Newsletter, May 1936.

MAD, F942. 733. FL1: Clarion Fellowship invitations and programmes, 1900.

MAD, MS 796. 51 Ha1: Hayfield and Kinder Scout Ancient Footpaths Association, Minute Book, 1876–77.

MAD, 796. 2, H. F.: Prospectuses, 1933–44.

MAD, 796. 51: Manchester Pedestrian Club, programme, rules, and bye-laws, 1904.

MAD, 796. 2. R37: Ramblers' Federation, Manchester and District, bulletin to affiliated club secretaries, delegates and associate members, May 1930 and May 1931.

Mitchell Library, Glasgow, TD 19. 6: small journal compiled by Adam Bald concerning Glasgow statistics, the weather and general notes of his reading.

Newcastle Local Studies Library, L796. 6: Brunswick Cycling Club (Newcastle), accounts, membership cards, letters to members.

Newcastle Local Studies Library, L506: Tyneside Naturalists' Field Club, minute book, 1875–6.

Newcastle University: Elliott, A., and Williams, G., eds, catalogue of the papers of Sir Charles Phillips Trevelyan, Bart, 1870–1958.

Newcastle University: Trevelyan, Sir C. P., personal papers of the Trevelyan family: CPT, 105, 148, 162, 175, 176, 214.

NMLH, Manchester: Clarion CC, programme of the twentieth annual meet at Shrewsbury, Easter 1914.

NMLH, Manchester: Clarion clubs map, n. d.

NMLH, Manchester: Clarion Field Club, London, leaflet describing Cinderella Home at Tatsfield, n. d.

NRA, 24458: CTC historical records (various), compiled by Centre for Urban and Regional Studies, Birmingham and Reading Universities.

PRO, R 34. 1: Jubb, M., 'Cocoa and Corsets', Victorian and Edwardian Posters.

Sheffield Local Studies Library, MP. 2317M: Clarion Call, an open letter.

Southern Veteran Cycling Club: letter from Mr D. Roberts of Mitcham, Surrey.

Tyne and Wear Archive Dept., Newcastle, Accession No. 213: Mabel Spence Watson family letters.

2. Newspapers and Periodicals

Accrington Weekly Advertiser, 1896.

Ashington Colliery Magazine, July 1932, September 1939.

Bicycle News and Sport and Play (Birmingham), 23 April 1895.

Biograph 1, January–June 1879.

Blackburn Gazette, 9 December 1935.

Blackburn Mail, 1825–7.

Blackburn Patriot, 1864.

Blackburn Standard, 1864.

Blackburn Times, 1866–7.

Bolton Chronicle, 1896.

Bolton Journal and Guardian, 1893, 1896, 1897, 1904, 1907, 1914, 1915, 1919, 1926.

Bradford Daily Argus, 24 August 1898.
Bradford Daily Telegraph, 1 February 1900.
Bradford Natural History and Microscopal Society, Syllabuses, 1881–95.
Bradford Scientific Association, Syllabuses, 1890–3.
Bradshaw's Journal III, 2, 14 May 1892.
Burnley Advertiser, 1855–61, 1872.
Burnley Express, 1883–4, 1990.
Burnley Express and News, 1956.
Burnley Gazette, 1876, 1884, 1892, 1896–7.
Burnley Literary and Scientific Club, Transactions, 1874–1919.
Burnley Mid-Week Gazette, 1888.
Burnley Natural History Society, Syllabuses, 1909–13, 1918–26.
Burnley News, 1913–20.
CHA, General Notes, 1918.
CHA Rambling Club (Newcastle District), Syllabuses and Rambling Programmes, 1902–1905, TWAD.
CHA, *Summer Holidays with the CHA, 1932* (Manchester, 1932).
Chorley and Leyland Advertiser, 26 February 1954.
Clarion, 1891–1932.
Clarion Cyclist, 1936–7.
Clarion Cyclists' Journal, August 1896–April 1897.
Colne Times, 1888–1911, 1948–9.
Commonweal, 1886, 1887, 1889.
Comradeship III, 2, November 1909–XI, 2, December 1917.
Contemporary Review XL, LXVIII, 1895; XCIV, 1908.
Cornhill Magazine, New Series, XXIV, January–June 1908.
Cricket and Football Field (Bolton), 1896–1908, 1932–5.
CTC Monthly Gazette, 1896–1939.
CTC, Year Book and Diary, 1908.
Cycle Magazine, 1895–7.
Daily Citizen, 31 December 1912.
Daily Herald, 1923, 1935, 1939.
Daily Mail, 3 July 1931.
Daily Worker, 1930–3.
Darwen News, 1878–96.
Darwen Post, 1896.
Darwen Weekly Advertiser, 1893–6.
Edinburgh Advertiser, 3 September 1847.
Ewen, G. T., *Manchester Rucksack Club Journal* 1, 1907–1910.
Federation of Rambling Clubs, Handbook (London, 1933).
Field, 22 March 1930.
Forward (Bradford), 11 August 1906.
Gateshead Herald, 1929–39.
Glasgow Herald, 1892, 1926.
Halifax Comet, 1898.
Halifax Courier, 1892–8, 1908.
Hill and Dale (Sheffield), June 1922.
Holme Valley Express, 18 May 1984.

Justice, 1890–1910.
King of the Road, April 1897–December 1897.
Labour Annual (Manchester), 1897.
Labour Journal (Blackburn), 1898–1907.
Labour Monthly, April 1931.
Labour Prophet and Labour Church Record, 1892–3, 1896–7.
Lakeland Rambler (Whitehaven), 1937.
Lancashire Daily Post, 1895–8.
Lang, L., *Rambles in the Burnley District*: newspaper cuttings of the late nineteenth century, Burnley Local Studies Library.
Leeds Mercury, 1878.
Leeds Patriot and Yorkshire Advertiser, 6 February 1830.
London and District Union of Clarion Cycling Clubs, Official Handbook, 1922.
M'Connochie, A. E., ed., *Cairngorm Club Journal*, July 1893–1915.
Manchester City News, 1898, 1904, 1920–2.
Manchester Evening Chronicle, 29 December 1910, 30 April 1923.
Manchester Field Naturalists' Society, Reports, 1860–73, Manchester Local Studies Library.
Manchester Gazette, 1827.
Manchester Guardian, 1830, 1850–1900, 1904, 1923–40.
Manchester Rucksack Club Handbook, 1922–39.
Manchester Times and Gazette, 17 October 1828–19 June 1830.
Manchester Union of Clarion Cycling Clubs, Official Handbook, 1914.
Midland Federation of Ramblers Handbook (Sutton Coldfield), 1934.
National Clarion Cycling Club Handbook, 1927–39.
National Home Reading Union, Monthly Journal, Artizan's Section, October 1889–May 1890.
Nelson Chronicle, 1890–7.
Nelson Leader, 1907–10, 1932–8.
Newcastle Daily Chronicle, 1898.
Newcastle Evening Chronicle, 25 August 1909.
Newcastle Journal, 1932.
Newspaper cuttings relating to Edwin Waugh, Lancashire writer and walker, Manchester Local Studies Library.
Newspaper cuttings, 1, p. 118; 3, pp. 99–101, Manchester Local Studies Library.
Nineteenth Century XIV, 1883.
Preston Guardian, 1856–67.
Progressive Rambler 1, 64, April 1940; 69, September 1940.
Putrell, J. W., Collection of Newspaper Cuttings, Sheffield Local Studies Library.
Rambling (London), 1933.
Ramblers' Federation (Manchester and District) Handbook, 1923–39.
Ramblers' Federation (Sheffield and District) Handbook, 1933–4.
Rochdale Express, 1896.
Rochdale Labour News, June 1899.
Rossendale Free Press, 1896.
Scottish Cycling News, 1936.

Scottish Cyclist, 1888–1918.
Scottish Cyclists' Road Book and Annual, 1894.
Scout, 1, May–June 1895.
Scrapbook of Newspaper Cuttings, 1907–16, Burnley Local Studies Library.
Sheffield Clarion Ramblers Handbook, 1914–15, 1928–39, 1958–9.
Sheffield Cooperative Ramblers, Syllabuses, 1921–34, Sheffield Local Studies
    Library.
Social Democrat II, 3, March 1898.
Sport and Play and Wheel Life, 1901–38.
Sports (Leamington Spa), 1895–7.
Sports and Games, January 1932.
Sports and Play and the Cycling World, January–February 1895.
Stott, J. G., ed., *Scottish Mountaineering Club Journal* (Edinburgh), 1891–1914.
Sunderland and Durham County Herald, 25 August and 8 September 1848, in
    Local Tracts 17, Durham, Newcastle Local Studies Library.
The Economist 7, 1849.
The Friend, 1932, 1933.
The Scotsman, 27 September 1930.
The Times, 1877, 1896–1913, 1932–9.
The Tramper and Cyclist, 1934–36.
The Worker (Huddersfield), 1905–8.
Trumpet 3, June 1943–62, May 1948.
Ward, H. S., and Riley, H. J., eds, *Practical Naturalist* (Bradford), 1883–94.
Wesleyan Methodist Quarterly Magazine, Edinburgh Circuit, January–March
    1891, Edinburgh Public Library.
Westminster Review CXXXV, 1891.
Wharfedale and Airedale Observer, 10 August 1917.
Wheelist Annual, 1897.
Willesden Call, 1914.
Workman's Times, 17 June 1893.
York Herald and General Advertiser, 1823–4.
Yorkshire Cyclists' Annual, 1892.
Yorkshire Post and Leeds Intelligencer, 1877.
Yorkshire Ramblers' Club, Annual Reports and List of Members, 1892–1907,
    Leeds Local Studies Library.
Yorkshire Ramblers' Club Journal 1–4, 1899–1902.

3. Parliamentary Papers and Official Publications

HMSO, Ministry of Town and Country Planning, Cmd. 7121, Report of the
    National Parks Committee (England and Wales), 1947.
HMSO, National Parks and Access to the Countryside Act, 1949.
Law Reports, Statutes, 1939, Chapter 30, Access to Mountains Act; 1949,
    Chapter 37, National Parks and Access to the Countryside Act.
PP, Select Committee on Public Walks, Report, Cd. 448 (1833).
PD, 3rd Series, 3 (1831); 5 (1831); 15 (1833); 19 (1833); 37 (1837); 41 (1838);
    82 (1845); 324 (1888).
PD, 4th Series, 2 (1892); 188 (1908).

PD, 5th Series, 6 (1908); 173 (1924); 175 (1924); 235 (1930); 252 (1931); 328 (1937); 341 (1938); 342 (1938); 346 (1939); 348 (1939); 349 (1939).
Public General Statutes, 1925, II (London, 1925), Clause 193, rights of the public over commons and waste lands.

4. Published Primary Sources

Andrews, W., ed., *North Country Poets. Poems and Biographies* (London, Manchester and Hull, 1888).
Arnold, M., *Culture and Anarchy* (London, 1869).
Atkinson, C. J. F., *Recollections from a Yorkshire Dale* (London, 1934).
Austin, A. B., *In Your Stride* (London, 1931).
Baker, E. A., *Moors, Crags and Caves of the High Peak* (London, 1903).
Banks, W. S., *Walks in Yorkshire* (London and Wakefield, 1871).
Barnes, P. A., *'Trespassers Will Be Prosecuted'. Views of the Forbidden Moorlands of the Peak District* (Sheffield, 1934).
Bates, J. ('Boshemengro'), *Rambles 'twixt Pendle and Holme* (Burnley, n.d.).
Bax, E. B., *The Religion of Socialism* (London, 1885).
Bird, P. H., *A Ramble by the Ribble and Hodder* (Preston, 1875).
Blatchford, R., *God and My Neighbour* (London, 1904).
Blatchford, R., *Merrie England* (London, 1893).
Blatchford, R., *My Eighty Years* (London, 1931).
Blatchford, R., *The New Religion* (Clarion pamphlet 9; London, 1892).
Blatchford, R., *The Sorcery Shop* (London, 1909).
Bogg, E., *A Thousand Miles of Wandering along the Roman Wall, the Old Border Region, Lakeland, and Ribblesdale* (Preston, 1898).
Bolton CCC, Scrapbook, 1896–1952, Bolton Local Studies Library.
Bolton Field Naturalists' Society, *The Natural History of Bolton* (Bolton, n.d.).
Booth T., *Holiday Rambles. By Mountain, Stream, and Sea* (Burnley, n.d.).
Borthwick, A., *Always a Little Further* (London, 1939).
Boswell, J., 'The Journal of a Tour to the Hebrides', in Johnson, S., and Boswell, J., *A Journey to the Western Islands and the Journal of a Tour to the Hebrides* (London, 1984).
Boyd, D. and Monkhouse, P., *Walking in the Pennines* (London, 1937).
Brown, A. J., *Moorland Tramping in West Yorkshire* (London, 1931).
Brown, A. J., *Striding Through Yorkshire* (London, 1938).
Burnett, W. H., *Holiday Rambles by Road and Field-path: Principally Near the River Ribble* (Blackburn and Manchester, 1889).
Buxton, R., *A Botanical Guide to the Flowering Plants, Ferns, Mosses, and Algae, found indigenous within sixteen miles of Manchester* (London and Manchester, 1859).
Byles, W., *Walks Round Bradford* (Bradford, 1911).
Cash, J., *Where There's a Will There's a Way! or Science in the Cottage. An Account of the Labours of Naturalists in Humble Life* (London, 1873).
Chancellor, V., ed., *Master and Artisan in Victorian England: The Diary of William Andrews and the Autobiography of Joseph Gutteridge* (New York and London, 1969).
Chandler, C. H., *Rambles Round Sheffield* (Sheffield, 1912).
Chorley, K., *Hills and Highways* (London, 1928).

Christian, G., ed., *A Victorian Poacher* (Oxford, 1961).

Clarion Song Book, National Museum of Labour History, Manchester.

Clarion, *The First Socialist Guest House: An Historical Sketch* (NMLH, Manchester, n.d.).

Clark, J. W. and McKenny Hughes, T., *The Life and Letters of the Reverend Adam Sedgwick*, vol. 2 (Cambridge, 1890).

Clarke, A., *Moorlands and Memories* (Blackpool, 1924).

Clarke, A., ed., *Teddy Ashton's Lancashire Annual, 1930–1931* (Blackpool, 1930).

Clarke, A., *Windmill Land* (Londom, 1916).

Cline, C. L., ed., *The Letters of George Meredith* (3 vols; Oxford, 1970).

Conyngham Greene, K., *The English Landscape* (London, 1932).

Cook, E. T. and Wedderburn, A., eds, *The Works of John Ruskin* XI, XVII, XXVII (London, 1905).

Cook, J., ed., *William Hazlitt: Selected Writings* (Oxford, 1991).

Cooper, A. N., *With Knapsack and Notebook* (London, 1906).

Cooper, A. N., *The Tramps of the 'Walking Parson'* (Newcastle, 1902).

Chandler, C. H., *More Rambles Round Sheffield* (Sheffield, 1915).

Crossland, C., *Pleasant Walks Around Halifax* (Halifax and London, 1910).

Darrah, J., jun., *The World Forgetting: A Record of the 4th Annual Whit-week Walk of the Manchester Pedestrian Club, 8–25 May, 1907* (Manchester, 1908).

Davies, C., *North Country Bred. A Working Class Family Chronicle* (London, 1963).

Dawson, S., *Incidents in the Course of a Long Cycling Career* (Lancaster, 1904).

DeQuincey, T., *Reminiscences of the English Lake Poets* (rev. edn; London, 1961).

Derry, J., *Twelve Rambles Near Sheffield* (Sheffield, 1926).

Dobson, W., *Rambles by the Ribble* (3 vols; Preston, 1864, 1877, 1883).

Elvin, H. H., *Socialism for Clerks* (pass on pamphlet, 26; Clarion, London, n.d.).

Ephemerides, *The Wheelman's Year-Book* (Newcastle, 1881).

Escott, T. H. S., *England; Its People, Polity and Pursuits* (London, 1885).

Escott, T. H. S., *Social Transformation of the Victorian Age* (London, 1897).

Evans, E., *Botany for Beginners* (1st edn; London, 1899).

Fabian Society, *Rights of Way, Common Lands, and Roadside Wastes* (Tract 4, 1895).

Fielding, J. T., *The Rambler: A Record of Rambles, Historical Facts, Legends, and Nature Notes* (Darwen, 1905).

Fifoot, C. H. S., ed., *The Letters of F. W. Maitland* (Cambridge, 1965).

Foley, A., *A Bolton Childhood* (Manchester, 1973).

Forman, M. B., ed., *The Letters of John Keats* (4th edn; London, 1952).

Fraser, B. S., 'Prentice Days', *Scottish Mountaineering Club Journal* XXX, 166 (Edinburgh, 1975), pp. 358–72.

Garside, L., *Kinder Scout with the Footpaths and Bridle Roads about Hayfield* (reprint; Oldham, 1980).

Gaskell, E., *Mary Barton: A Tale of Manchester Life* (London, 1848).

Glasser, R., *Gorbals Boy* (London, 1986).

Green, H., *Rambles by Highway, Lane and Field Path* (Burnley, 1920).

Grindon, L. H., *Country Rambles and Manchester Walks and Wild Flowers* (Manchester, 1882).

Grindon, L. H., *Manchester Walks and Wild Flowers* (Manchester, 1860).

Hall, R. W., *The Art of Mountain Tramping* (London, 1932).

Hamerton, P. G., *A Painters' Camp in the Highlands*, vol. 1 (London, 1862).

Hampson, T., *Horwich, its History, Legends, and Church* (Wigan, 1883).

Hanley, K., ed., *George Meredith. Selected Poems* (Manchester, 1983).

Hardy T., *The Return of the Native* (London, 1909).

Hayfield and Kinder Scout Footpaths Association, *The Guide to Hayfield and Kinder Scout* (Manchester and London, 1877).

Hobkirk, C. P., *Huddersfield: Its History and Natural History* (London, 1859).

Holiday Fellowship, Introductory Leaflet, September 1913, British Library.

Houlding, H., *From Lancashire to London On Foot* (Burnley, 1896).

Houlding, H., 'Reminiscences of local flora', *Burnley Literary and Scientific Club Transactions* V (1887), pp. 35–8.

Howe, M. D., ed., *The Pollock–Holmes Letters, Correspondence of Sir Frederick Pollock and Mr. Justice Holmes, 1874–1932* (2 vols; Cambridge, 1942).

Humble, B. H., *Tramping in Skye* (Edinburgh, 1933).

Hutton, R. H., *Holiday Rambles in Ordinary Places. By a Wife with her Husband* (London, 1877).

Joad, C. E. M., *A Charter For Ramblers* (London, 1934).

Joad, C. E. M., *The Untutored Townsman's Invasion of the Country* (London, 1946).

Johnson, T., *The East Lancashire Cyclists' Road Book and Guide. Over 100 Routes and Tours* (Accrington, n.d.).

Jowett, F. W., *What Made Me A Socialist* (Glasgow, 1941).

Kay, B., ed., *Odyssey: Voices from Scotland's Recent Past* (Edinburgh, 1980).

Lancashire and Yorkshire Railway Company, *Walking and Cycling Tours in Lancashire and Yorkshire* (Manchester, 1906).

Lodge, E., ed., *The Yorkshire Wayfarers' Yearbook* (Leeds, 1933).

London and North Eastern Railway Company, *Walking and Cycling Tours in the District of Manchester* (3rd edn; 1935).

Macauley, J., *Fifty Country Walks by Path and Field, Within Easy Reach of Manchester* (Manchester, 1914).

Macauley, J., *Sixty Country Walks by Path and Field, Within Easy Reach of Manchester and the East Lancashire Towns* (Manchester, 1928).

MacDonald, H., *Rambles Round Glasgow* (Glasgow, 1854; new edn, 1878).

Mais, S. P. B., *This Unknown Island* (London, 1932).

Marr, J. E., *The Geology of the Lake District* (Cambridge 1916).

Marr, J. E., *The Scientific Study of Scenery* (London, 1900).

Martineau, H., *Bibliographical Sketches. 1852–1875* (new edn; London, 1885).

Masson, D., ed., *The Collected Writings of Thomas De Quincey*, vol. III (Edinburgh, 1890).

Masterman, C. F. G., *The Condition of England* (London, 1909).

Mather, Rev. J. M., *Rambles Round Rossendale* (2 vols; Rawtenstall, 1880 and 1894).

Mayer, A. J., *The Persistence of the Old Regime* (Beckenham, 1981).

Meredith, G., *The Egoist* (London, 1947).

Miller, A., *Cycle Tours for Manchester and District Cyclists* (Manchester, 1937).

Miller, W. J. C., *Essays and Nature Studies. With Lectures* (London, 1899).

Mitchell, H., *The Hard Way Up* (London, 1968).

Monkhouse, P., *On Foot in the Peak* (London, 1932).

Moorhouse, S., *Walking Tours and Hostels in England* (London, 1936).

Morris, W., 'How we live and how we might live', *Commonweal*, 18 June 1887, p. 195.

Morris, W., *News From Nowhere* (London, 1891).

Morrison, J. H., ed., *The Northern Cyclists' Pocket Guide: A Compendium for North of England Clubmen, Tourists and Path Racers* (Newcastle, 1897).

Morton, H. V., *In Search of England* (London, 1929).

Narrative of the Proceedings in the Case of Rodgers and Others versus Harvie for the Recovery of the Liberty of the Banks of the Clyde (Glasgow, 1829).

Palmer, W. T., *Lake-Country Rambles* (London, 1902).

Palmer, W. T., *The Complete Hill Walker* (London, 1934).

Palmer, W. T., *Tramping in Derbyshire* (London, 1934).

Palmer, W. T., *Tramping in Lakeland* (London, 1934).

Partington, S., *Five 'Truth' Pamphlets* (Bolton, 1902).

Partington, S., *My Three Years Councillorship for West Ward* (Bolton, 1907).

Partington, S., *Winter Hill Dispute, 'Truth' Pamphlet No. 3* (Bolton, 1900).

Perry, H., *Road and Lane. A Handbook for Manchester Cyclists and Tourists* (Manchester, 1896).

Phillips, G. S., *Walks Round Huddersfield* (Huddersfield, 1848).

Pleasant Walks Around Blackburn (Burnley Local Studies Library, n.d.).

Plomer, W., ed., *Kilvert's Diary, Selections from the Diary of the Reverend Francis Kilvert, 1 January 1870–19 August 1871* (London, 1938).

Poucher, W. A., *Escape to the Hills* (London, 1943).

Poucher, W. A., *Peak Panorama, Kinder Scout to Dovedale* (London, 1946).

Poucher, W. A., *Snowdon Holiday* (London, 1943).

Price, N., *Vagabond's Way* (London, 1914).

Priestley, J. B., *English Journey* (new edn; London, 1984).

Prince, J. C., 'Rambles of a Rhymester; or Wandering Through England', *Bradshaw's Journal* III, 2 (14 May 1842), p. 1.

Rawnsley, Reverend H. D., *By Fell and Dale* (Glasgow, 1911).

Riley, W., *The Yorkshire Pennines of the North-West. The Open Roads of the Yorkshire Highlands* (London, 1934).

Robinson, E., ed., *John Clare's Autobiographical Writings* (Oxford, 1983).

Rosenberg, J. D., ed., *The Genius of John Ruskin: Selections from his Writings* (London, 1979).

Rothman, B., *The 1932 Kinder Trespass. A Personal View* (Timperley, Cheshire, 1982).

Rothstein, T., 'Why is Socialism in England at a Discount?', *Social Democrat* II, 3 (March 1898), pp. 69–70.

Rowley, C., *Fifty Years of Work Without Wages* (London, 1911).

Rowntree, S., *Poverty and Progress* (London, 1941).

Russell, C. E. B., *Manchester Boys. Sketches of Manchester Lads at Work and Play* (Manchester, 1905).

Sampson, G., ed., *Hazlitt: Selected Essays* (Cambridge, 1959).

Sandford, F. B., ed., *CTC British Road Book* (new series), vol. V, *North-East England* (London, Edinburgh, and Dublin, 1913).

Shaw, J. G., *History and Traditions of Darwen and its People* (Blackburn and London, 1889).

Sidgwick, A. H., *Walking Essays* (London, 1912).

Sidgwick and Jackson, eds, *The Footpath Way: An Anthology for Walkers* (London, 1911).

Smith, C. G. (pseud. Ichabod Tristram Jones), *Rural Rambles in Cheshire; or walks, rides and drives for Manchester and other people: a guide book to the scenery, antiquities, and gentlemen's seats within walking distance of the Altrincham and Cheshire Midland Railways* (Manchester, 1862).

Stansfield, A., *Essays and Sketches* (Manchester, 1897).

Stephen, Sir L., *Hours in a Library*, III (London, 1909).

Stephen, Sir L., *The Playground of Europe* (Oxford, 1936).

Sturmey, H., ed., *The Cyclist Annual and Year Book* (London, 1893).

Sugden, J., *Slaithwaite Notes of the Past and Present* (3rd edn; Manchester, 1905).

Sutter, J., *A Colony of Mercy or Social Christianity at Work* (London, 1893).

Swainson, W., *A Preliminary Discourse on the Study of Natural History* (London, 1834).

Taylor, J. E., *Mountain and Moor; Natural History Rambles* (Manchester, 1884).

Tudor, T. L., *The High Peak to Sherwood* (London and Philadelphia, 1926).

Turner, W., *A Springtime Saunter in Brontëland* (Halifax, 1913).

Vale, E., *The Face of Britain: North Country* (London, 1937).

Walshaw, P., *The Ramblers' Way* (2 vols; Burnley, n. d.).

Waugh, E., *Lancashire Sketches* (London and Manchester, 1892).

Waugh, E., *Poems and Lancashire Songs* (Manchester and London, 1876).

Waugh, E., *Rambles in the Lake Country* (London, 1861).

Wells, H. G., *The Wheels of Chance* (London, 1896).

Whitman, W., *Leaves of Grass* (New York, 1855).

Winder, T. H., *A Life's Adventure* (London, 1921).

Wood, J., *Mountain Trail. The Pennine Way from the Peak District to the Cheviots* (London, 1947).

Wrigley, A., *Rakings Up. An Autobiography* (Rochdale, 1949).

Wrigley, A., *Songs of the Pennine Hills* (Stalybridge, 1938).

Wrigley, A., *The Wind Among the Heather* (Huddersfield, 1916).

5. Oral Sources

Mr R. Courtney, Northumberland.

Mr J. Jones, Newcastle.

Mrs D. Raulson, Halifax.

Mr D. Roberts, Surrey.

Mr K. Spencer, Burnley.

Mr J. Taylor, Newcastle.

Secondary Sources

1. Newspapers and Periodicals

Burnley Express, 11 January 1991, newspaper cutting from Mr K. Spencer of Burnley.

Country Life, 5 July 1973, pp. 38–40.

Daily Telegraph, 5 January 1970, p. 10.

Huddersfield Daily Examiner, 13 October 1986, p. 7.
Lancashire Life 25 (May 1977), p. 76.
Rambling Today (Spring 1993), pp. 38–9, 62.
The Guardian, 1990–3.
The Guardian (Weekend Supplement), 27 July 1991, pp. 20–1.
The Observer, 9 August 1970, p. 17; 25 April 1982, p. 3; 21 July 1991, p. 4.
The Open Air in Scotland 1, 2 (Spring 1946), pp. 56–7, EPL.

2. Books and Pamphlets

Abercrombie, N., Hill. H. and Turner, B. S., *The Dominant Ideology Thesis* (London, 1980).

Adams, G., *A History of Bridgeton and Dalmarnock* (Glasgow, n.d.).

a'Green, G., *This Great Club of Ours* (London, 1953).

Allen, D. E., *The Naturalist in Britain, A Social History* (London, 1976).

Anderson, G. L., *Victorian Clerks* (Manchester, 1976).

Annan, N. G., *Leslie Stephen: His Thought and Character in Relation to his Time* (Harvard, 1952).

Anthony, P. D., *John Ruskin's Labour: A Study of Ruskin's Social Theory* (Cambridge, 1983).

Aspin, C., *Lancashire, the First Industrial Society* (London, 1969).

Bailey, P., *Leisure and Class in Victorian England. Rational Recreation and the Contest for Control, 1830–1885* (London, 1978).

Baker, E. A., *The Forbidden Land* (London, 1924).

Barber, L., *The Heyday of Natural History* (London, 1980).

Barlow, T. M., *A History of Manchester Wheelers' Club, Formerly Manchester Athletic Bicycle Club* (Manchester, 1933).

Barlow, T. M. and Fletcher, J. R., *A History of Manchester Wheelers' Club* (new edn; Manchester, 1983).

Barrell, J., *The Idea of Landscape and the Sense of Place, 1730–1840* (Cambridge, 1972).

Barrow, L., *Independent Spirits: Spiritualism and English Plebeians, 1850–1910* (London and New York, 1986).

Basterfield, G., *Mountain Lure* (Kendal, 1947).

Bates, J. ('Boshemengro'), *Joe's Your Uncle* (Lancashire Libraries, 1946).

Beer, M., *A History of British Socialism* II (London, 1929).

Beith, G., ed., *Edward Carpenter: In Appreciation* (London, 1931).

Bellamy, R., ed, *Victorian Liberalism. Nineteenth-century Political Thought and Practice* (London and New York, 1990).

Bennett, T., 'Hegemony, Ideology, Pleasure: Blackpool', in Bennett *et al.*, eds, *Popular Culture: Past and Present* (London, 1982).

Bennett, W., *The History of Burnley* 4 (Burnley, 1951).

Bennett, W., *The History of Marsden and Nelson* (Nelson, 1957).

Beresford, M., *East End, West End: The Face of Leeds During Urbanisation, 1684–1842* (Leeds, 1988).

Bloom, H., *Figures of Capable Imagination* (New York, 1976).

Bolton Local Studies Library, *Bolton People's History* (Bolton, 1984).

Booth, C., ed., *Life and Labour of the People in London* (London, 1897).

Bowden, K. F., ed., *A Second Bacup Miscellany* (Lancashire Libraries, 1975).

Bradford Scientific Association, *One Hundred Years Old, 1875–1975* (Bradford, 1975).

Branson, N. and Heinemann, M., *Britain in the Nineteen Thirties* (St Albans, 1973).

Brierley, B., *Tales and Sketches of Lancashire Life* (Manchester, n.d.).

Briggs, A., *Collected Essays* 2 (Brighton, 1985).

Briggs, A., *Victorian People* (London, 1955).

Brown, S., *A History of the London CHA Club From Its Inception in 1901 to the Diamond Jubilee in 1961* (London, 1965).

Bullock, A., *The Liberal Tradition from Fox to Keynes* (London, 1956).

Burgess, W. V., *Chorlton Road Sunday School, 1857–1907* (London and Manchester, 1908).

Burns, T., 'Leisure in Industrial Society', in Smith, M. A. *et al.*, eds, *Leisure and Society in Britain* (London, 1973), pp. 40–65.

Butt, J. and Clarke, I. F., *The Victorians and Social Protest* (Newton Abbot, 1973).

Cannadine, D., *Lords and Landlords: The Aristocracy and the Towns, 1774–1967* (Leicester, 1980).

Carpenter, E., *Towards Democracy* (complete edn; London, 1915).

Checkland, S. G., *The Rise of Industrial Society in England 1815–1885* (London, 1964).

Chesterton, G. K., *The Victorian Age in Literature* (London, 1913).

Clarke, J. and Critcher, C., *The Devil Makes Light Work: Leisure in Capitalist Britain* (London, 1985).

Clarke, P. F., *Lancashire and the New Liberalism* (Cambridge, 1971).

Clarke, P. F., *Liberals and Social Democrats* (Cambridge, 1978).

Clewlow, N., *The Moors were Changeless* (Lancashire Libraries, n.d.).

Cole, G. D. H., *A History of Socialist Thought*, pt. 1 (London, 1956).

Collins, H. C., *Rochdale Roundabout* (Rochdale, 1960).

Colls, R., and Dodd, P., eds, *Englishness: Politics and Culture, 1880–1920* (London, 1986).

Concise Dictionary of National Biography (3 vols; Oxford, 1992).

Consett and District Field Naturalists' Club, *History and Transactions* (1954), Newcastle Local Studies Library.

Corder, P., *The Life of Robert Spence Watson* (2nd edn; London, 1914).

Cosgrove, D. E., *Social Formation and Symbolic Landscape* (London, 1985).

Craig, D., *On the Crofters' Trail. In Search of the Clearance Highlanders* (London, 1990).

Craig, F. W. S., *British Electoral Facts, 1832–1987* (London, 1987).

Crossick, G., ed., *The Lower Middle Class in Britain* (London, 1977).

Crossick, G., 'The petite bourgeoisie in nineteenth century Britain: the urban and liberal case', in Crossick, G. and Haupt, H-G., eds, *Shopkeepers and Master Artisans in Nineteenth Century Europe* (London, 1984).

Cunningham, H., *Leisure in the Industrial Revolution, c. 1780 to c. 1880* (London, 1980).

Dahrendorf, R., *After Social Democracy* (London, 1981).

Dictionary of National Biography.

Digby, R., *A Rossendale Anthology* (Rawtenstall, 1969).

Dodgshon, R. A., *Land and Society in Early Modern Scotland* (Oxford, 1981).

Dormer, K. J., and Tallis, J. H., 'Interesting Features of the Local Vegetation and Flora', in Carter, C. F., ed., *Manchester and its Region. A survey prepared for the meeting of the British Association for the Advancement of Science* (Manchester, 1962).

Douglas, R., *Land, People, and Politics* (London, 1976).

Dyson, T., *The History of Huddersfield and District* (Huddersfield, 1951).

Eccleshall, R. *et al.*, *Political Ideologies* (London, 1984).

Eden, R., *Going to the Moors* (London, 1979).

Elbourne, R., *Music and Tradition in Early Industrial Lancashire, 1780–1840* (Woodbridge, Suffolk, 1980).

Elson, M. J., *Green Belts: Conflict Mediation in the Urban Fringe* (London, 1986).

Ensor, R. C. K., *England 1870–1914* (Oxford, 1941).

Firth, G., Laybourn, K. and O'Connell, J., eds, *Yorkshire Labour Movements c. 1780–1926. A Guide to the Historical Sources and their Uses* (Leeds, n.d.).

Fisher, H. A. L., *James Bryce* (2 vols; London, 1927).

Fraser, D., ed., *A History of Modern Leeds* (Manchester, 1980).

Gaitskell, H., 'Recollections of GDH Cole. (ii): At Oxford in the Twenties', in Briggs, A. and Saville, J., eds, *Essays in Labour History. In Memory of G. D. H. Cole* (London, 1960).

Gatrell, V. A. C., 'Incorporation and the Pursuit of Liberal Hegemony in Manchester, 1790–1839', in Fraser, D., *Municipal Reform and the Industrial City* (Leicester, 1982).

Goddard, T. R., *History of the Natural History Society of Northumberland, Durham, and Newcastle upon Tyne, 1829–1929* (Newcastle, 1929).

Golby, J. M. and Purdue, A. W., *The Civilisation of the Crowd. Popular Culture in England, 1750–1900* (London, 1984).

Gould, P. C., *Early Green Politics. Back to Nature, Back to the Land, and Socialism in Britain* (Brighton, 1988).

Graham, F., *The History of a Society* (Huddersfield, 1968).

Graves, R., and Hodge, A., *The Long Weekend* (New York, 1963).

Grindon, L. H., *Lancashire: Brief Historical and Descriptive Notes* (Manchester, 1892).

Groom, T., *National Clarion Cycling Club, 1894–1944* (Halifax, 1944).

Grosskurth, P., *Leslie Stephen* (Harlow, Essex, 1968).

Hall, S., 'Popular Culture and the State', in Bennett, T., Mercer, C., and Woollacott, J., eds, *Popular Culture and Social Relations* (Open University, 1986).

Hamilton, R., *Hilaire Belloc* (London, 1945).

Hammond, J. L. and B., *The Bleak Age* (London, 1934).

Hardy, D. and Ward C., *Arcadia for All* (London, 1984).

Harrison, R. J., *Before the Socialists; Studies in Labour and Politics, 1861–1881* (London, 1965).

Harvie, C. T. *et al.*, eds, *Industrialisation and Culture, 1830–1914* (Open University, 1970).

Harvie, C. T., *The Lights of Liberalism. University Liberals and the Challenge of Democracy* (London, 1976).

Hewison, R., *The Heritage Industry: Britain in the Age of Decline* (London, 1987).

Hill, H., *Freedom to Roam* (Ashbourne, 1980).

Hobsbawm, E. J. and Ranger, T., *The Invention of Tradition* (Cambridge, 1983).

Hodgson, J. H., 'An Appreciation of Mr. Earl Binns', in Binns, E., *Colne Naturalist Rambles, 1926–1953* (Colne, 1953).

Hoggart, R., *The Uses of Literacy* (London, 1971).

Holt, A., ed., *Making Tracks. A Celebration of Fifty Years of the Ramblers' Association* (London, 1985).

Holt, R., *Sport and the British: a Modern History* (Oxford, 1989).

Holt, R., ed., *Sport and the Working Class in Modern Britain* (Manchester, 1990).

Hopkins, H., *The Long Affray; The Poaching Wars, 1760–1914* (London, 1985).

Hoskins, W. G. and Dudley Stamp, L., *The Common Lands of England and Wales* (London, 1963).

Hoskins, W. G., *The Making of the English Landscape* (London, 1975).

Howe, A. C., *The Cotton Masters, 1830–1860* (Oxford, 1984).

Howell, D., *British Workers and the ILP, 1885–1906* (Manchester, 1983).

Howkins, A. and Lowerson, J., *Trends in Leisure, 1919–1939* (Sports Council; Social Services Research Council, 1979).

Hudson, J. W., *The History of Adult Education* (London, 1869).

Hughes, G., *Millstone Grit* (London, 1975).

Illingworth, J. and Routh J., eds, *Reginald Farrer. Dalesman, Planthunter, Gardener* (Lancaster, 1991).

Irving, R. L. G., *The Mountain Way. An Anthology in Prose and Verse* (London, 1938).

Iveson, S. and Brown, R., *ILP Clarion House: A Monument to a Movement* (Burnley, n. d.).

James, D., *Bradford* (Halifax, 1990).

Johnson, C., *The History of the Holiday Fellowship, Parts 1 & 2* (London, 1981).

Johnston, J., *Walt Whitman*: The Poet of Nature (London, 1910).

Johnston, T., *The History of the Working Classes in Scotland* (2nd edn; Glasgow, 1929).

Jones, B., *Holiday Fellowship: The First Sixty Years* (Bolton, 1983).

Jones, S. G., *Sport, Politics and the Working Class* (Manchester, 1988).

Jones, S. G., *Workers at Play: A Social History of Leisure, 1918–1939* (London, 1986).

Joyce, P., *Visions of the People. Industrial England and the Question of Class, 1840–1914* (Cambridge, 1991).

Joyce, P., *Work, Society and Politics. The Culture of the Factory in Later Victorian England* (Brighton, 1980).

Kershaw, E., *Manchester Pedestrians, 1903–1970* (Manchester, 1971).

Langton, D. H., *A History of the Parish of Flixton* (Manchester, 1898).

Lawson, R., *A History of Flixton, Urmston and Davyhulme* (Manchester, 1898).

Lawson, Z., 'Wheels Within Wheels – the Lancashire Cycling Clubs of the 1880s and '90s', in Crosby, A., ed., *Lancashire Local Studies in Honour of Diana Winterbottom* (Preston, 1993).

Laybourn, K., *The British Labour Party 1881–1951* (Gloucester, 1988).

Laybourn, K., *The Rise of Labour. The British Labour Party 1890–1979* (London, 1988).

Laybourn, K. and Reynolds, J., *Liberalism and the Rise of Labour* (Beckenham, 1984).

Lee, D. W., *The Flixton Footpath Battle* (Manchester, 1976).

LeMahieu, D. L., *A Culture for Democracy. Mass Communication and the Cultivated Mind in Britain Between the Wars* (Oxford, 1988).

Leonard, T. A., *Adventures in Holiday-Making; Being the Story of the Rise and Development of a People's Holiday Movement* (London, 1934).

Levy, C., 'Education and Self-Education: Staffing the Early I. L. P.', in Levy, C., ed., *Socialism and the Intelligentsia, 1880–1914* (London, 1987).

Lightwood, J. T., *Romance of the CTC* (London, 1928).

Longrigg, R., *The English Squire and his Sport* (London, 1977).

Lowerson, J., 'Battles for the Countryside', in Gloversmith, F., ed., *Class, Culture, and Social Change: A New View of the 1930s* (Brighton, 1980).

Lowerson, J., 'Middle Class Sports 1870–1914', in Cox, R. W., ed., *Aspects of the Social History of Nineteenth Century Sport* (Liverpool, 1982).

Luckin, B., *Pollution and Control. A social history of the Thames in the Nineteenth Century* (Bristol, 1986).

Lynd, H. M., *England in the Eighteen-Eighties. Towards a Social Basis for Freedom* (London, 1945).

Lyons, N. A., *Robert Blatchford – The Sketch of a Personality* (London, 1910).

MacCarthy, F., *The Simple Life. C. R. Ashbee in the Cotswolds* (London, 1981).

MacDonald, H., *On Foot* (London, 1942).

MacKenzie, J., ed., *Cycling* (Oxford, 1981).

Mackenzie, O. H., *A Hundred Years in the Highlands* (London, 1921).

McKibbin, R., *The Ideologies of Class. Social Relations in Britain, 1880–1950* (Oxford, 1990).

McLeod, H., *Class and Religion in the Late Victorian City* (London, 1974).

McLeod, H., *Religion and the Working Class in Nineteenth Century Britain* (London, 1984).

Marples, M., *Shanks's Pony* (London, 1959).

Marsh, J., *Back to the Land* (London, 1982).

Marshall, J. D., ed., *Samuel Bamford, Walks in South Lancashire and its Borders* (Brighton, 1972).

Mayall, D., *Gypsy-Travellers in Nineteenth Century Society* (Cambridge, 1988).

Mayer, A. J., *The Persistence of the Old Regime* (Beckenham, 1981).

Meller, H. E., *Leisure and the Changing City, 1870–1914* (London, 1976).

Miller, G. C., *Blackburn: The Evolution of a Cotton Town* (Blackburn, 1951).

Miller, G. C., *Blackburn Worthies of Yesterday: A Biographical Galaxy* (Blackburn, 1959).

Milward, R., *Lancashire: An Illustrated Essay on the History of the Landscape* (London, 1955).

Mingay, G. E., ed., *The Victorian Countryside*, vols 1 and 2 (London, 1981).

Mitchell, W. R., *Lancashire Milltown Memories: Colne-Nelson-Burnley* (Clapham, Yorkshire, 1987).

Morris, R. J., *Class, Sect, and Party: The Making of the British Middle Class: Leeds, 1820–1950* (Manchester, 1990).

Nicholson, N., *The Lakers* (London, 1955).

Nicholson, T. R., *Wheels on the Road* (Norwich, 1983).

Nield Chew, D., *The Life and Writings of Ada Nield Chew* (London, 1982).

Ogden, J., *Keighley Naturalists' One Hundred Years, 1868–1968* (Bradford, 1968).

Orr, W., *Deer Forests, Landlords and Crofters. The West Highlands in Victorian and Edwardian Times* (Edinburgh, 1982).

Pateman, T. W., *Dunshaw. A Lancashire Background* (London, 1948).

Paton, J. L., *John Brown Paton. A Biography* (London, 1914).

Pelling, H., *The Origins of the Labour Party, 1880–1900* (2nd edn; Oxford, 1965).

Perkin, H., *Professionalism, Property, and English Society since 1880* (Reading, 1981).

Perkin, H., *The Age of the Automobile* (London, 1976).

Perkin, H., *The Age of the Railway* (London, 1971).

Perkin, H., *The Origins of Modern English Society, 1780–1880* (London, 1969).

Phillips, G. S., *Ebenezer Elliott* (Huddersfield, 1852).

Pierson, S., *Marxism and the Origins of British Socialism* (London, 1973).

Pilkington, W., *History of the Preston CC and Longridge Golf Club* (Preston, 1928).

Pimlott, B., ed., *Fabian Essays in Socialist Thought* (London, 1987).

Pimlott, B. *Hugh Dalton* (London, 1985).

Pimlott, J. A. R., *Recreations* (London, 1968).

Pimlott, J. A. R., *The Englishman's Holiday: A Social History* (Brighton, 1976).

Pollard, S., *A History of Labour in Sheffield* (Liverpool, 1959).

Porritt, J., *Seeing Green. The Politics of Ecology Explained* (Oxford, 1984).

Powis, J., *Aristocracy* (Oxford, 1984).

Prebble, J., *The Highland Clearances* (London, 1963).

Prentice, A., *Historical Sketches and Personal Recollections of Manchester* (London and Manchester, 1851).

Pugh, M., *The Tories and the People, 1880–1935* (Oxford, 1985).

Ramblers' Association, *In Memory of T. Arthur Leonard* (London, 1948).

Ramblers' Association, *Tom Stephenson* (London, n. d.).

Redford, A., *Labour Migration in England, 1800–1850* (Manchester, 1926).

Reid, C., 'Middle Class Values and Working Class Culture in Nineteenth Century Sheffield. The Pursuit of Respectability', in Pollard, S. and Holmes, C., eds, *Essays in the Economic and Social History of South Yorkshire* (Sheffield, 1976).

Richards, E., *A History of the Highland Clearances, 1746–1886* (London, 1982).

Rickwood, P., *The Story of Access in the Peak District* (Bakewell, 1982).

Roberts, D., *This Veteran Business* (Southern Veteran CC, 1984).

Roberts, J. M., *Europe, 1880–1945* (2nd edn; London, 1989).

Royle, C., *Modern Britain. A Social History, 1750–1985* (London, 1987).

Salveson, P., *Lancashire's Links to Walt Whitman* (Bolton, 1984).

Salveson, P., *Mill Towns and Moorlands: Rural Themes in Lancashire Working Class Culture* (Salford, 1986).

Salveson, P., *Will yo come o Sunday morning* (Bolton, 1982).

Selbie, W. B., *Congregationalism* (London, 1927).

Shaw, C. and Chase, M., *The Imagined Past: History and Nostalgia* (Manchester, 1989).

Shaw-Lefevre, G. J. (Lord Eversley), *Commons, Forests and Footpaths* (London, 1910).

Shaw-Lefevre, G. J., *English Commons and Forests, the story of the battle during the last thirty years for public rights over the commons and forests of England and Wales* (London, 1894),

Sheail, J., *Rural Conservation in Inter-war Britain* (Oxford, 1981).

Sheffield Campaign for Access to Moorland, *Freedom of the Moors* (Sheffield, 1988).

Shepherd, R. G., *In The Country* (Blackpool, 1977).

Shepherd, R. G., *Village Year* (Blackpool, 1978).

Shoard, M., 'The Lure of the Moors', in Gold, J. R. and Burgess, J., eds, *Valued Environments* (London, 1982).

Shoard, M., *This Land is Our Land* (London, 1983).

Smout, T. C., *A Century of the Scottish People, 1830–1950* (London, 1987).

Spear, J. L., *Dreams of an English Eden: Ruskin and his Tradition of Social Criticism* (New York, 1984).

Sports Council, Countryside Commission, *Digest of Countryside Recreation and Statistics* (Countryside Commission, 1974).

Springhall, J., *Youth, Empire, and Society: British Youth Movements, 1883–1940* (London, 1977).

Stephenson, T., *Forbidden Land. The Struggle for Access to Mountain and Moorland* (Manchester, 1989).

Stephenson, T., *The Pennine Way* (London, 1980).

Stevenson, J., *British Society, 1914–45* (London, 1984).

Stevenson, J. and Cook, C., *The Slump* (London, 1977).

Storch, R. D., ed., *Popular Culture and Custom in Nineteenth Century England* (London, 1982).

Sykes, M., *In the Steps of Leo Grindon* (Manchester Local Studies Library, n.d.).

Taylor, H., 'Sporting Heroes', in Colls, R. and Lancaster, B., *Geordies: Roots of Regionalism* (Edinburgh, 1992).

Tholfsen, T., *Working Class Radicalism in Mid-Victorian England* (London, 1976).

Thomas, K., *Man and the Natural World. Changing Attitudes in England, 1500–1800* (London, 1983).

Thomis, M. I., *Responses to Industrialisation. The British Experience, 1780–1850* (Newton Abbot, 1976).

Thompson, E. P., *Whigs and Hunters* (London, 1975).

Thompson, E. P., *William Morris: Romantic to Revolutionary* (rev. edn; London, 1977).

Thompson, F. M. L., *The Rise of Respectable Society. A Social History of Victorian Britain, 1830–1900* (London, 1988).

Tibble, J. and A., *John Clare: His Life and Poetry* (London, 1956).

Tomlinson, A., ed., *Leisure and Social Control* (Brighton, 1981).

Trayner, B., *A Short History of the YHA* (St Albans, 1979).

Tsuzuki, C., *Edward Carpenter, 1844–1929. Prophet of Human Fellowship* (Cambridge, 1980).

Tudor Jones, R., *Congregationalism in England, 1662–1962* (London, 1962).

Tupling, G. H., *The Economic History of Rossendale* (Manchester, 1927).

Tylecote, M., *The Mechanics' Institutes of Lancashire and Yorkshire before 1851* (Manchester, 1957).

Tyne and Wear County Council, *Cycle Clips* (TWAD, n. d.).

Vicinus, M., *The Ambiguities of Self-Help; Concerning the Life and Work of the Lancashire Dialect Writer Edwin Waugh* (Manchester, 1984).

Vicinus, M., *The Industrial Muse* (London, 1974).

Walker, C. K., *Walking North With Keats* (Yale, 1992).

Walton, J. K., *Lancashire. A Social History* (Manchester, 1987).

Walton, J. K., 'Residential Amenity, Respectable Morality and the Rise of the Entertainment Industry; the case of Blackpool 1860–1914', in Bennett, T. et al., eds, *Popular Culture: Past and Present* (London, 1982).

Walton, J. K., *The English Seaside Resort. A Social History, 1750–1914* (Leicester, 1983).

Walton, J. K., 'The Windermere Tourist Trade in the Age of the Railway, 1847–1912', in Westall, O. M., ed., *Windermere in the Nineteenth Century* (Lancaster, 1991).

Walton, J. K. and Walvin, J., eds, *Leisure in Britain, 1780–1939* (Manchester, 1983).

Walvin, J., *English Urban Life, 1776–1851* (London, 1984).

Walvin, J., *Leisure and Society, 1830–1950* (London, 1978).

Ward, C. and Hardy, D., *Arcadia for All: The Legacy of a Makeshift Landscape* (London, 1984).

Ward, S., *The Countryside Between the Wars, 1918–1940: A Photographic Record* (London, 1984).

Waters, C., *British Socialists and the Politics of Popular Culture, 1884–1914* (Manchester, 1990).

Watson, R. and Gray, M., *The Penguin Book of the Bicycle* (London, 1978).

Webb, S. and B., *The Story of the King's Highway* (London, 1913).

Weir, T., *Highland Days* (Edinburgh, 1991).

Whatmore, J., *The CTC Book of Cycling* (Newton Abbot, 1983).

Whittle, P. A., *Bolton-le-Moors, and the Townships in the Parish* (Bolton, 1855).

Who Was Who, 1897–1916 (London, 1920).

Wiener, M. J., *English Culture and the Decline of the Industrial Spirit* (London, 1981).

Wigley, J., *The Rise and Fall of the Victorian Sunday* (Manchester, 1980).

Williams-Ellis, C., ed., *Britain and the Beast* (London, 1937).

Williams, D., *George Meredith. His Life and Lost Love* (London, 1977).

Williams, J., *Journey into Adventure* (London, 1960).

Williams, R., *Culture and Society, 1780–1950* (London, 1963).

Williams, R., *The Country and the City* (new edn; London, 1985).

Williams, W. H., *The Commons, Open Spaces and Footpaths Preservation Society* (London, 1965).

Wilson, A. N., *Hilaire Belloc* (London, 1984).

Wilson, J., *Green Shadows. The Life of John Clare* (London, 1951).

Wilt, J., *The Readable People of George Meredith* (Princeton, 1975).

Winstanley, A., *Golden Days Awheel* (Wigan, 1991).

Woodforde, J., *The Story of the Bicycle* (London, 1970).

Wright, P., *On Living in an Old Country: The National Past in Contemporary Britain* (London, 1985).

Yeo, E. and S., eds, *Popular Culture and Class Conflict, 1590–1914* (Brighton, 1981).

Yorkshire Ramblers' Club, *Library List*, Leeds Local Studies Library.

Youth Hostels Association (England and Wales), *Ah, Happy Days! A Nostalgic Look at the Youth Hostels Association 1930–1980* (St Albans, 1980).

3. Articles

Aitken, R., 'Stravagers and marauders', *Scottish Mountaineering Club Journal* XXX, 166 (1975), pp. 351–8.

Bailey, P., '"Will the real Bill Banks stand up?" Towards a role analysis of mid-Victorian working-class respectability', *Journal of Social History* 12, 3 (1978–9), pp. 338–53.

Barrow, L., 'The origins of Robert Blatchford's social imperialism', *Bulletin of the Society for the Study of Labour History* 19 (1969), p. 9.

Baxendale, J., 'Review; Wiener, M. J., English Culture and the Decline of the Industrial Spirit', *History Workshop Journal* 21 (Spring 1986), pp. 171–4.

Coppock, J. T., 'The recreational use of land and water in rural Britain', *Journal of Economic and Social Geography (Tijdschrift Voor Economische en Sociale Geografie)* 57 (1966), p. 56.

Cosgrove, D. E., 'John Ruskin and the geographical imagination', *The Geographical Review* 69, 1 (1979), pp. 43–62.

Crossick, G., 'The labour aristocracy and its values: a study of mid-Victorian Kentish London', *Victorian Studies* 19, 3 (March 1976), pp. 301–28.

Donnelly, P., 'The paradox of the parks', *Leisure Studies* 5 (1986), pp. 211–31.

Dower, M., 'Leisure; its impact on man and the land', *Geography* 55 (July 1970), pp. 253–60.

Garnett, H., 'Richard Buxton. An old-time Manchester botanist, *North Western Naturalist* 6 (Manchester, 1931), pp. 18–21.

Gregory, D., 'The production of regions in England's industrial revolution', *Journal of Historical Geography* 14 (1988), pp. 50–8.

Harrison, B., 'Religion and recreation in ninteenth century England', *Past and Present* 38 (December, 1967), p. 98.

Higgs, E., 'Leisure and the state: the history of popular culture as reflected in the public records', *History Workshop Journal* 15 (Spring 1983), pp. 141–50.

Hill, H., 'Who is Bert Ward?', *The Holberry Society for the Study of Sheffield Labour History* 3 (November 1979), p. 8.

Holt, A., 'Hikers and ramblers; surviving a thirties fashion', *International Journal of Sports History* 4, 1 (May 1987), pp. 56–67.

Jenkins, J., 'The roots of the National Trust', *History Today* 45, 1 (January 1995), pp. 3–9.

Jones, M., 'Padiham Field Naturalists Society', *Retrospect* (Journal of Burnley and District History Society) 7 (1987), p. 3.

Jones, S. G., 'Sport, politics and the labour movement: the BWSF, 1923–35', *British Journal of Sports History* 2, 2 (September 1985).

Jones, S. G., 'Trade union policy between the wars. The case of holidays with pay in Britain', *International Review of Social History* 31, 1 (1986), pp. 40–67.

Kirk, N., 'Traditional working-class culture and the rise of labour: some preliminary questions and observations', *Social History* 16, 2 (May 1991), pp. 203–16.

Langton J., 'The industrial revolution and the regional geography of England', *Transactions of the Institute of British Geographers* 9 (1984), pp. 145–67.

Langton, J. v. Gregory, D., 'Debate. The production of regions in England's Industrial Revolution, a) a response, b) a reply', *Journal of Historical Geography* 14 (1988), pp. 170–6.

Lowenthal, D., 'Finding valued landscapes', *Progress in Human Geography* 2, 3 (1978), pp. 373–418.

Lowenthal, D. and Prince, H. C., 'English landscape tastes', *Geographical Review* 55 (1965), pp. 185–222.

Lowerson, J., 'Sport and the Victorian Sunday: the beginnings of middle class apostasy', *British Journal of Sports History* 1, 2 (September 1984), pp. 202–20.

Mackay, I. R., 'The Pet Lamb Case', *Transactions of the Gaelic Society of Inverness* 48 (1972–4), pp. 188–200.

McKibbin, R., 'Why was there no Marxism in Great Britain?', *English Historical Review* XCIX (1984), pp. 306–10.

Pahl, R., 'New rich, old rich, stinking rich? – Review essay; Rubinstein, D., Wealth and inequality in Britain', *Social History* 15, 2 (May 1990), pp. 229–39.

Percy, J., 'Scientists in humble life: the artisan naturalists of south Lancashire', *Manchester Region History Review* V, 1 (Spring/Summer 1991), pp. 3–10.

Porter, B., 'Cragside. Arms and the man', *History Today* 45, 1 (January 1995), pp. 46–52.

Price, C., 'Subjectivity and objectivity in landscape evaluation', *Environment and Planning* 8 (1976), pp. 829–38.

Prynn, D., 'The Clarion clubs, rambling, and the holiday associations in Britain', *Journal of Contemporary History* 11 (July 1976), pp. 65–77.

Pye, D., 'Fellowship is Life: Bolton Clarion CC', *North West Labour History Society Bulletin* (1984), p. 20.

Reid, D., 'Leisure and recreation', *History* 65 (1980), pp. 52–7.

Reynolds, J. and Laybourn, K., 'The emergence of the Independent Labour Party in Britain', *International Review of Social History* XX (1975), pp. 313–46.

Rich, P., 'The quest for Englishness', *History Today* 31 (June 1987), pp. 24–30.

Rubinstein, D., 'Cycling in the 1890s', *Victorian Studies* 21 (Autumn 1977), pp. 47–71.

Rubinstein, D., 'Interview with Tom Stephenson', *Bulletin of the Society for the Study of Labour History* 22 (1971), pp. 27–32.

Rubinstein, D., 'Sport and the sociologist', *British Journal of Sports History* 1, 1 (May 1984), pp. 14–23.

Rubinstein, D., 'The struggle for ramblers' rights', *New Society*, 15 April 1982, pp. 85–7.

Salveson, P., 'When socialism was popular', *The Chartist* (June–August 1984), pp. 22–5.

Sandbach, F. R., 'Campaign for the Lake District National Park', *Transactions of the Institute of British Geographers*, New Series, 3 (1978), p. 498.

Shimwell, D. W., 'Images of moorland, amenity recreation and wildlife', *Manchester Geographer*, New Series, 4 (1983), pp. 24–37.

Shimwell, D. W., 'Images of the Peak District', *Manchester Geographer*, New Series (Winter 1980), pp. 19–38.

Stedman-Jones, G., 'Class expression versus social control? A critique of recent trends in the social history of leisure', *History Workshop Journal* 4 (1977), pp. 162–70.

Sykes, M., 'The botanists', *Lancashire Life* 21 (1973), p. 97.

Taylor, H., 'Footpath protection societies in mid-nineteenth century textile Lancashire', *Manchester Region History Review* IX (1995), pp. 25–31.

Thursby, Sir J. O. S., 'The Lancashire borderland: the Towneley Moors', *The Badminton Magazine* 23, 133 (August 1906), p. 2.
Todd, R., 'Women Walkers', *Rambling Today* (Spring 1993).
Trentmann, F., 'Civilisation and its Discontents: English Neo-Romanticism and the Transformation of Anti-Modernism in Twentieth-Century Western Culture', *Journal of Contemporary History* 29, 4 (October 1994).
Walker, H., 'The popularisation of the outdoor movement, 1900–1940, *British Journal of Sports History* 2, 2 (September 1985), pp. 140–53.
Walker, H., 'The Workers' Travel Association, 1921–1939', *Bulletin of the Society for the Study of Labour History* 50 (1985), pp. 9–10.
Walker, W., 'Kinder Scout: The reclamation and preservation of its footpaths', *Manchester Literary Club Papers* 6 (1880), pp. 275–78.
Walvin, J., 'Sport, social history and the historian', *British Journal of Sports History* 1, 1 (May 1984), pp. 5–13.
Wild, H., 'The Manchester Society for the Preservation of Ancient Footpaths', *Manchester Review* 10 (Winter 1965–6).
Wyborn, T., 'Parks for the people: the development of public parks in Victorian Manchester', *Manchester Region History Review* IX (1995), pp. 3–14.
Yeo, S., 'A new life: The religion of socialism in Britain, 1883–1896', *History Workshop Journal* 4 (Autumn 1977), pp. 5–49.

4. Theses

Cook, R. P., 'Political Elites and Electoral Politics in late Nineteenth Century Burnley', unpublished MA thesis, University of Lancaster, 1974.
Evans, G., 'Social Leadership and Social Control: Bolton 1870–1898', unpublished MA thesis, University of Lancaster, 1974.
Fincher, J. A., 'The Clarion Movement: A Study of a Socialist Attempt to Implement the Co-operative Commonwealth in England, 1891–1944', unpublished MA thesis, University of Manchester, 1971.
Handy, S. D., 'Burnley Society and the Politics of Change, 1885–1914', unpublished MA thesis, University of Lancaster, 1979.
Harris, P. A., 'Class conflict, the trade unions and working class politics in Bolton, 1875–1896', unpublished MA thesis, University of Lancaster, 1971.
Harris, P. A., 'Social Leadership and Social Attitudes in Bolton, 1919–1939', unpublished Ph.D. thesis, University of Lancaster, 1973.
McGloin, P., 'The impact of the railway on the development of Keswick as a tourist resort, 1860–1914', unpublished MA thesis, University of Lancaster, 1977.
O'Leary, M., 'New Liberalism and the Bolton Working Class, 1906–1914', unpublished MA thesis, University of Lancaster, 1982.
Rickwood, P. W., 'Public Enjoyment of Open Countryside in England and Wales, 1919–1939', unpublished Ph.D. thesis, University of Leicester, 1973.
Walker, H., 'The Outdoor Movement in England and Wales, 1900–1939', unpublished Ph.D. thesis, University of Sussex, 1988.

Index